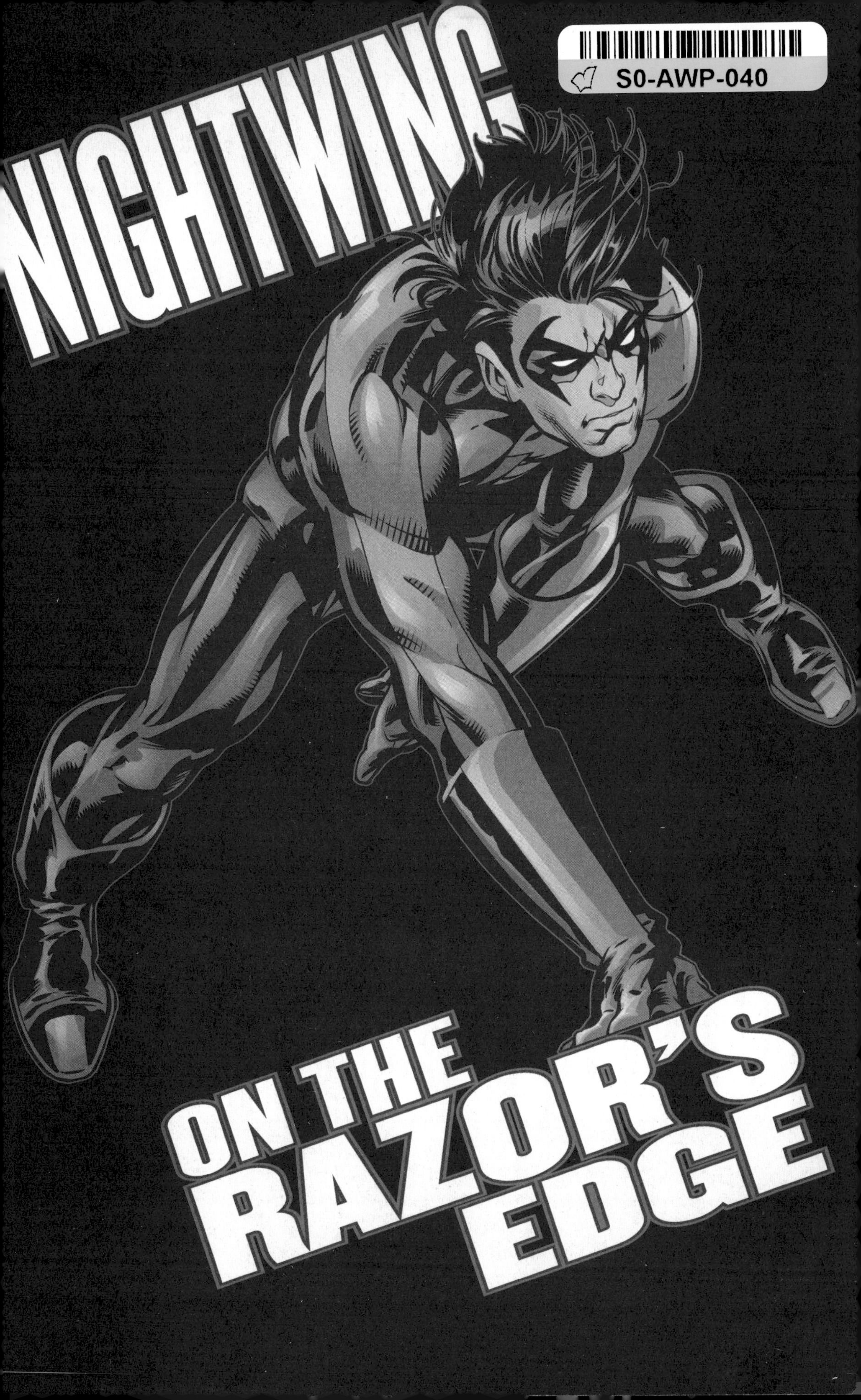
NIGHTWING:
ON THE
RAZOR'S
EDGE

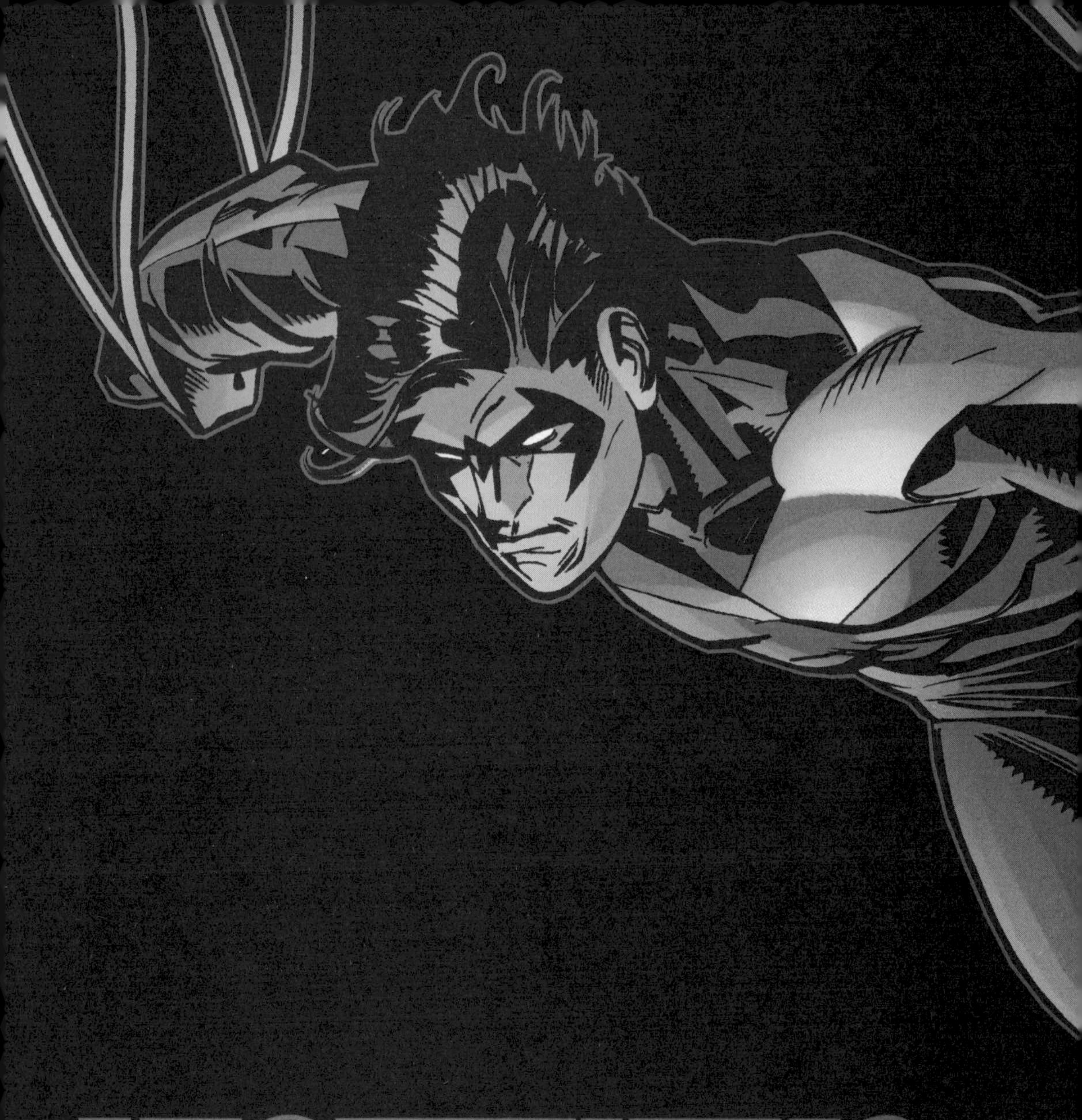

NIGHTWING

DAN DiDIO VP-Executive Editor BOB SCHRECK, MICHAEL WRIGHT Editors-original series ROBERT GREENBERGER Senior Editor-collected edition ROBBIN BROSTERMAN Senior Art Director PAUL LEVITZ President & Publisher GEORG BREWER VP-Design & Retail Product Development RICHARD BRUNING Senior VP-Creative Director PATRICK CALDON Senior VP-Finance & Operations CHRIS CARAMALIS VP-Finance TERRI CUNNINGHAM VP-Managing Editor STEPHANIE FIERMAN Senior VP-Sales & Marketing ALISON GILL VP-Manufacturing RICH JOHNSON VP-Book Trade Sales HANK KANALZ VP-General Manager, WildStorm LILLIAN LASERSON Senior VP & General Counsel JIM LEE Editorial Director-WildStorm PAULA LOWITT Senior VP-Business & Legal Affairs DAVID McKILLIPS VP-Advertising & Custom Publishing JOHN NEE VP-Business Development GREGORY NOVECK Senior VP-Creative Affairs CHERYL RUBIN Senior VP-Brand Management BOB WAYNE VP-Sales

ISBN: 1-4012-0437-6. Cover illustration by J. G. Jones, Greg Land and Drew Geraci. Publication design by Peter Hamboussi.

ON THE RAZOR'S EDGE

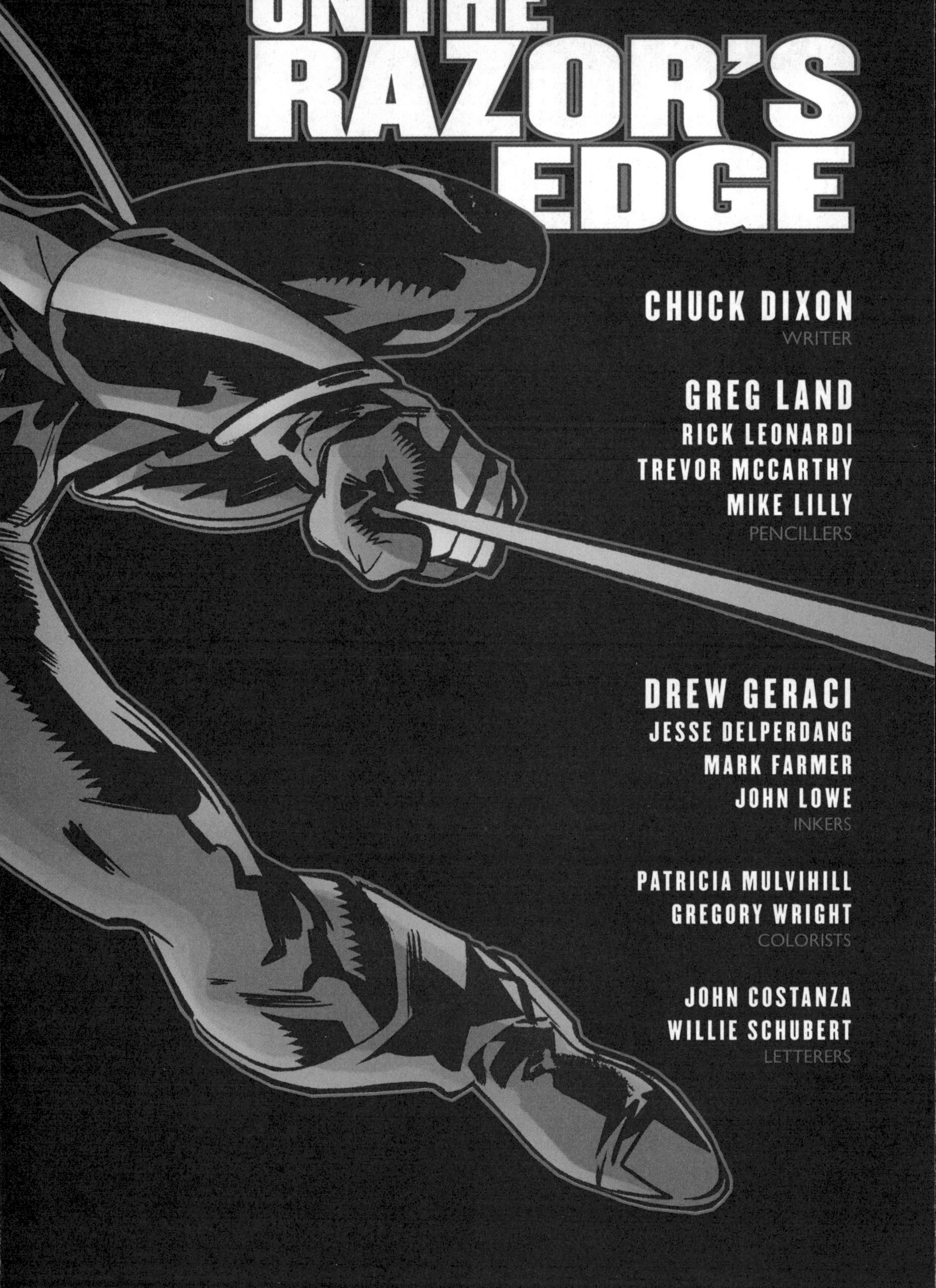

CHUCK DIXON
WRITER

GREG LAND
RICK LEONARDI
TREVOR McCARTHY
MIKE LILLY
PENCILLERS

DREW GERACI
JESSE DELPERDANG
MARK FARMER
JOHN LOWE
INKERS

PATRICIA MULVIHILL
GREGORY WRIGHT
COLORISTS

JOHN COSTANZA
WILLIE SCHUBERT
LETTERERS

CAST OF CHARACTERS

WHO'S WHO AND WHERE THEY ARE AT THE TIME OF THIS STORY

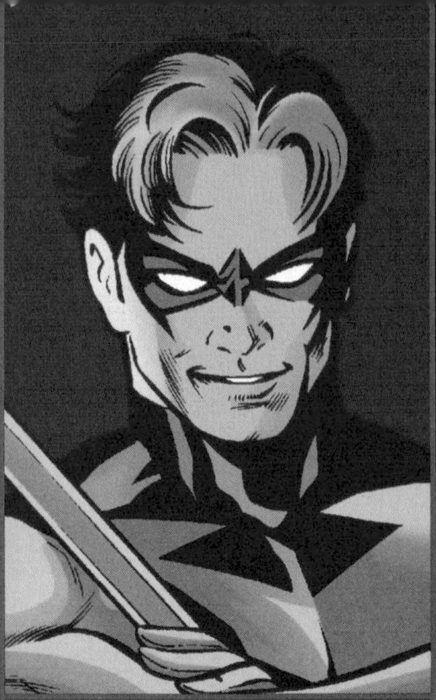

NIGHTWING

Dick Grayson's life changed forever when he witnessed his aerialist parents fall to their death, the victims of an extortion scheme. Knowing the pain of such a loss, the wealthy Bruce Wayne took in the youth, and in a short time Dick was being trained to work alongside Gotham City's famed crime-fighter, Batman. Befitting his circus heritage, Dick chose a more colorful outfit than that of his new partner, and became Robin, the Boy Wonder. Batman and Robin proved to be a perfect crime-fighting team, but, as he grew to manhood, Dick began to separate himself from his mentor, unwilling to become a copy of the obsessed Bruce Wayne.

Asserting his independence, he changed his persona from Robin to Nightwing, and then left Gotham for the nearby city of Blüdhaven. Wanting to gain access to places Nightwing could not go, Dick Grayson trained to join the city's police, only to discover that he couldn't get a job with the corrupt force.

Nightwing is a master of a half-dozen martial arts disciplines with an emphasis on aikido. He is also armed with twin escrima sticks made from an unbreakable polymer and carries several dozen modified batarangs along with de-cel jumplines and gas capsules.

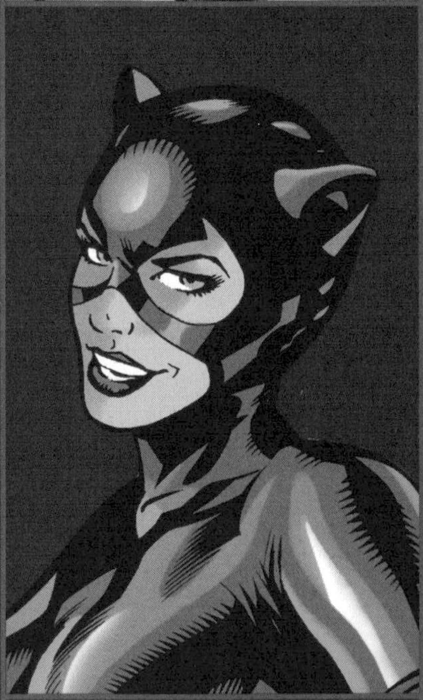

CATWOMAN

Selina Kyle's life had gone from bad to worse until she found herself in a Gotham City ghetto, selling herself to pay the rent. Then she saw the television reports of a caped character terrorizing the police. Inspired, she donned a complementary cat-suit and sought out the bat-man. Thus began one of the most complicated relationships in modern times. Catwoman has been a cat-thief, master criminal, politician, financier, and protector of Gotham's East Side. When her city is at its most vulnerable, Catwoman is usually found on the side of the angels, but not without an agenda of her own.

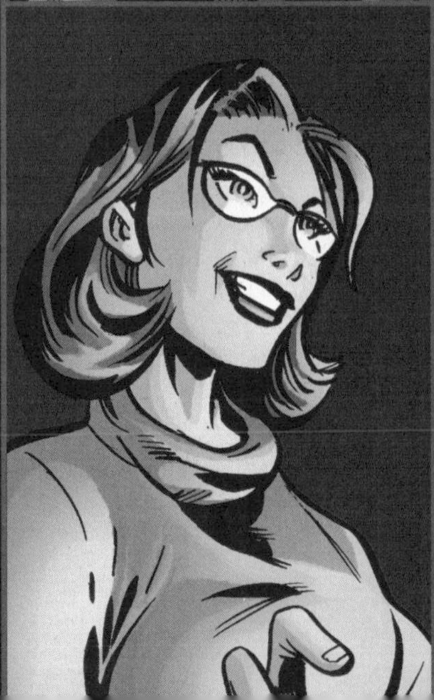

ORACLE

The niece and adopted daughter of Gotham City Police Commissioner James Gordon, Barbara Gordon was entranced by her uncle's clandestine associations with Gotham's mysterious guardian Batman. Inspired by the Dark Knight to create her own costumed identity, Barbara began aiding and abetting Batman's war on crime as Batgirl. But a bullet from the psychotic Joker ended all that. Now paralyzed from the waist down, Barbara nevertheless refuses to live a sedentary life in a wheelchair. With a vast computer network and her own photographic memory, Barbara Gordon has become the all-seeing Oracle — information broker to costumed crimefighters. And no longer content to remain on the sidelines of crime-fighting, Oracle is itching to take a more *proactive* role in troubleshooting global crises.

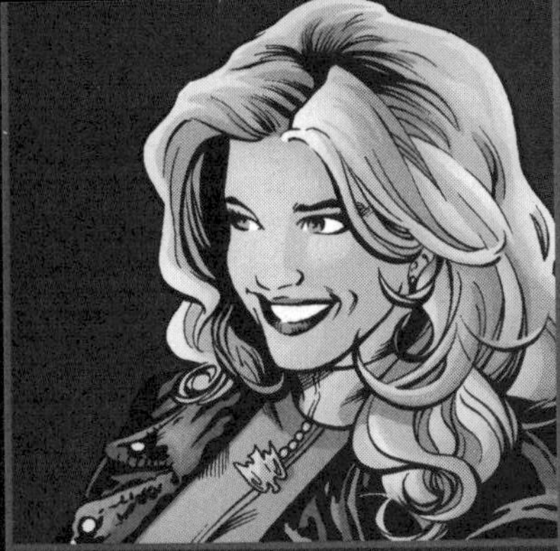

BLACK CANARY

Dinah Lance grew up in the shadow of the legendary Justice Society of America, inheriting the role of Black Canary from her well-intentioned but domineering mother. Armed with a super-powered sonic cry and a mastery of several martial arts, Dinah helped found the JSA's successor, the Justice League of America. When her relationship with Oliver Queen — Green Arrow — soured, Dinah left the Emerald Archer to blaze her own path. Now, with little direction and having lost her sonic cry, Dinah strives to rediscover what the mantle of Black Canary means to her and to the world. She has been partnered with Oracle and recently met her in person for the first time.

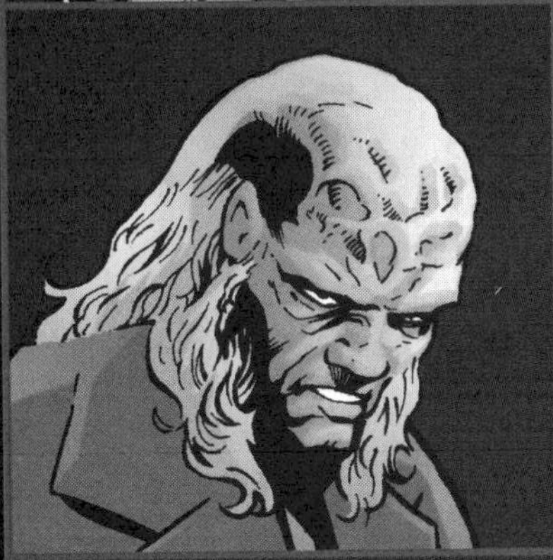

BLOCKBUSTER

Roland Desmond is Blüdhaven's undisputed crime boss, amassing enough money and connections to ultimately gain control of Gotham City's underworld. Desmond's key attribute is his mind. He gained his body's bulk as a result of experimental steroids to cure a debilitating heart disease. His vast fortune has been raided time and again by Oracle, and he has sworn to bring her down. Blockbuster is not above using costumed vigilantes to do his bidding. In recent times, his heart could no longer handle the strain of his bulk, making a transplant an absolute necessity. This was accomplished with more than a little difficulty. Renewed, he works hard to retain his grip on Blüdhaven.

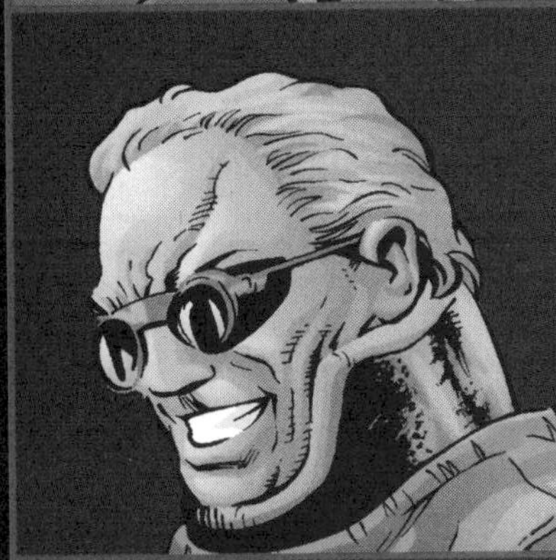

TORQUE

In a city full of dirty cops, Dudley Soames was the dirtiest. He played all sides, including feeding information on crime boss Blockbuster to Nightwing. The price he paid for his actions was having his head rotated 180 degrees — permanently. For anyone else that would have meant instant death, but thanks to the radical drug therapy of Dr. Sandra Pavaar, Soames lived. Having mastered his new world-view, Soames took the name Torque and now seeks vengeance on everyone who wronged him. His only agenda is mayhem.

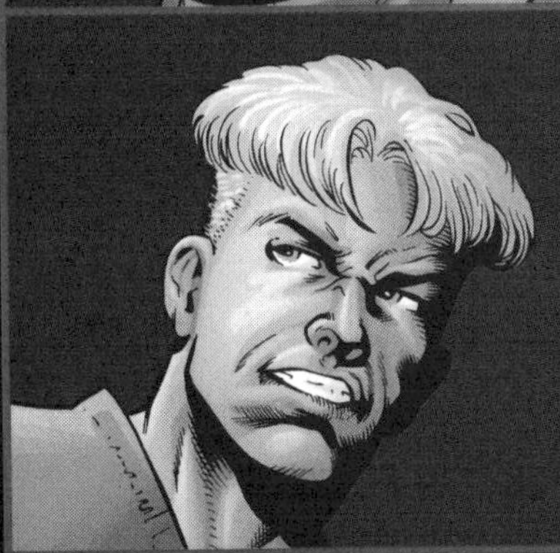

NITE-WING

The city of Blüdhaven does not function very well, as seen in its daily failures at public services. This is nothing new — just ask Tad Ryerstad, who was raised under the auspices of the Child Services Department. After shuttling through a series of foster homes, Tad ran away at age twelve and the department never noticed. This indifferent upbringing twisted Tad into a sociopath, schooled as much on comic books and television as he was in any educational setting. His view of the world is warped, and he metes out his personal brand of "justice" far more violently than his costumed inspiration. Recently, Nightwing tried to train him, channeling the aggression into something positive. Instead, Nite-Wing killed an FBI agent and is now serving time for the crime.

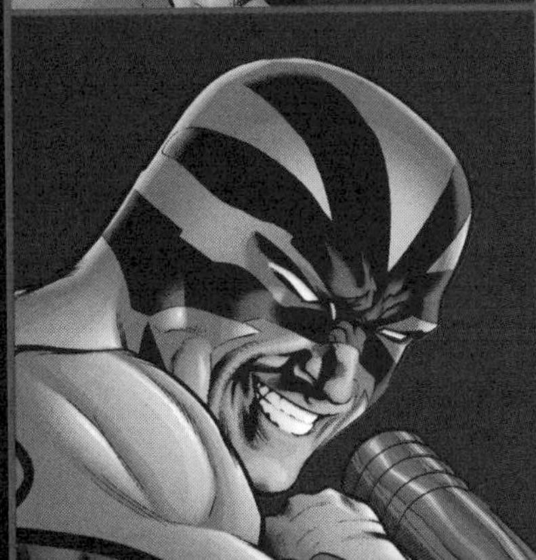

SHRIKE

They knew each other as boys, were friends, but then took different paths. Dick Grayson grew up to become Nightwing and the other youth turned to crime, ultimately inheriting the costume of Shrike, fourth to use that name. Trained by the League of Assassins, the new Shrike is one of the best known, deadly mercenaries in the world.

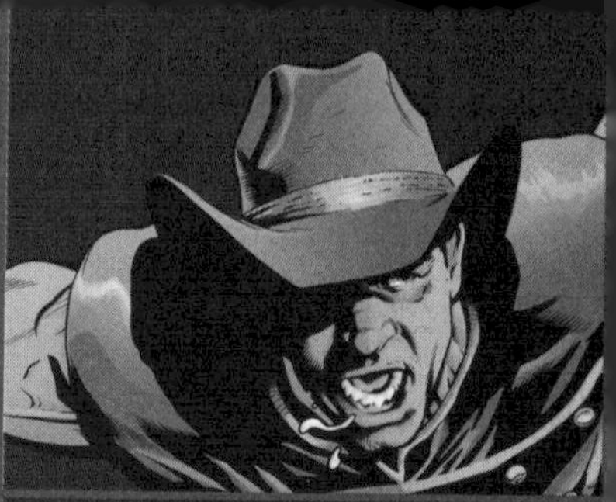

STALLION

Blockbuster will hire his muscle without regard to their intellectual prowess, which is a good thing for Rudy Hanrahan, one of the dimmest mercenaries ever to visit Blüdhaven.

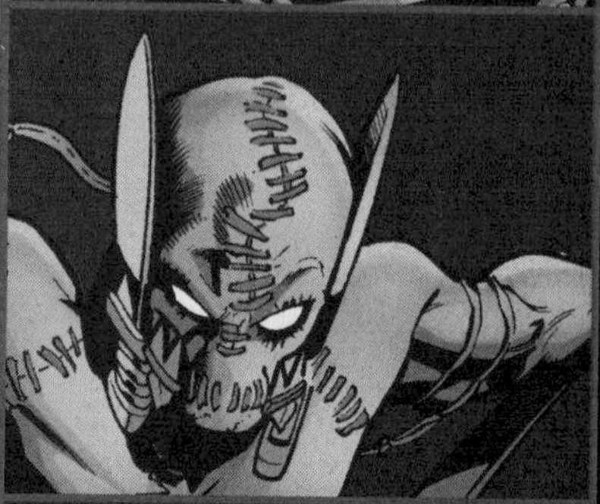

BRUTALE

An expert at torture with blades, Guillermo Barrera was the most effective interrogator in Hasaragua. When the government changed hands, he adopted the identity of Brutale and sold his services on the open market.

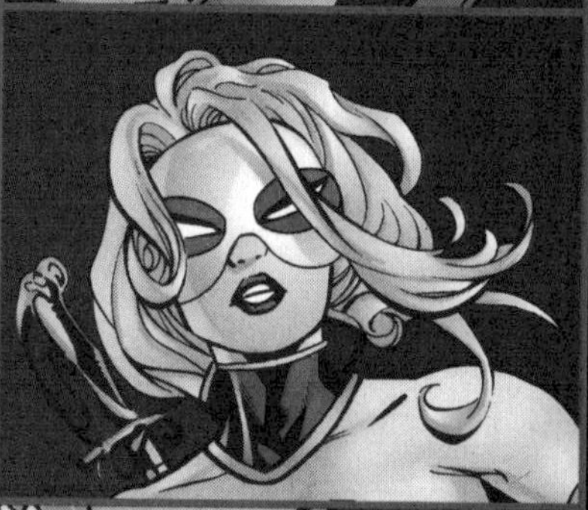

LADY VIC

Lady Elaine Marsh-Morton took the name Lady Vic — short for Victim — when she entered into her family's long tradition of mercenary work. In addition to her international clients, she serves on retainer to Blockbuster.

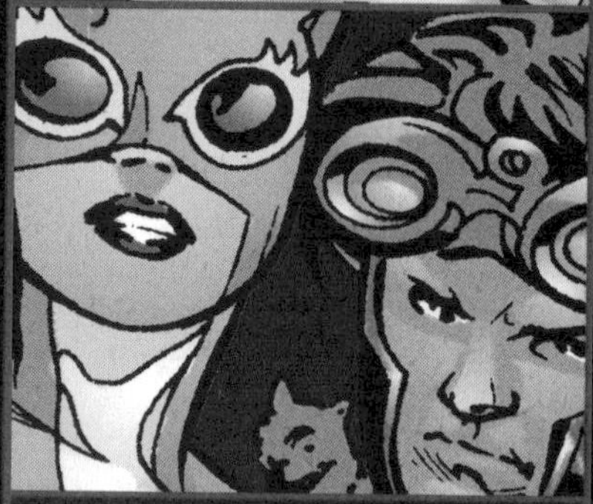

MOUSE AND GIZ

Despite their outlandish costumes, this mercenary pair are experts with computers and electronic surveillance. In Blockbuster's employ, they have effectively put his criminal rivals out of commission.

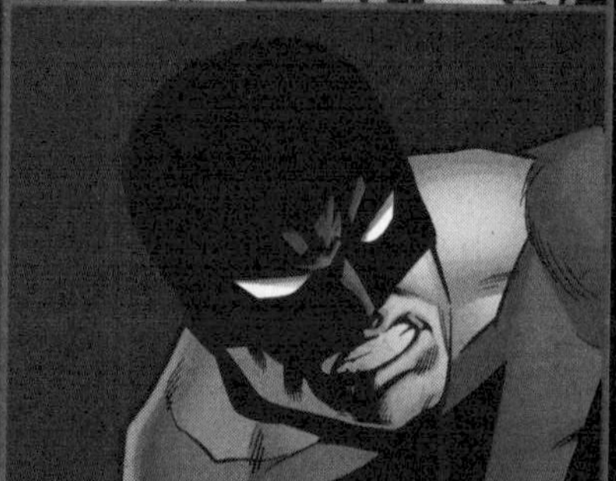

ELECTROCUTIONER

Lester Buchinsky went into the family business, replacing his dead brother as the second Electrocutioner. Following a warped sense of justice, Buchinsky used the exoskeleton with its electricity-emitting ability to control crime. He quickly fell under Blockbuster's sway, serving the underworld boss and being beaten time and again by Nightwing, not to mention Batman and Robin.

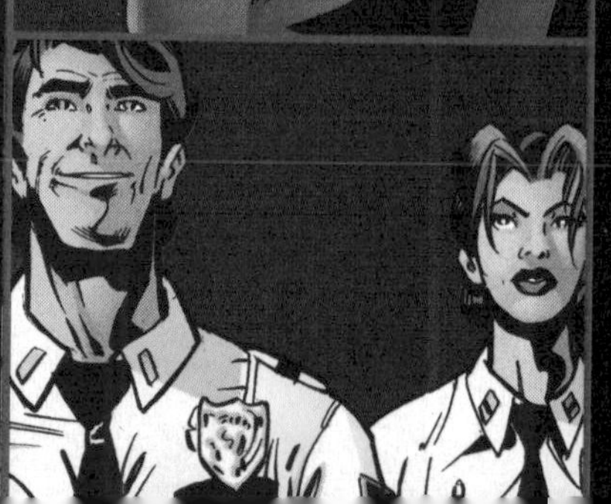

BLÜDHAVEN POLICE DEPT.

Like everything else in the city, the Blüdhaven P.D. is corrupt from top to bottom. A 1971 anti-corruption committee eliminated the post of Police Commissioner when the position's power and influence began to rival that of the mayor. Today, Police Chief Francis Alexander Redhorn is still more powerful than the mayor but at a lower (official) pay grade. A laundry list of federal agencies has been, for decades, investigating Redhorn and his department's connection to organized crime. Most recently, this investigation turned to the operations of Roland Desmond. Stories of secret offshore "retirement" funds, intentionally bungled investigations, and entire precincts on the take lead nowhere as the FBI, DEA, and Treasury Department are led on countless wild-goose chases down innumerable blind alleys. The Blüdhaven P.D. continues to have the highest rate of early retirement of any police department in the country. Incriminating records were recently found by Nightwing, implicating Redhorn, who abandoned his force, leaving things in greater disarray than usual.

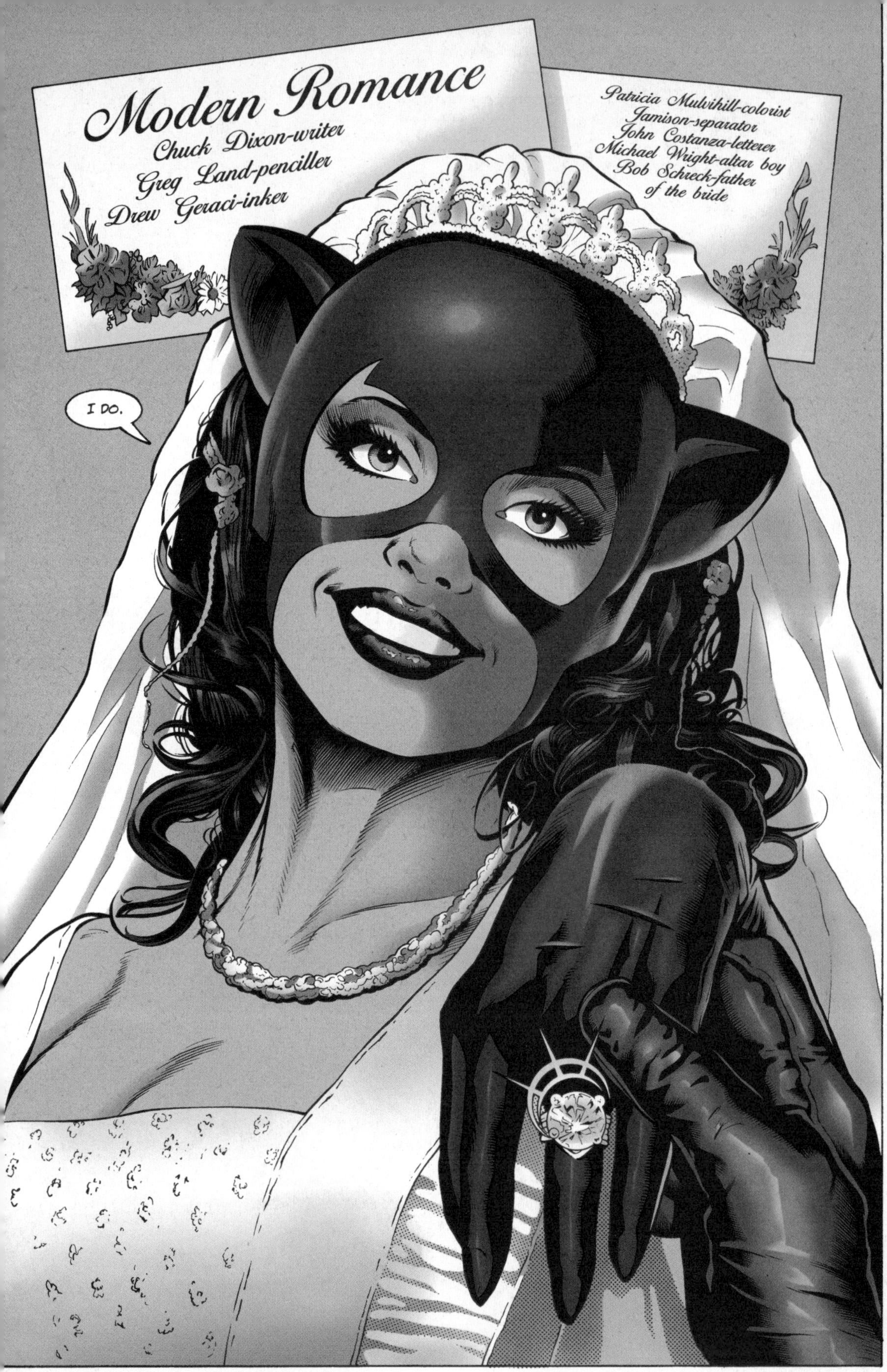

Modern Romance
Chuck Dixon-writer
Greg Land-penciller
Drew Geraci-inker
Patricia Mulvihill-colorist
Jamison-separator
John Costanza-letterer
Michael Wright-altar boy
Bob Schreck-father of the bride
I DO.

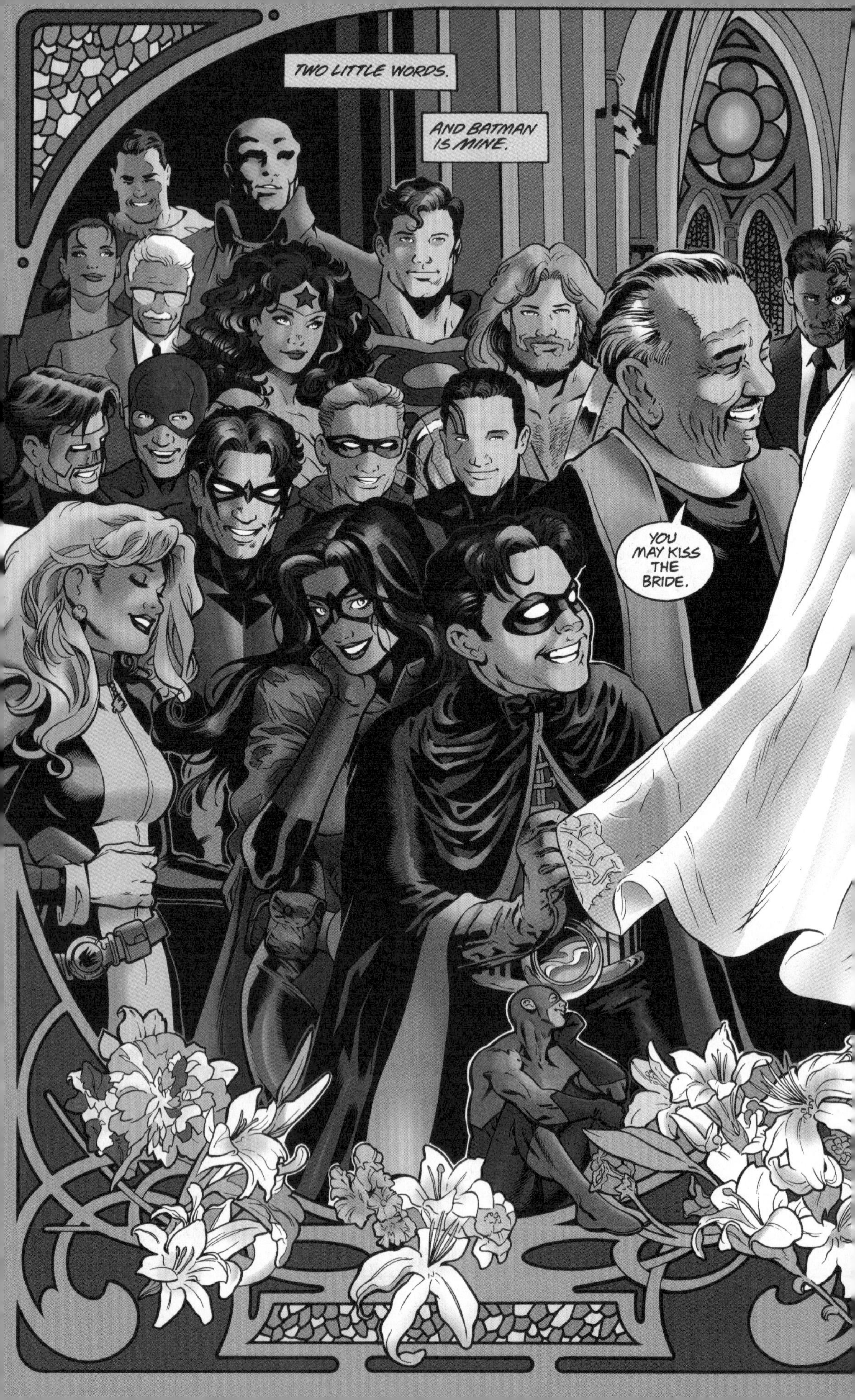
TWO LITTLE WORDS.
AND BATMAN IS MINE.
YOU MAY KISS THE BRIDE.

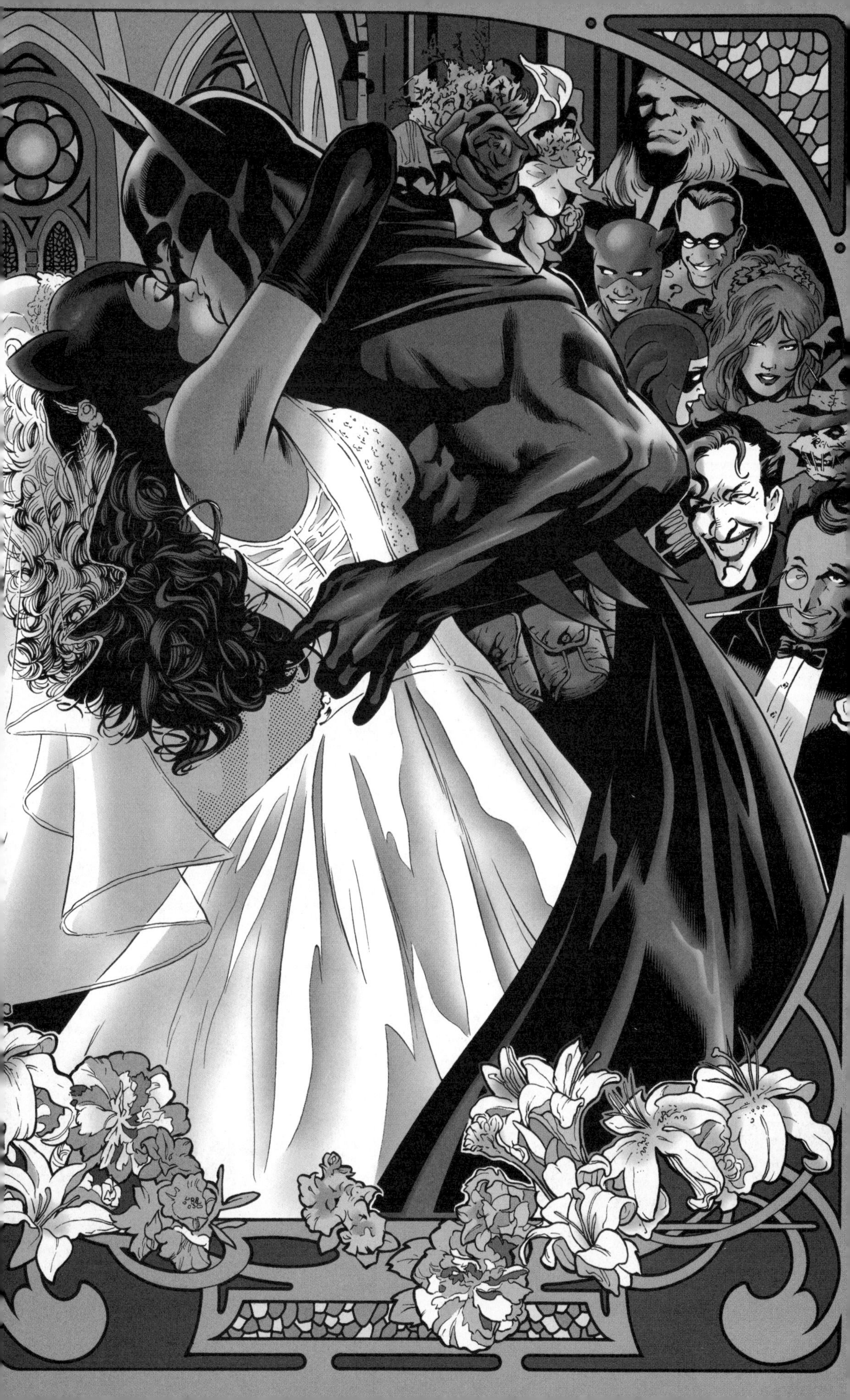

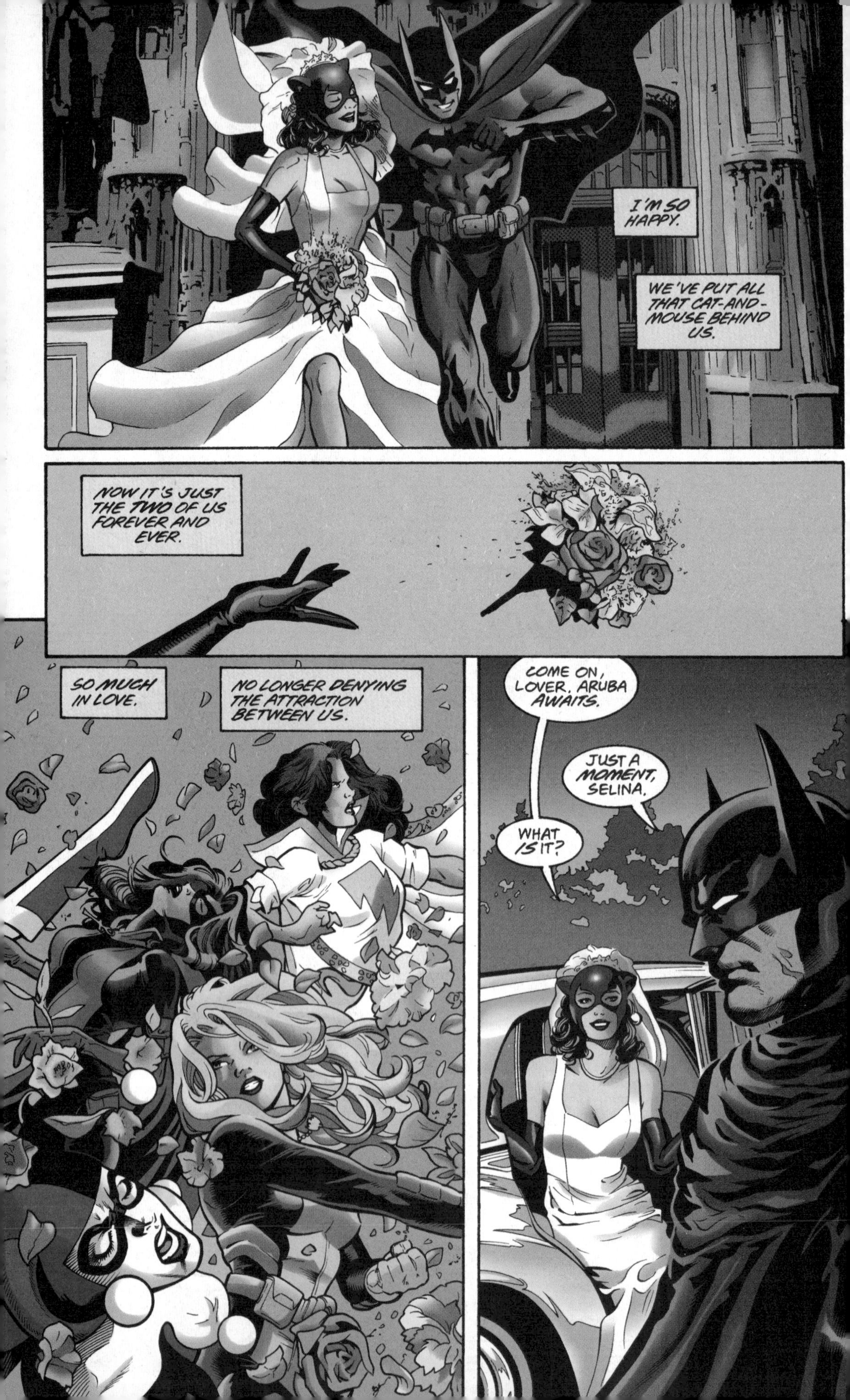
I'M SO HAPPY.
WE'VE PUT ALL THAT CAT-AND-MOUSE BEHIND US.
NOW IT'S JUST THE TWO OF US FOREVER AND EVER.
SO MUCH IN LOVE.
NO LONGER DENYING THE ATTRACTION BETWEEN US.
COME ON, LOVER. ARUBA AWAITS.
JUST A MOMENT, SELINA.
WHAT IS IT?

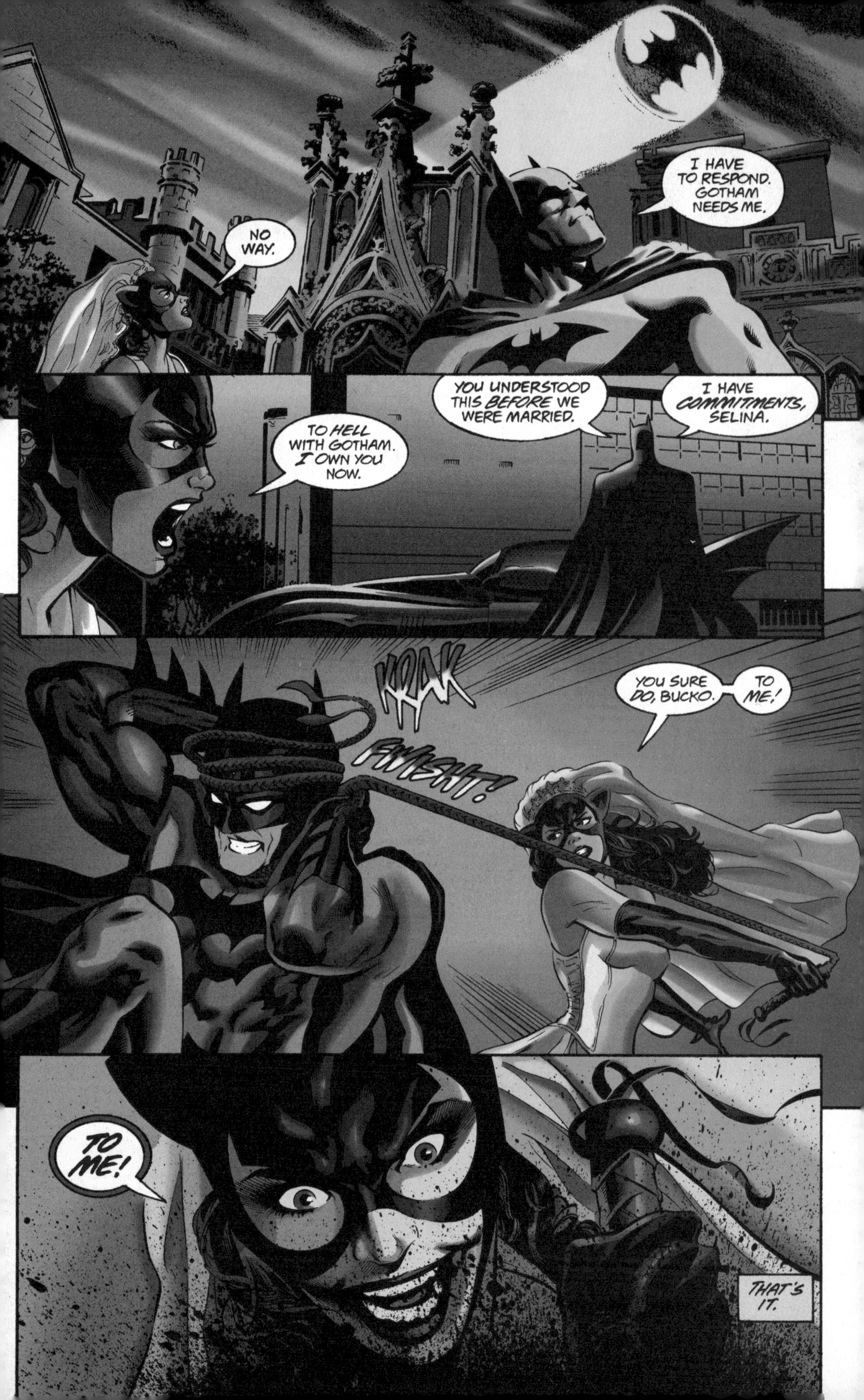
NO WAY.
I HAVE TO RESPOND. GOTHAM NEEDS ME.
TO HELL WITH GOTHAM. I OWN YOU NOW.
YOU UNDERSTOOD THIS BEFORE WE WERE MARRIED.
I HAVE COMMITMENTS, SELINA.
KRAK
FWISHT!
YOU SURE DO, BUCKO.
TO ME!
TO ME!
THAT'S IT.

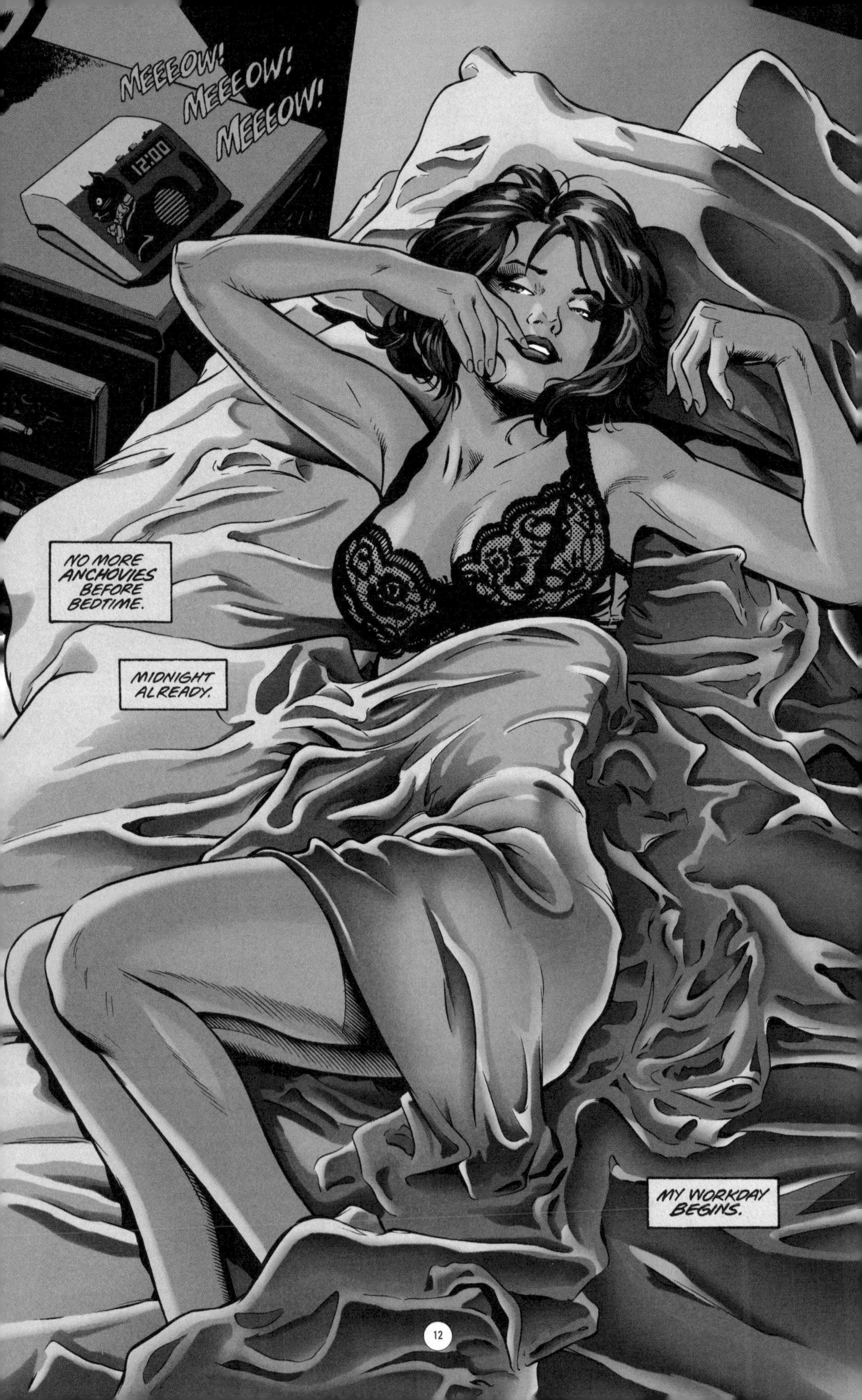
MEEEOW! MEEEOW! MEEEOW!
12:00
NO MORE ANCHOVIES BEFORE BEDTIME.
MIDNIGHT ALREADY.
MY WORKDAY BEGINS.

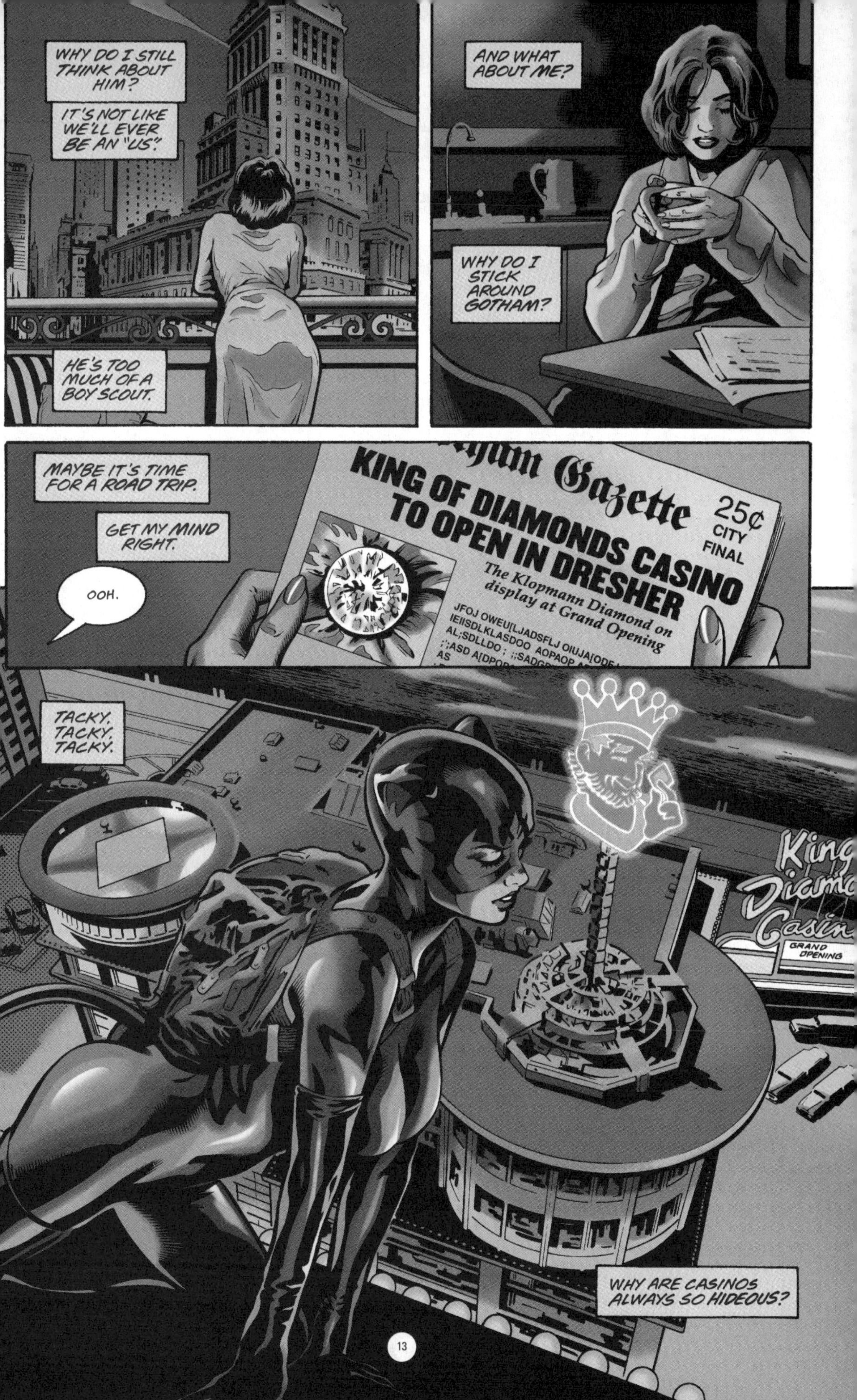
WHY DO I STILL THINK ABOUT HIM?
IT'S NOT LIKE WE'LL EVER BE AN "US."
HE'S TOO MUCH OF A BOY SCOUT.
AND WHAT ABOUT ME?
WHY DO I STICK AROUND GOTHAM?
MAYBE IT'S TIME FOR A ROAD TRIP.
GET MY MIND RIGHT.
OOH.
Gazette
25¢
CITY FINAL
KING OF DIAMONDS CASINO TO OPEN IN DRESHER
The Klopmann Diamond on display at Grand Opening
TACKY. TACKY. TACKY.
GRAND OPENING
WHY ARE CASINOS ALWAYS SO HIDEOUS?

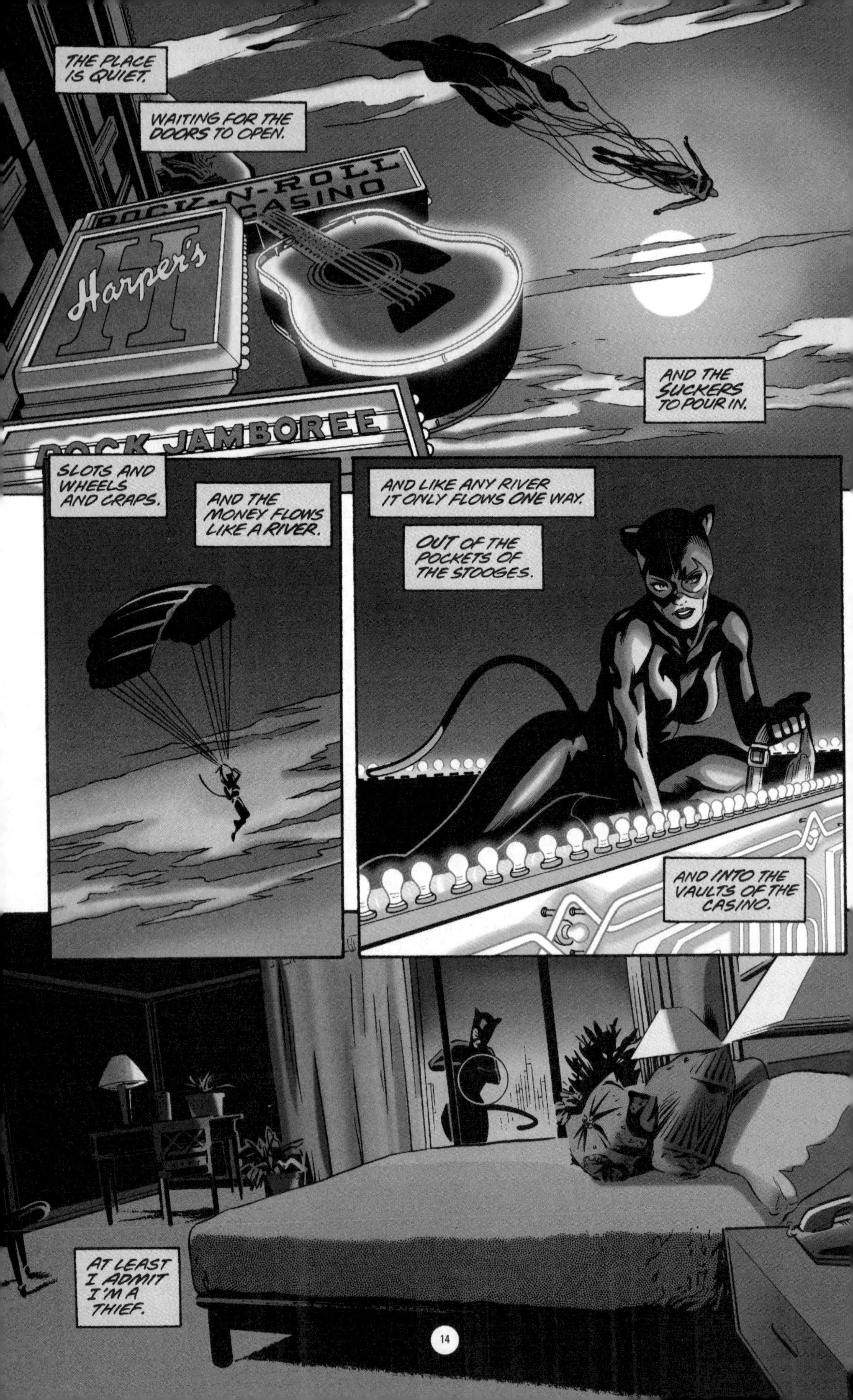
THE PLACE IS QUIET.
WAITING FOR THE DOORS TO OPEN.
Harper's
AND THE SUCKERS TO POUR IN.
SLOTS AND WHEELS AND CRAPS.
AND THE MONEY FLOWS LIKE A RIVER.
AND LIKE ANY RIVER IT ONLY FLOWS ONE WAY.
OUT OF THE POCKETS OF THE STOOGES.
AND INTO THE VAULTS OF THE CASINO.
AT LEAST I ADMIT I'M A THIEF.

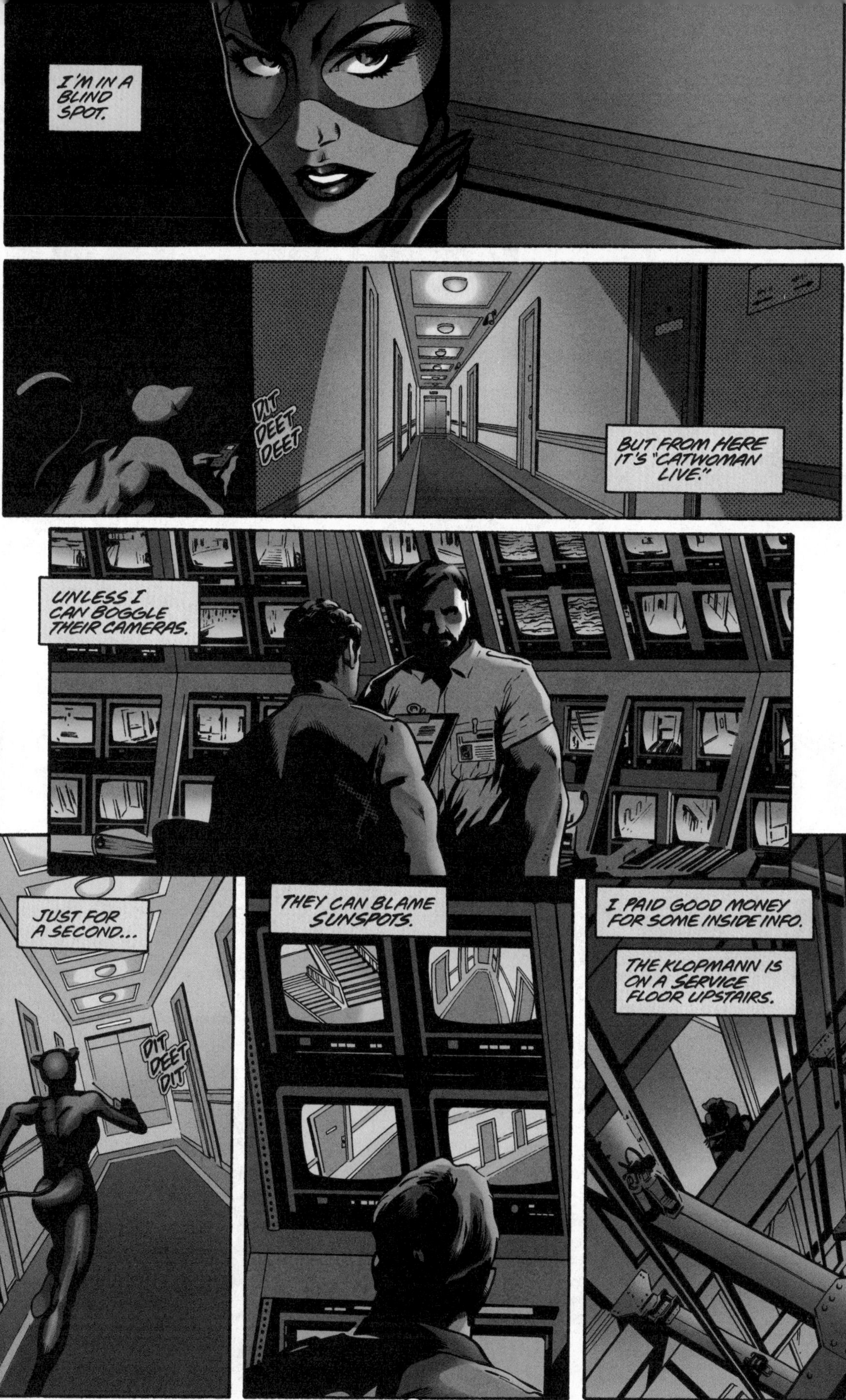
I'M IN A BLIND SPOT.
DIT DEET DEET
BUT FROM HERE IT'S "CATWOMAN LIVE."
UNLESS I CAN BOGGLE THEIR CAMERAS.
JUST FOR A SECOND...
DIT DEET DIT
THEY CAN BLAME SUNSPOTS.
I PAID GOOD MONEY FOR SOME INSIDE INFO.
THE KLOPMANN IS ON A SERVICE FLOOR UPSTAIRS.

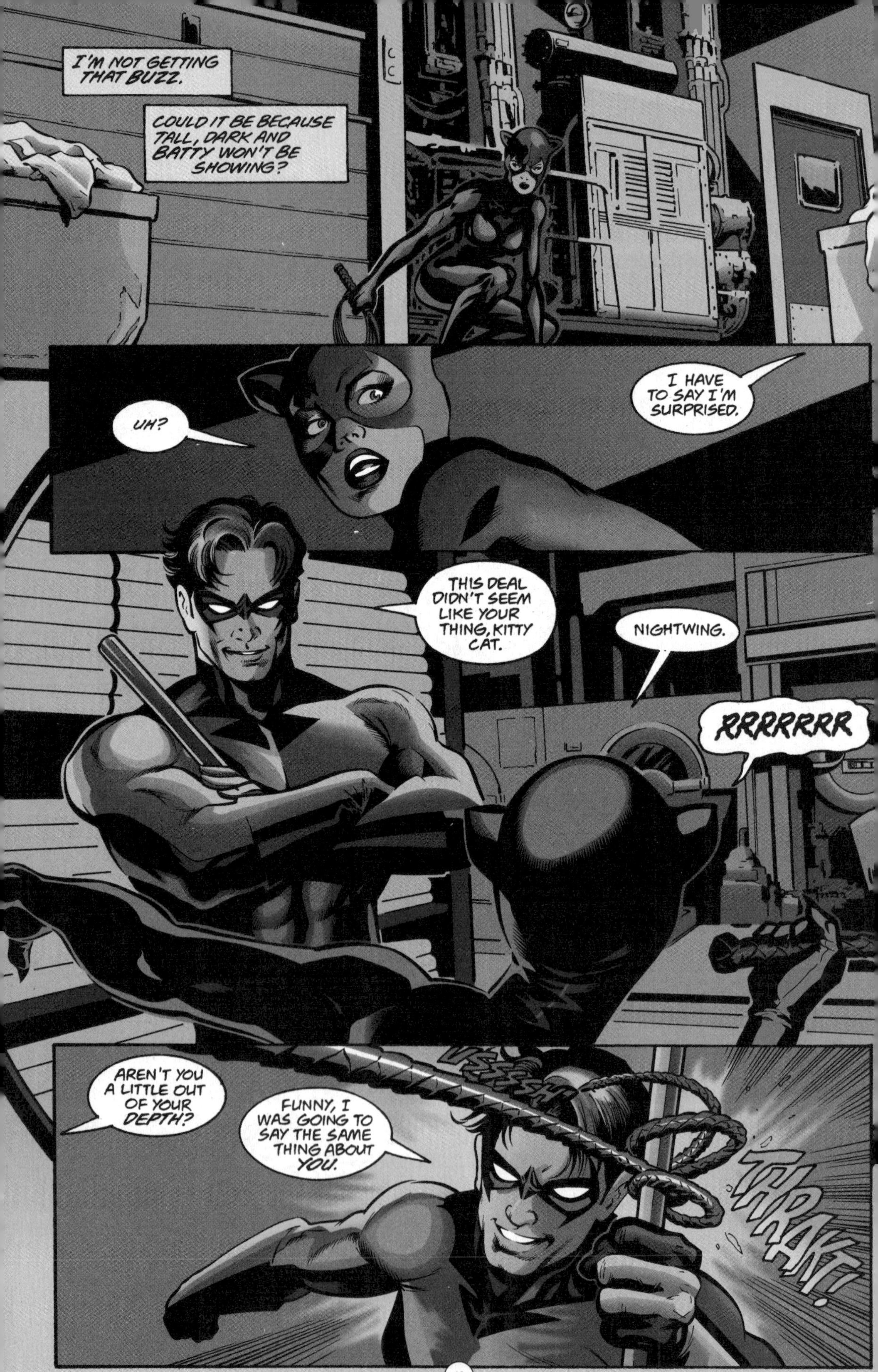
I'M NOT GETTING THAT BUZZ.
COULD IT BE BECAUSE TALL, DARK AND BATTY WON'T BE SHOWING?
UH?
I HAVE TO SAY I'M SURPRISED.
THIS DEAL DIDN'T SEEM LIKE YOUR THING, KITTY CAT.
NIGHTWING.
RRRRRRR
AREN'T YOU A LITTLE OUT OF YOUR DEPTH?
FUNNY, I WAS GOING TO SAY THE SAME THING ABOUT YOU.
THRAK!

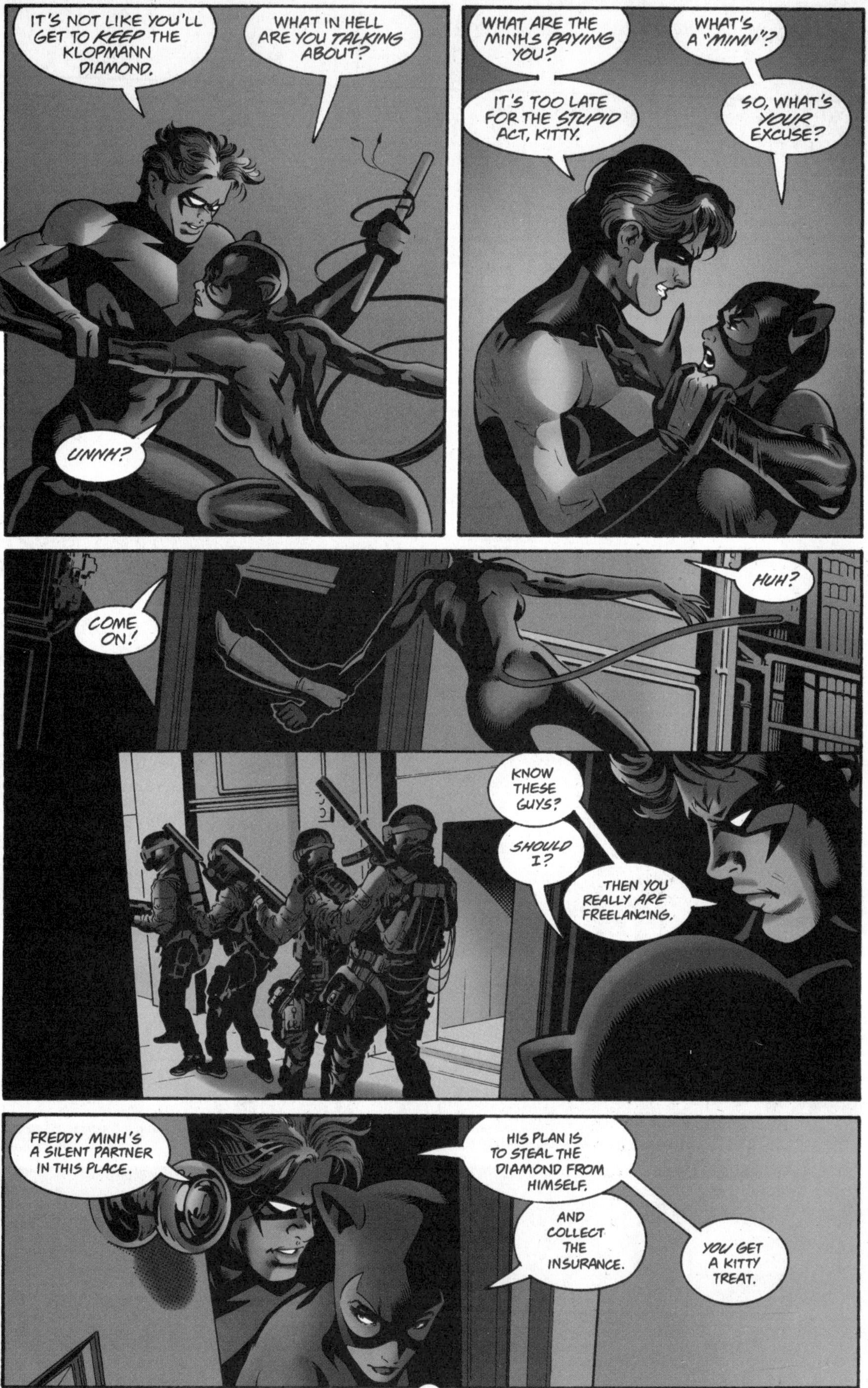
IT'S NOT LIKE YOU'LL GET TO KEEP THE KLOPMANN DIAMOND.
WHAT IN HELL ARE YOU TALKING ABOUT?
UNNH?
WHAT ARE THE MINHS PAYING YOU?
IT'S TOO LATE FOR THE STUPID ACT, KITTY.
WHAT'S A "MINN"?
SO, WHAT'S YOUR EXCUSE?
COME ON!
HUH?
KNOW THESE GUYS?
SHOULD I?
THEN YOU REALLY ARE FREELANCING.
FREDDY MINH'S A SILENT PARTNER IN THIS PLACE.
HIS PLAN IS TO STEAL THE DIAMOND FROM HIMSELF.
AND COLLECT THE INSURANCE.
YOU GET A KITTY TREAT.

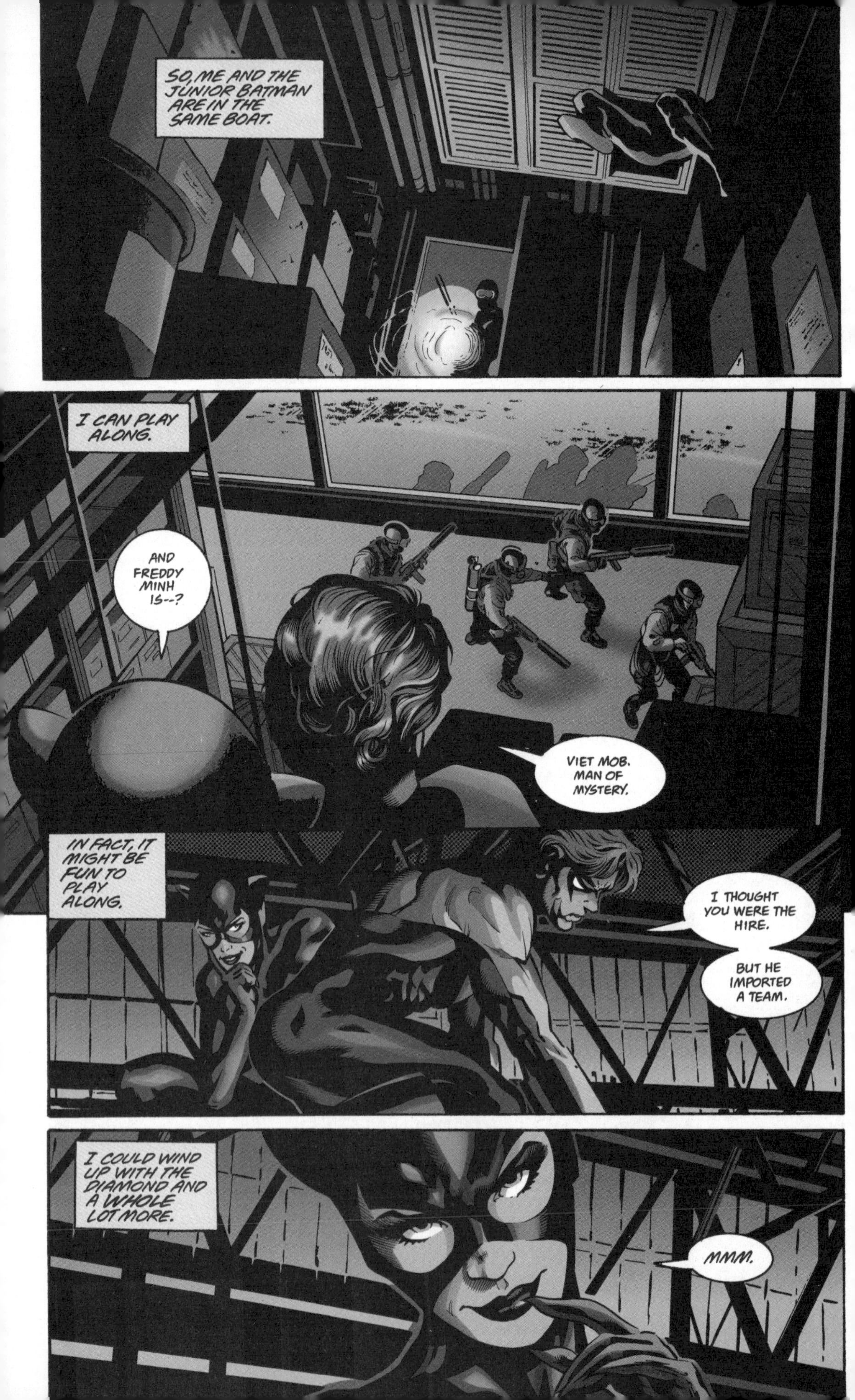
SO, ME AND THE JUNIOR BATMAN ARE IN THE SAME BOAT.
I CAN PLAY ALONG.
AND FREDDY MINH IS--?
VIET MOB. MAN OF MYSTERY.
IN FACT, IT MIGHT BE FUN TO PLAY ALONG.
I THOUGHT YOU WERE THE HIRE.
BUT HE IMPORTED A TEAM.
I COULD WIND UP WITH THE DIAMOND AND A WHOLE LOT MORE.
MMM.

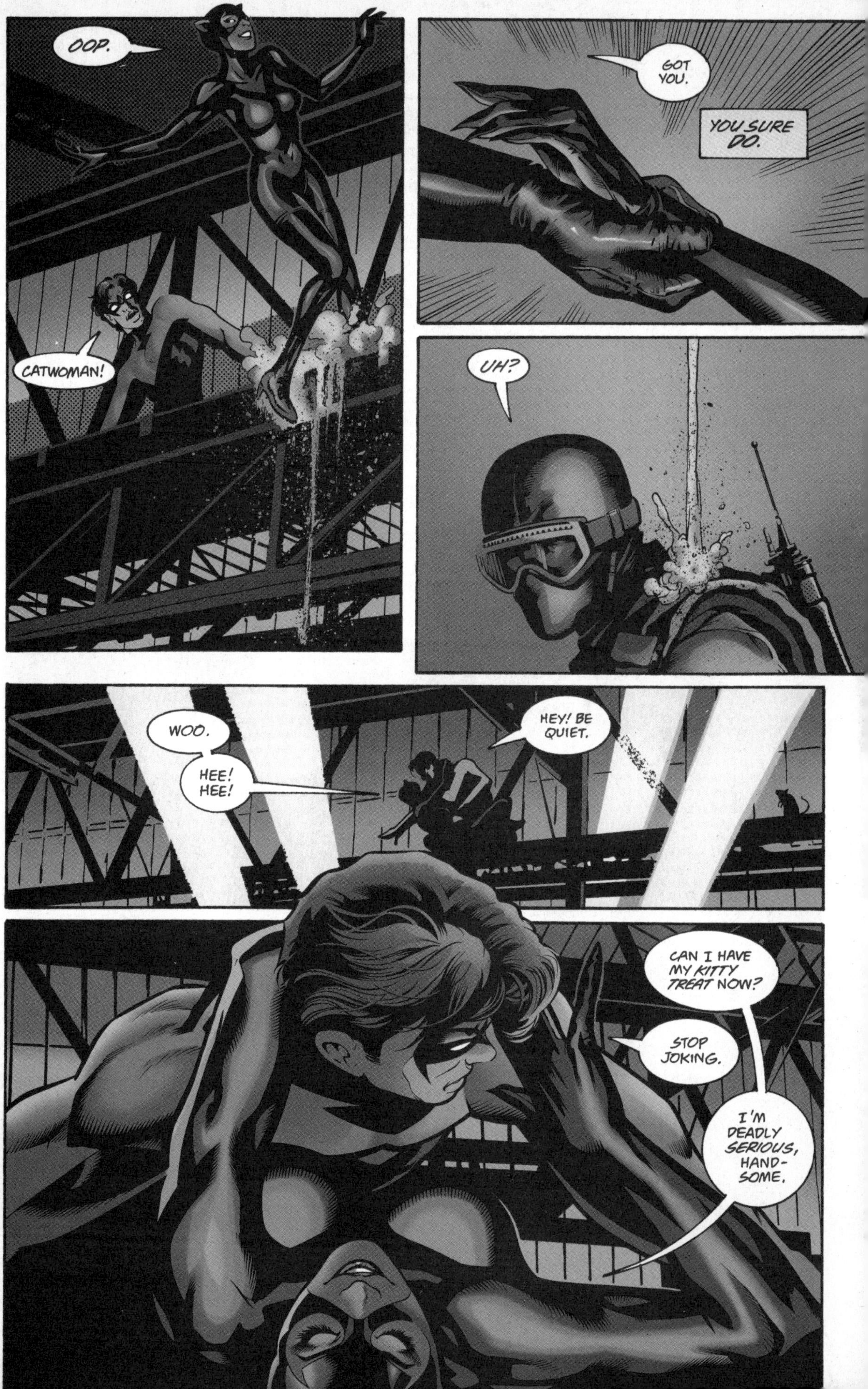
OOP.
CATWOMAN!
GOT YOU.
YOU SURE DO.
UH?
WOO.
HEE! HEE!
HEY! BE QUIET.
CAN I HAVE MY KITTY TREAT NOW?
STOP JOKING.
I'M DEADLY SERIOUS, HAND-SOME.

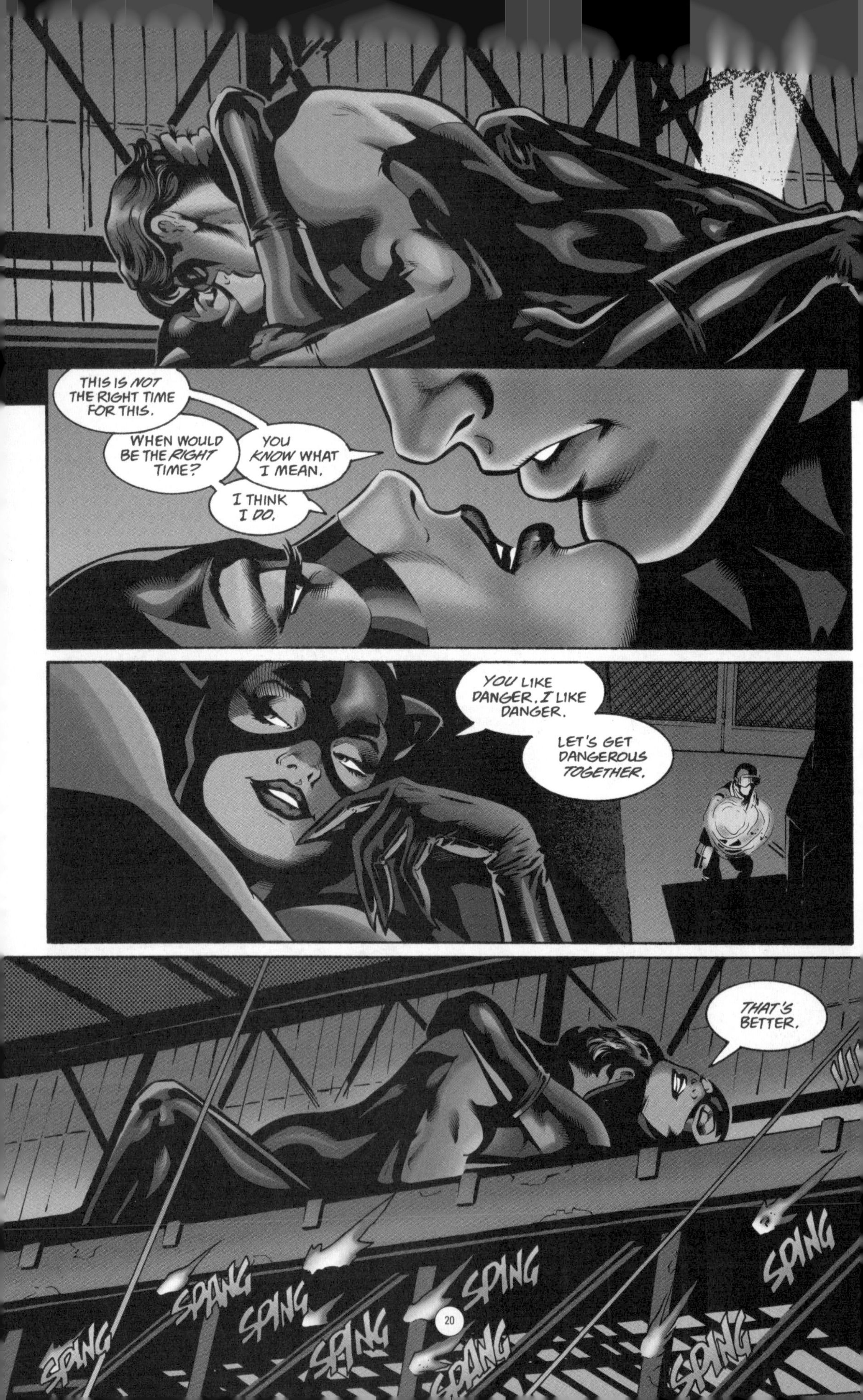
THIS IS NOT THE RIGHT TIME FOR THIS.
WHEN WOULD BE THE RIGHT TIME?
YOU KNOW WHAT I MEAN.
I THINK I DO.
YOU LIKE DANGER. I LIKE DANGER.
LET'S GET DANGEROUS TOGETHER.
THAT'S BETTER.
SPING
SPING
SPING
SPING
SPING
SPING
SPING
SPING
SPING
SPING

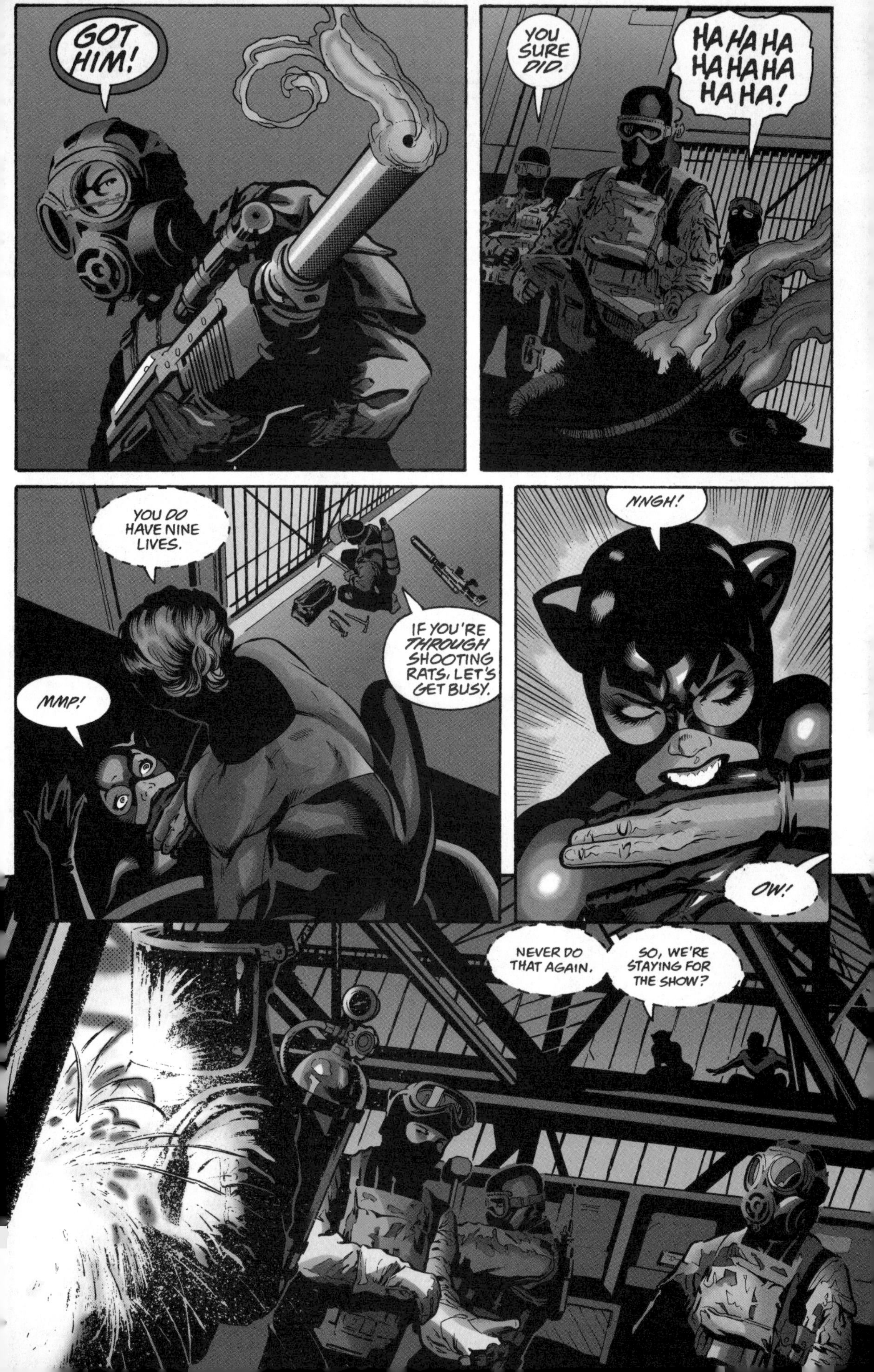
GOT HIM!
YOU SURE DID.
HA HA HA HA HA HA HA HA!
YOU DO HAVE NINE LIVES.
IF YOU'RE THROUGH SHOOTING RATS, LET'S GET BUSY.
MMP!
NNGH!
OW!
NEVER DO THAT AGAIN.
SO, WE'RE STAYING FOR THE SHOW?

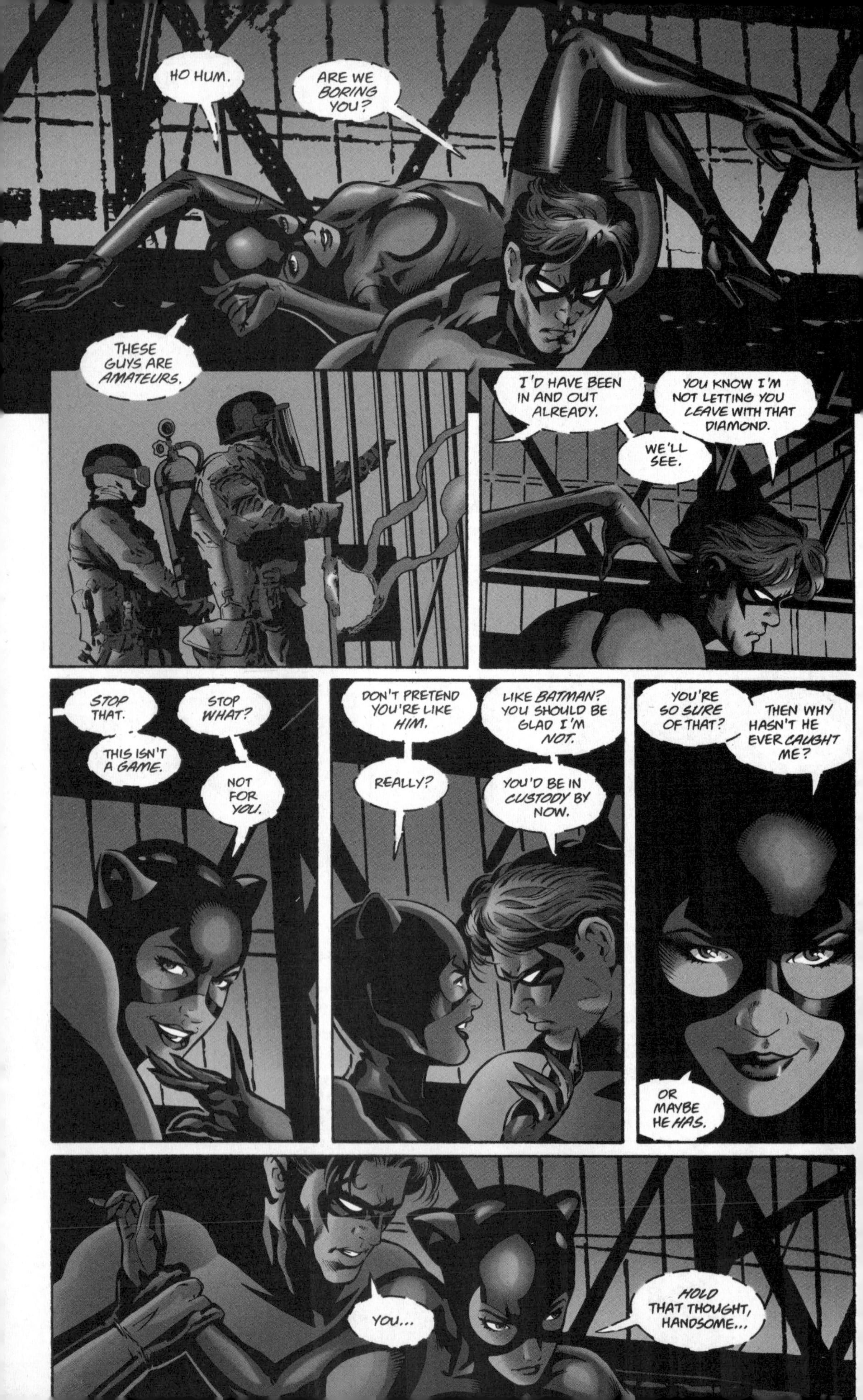
HO HUM.
ARE WE BORING YOU?
THESE GUYS ARE AMATEURS.
I'D HAVE BEEN IN AND OUT ALREADY.
YOU KNOW I'M NOT LETTING YOU LEAVE WITH THAT DIAMOND.
WE'LL SEE.
STOP THAT.
STOP WHAT?
THIS ISN'T A GAME.
NOT FOR YOU.
DON'T PRETEND YOU'RE LIKE HIM.
LIKE BATMAN? YOU SHOULD BE GLAD I'M NOT.
REALLY?
YOU'D BE IN CUSTODY BY NOW.
YOU'RE SO SURE OF THAT?
THEN WHY HASN'T HE EVER CAUGHT ME?
OR MAYBE HE HAS.
YOU...
HOLD THAT THOUGHT, HANDSOME...

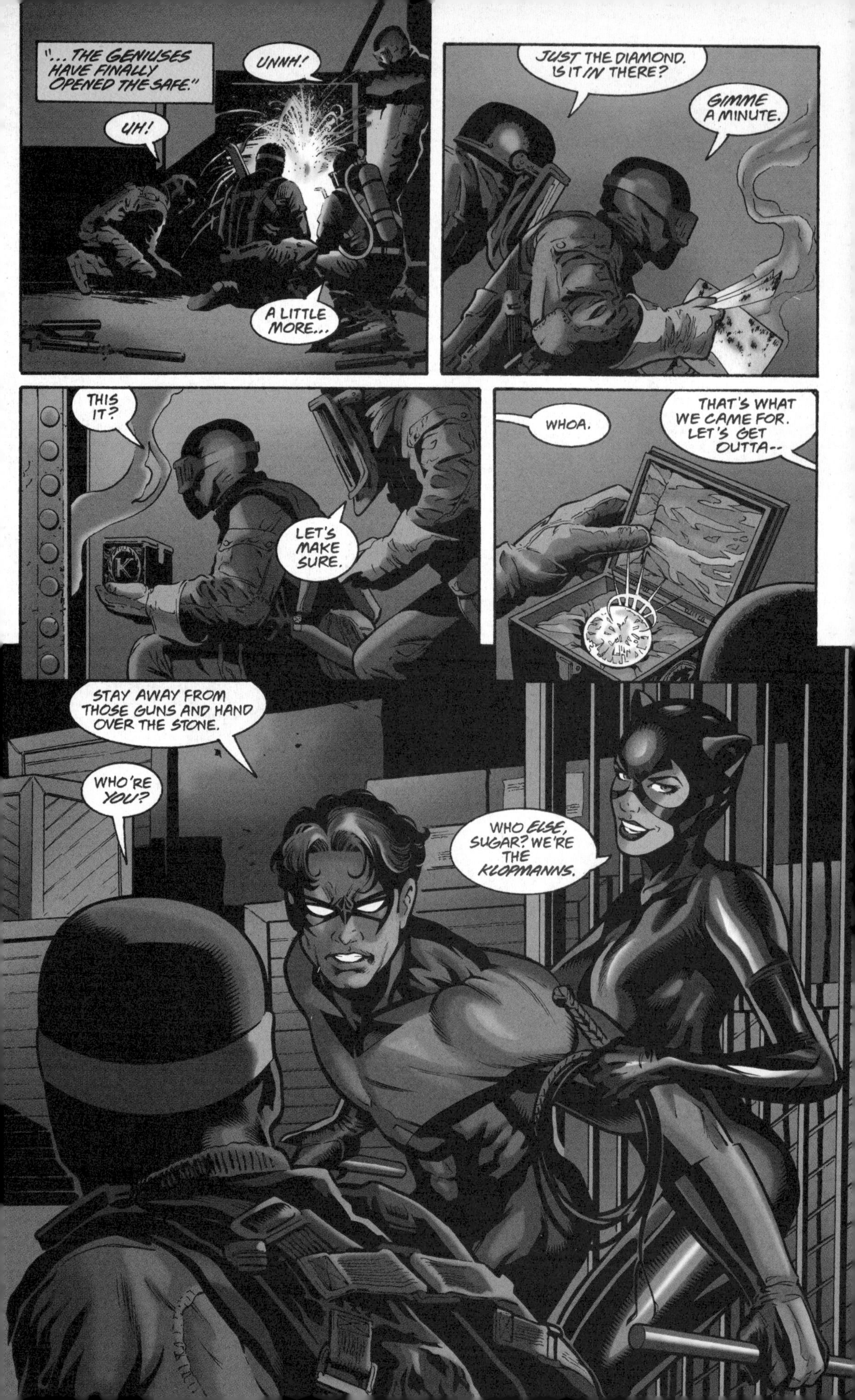
"...THE GENIUSES HAVE FINALLY OPENED THE SAFE."
UNNH!
UH!
A LITTLE MORE...
JUST THE DIAMOND. IS IT IN THERE?
GIMME A MINUTE.
THIS IT?
LET'S MAKE SURE.
WHOA.
THAT'S WHAT WE CAME FOR. LET'S GET OUTTA--
STAY AWAY FROM THOSE GUNS AND HAND OVER THE STONE.
WHO'RE YOU?
WHO ELSE, SUGAR? WE'RE THE KLOPMANNS.

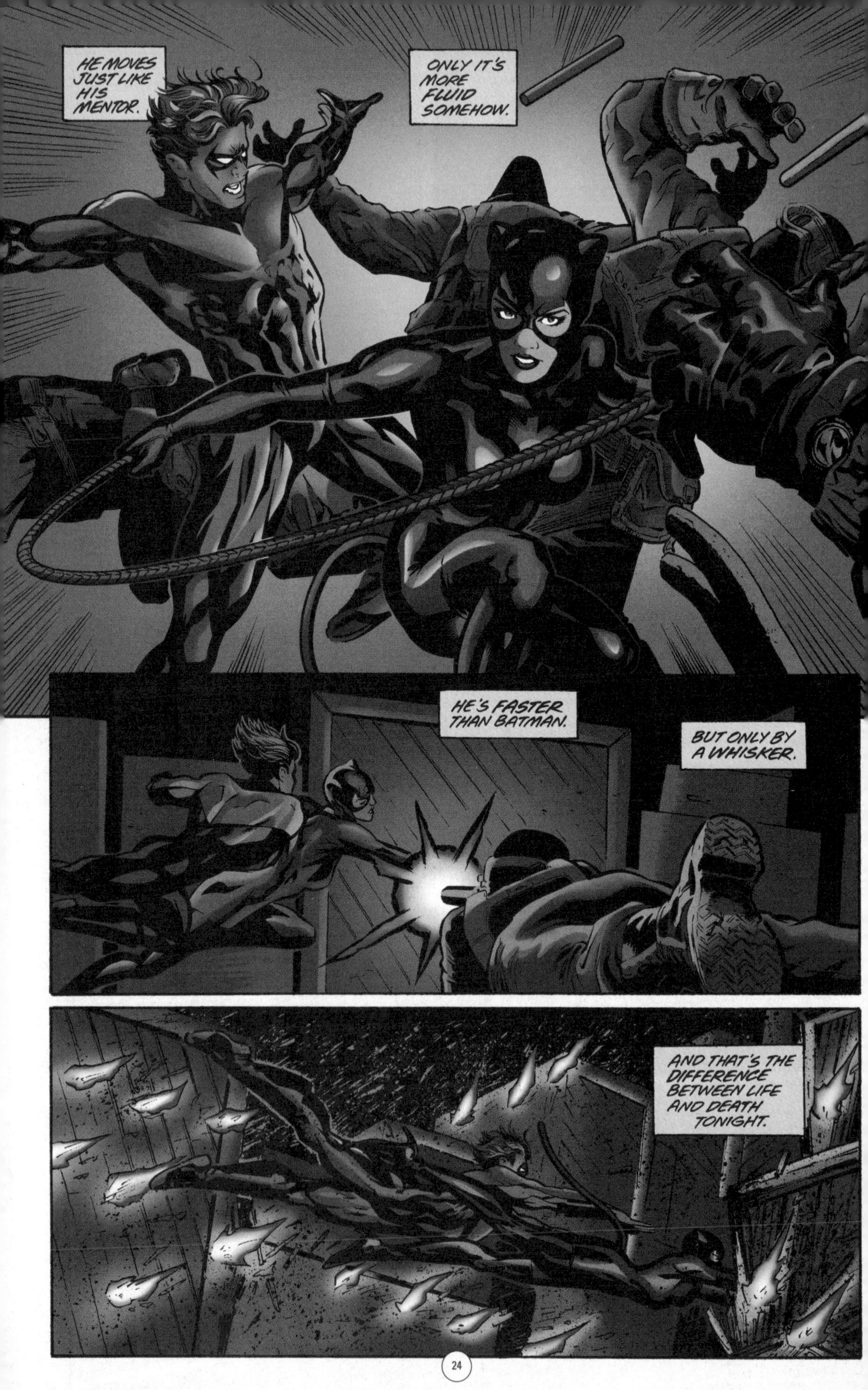
HE MOVES JUST LIKE HIS MENTOR.
ONLY IT'S MORE FLUID SOMEHOW.
HE'S FASTER THAN BATMAN.
BUT ONLY BY A WHISKER.
AND THAT'S THE DIFFERENCE BETWEEN LIFE AND DEATH TONIGHT.

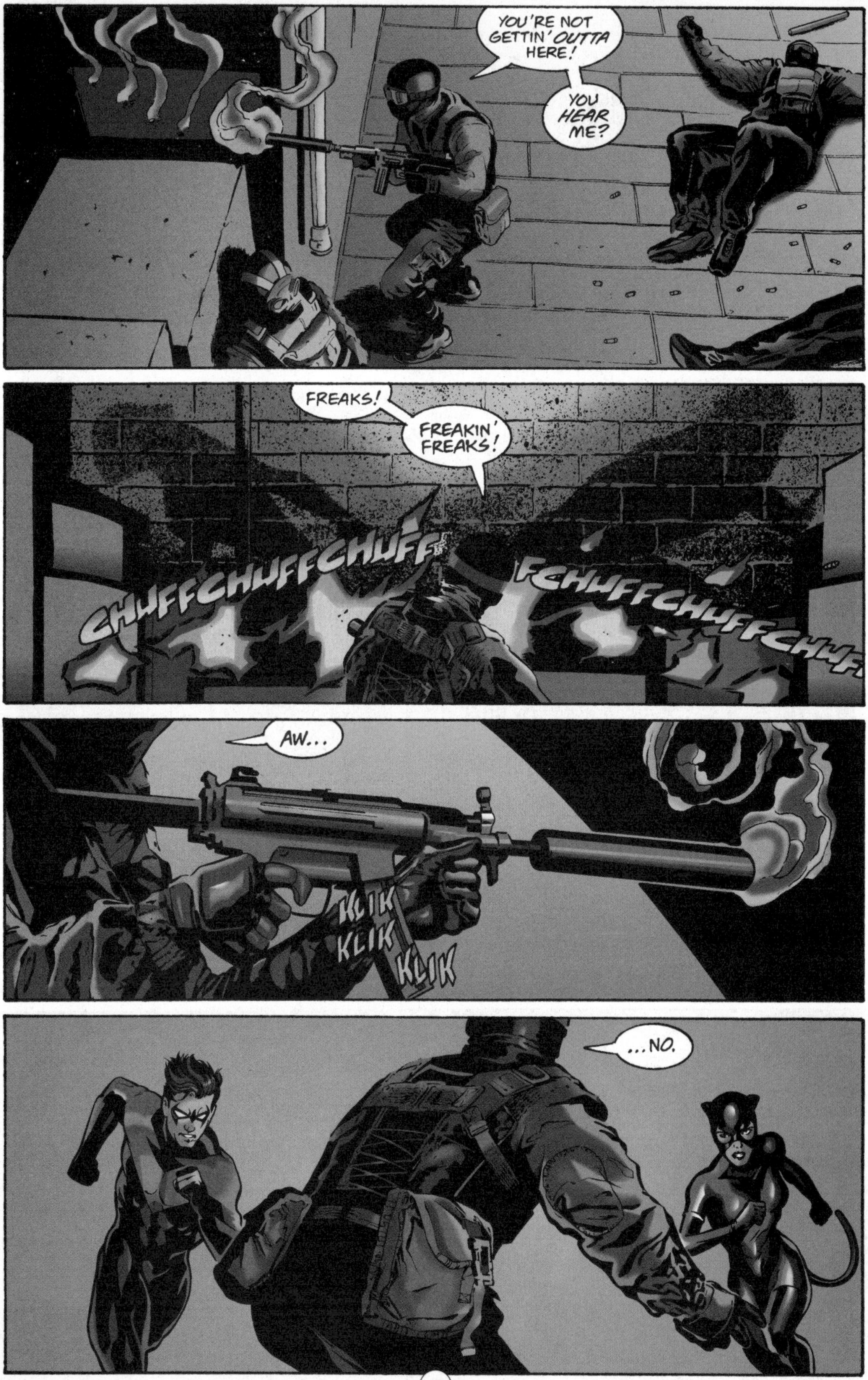
YOU'RE NOT GETTIN' OUTTA HERE!
YOU HEAR ME?
FREAKS!
FREAKIN' FREAKS!
CHUFFCHUFFCHUFF
FCHUFFCHUFFCHUFF
AW...
KLIK KLIK
KLIK
...NO.

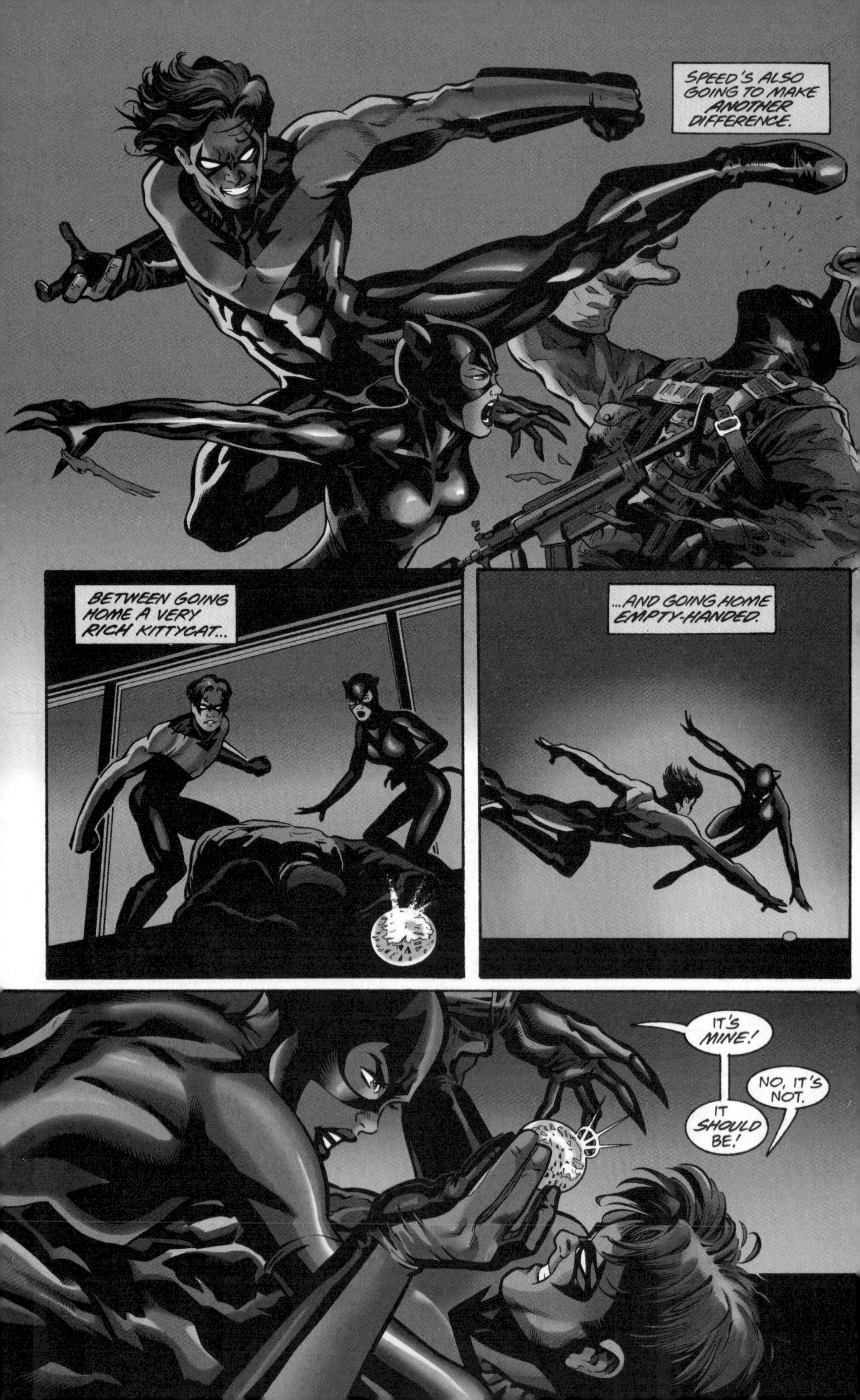
SPEED'S ALSO GOING TO MAKE ANOTHER DIFFERENCE.
BETWEEN GOING HOME A VERY RICH KITTYCAT...
...AND GOING HOME EMPTY-HANDED.
IT'S MINE!
IT SHOULD BE!
NO, IT'S NOT.

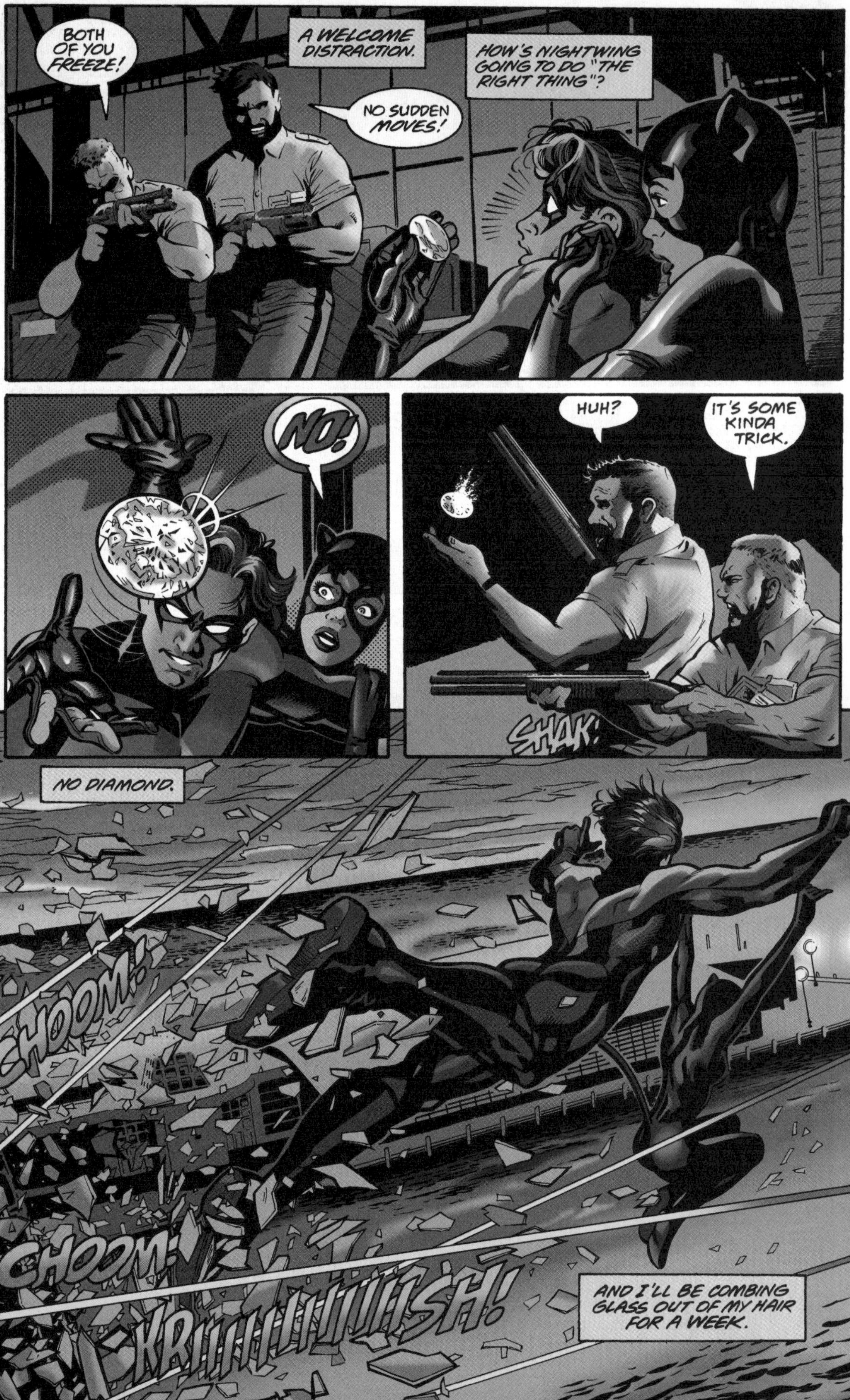
BOTH OF YOU FREEZE!
A WELCOME DISTRACTION.
NO SUDDEN MOVES!
HOW'S NIGHTWING GOING TO DO "THE RIGHT THING"?
NO!
HUH?
IT'S SOME KINDA TRICK.
SHAK!
NO DIAMOND.
CHOOM!
CHOOM!
KRIIIIIIIIIIISH!
AND I'LL BE COMBING GLASS OUT OF MY HAIR FOR A WEEK.

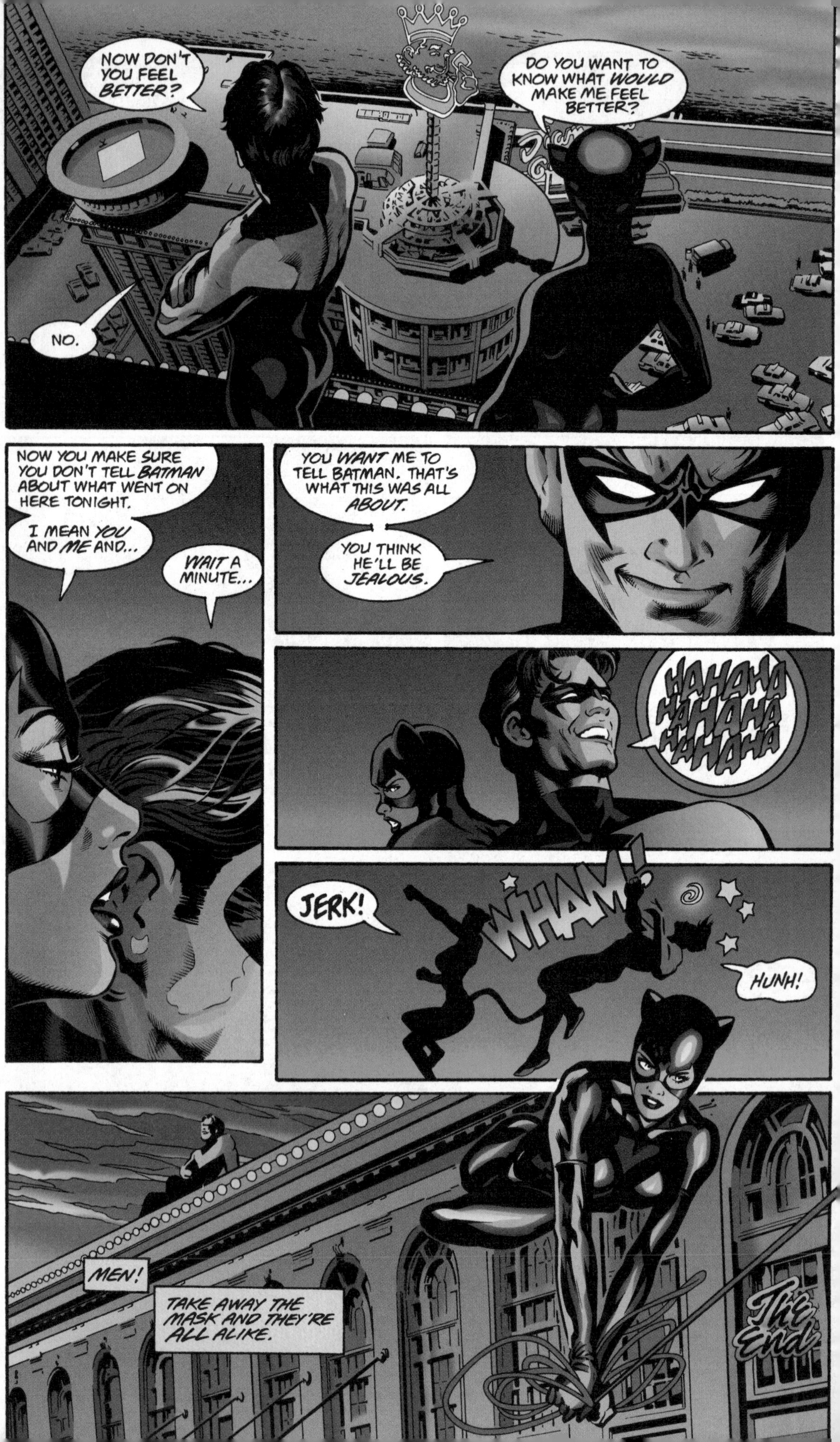
NOW DON'T YOU FEEL BETTER?
DO YOU WANT TO KNOW WHAT WOULD MAKE ME FEEL BETTER?
NO.
NOW YOU MAKE SURE YOU DON'T TELL BATMAN ABOUT WHAT WENT ON HERE TONIGHT.
I MEAN YOU AND ME AND...
WAIT A MINUTE...
YOU WANT ME TO TELL BATMAN. THAT'S WHAT THIS WAS ALL ABOUT.
YOU THINK HE'LL BE JEALOUS.
HAHAHA HAHAHA HAHAHA
JERK!
WHAM!
HUNH!
MEN!
TAKE AWAY THE MASK AND THEY'RE ALL ALIKE.
The End

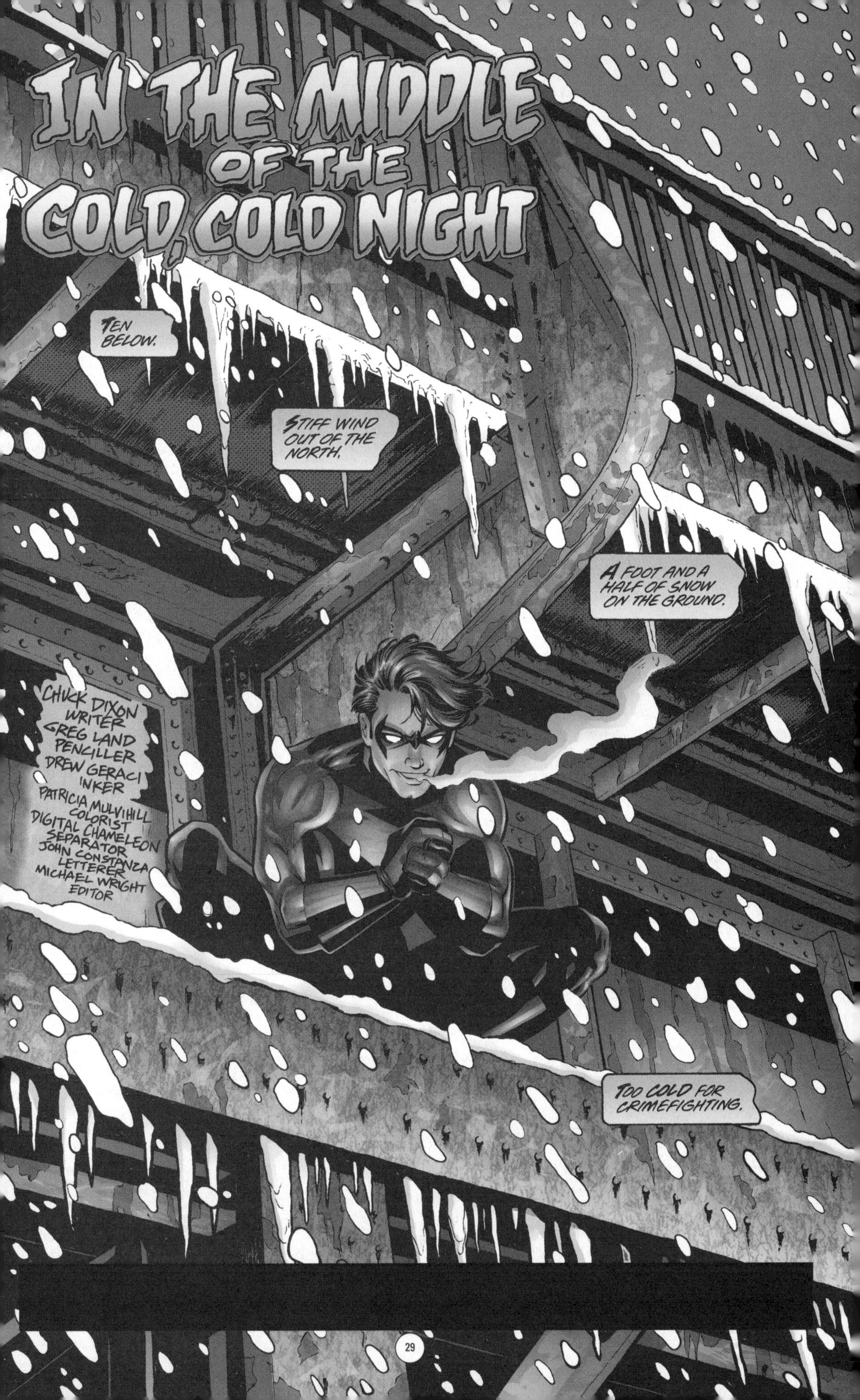
IN THE MIDDLE OF THE COLD, COLD NIGHT
TEN BELOW.
STIFF WIND OUT OF THE NORTH.
A FOOT AND A HALF OF SNOW ON THE GROUND.
CHUCK DIXON WRITER
GREG LAND PENCILLER
DREW GERACI INKER
PATRICIA MULVIHILL COLORIST
DIGITAL CHAMELEON SEPARATOR
JOHN CONSTANZA LETTERER
MICHAEL WRIGHT EDITOR
TOO COLD FOR CRIMEFIGHTING.

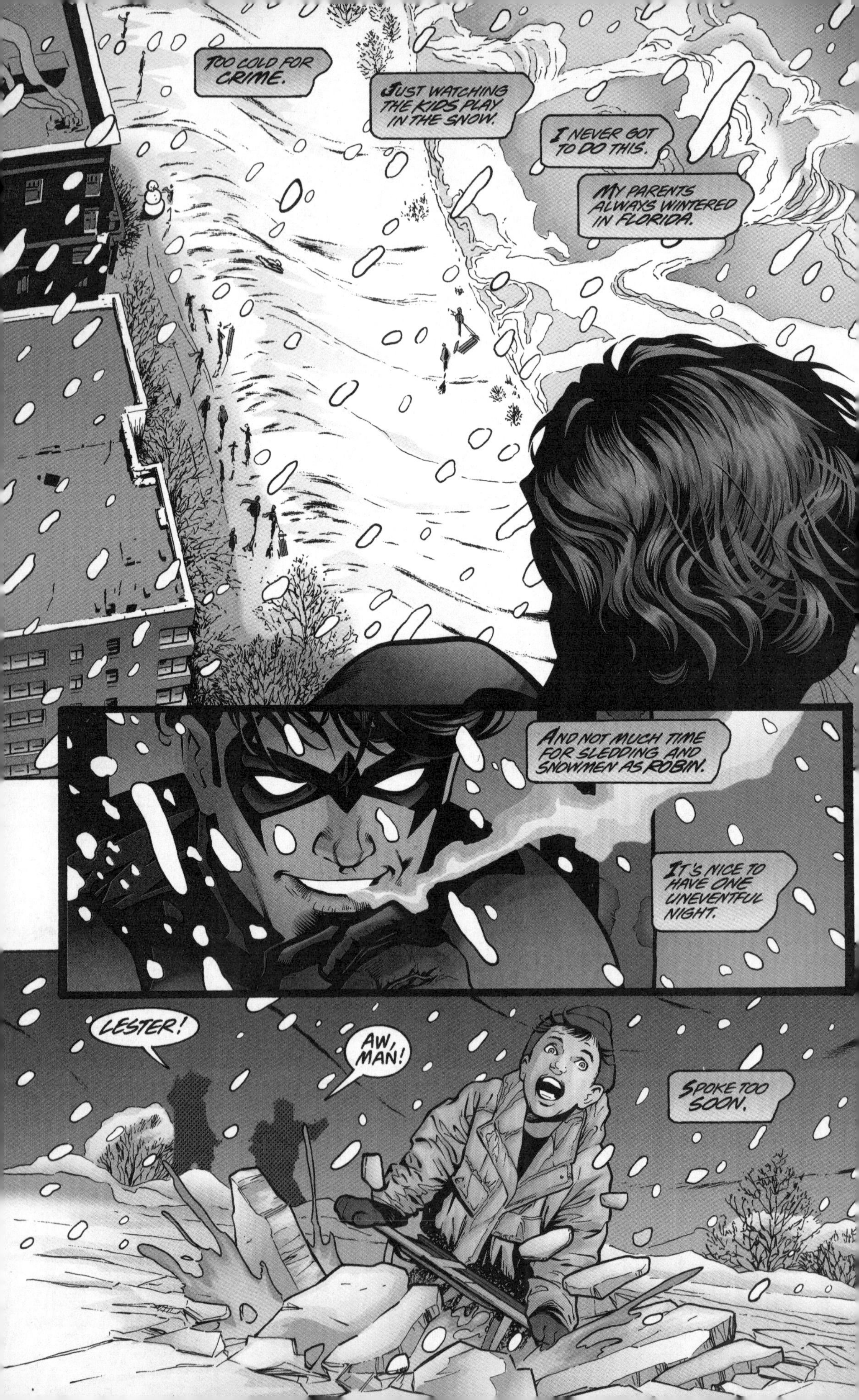
TOO COLD FOR CRIME.
JUST WATCHING THE KIDS PLAY IN THE SNOW.
I NEVER GOT TO DO THIS.
MY PARENTS ALWAYS WINTERED IN FLORIDA.
AND NOT MUCH TIME FOR SLEDDING AND SNOWMEN AS ROBIN.
IT'S NICE TO HAVE ONE UNEVENTFUL NIGHT.
LESTER!
AW, MAN!
SPOKE TOO SOON.

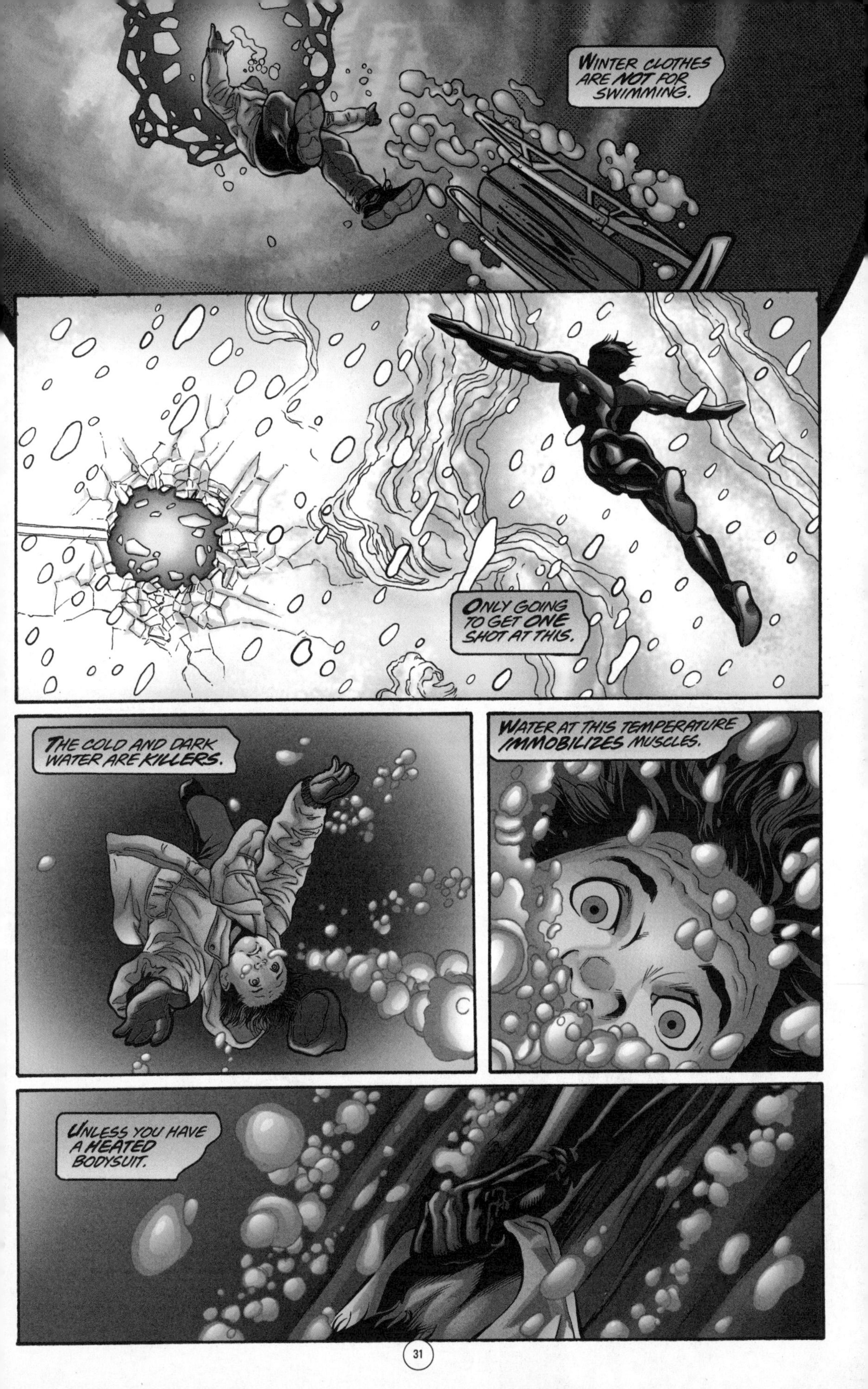
WINTER CLOTHES ARE NOT FOR SWIMMING.
ONLY GOING TO GET ONE SHOT AT THIS.
THE COLD AND DARK WATER ARE KILLERS.
WATER AT THIS TEMPERATURE IMMOBILIZES MUSCLES.
UNLESS YOU HAVE A HEATED BODYSUIT.

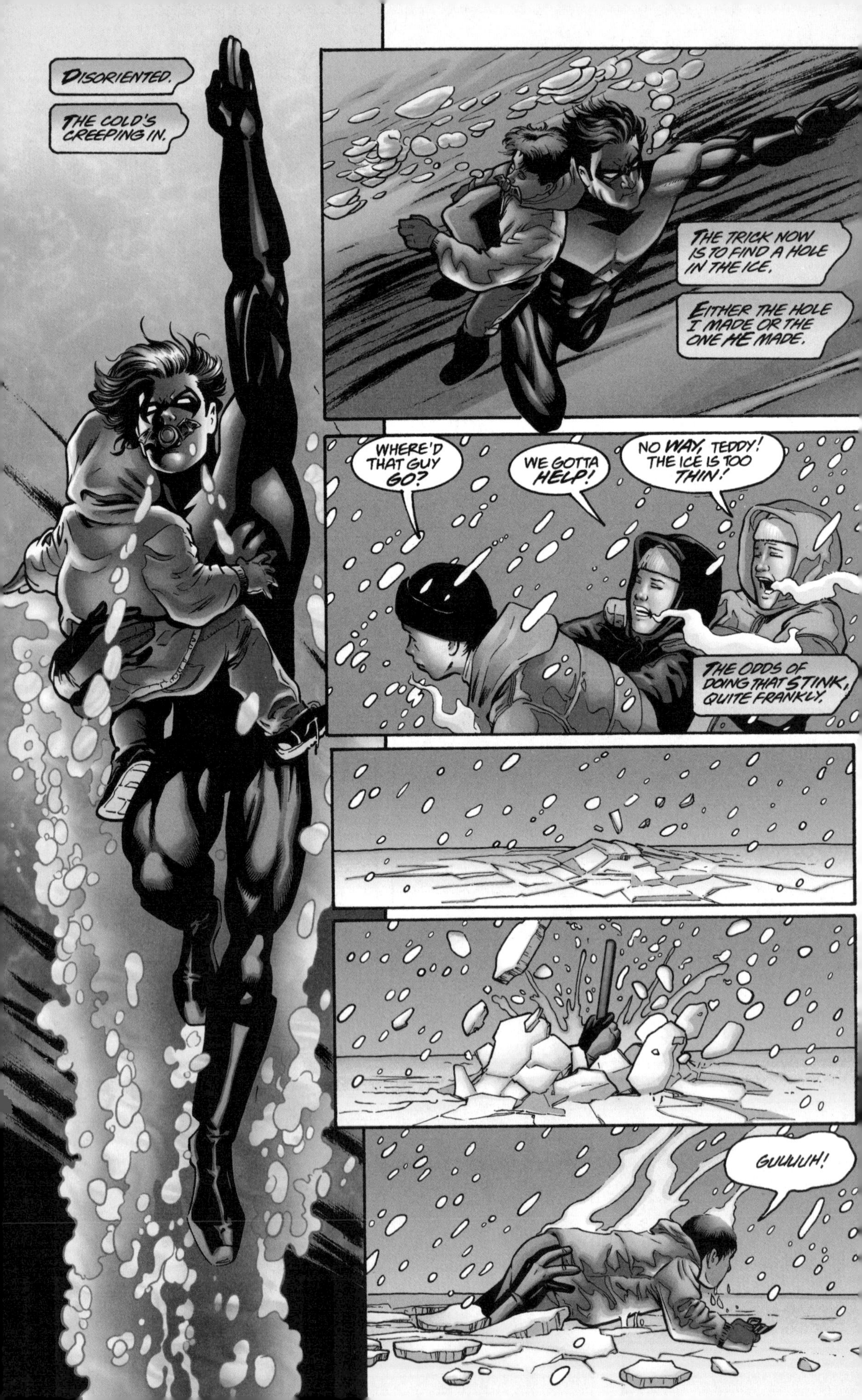
DISORIENTED.
THE COLD'S CREEPING IN.
THE TRICK NOW IS TO FIND A HOLE IN THE ICE.
EITHER THE HOLE I MADE OR THE ONE HE MADE.
WHERE'D THAT GUY GO?
WE GOTTA HELP!
NO WAY, TEDDY! THE ICE IS TOO THIN!
THE ODDS OF DOING THAT STINK, QUITE FRANKLY.
GUUUUH!

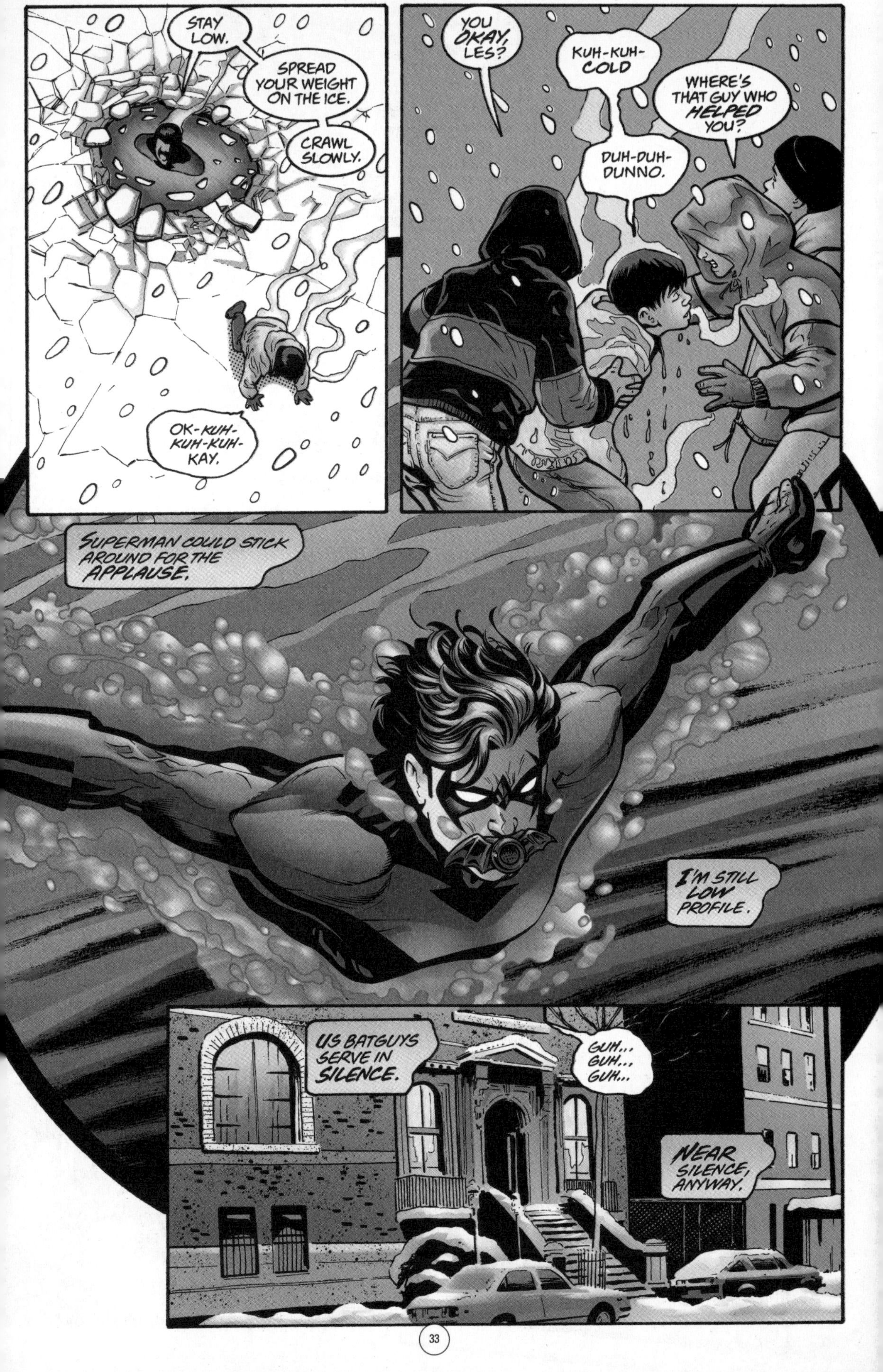
STAY LOW.
SPREAD YOUR WEIGHT ON THE ICE.
CRAWL SLOWLY.
OK-KUH-KUH-KUH-KAY.
YOU OKAY, LES?
KUH-KUH-COLD
DUH-DUH-DUNNO.
WHERE'S THAT GUY WHO HELPED YOU?
SUPERMAN COULD STICK AROUND FOR THE APPLAUSE.
I'M STILL LOW PROFILE.
US BATGUYS SERVE IN SILENCE.
GUH... GUH... GUH...
NEAR SILENCE, ANYWAY.

LOOKS LIKE REDHORN'S MAKING A COMEBACK.

GUH...
GUH...
GUH...

Blud News $1.50 edition

CHIEF REDHORN RETURNS
In Wake of Ebersol Murder, Former Chief to Take the Reins

BULLIES STINK ON ICE
3-0 LOSS ADDS TO STREAK

GICHOOOO!

I GUESS HE BELIEVED ME.

--A CRISIS OF FAITH IN THE BLÜDHAVEN POLICE DEPARTMENT.

HIS PROBLEMS WITH BLOCKBUSTER ARE ANCIENT HISTORY BY NOW.

BACK TO THE STATUS QUO WITH THE 'HAVEN'S FINEST.

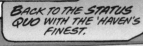

I FEEL A RESPONSIBILITY TO THIS CITY. IT'S MY HOMETOWN. IT'S WHERE I WAS BORN.

LIVE NEWS COVERAGE
ACTION 12

HOW CAN I RETIRE WHEN MY BOYS NEED ME?

HOW CAN I NOT HEED THE CALL?

RETIRE? THAT'S A GOOD ONE.

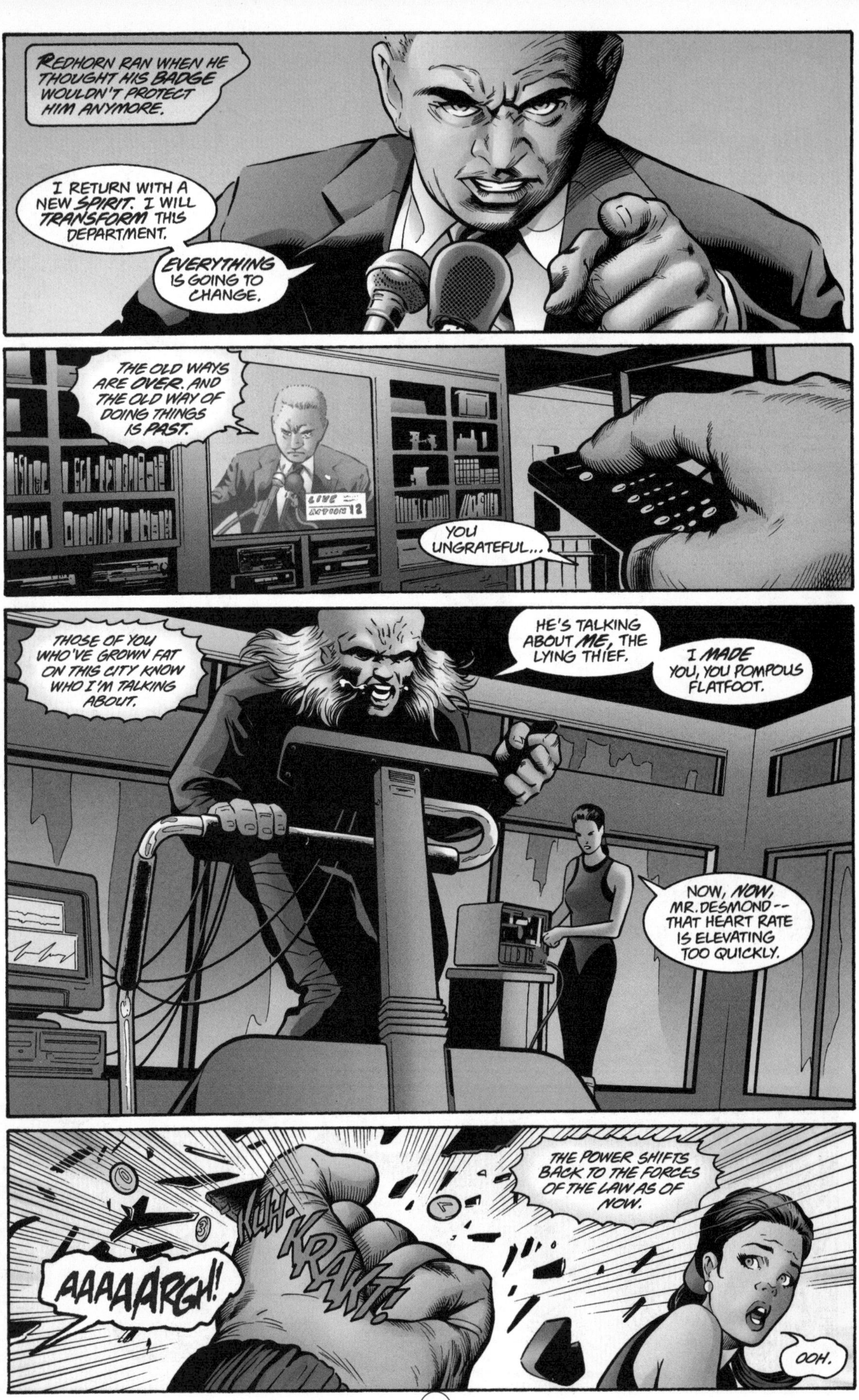

REDHORN RAN WHEN HE THOUGHT HIS BADGE WOULDN'T PROTECT HIM ANYMORE.
I RETURN WITH A NEW SPIRIT. I WILL TRANSFORM THIS DEPARTMENT.
EVERYTHING IS GOING TO CHANGE.
THE OLD WAYS ARE OVER. AND THE OLD WAY OF DOING THINGS IS PAST.
LIVE
ACTION 12
YOU UNGRATEFUL...
THOSE OF YOU WHO'VE GROWN FAT ON THIS CITY KNOW WHO I'M TALKING ABOUT.
HE'S TALKING ABOUT ME, THE LYING THIEF.
I MADE YOU, YOU POMPOUS FLATFOOT.
NOW, NOW, MR. DESMOND -- THAT HEART RATE IS ELEVATING TOO QUICKLY.
THE POWER SHIFTS BACK TO THE FORCES OF THE LAW AS OF NOW.
KUH-KRAK!
AAAAARGH!
OOH.

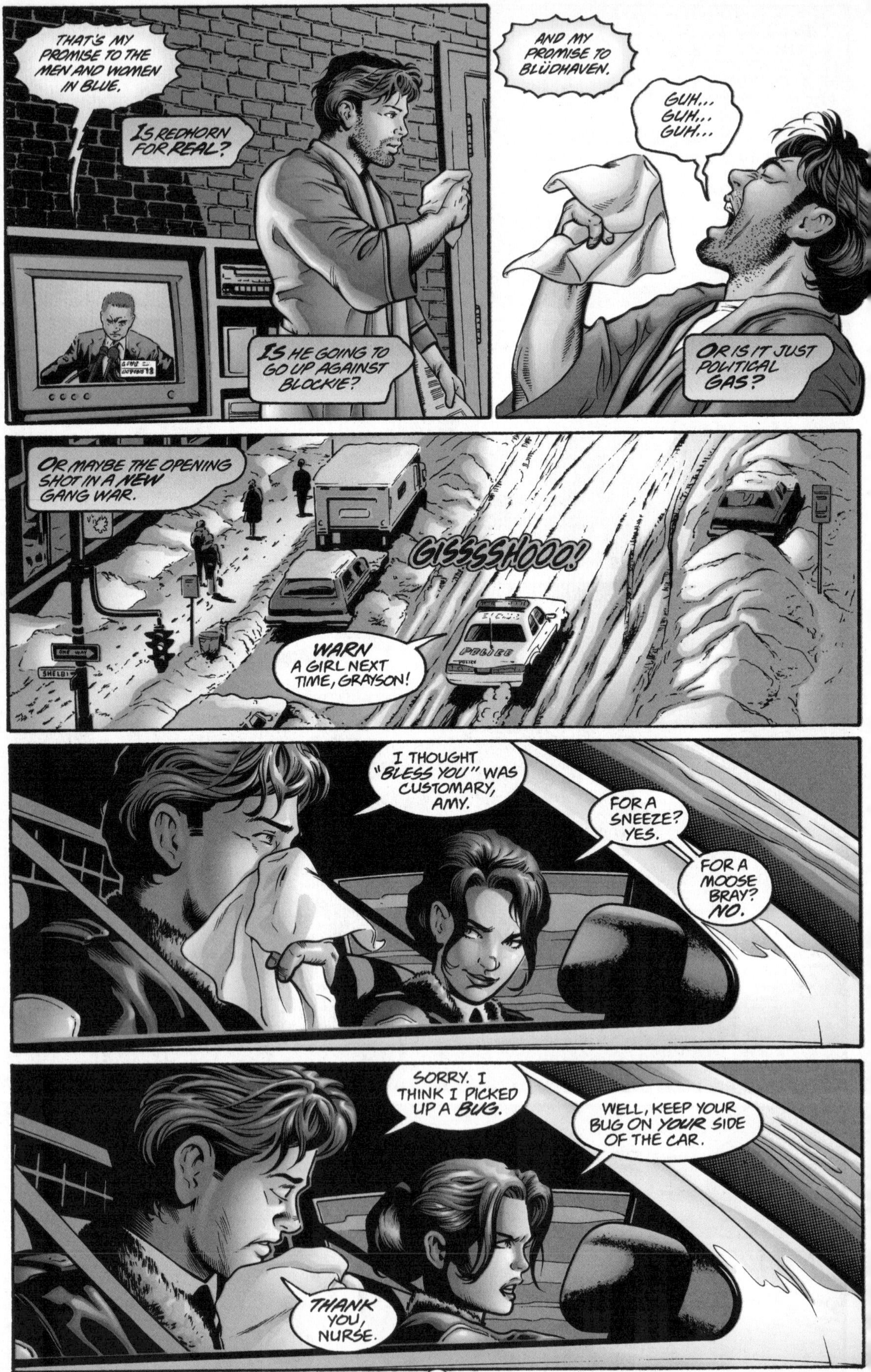
THAT'S MY PROMISE TO THE MEN AND WOMEN IN BLUE.
IS REDHORN FOR REAL?
IS HE GOING TO GO UP AGAINST BLOCKIE?
AND MY PROMISE TO BLÜDHAVEN.
GUH... GUH... GUH...
OR IS IT JUST POLITICAL GAS?
OR MAYBE THE OPENING SHOT IN A NEW GANG WAR.
GISSSSHOOO!
WARN A GIRL NEXT TIME, GRAYSON!
ONE WAY
POLICE
I THOUGHT "BLESS YOU" WAS CUSTOMARY, AMY.
FOR A SNEEZE? YES.
FOR A MOOSE BRAY? NO.
SORRY. I THINK I PICKED UP A BUG.
WELL, KEEP YOUR BUG ON YOUR SIDE OF THE CAR.
THANK YOU, NURSE.

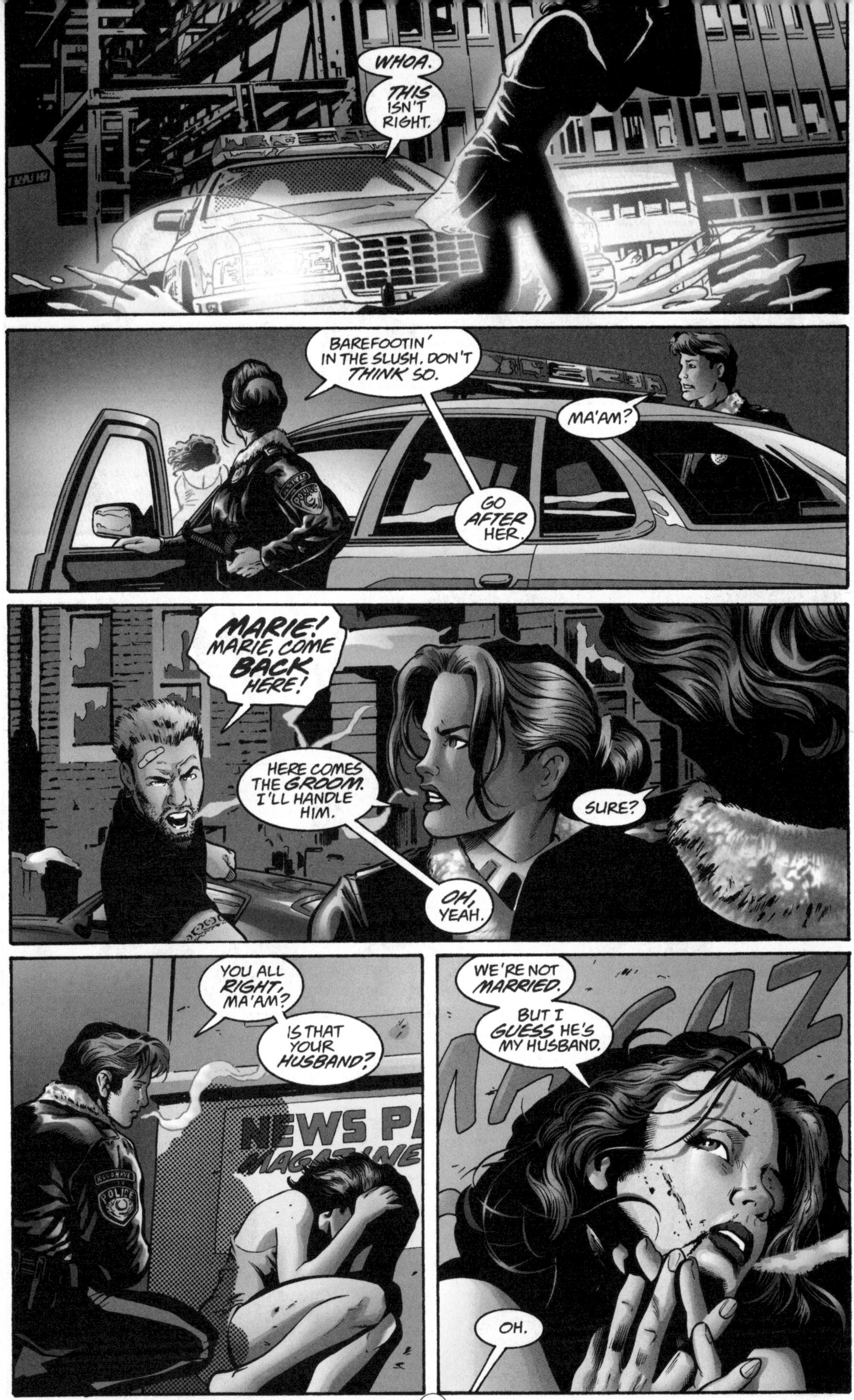
WHOA.
THIS ISN'T RIGHT.
BAREFOOTIN' IN THE SLUSH. DON'T THINK SO.
MA'AM?
GO AFTER HER.
MARIE! MARIE, COME BACK HERE!
HERE COMES THE GROOM. I'LL HANDLE HIM.
SURE?
OH, YEAH.
YOU ALL RIGHT, MA'AM?
IS THAT YOUR HUSBAND?
NEWS
WE'RE NOT MARRIED.
BUT I GUESS HE'S MY HUSBAND.
OH.

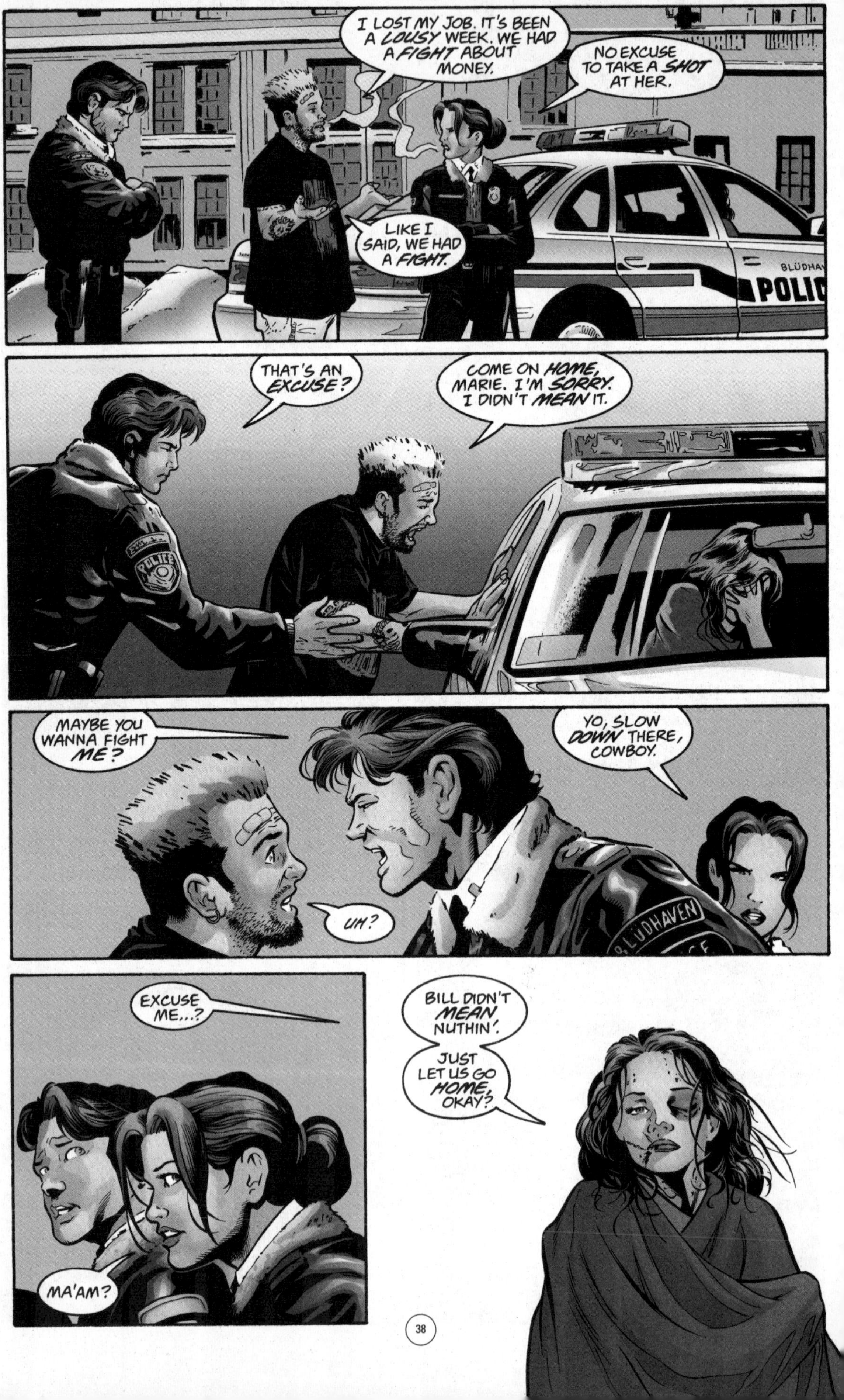
I LOST MY JOB. IT'S BEEN A LOUSY WEEK. WE HAD A FIGHT ABOUT MONEY.
NO EXCUSE TO TAKE A SHOT AT HER.
LIKE I SAID, WE HAD A FIGHT.
BLÜDHAVEN POLIC
THAT'S AN EXCUSE?
COME ON HOME, MARIE. I'M SORRY. I DIDN'T MEAN IT.
POLICE
MAYBE YOU WANNA FIGHT ME?
YO, SLOW DOWN THERE, COWBOY.
UH?
BLÜDHAVEN
EXCUSE ME...?
MA'AM?
BILL DIDN'T MEAN NUTHIN'.
JUST LET US GO HOME, OKAY?

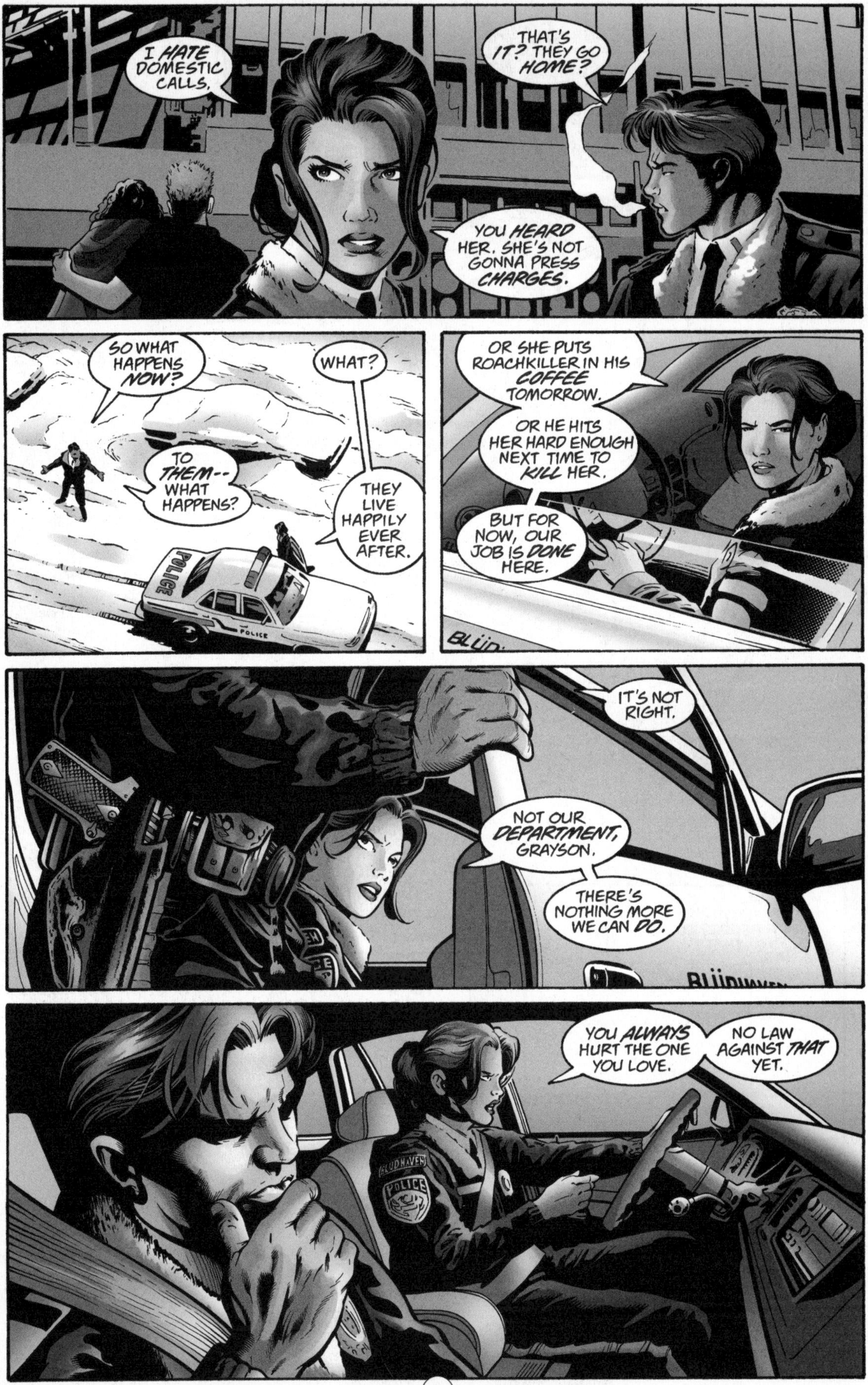
I HATE DOMESTIC CALLS.
THAT'S IT? THEY GO HOME?
YOU HEARD HER. SHE'S NOT GONNA PRESS CHARGES.
SO WHAT HAPPENS NOW?
WHAT?
TO THEM-- WHAT HAPPENS?
THEY LIVE HAPPILY EVER AFTER.
POLICE
OR SHE PUTS ROACHKILLER IN HIS COFFEE TOMORROW.
OR HE HITS HER HARD ENOUGH NEXT TIME TO KILL HER.
BUT FOR NOW, OUR JOB IS DONE HERE.
IT'S NOT RIGHT.
NOT OUR DEPARTMENT, GRAYSON.
THERE'S NOTHING MORE WE CAN DO.
YOU ALWAYS HURT THE ONE YOU LOVE.
NO LAW AGAINST THAT YET.
POLICE

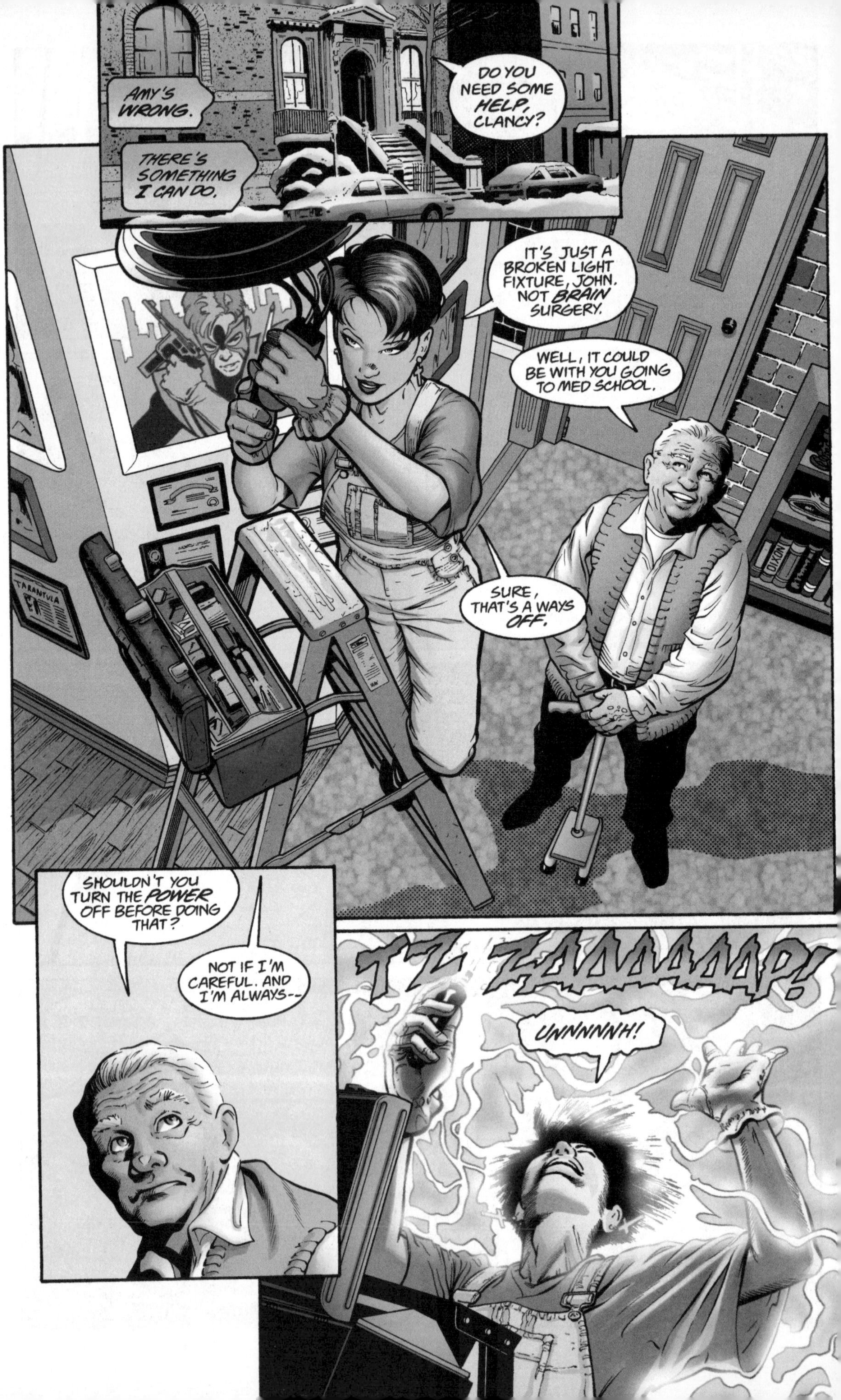
AMY'S WRONG.
THERE'S SOMETHING I CAN DO.
DO YOU NEED SOME HELP, CLANCY?
IT'S JUST A BROKEN LIGHT FIXTURE, JOHN. NOT BRAIN SURGERY.
WELL, IT COULD BE WITH YOU GOING TO MED SCHOOL.
SURE, THAT'S A WAYS OFF.
TARANTULA
DIXON
SHOULDN'T YOU TURN THE POWER OFF BEFORE DOING THAT?
NOT IF I'M CAREFUL. AND I'M ALWAYS--
TZ ZAAAAAAP!
UNNNNNH!

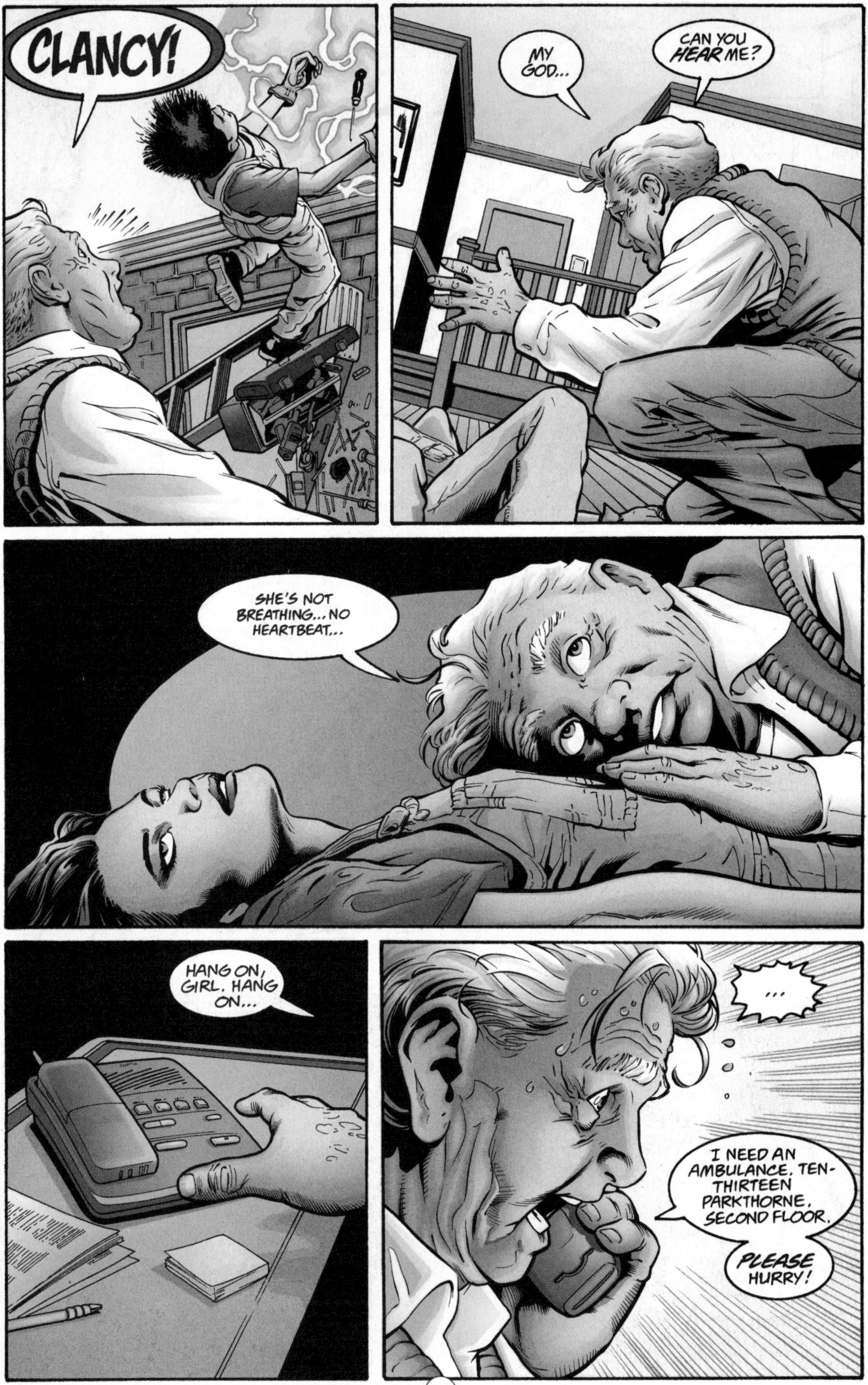
CLANCY!
MY GOD...
CAN YOU HEAR ME?
SHE'S NOT BREATHING... NO HEARTBEAT...
HANG ON, GIRL. HANG ON...
...
I NEED AN AMBULANCE. TEN-THIRTEEN PARKTHORNE, SECOND FLOOR.
PLEASE HURRY!

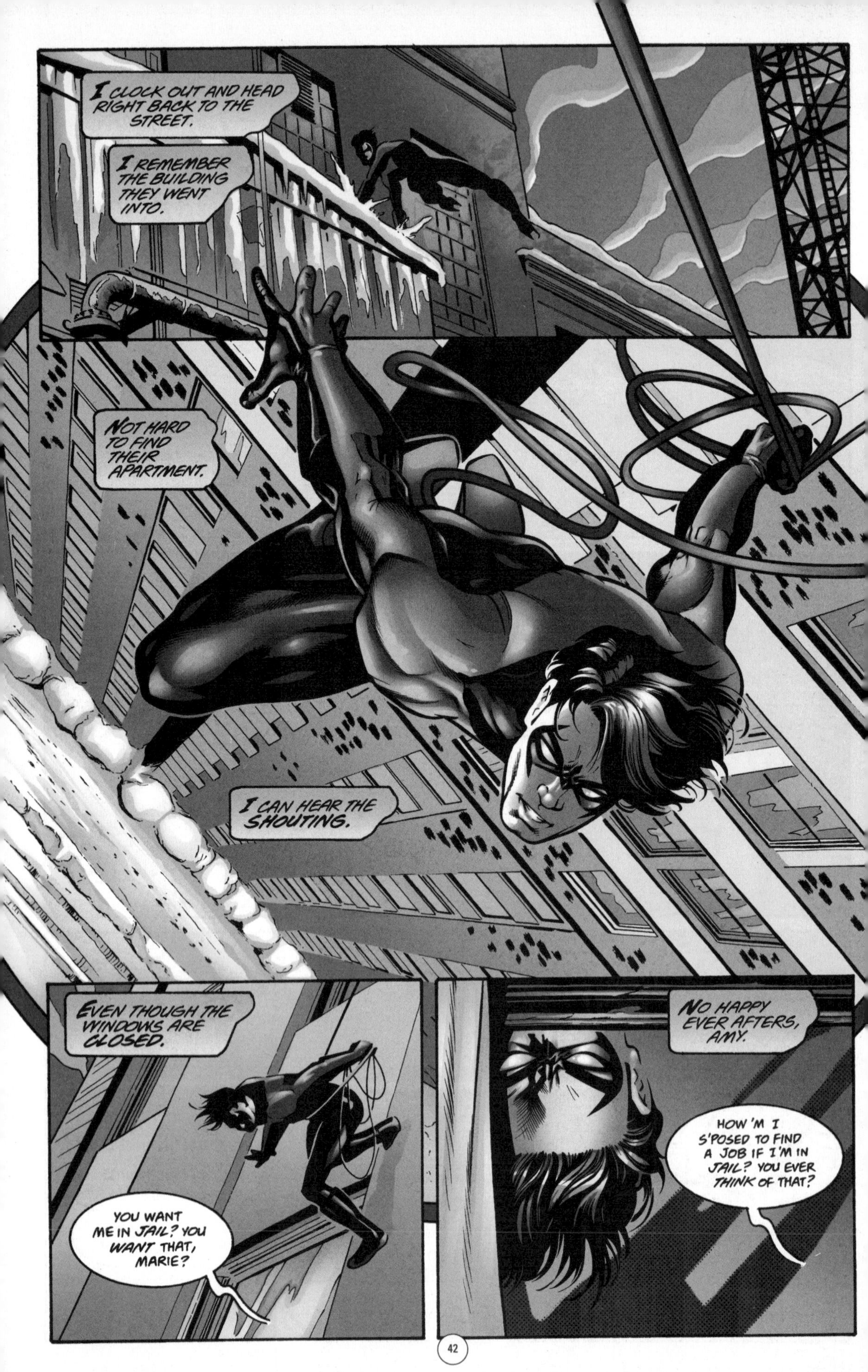
I CLOCK OUT AND HEAD RIGHT BACK TO THE STREET.
I REMEMBER THE BUILDING THEY WENT INTO.
NOT HARD TO FIND THEIR APARTMENT.
I CAN HEAR THE SHOUTING.
EVEN THOUGH THE WINDOWS ARE CLOSED.
YOU WANT ME IN JAIL? YOU WANT THAT, MARIE?
NO HAPPY EVER AFTERS, AMY.
HOW 'M I S'POSED TO FIND A JOB IF I'M IN JAIL? YOU EVER THINK OF THAT?

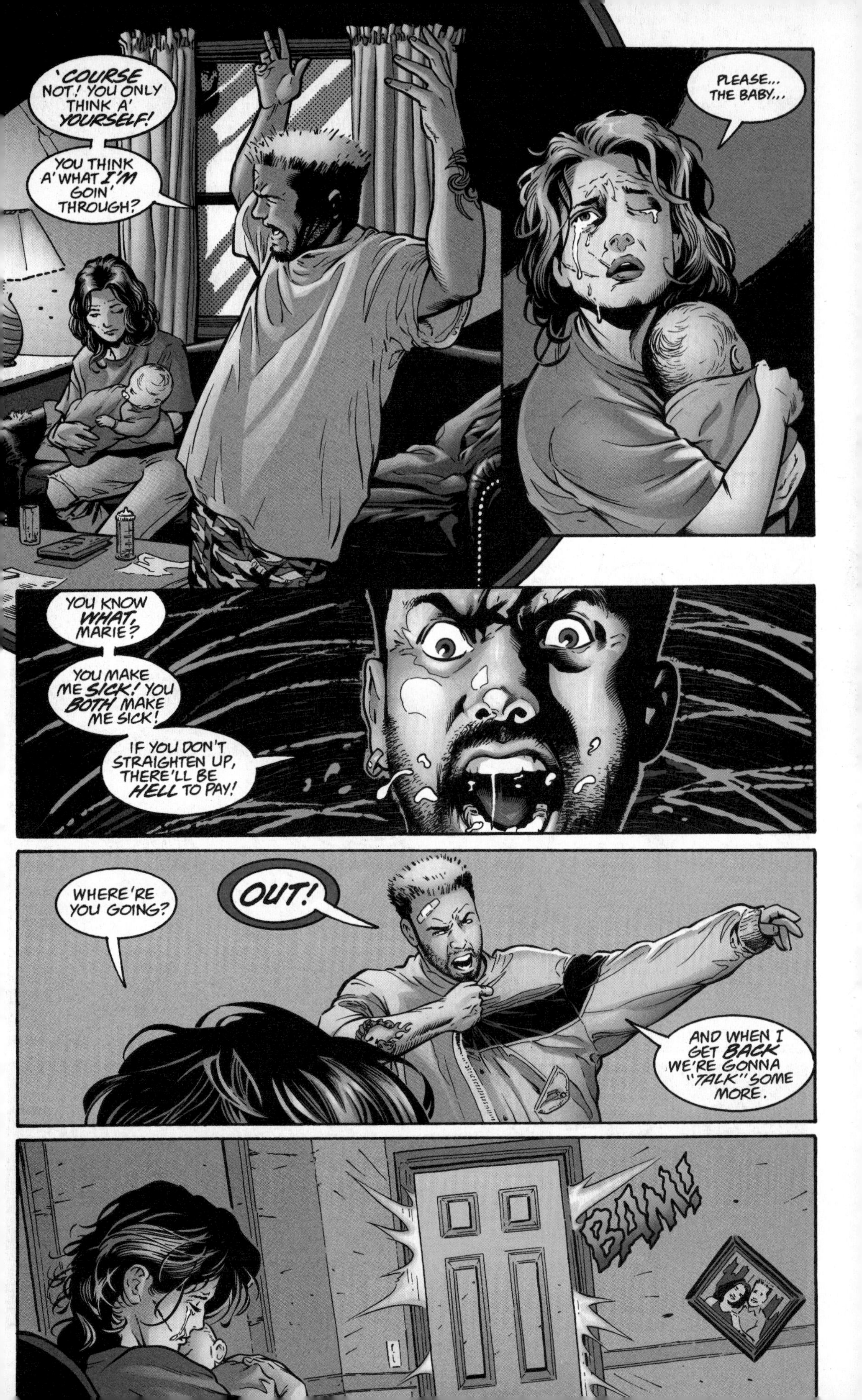
'COURSE NOT! YOU ONLY THINK A' YOURSELF!
YOU THINK A' WHAT I'M GOIN' THROUGH?
PLEASE... THE BABY...
YOU KNOW WHAT, MARIE?
YOU MAKE ME SICK! YOU BOTH MAKE ME SICK!
IF YOU DON'T STRAIGHTEN UP, THERE'LL BE HELL TO PAY!
WHERE'RE YOU GOING?
OUT!
AND WHEN I GET BACK WE'RE GONNA "TALK" SOME MORE.
BAM!

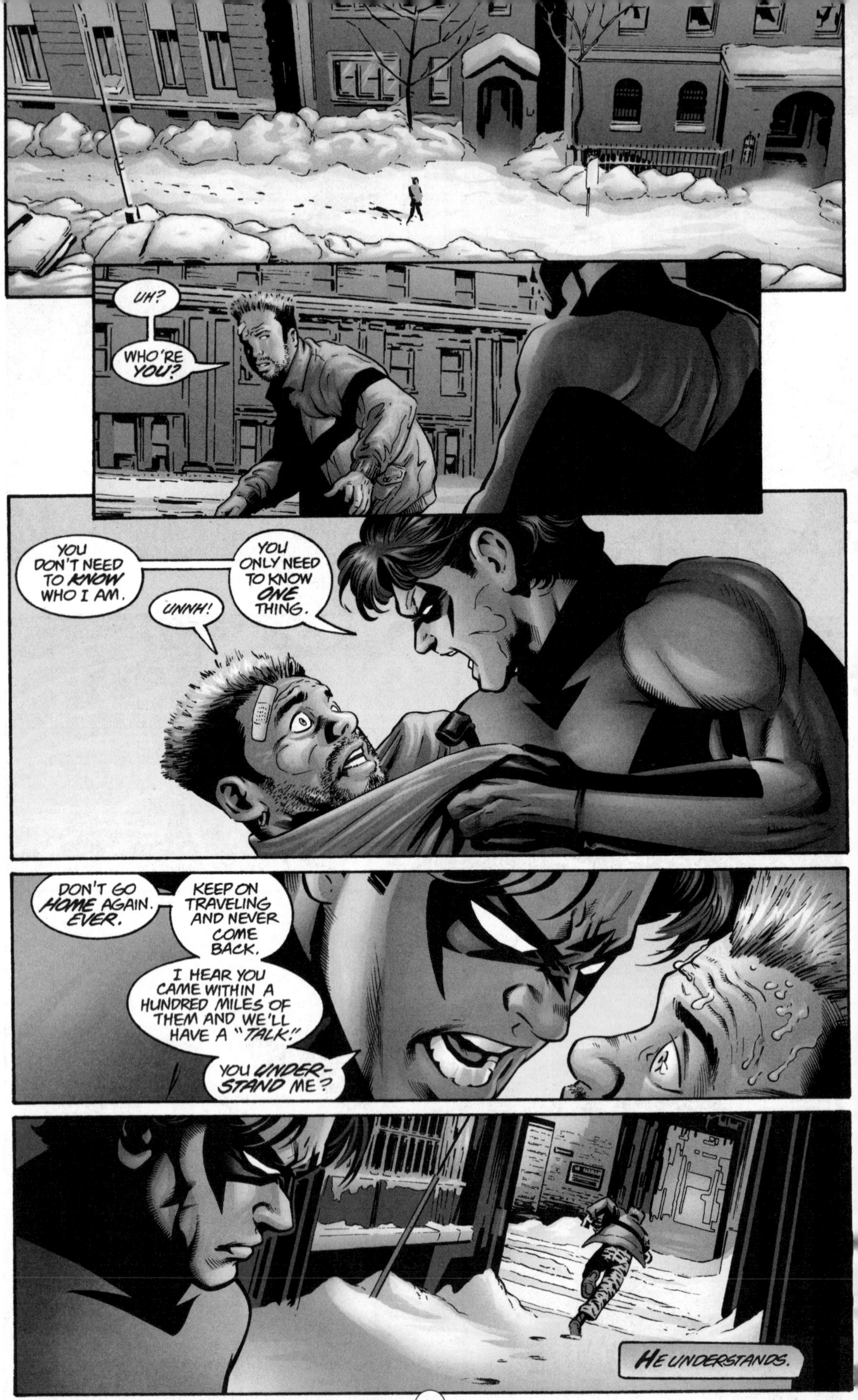
UH?
WHO'RE YOU?
YOU DON'T NEED TO KNOW WHO I AM.
YOU ONLY NEED TO KNOW ONE THING.
UNNH!
DON'T GO HOME AGAIN. EVER.
KEEP ON TRAVELING AND NEVER COME BACK.
I HEAR YOU CAME WITHIN A HUNDRED MILES OF THEM AND WE'LL HAVE A "TALK."
YOU UNDERSTAND ME?
HE UNDERSTANDS.

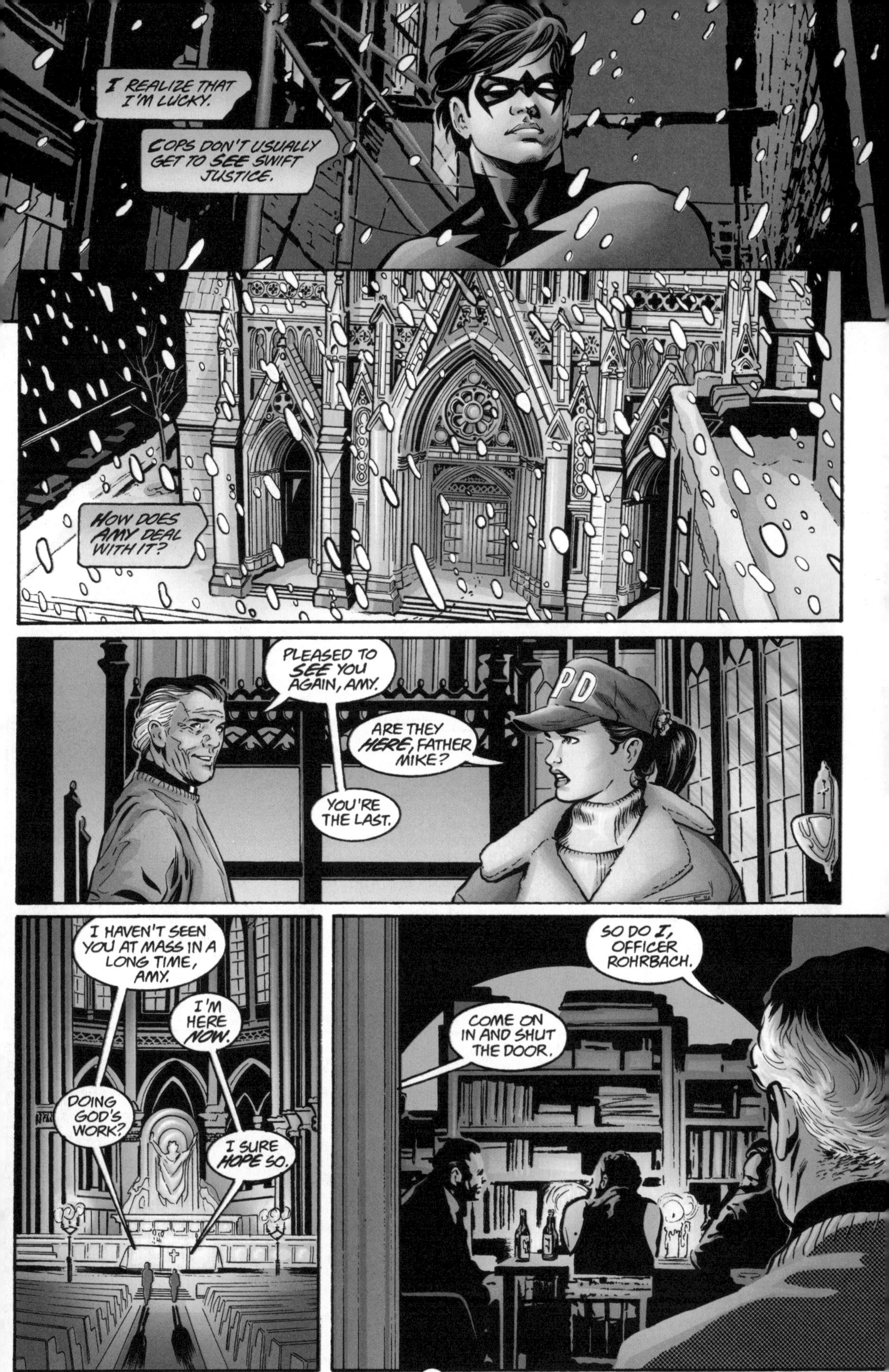
I REALIZE THAT I'M LUCKY.
COPS DON'T USUALLY GET TO SEE SWIFT JUSTICE.
HOW DOES AMY DEAL WITH IT?
PLEASED TO SEE YOU AGAIN, AMY.
ARE THEY HERE, FATHER MIKE?
YOU'RE THE LAST.
PD
I HAVEN'T SEEN YOU AT MASS IN A LONG TIME, AMY.
I'M HERE NOW.
DOING GOD'S WORK?
I SURE HOPE SO.
SO DO I, OFFICER ROHRBACH.
COME ON IN AND SHUT THE DOOR.

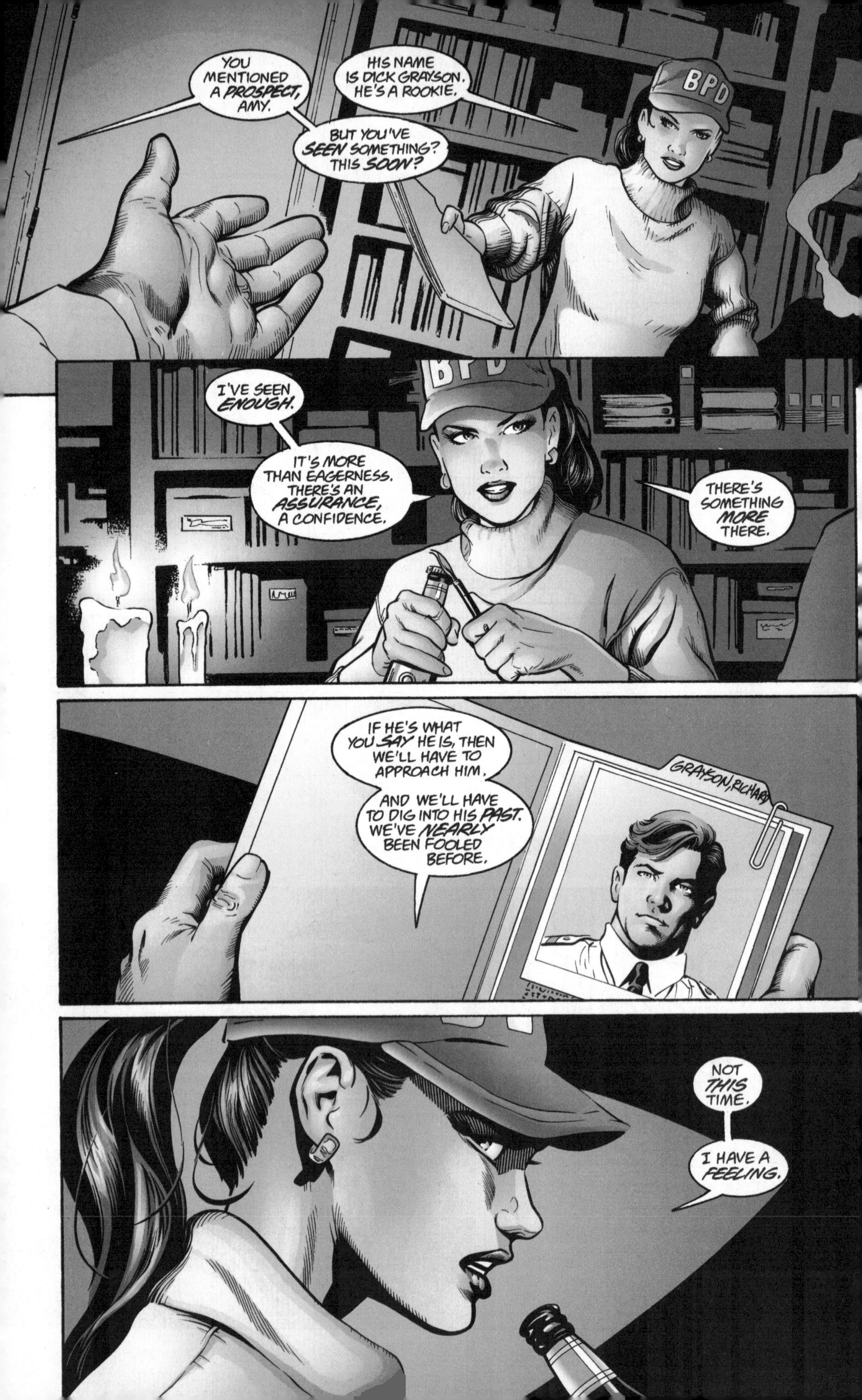

YOU MENTIONED A PROSPECT, AMY.
HIS NAME IS DICK GRAYSON. HE'S A ROOKIE.
BUT YOU'VE SEEN SOMETHING? THIS SOON?
BPD
I'VE SEEN ENOUGH.
IT'S MORE THAN EAGERNESS. THERE'S AN ASSURANCE, A CONFIDENCE.
THERE'S SOMETHING MORE THERE.
IF HE'S WHAT YOU SAY HE IS, THEN WE'LL HAVE TO APPROACH HIM.
AND WE'LL HAVE TO DIG INTO HIS PAST. WE'VE NEARLY BEEN FOOLED BEFORE.
GRAYSON, RICHARD
NOT THIS TIME.
I HAVE A FEELING.

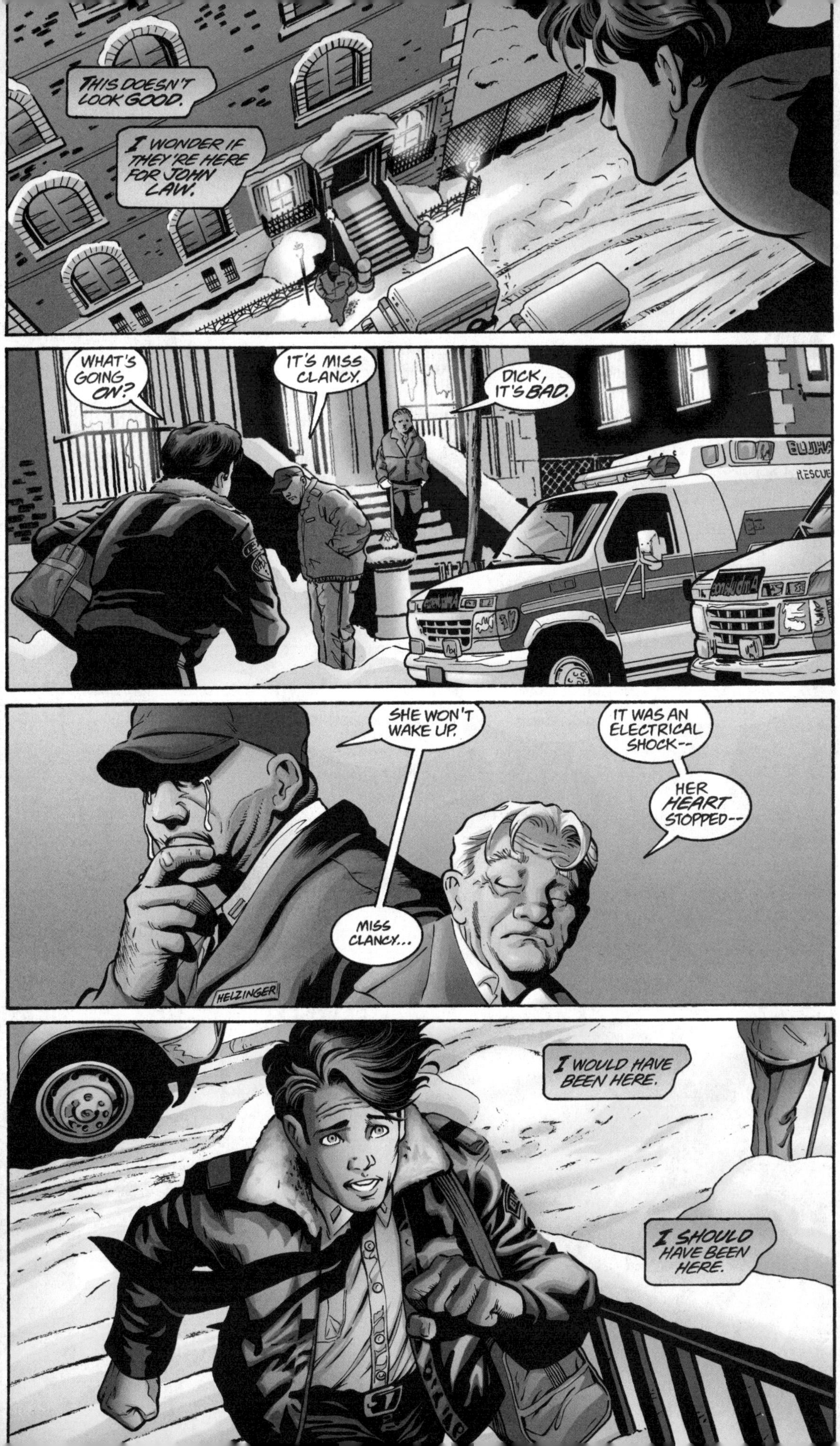
THIS DOESN'T LOOK GOOD.
I WONDER IF THEY'RE HERE FOR JOHN LAW.
WHAT'S GOING ON?
IT'S MISS CLANCY.
DICK, IT'S BAD.
RESCUE
SHE WON'T WAKE UP.
MISS CLANCY...
IT WAS AN ELECTRICAL SHOCK--
HER HEART STOPPED--
HELZINGER
I WOULD HAVE BEEN HERE.
I SHOULD HAVE BEEN HERE.

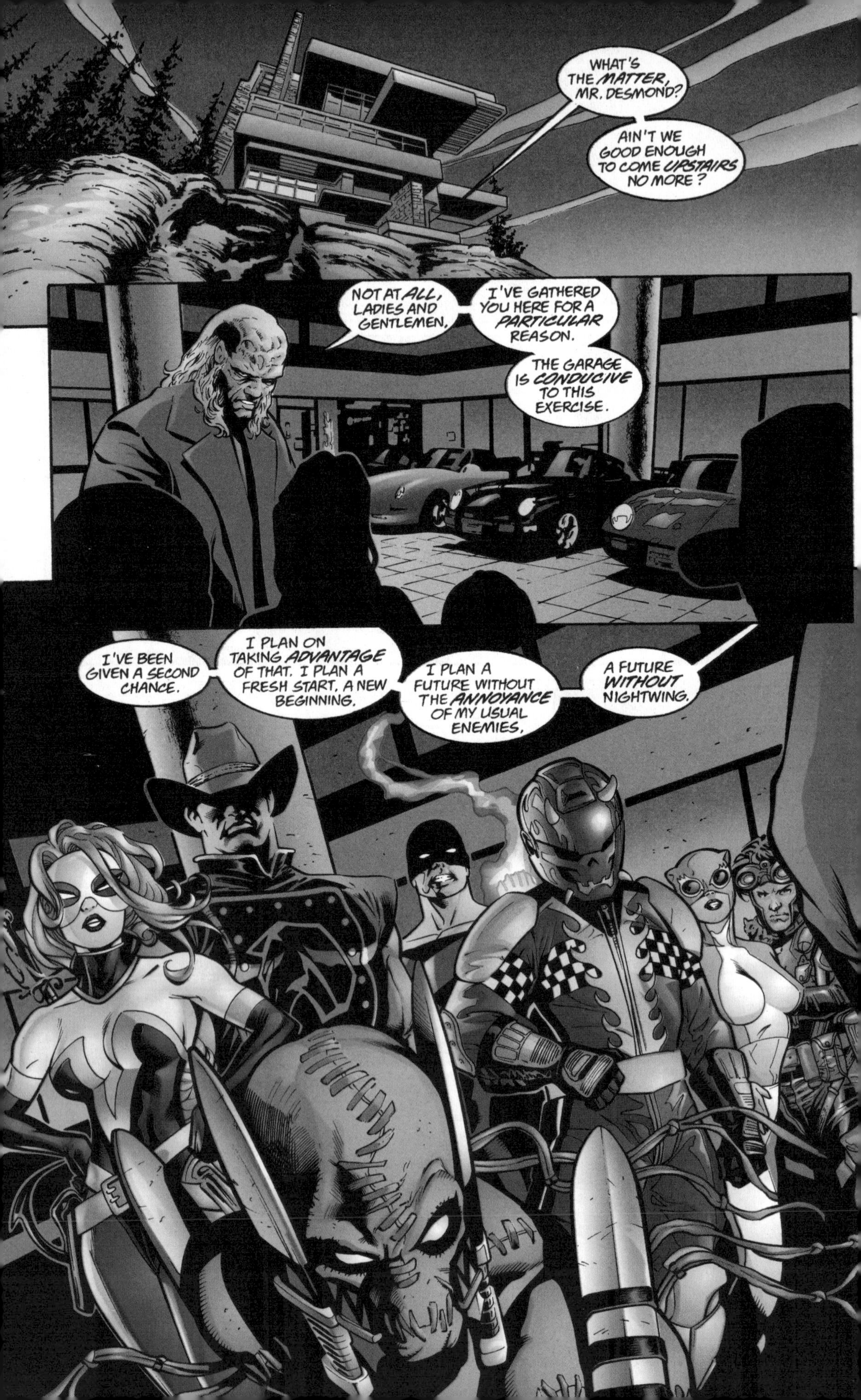
WHAT'S THE MATTER, MR. DESMOND?
AIN'T WE GOOD ENOUGH TO COME UPSTAIRS NO MORE?
NOT AT ALL, LADIES AND GENTLEMEN,
I'VE GATHERED YOU HERE FOR A PARTICULAR REASON.
THE GARAGE IS CONDUCIVE TO THIS EXERCISE.
I'VE BEEN GIVEN A SECOND CHANCE.
I PLAN ON TAKING ADVANTAGE OF THAT. I PLAN A FRESH START. A NEW BEGINNING.
I PLAN A FUTURE WITHOUT THE ANNOYANCE OF MY USUAL ENEMIES.
A FUTURE WITHOUT NIGHTWING.

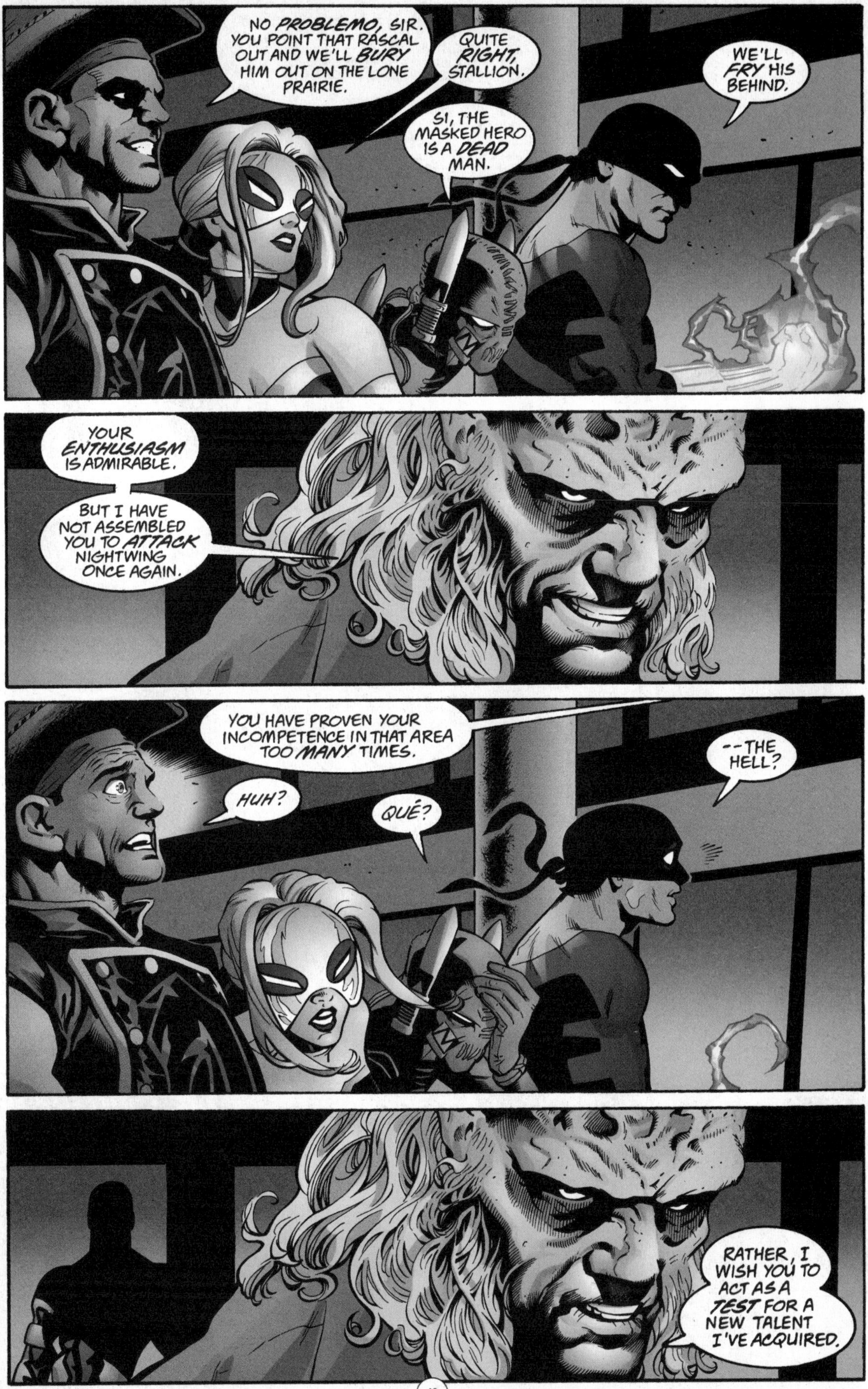
NO PROBLEMO, SIR. YOU POINT THAT RASCAL OUT AND WE'LL BURY HIM OUT ON THE LONE PRAIRIE.
QUITE RIGHT, STALLION.
SI, THE MASKED HERO IS A DEAD MAN.
WE'LL FRY HIS BEHIND.
YOUR ENTHUSIASM IS ADMIRABLE.
BUT I HAVE NOT ASSEMBLED YOU TO ATTACK NIGHTWING ONCE AGAIN.
YOU HAVE PROVEN YOUR INCOMPETENCE IN THAT AREA TOO MANY TIMES.
HUH?
QUÉ?
--THE HELL?
RATHER, I WISH YOU TO ACT AS A TEST FOR A NEW TALENT I'VE ACQUIRED.

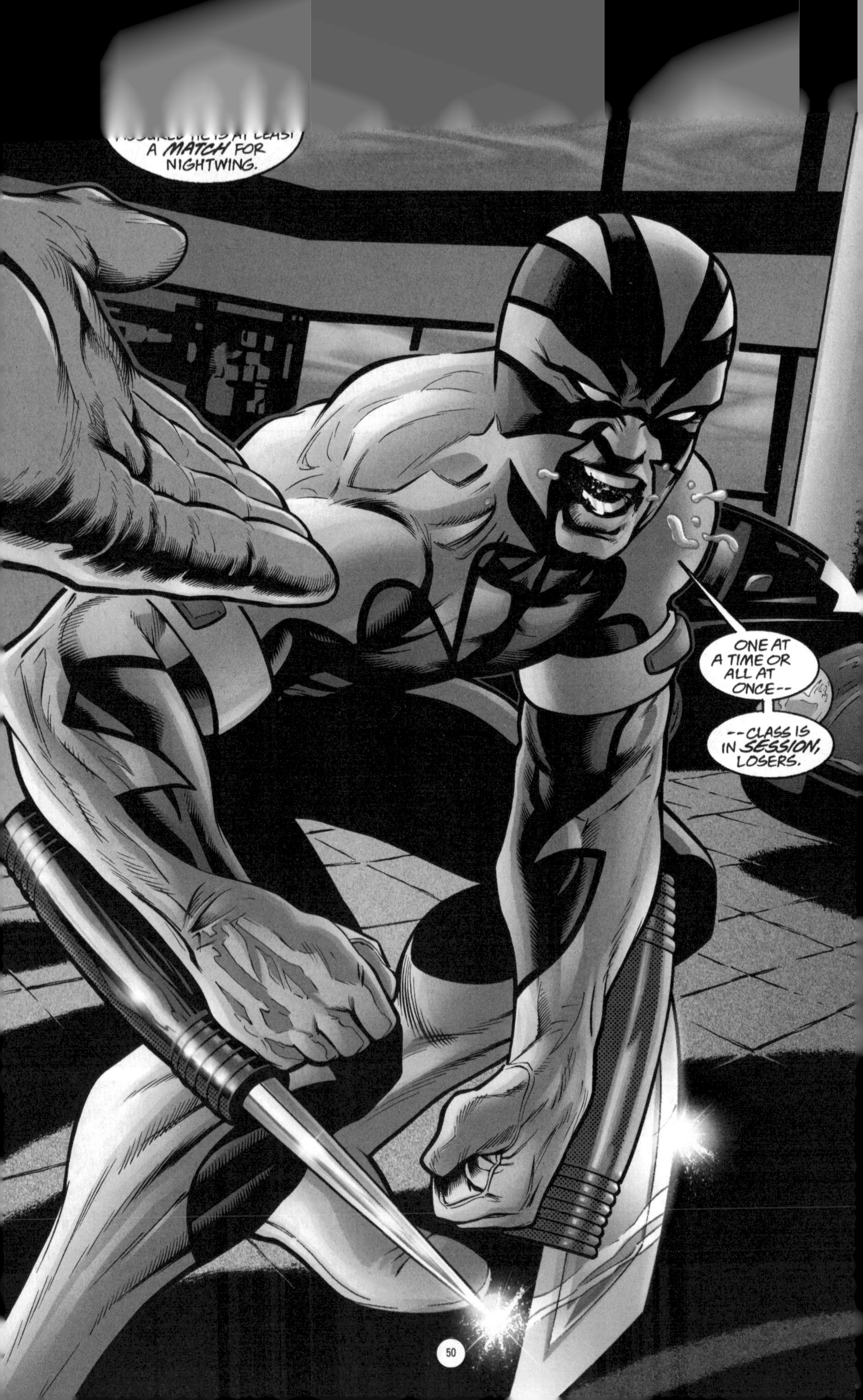
A MATCH FOR
NIGHTWING.
ONE AT
A TIME OR
ALL AT
ONCE--
--CLASS IS
IN SESSION,
LOSERS.

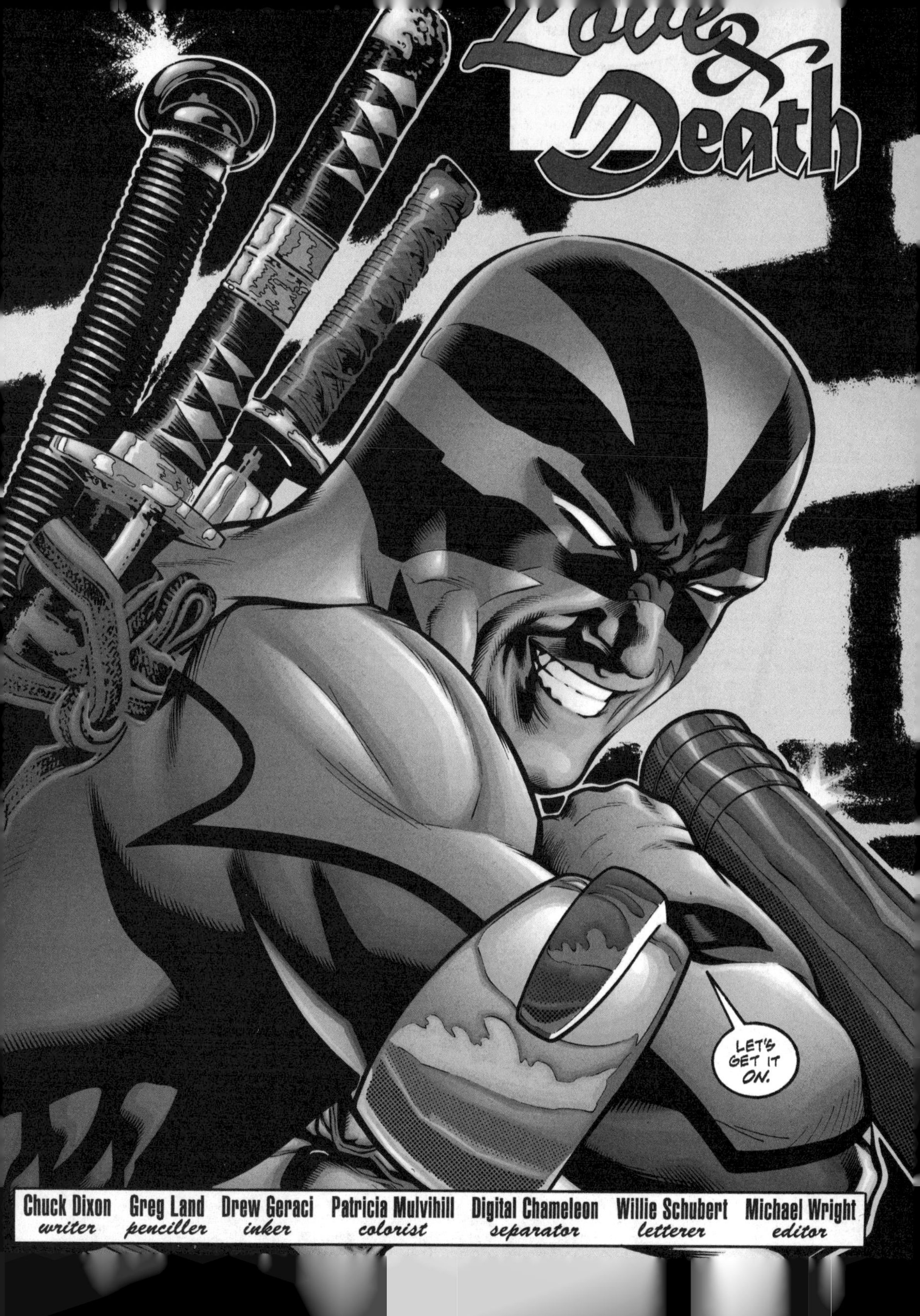
Love & Death
LET'S GET IT ON.
Chuck Dixon writer
Greg Land penciller
Drew Geraci inker
Patricia Mulvihill colorist
Digital Chameleon separator
Willie Schubert letterer
Michael Wright editor

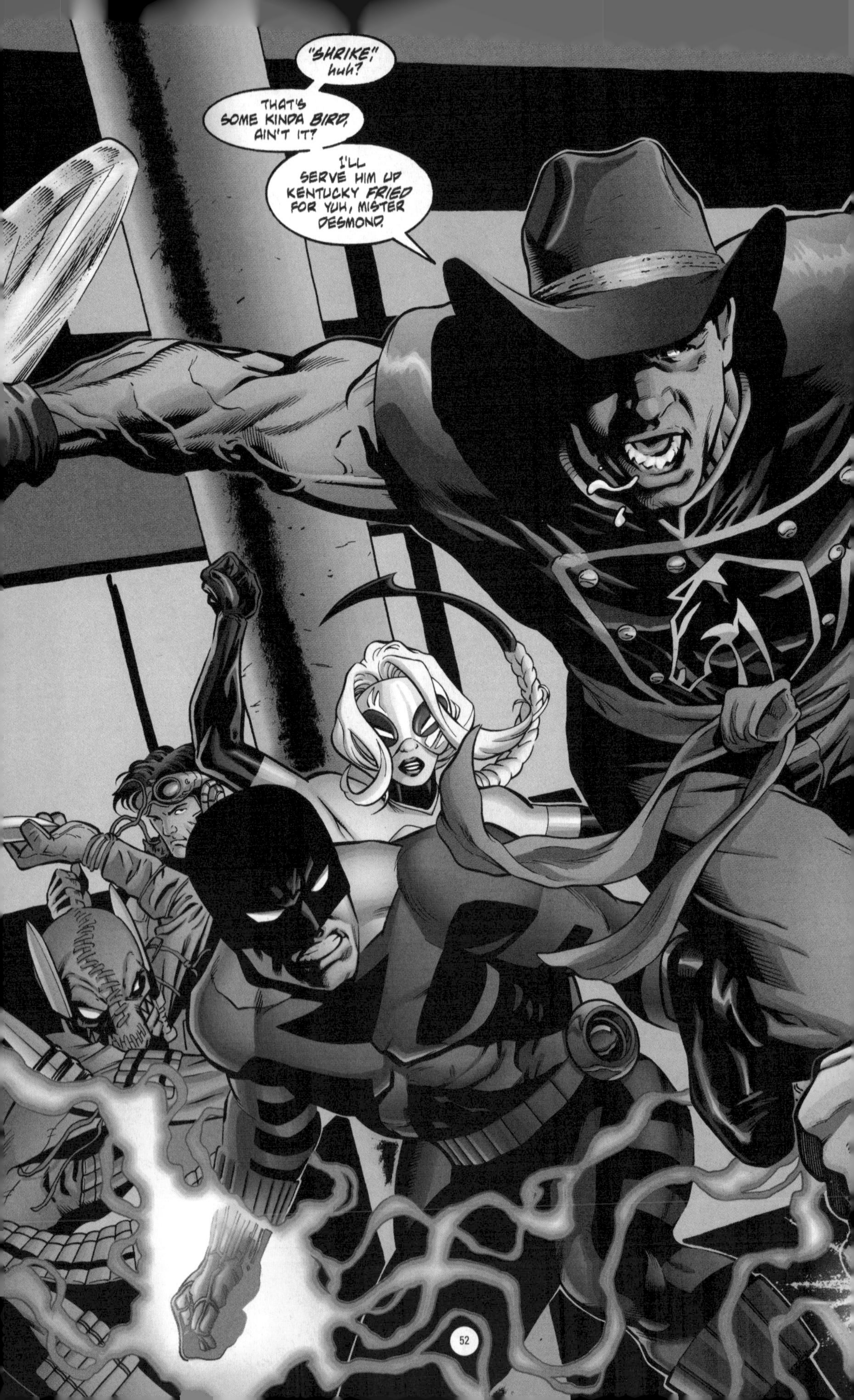
"SHRIKE," huh?
THAT'S SOME KINDA BIRD, AIN'T IT?
I'LL SERVE HIM UP KENTUCKY FRIED FOR YUH, MISTER DESMOND.

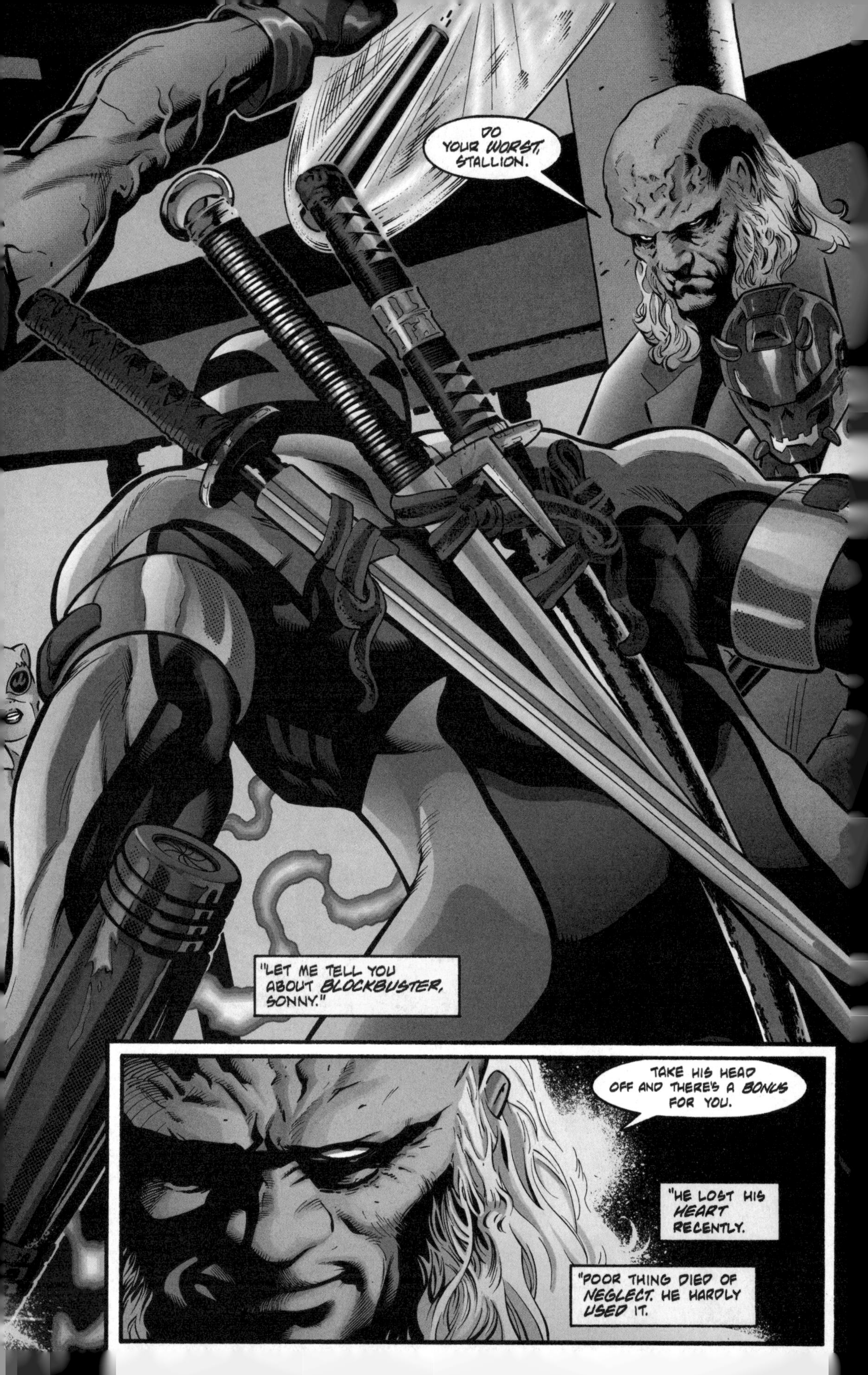
DO YOUR WORST, STALLION.
"LET ME TELL YOU ABOUT BLOCKBUSTER, SONNY."
TAKE HIS HEAD OFF AND THERE'S A BONUS FOR YOU.
"HE LOST HIS HEART RECENTLY.
"POOR THING DIED OF NEGLECT. HE HARDLY USED IT.

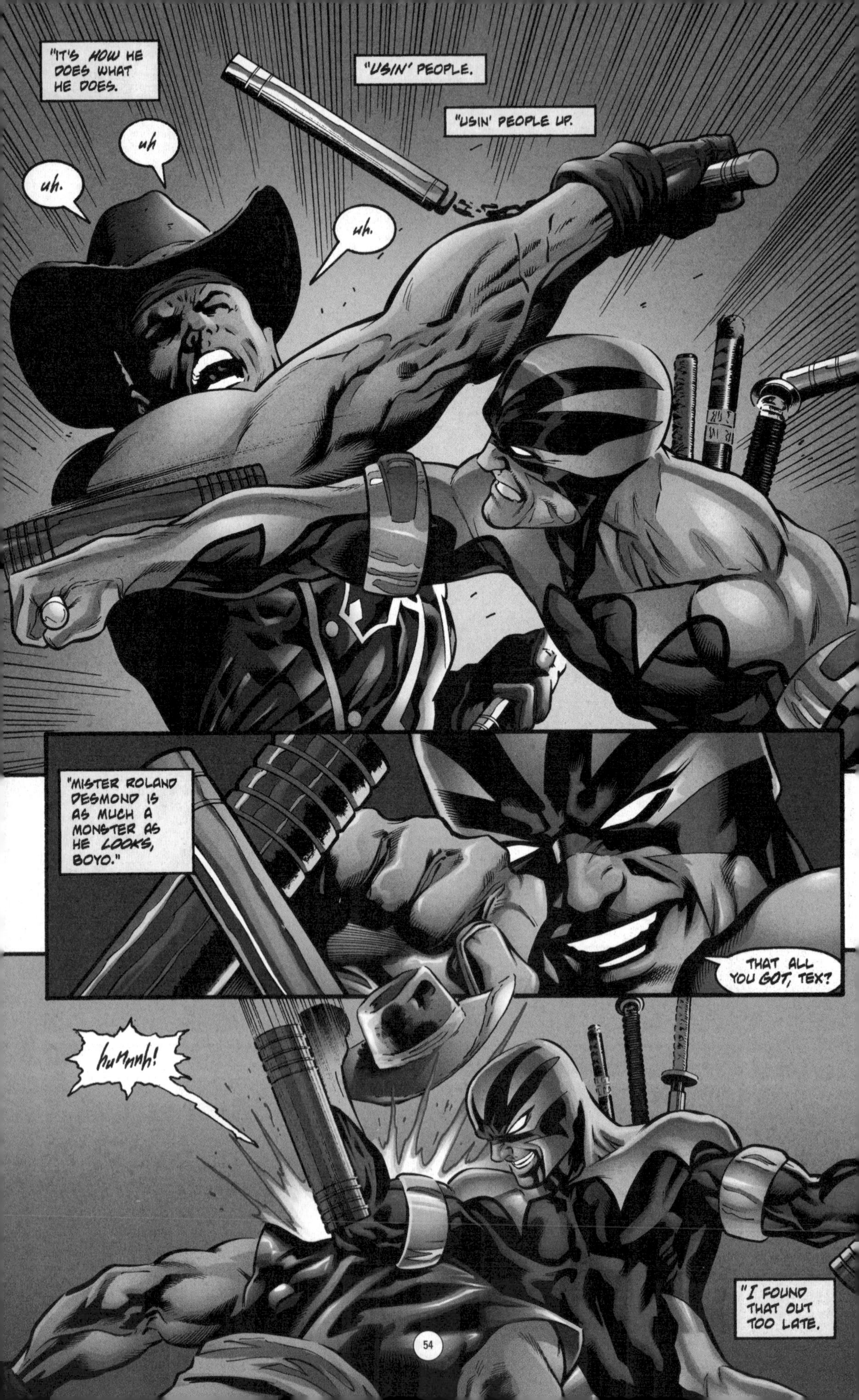
"IT'S HOW HE DOES WHAT HE DOES.
"USIN' PEOPLE.
"USIN' PEOPLE UP.
uh.
uh
uh.
"MISTER ROLAND DESMOND IS AS MUCH A MONSTER AS HE LOOKS, BOYO."
THAT ALL YOU GOT, TEX?
hunnnh!
"I FOUND THAT OUT TOO LATE.

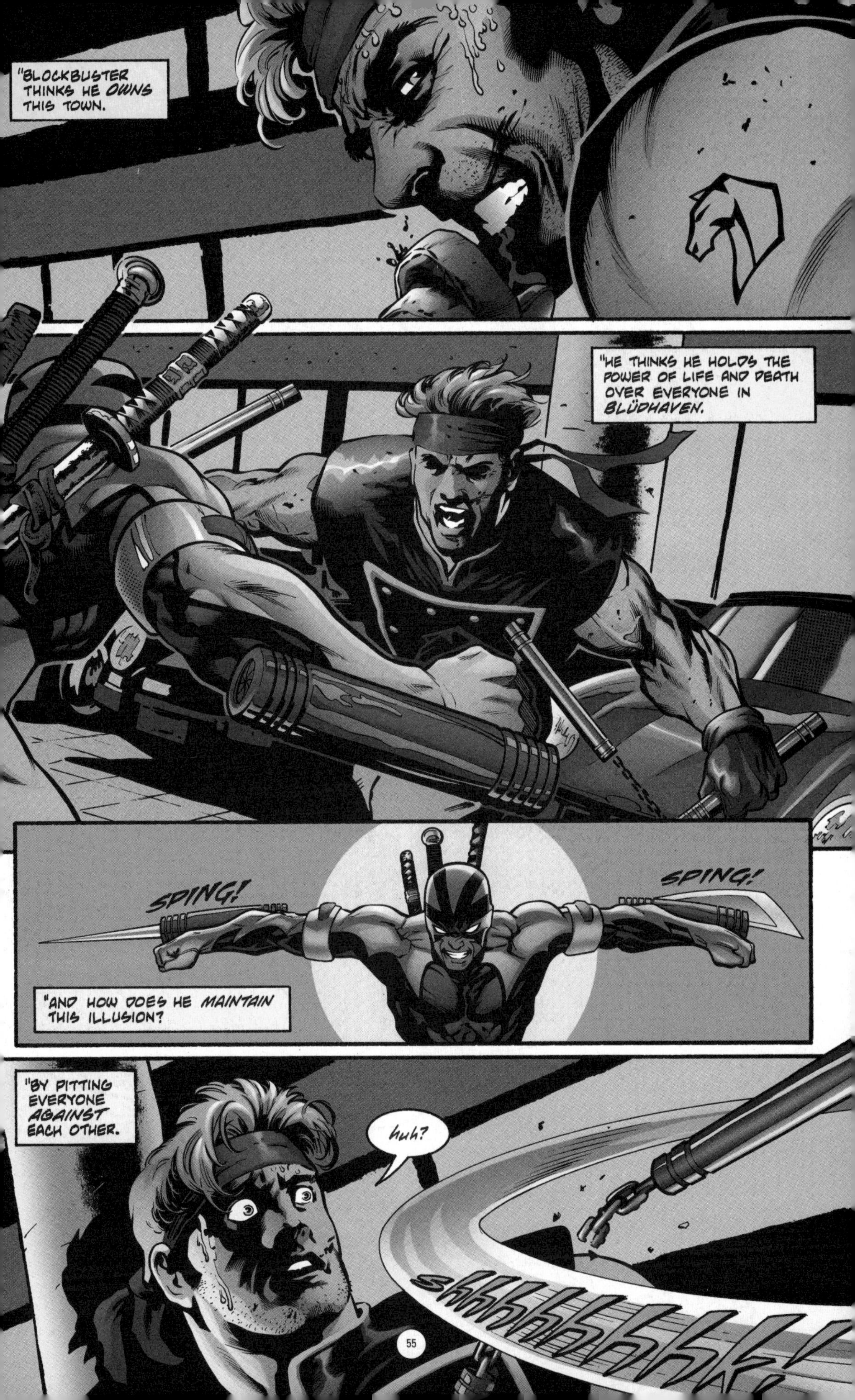

"BLOCKBUSTER THINKS HE OWNS THIS TOWN.
"HE THINKS HE HOLDS THE POWER OF LIFE AND DEATH OVER EVERYONE IN BLÜDHAVEN.
SPING!
SPING!
"AND HOW DOES HE MAINTAIN THIS ILLUSION?
"BY PITTING EVERYONE AGAINST EACH OTHER.
huh?
SHHHHHHHHK!

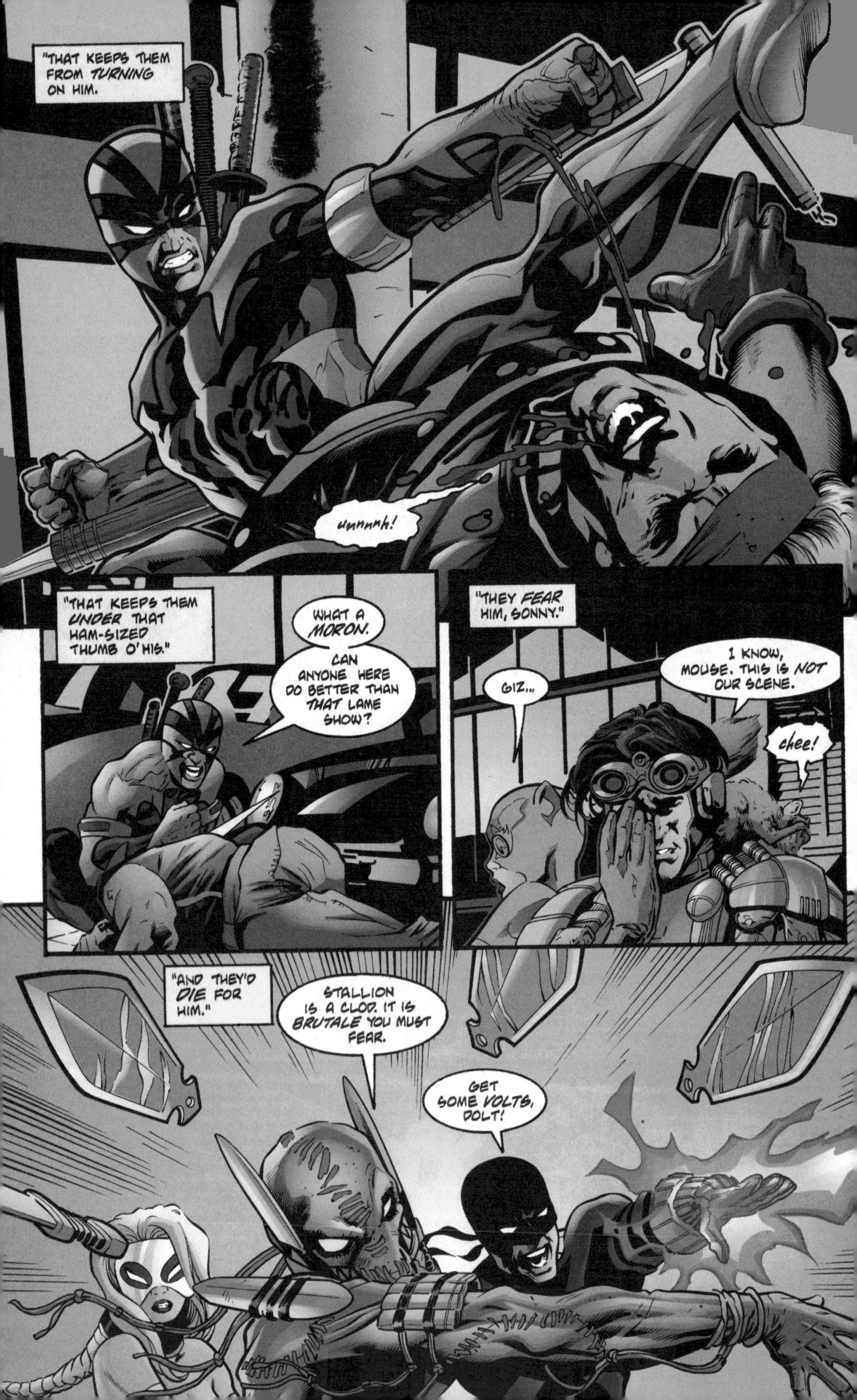
"THAT KEEPS THEM FROM TURNING ON HIM.
unnnnh!
"THAT KEEPS THEM UNDER THAT HAM-SIZED THUMB O' HIS."
WHAT A MORON.
CAN ANYONE HERE DO BETTER THAN THAT LAME SHOW?
"THEY FEAR HIM, SONNY."
GIZ...
I KNOW, MOUSE. THIS IS NOT OUR SCENE.
chee!
"AND THEY'D DIE FOR HIM."
STALLION IS A CLOD. IT IS BRUTALE YOU MUST FEAR.
GET SOME VOLTS, DOLT!

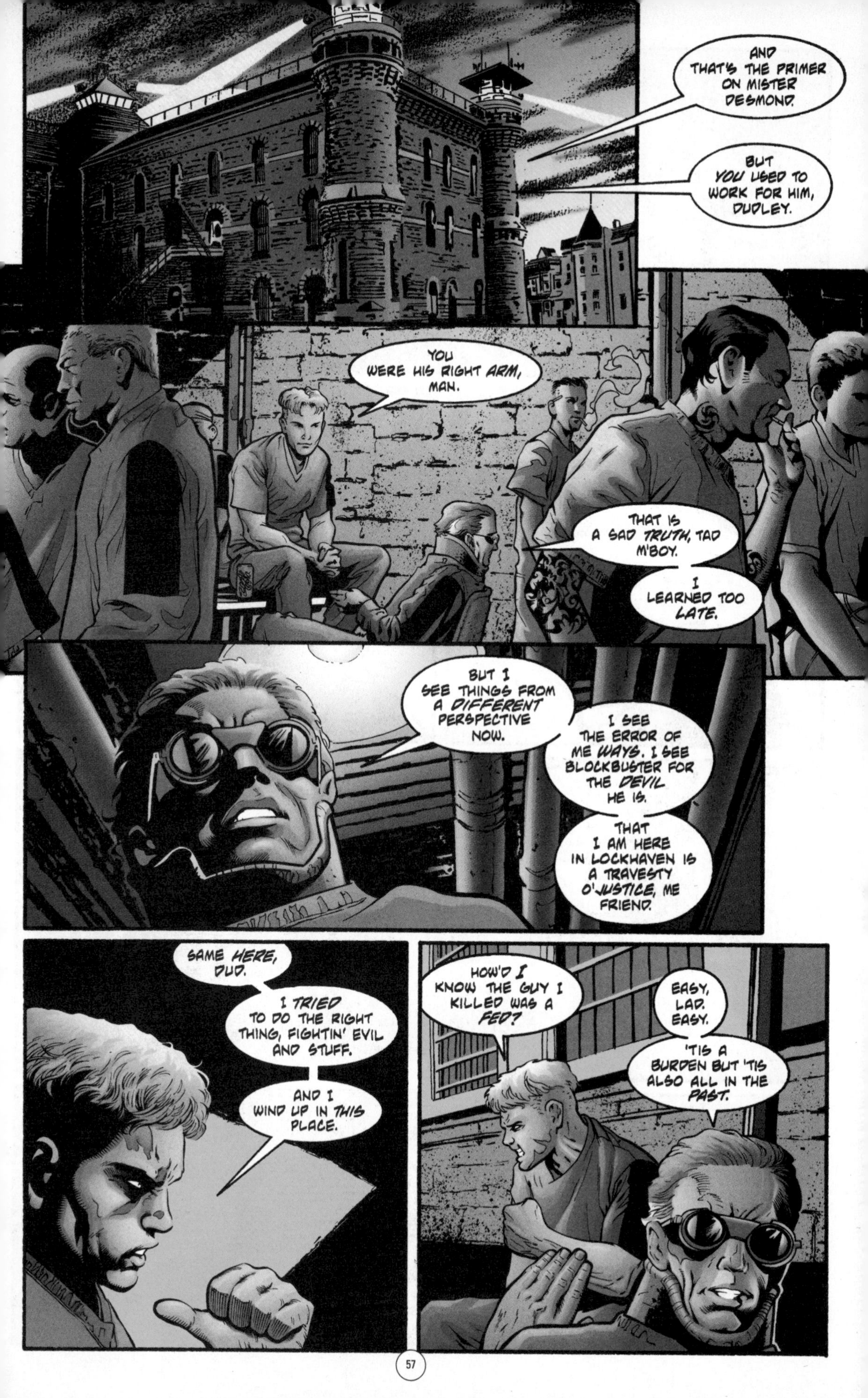
AND THAT'S THE PRIMER ON MISTER DESMOND.
BUT YOU USED TO WORK FOR HIM, DUDLEY.
YOU WERE HIS RIGHT ARM, MAN.
THAT IS A SAD TRUTH, TAD M'BOY.
I LEARNED TOO LATE.
BUT I SEE THINGS FROM A DIFFERENT PERSPECTIVE NOW.
I SEE THE ERROR OF ME WAYS. I SEE BLOCKBUSTER FOR THE DEVIL HE IS.
THAT I AM HERE IN LOCKHAVEN IS A TRAVESTY O'JUSTICE, ME FRIEND.
SAME HERE, DUD.
I TRIED TO DO THE RIGHT THING, FIGHTIN' EVIL AND STUFF.
AND I WIND UP IN THIS PLACE.
HOW'D I KNOW THE GUY I KILLED WAS A FED?
EASY, LAD. EASY.
'TIS A BURDEN BUT 'TIS ALSO ALL IN THE PAST.

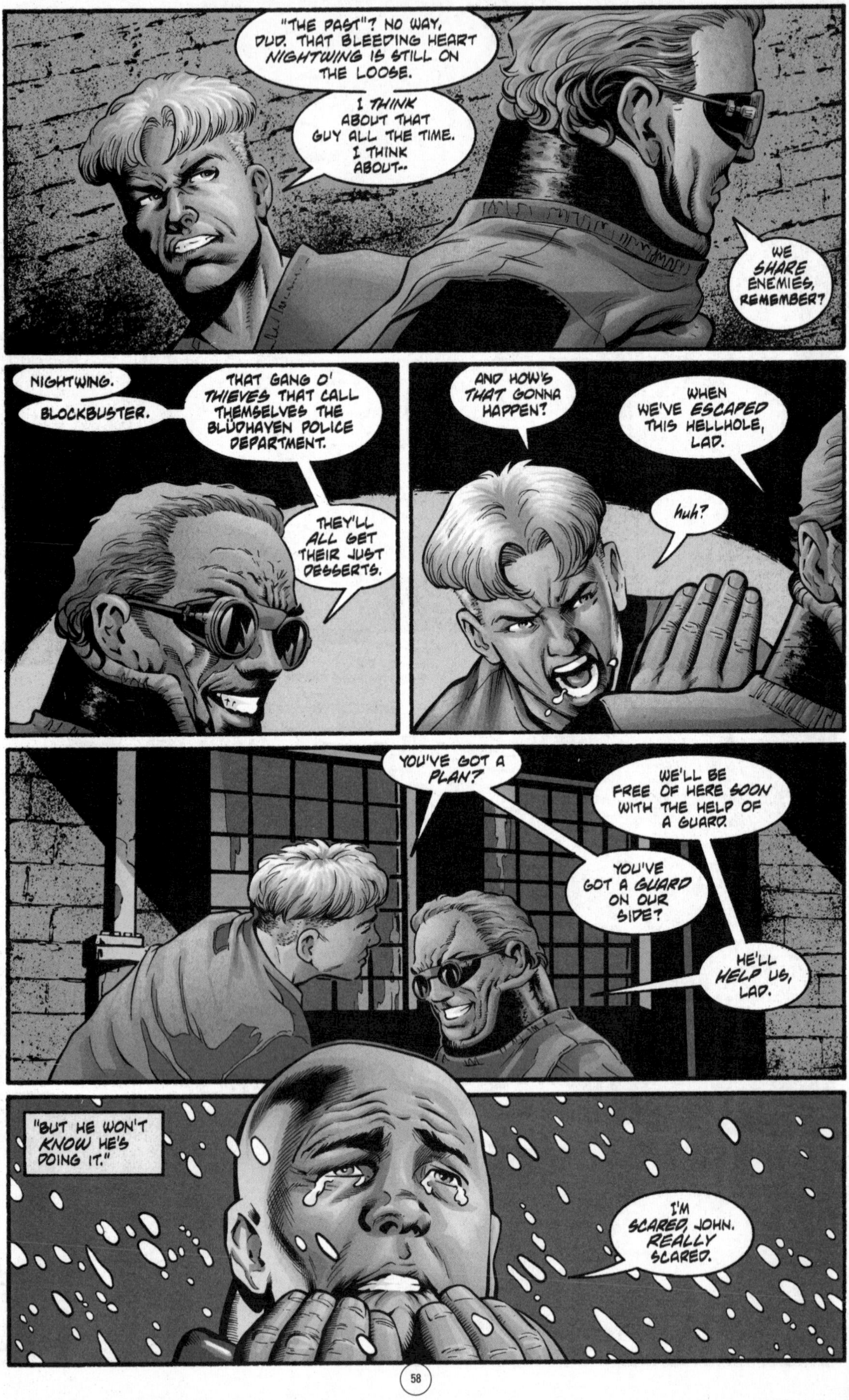
"THE PAST"? NO WAY, DUD. THAT BLEEDING HEART NIGHTWING IS STILL ON THE LOOSE.
I THINK ABOUT THAT GUY ALL THE TIME. I THINK ABOUT--
WE SHARE ENEMIES, REMEMBER?
NIGHTWING.
BLOCKBUSTER.
THAT GANG O' THIEVES THAT CALL THEMSELVES THE BLÜDHAVEN POLICE DEPARTMENT.
THEY'LL ALL GET THEIR JUST DESSERTS.
AND HOW'S THAT GONNA HAPPEN?
WHEN WE'VE ESCAPED THIS HELLHOLE, LAD.
huh?
YOU'VE GOT A PLAN?
WE'LL BE FREE OF HERE SOON WITH THE HELP OF A GUARD.
YOU'VE GOT A GUARD ON OUR SIDE?
HE'LL HELP US, LAD.
"BUT HE WON'T KNOW HE'S DOING IT."
I'M SCARED, JOHN. REALLY SCARED.

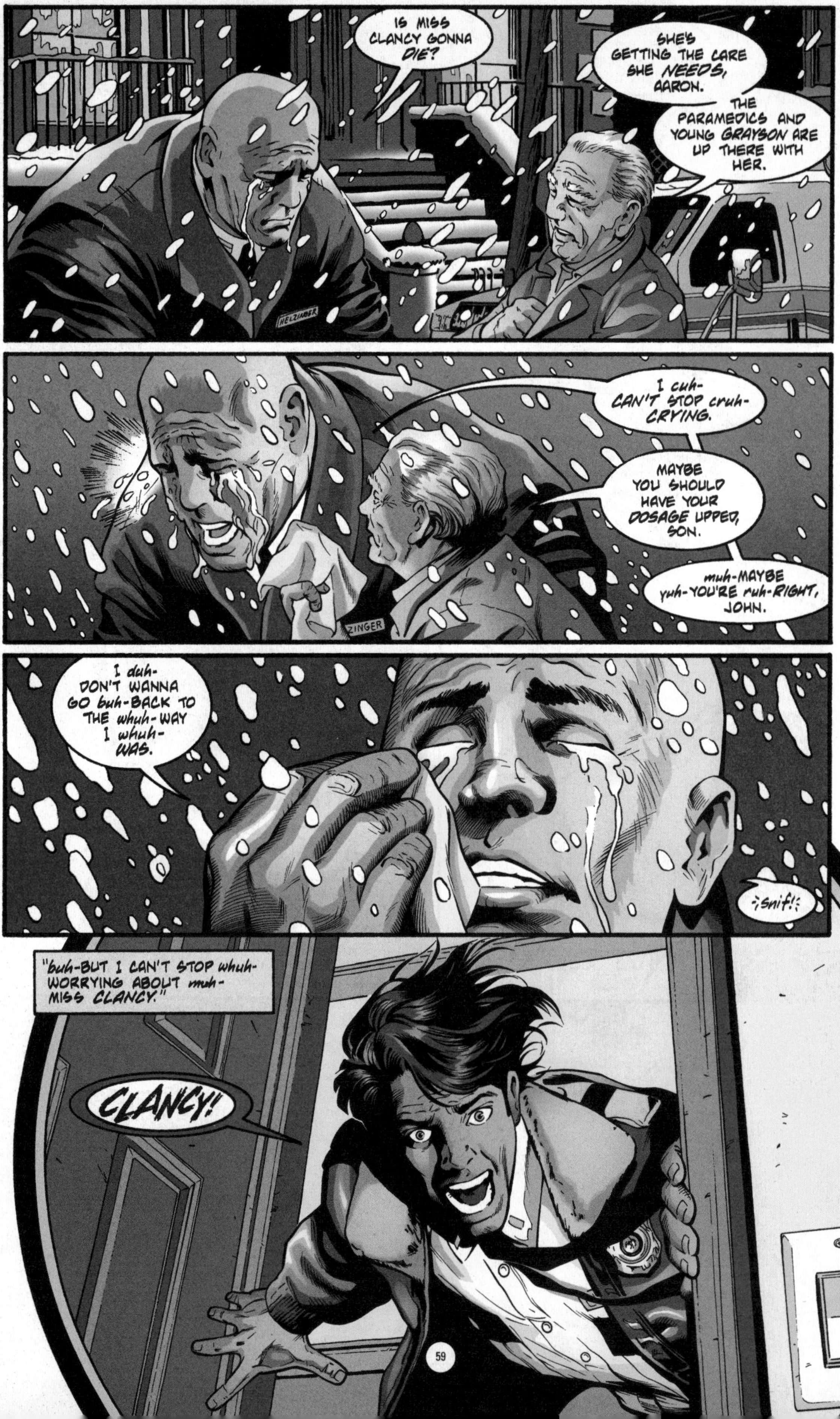

IS MISS CLANCY GONNA DIE?
SHE'S GETTING THE CARE SHE NEEDS, AARON.
THE PARAMEDICS AND YOUNG GRAYSON ARE UP THERE WITH HER.
HELZINGER
I cuh-CAN'T STOP cruh-CRYING.
MAYBE YOU SHOULD HAVE YOUR DOSAGE UPPED, SON.
muh-MAYBE yuh-YOU'RE ruh-RIGHT, JOHN.
ZINGER
I duh-DON'T WANNA GO buh-BACK TO THE whuh-WAY I whuh-WAS.
snif!
"buh-BUT I CAN'T STOP whuh-WORRYING ABOUT muh-MISS CLANCY."
CLANCY!

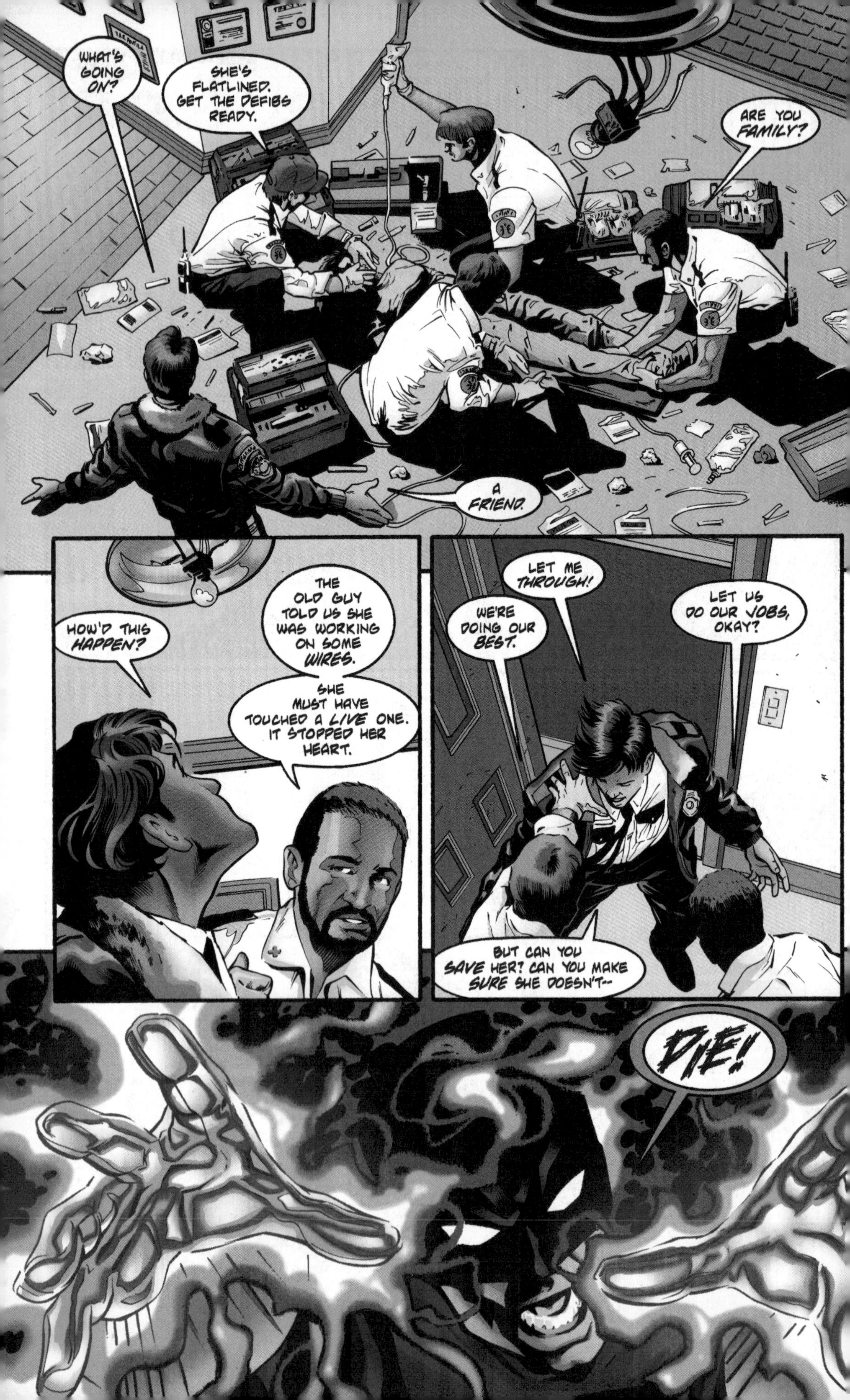
WHAT'S GOING ON?
SHE'S FLATLINED. GET THE DEFIBS READY.
ARE YOU FAMILY?
A FRIEND.
HOW'D THIS HAPPEN?
THE OLD GUY TOLD US SHE WAS WORKING ON SOME WIRES.
SHE MUST HAVE TOUCHED A LIVE ONE. IT STOPPED HER HEART.
LET ME THROUGH!
WE'RE DOING OUR BEST.
LET US DO OUR JOBS, OKAY?
BUT CAN YOU SAVE HER? CAN YOU MAKE SURE SHE DOESN'T--
DIE!

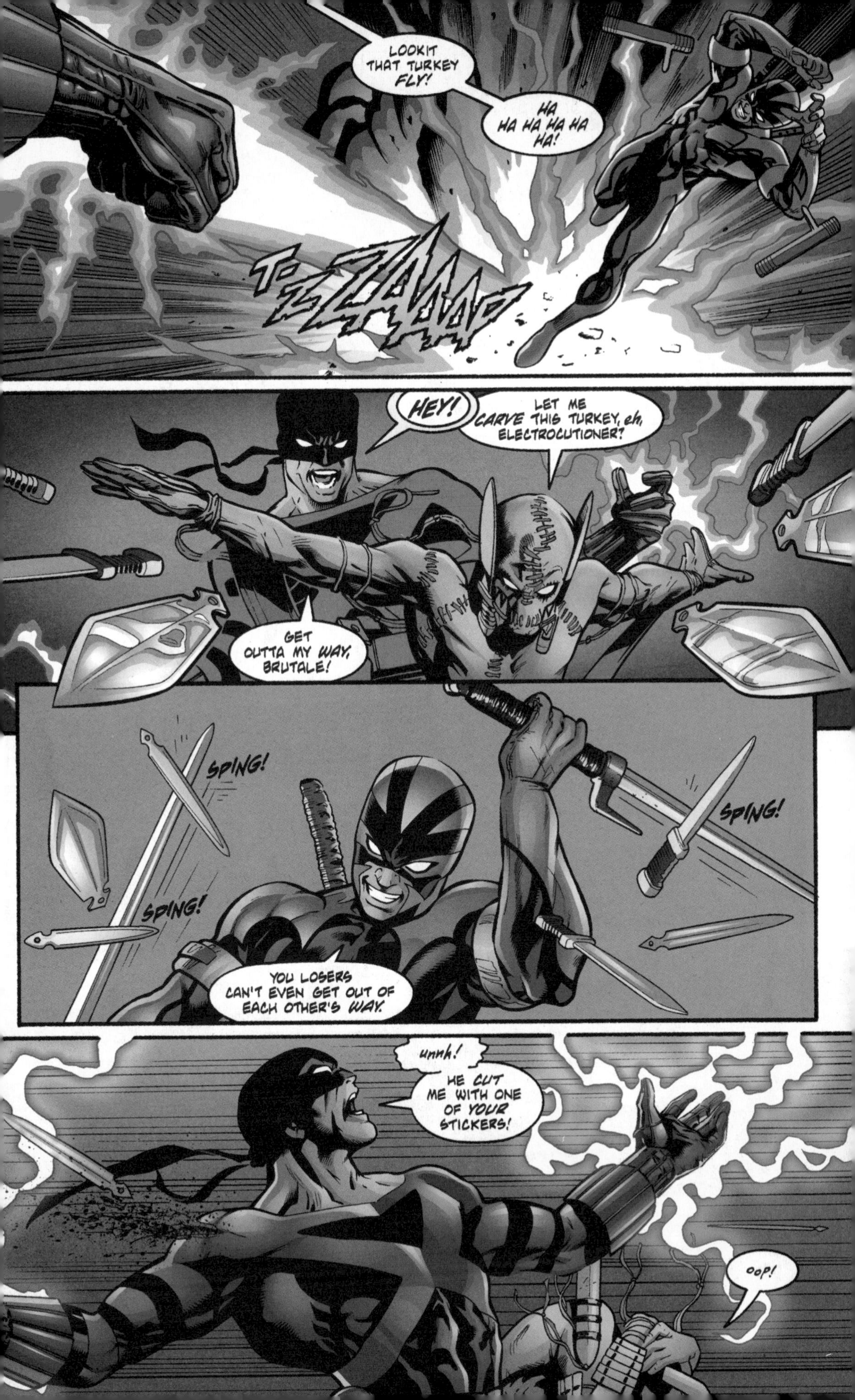
LOOKIT THAT TURKEY FLY!
HA HA HA HA HA HA HA!
TZZAAAP
HEY!
LET ME CARVE THIS TURKEY, eh, ELECTROCUTIONER?
GET OUTTA MY WAY, BRUTALE!
SPING!
SPING!
SPING!
YOU LOSERS CAN'T EVEN GET OUT OF EACH OTHER'S WAY.
unnh!
HE CUT ME WITH ONE OF YOUR STICKERS!
oop!

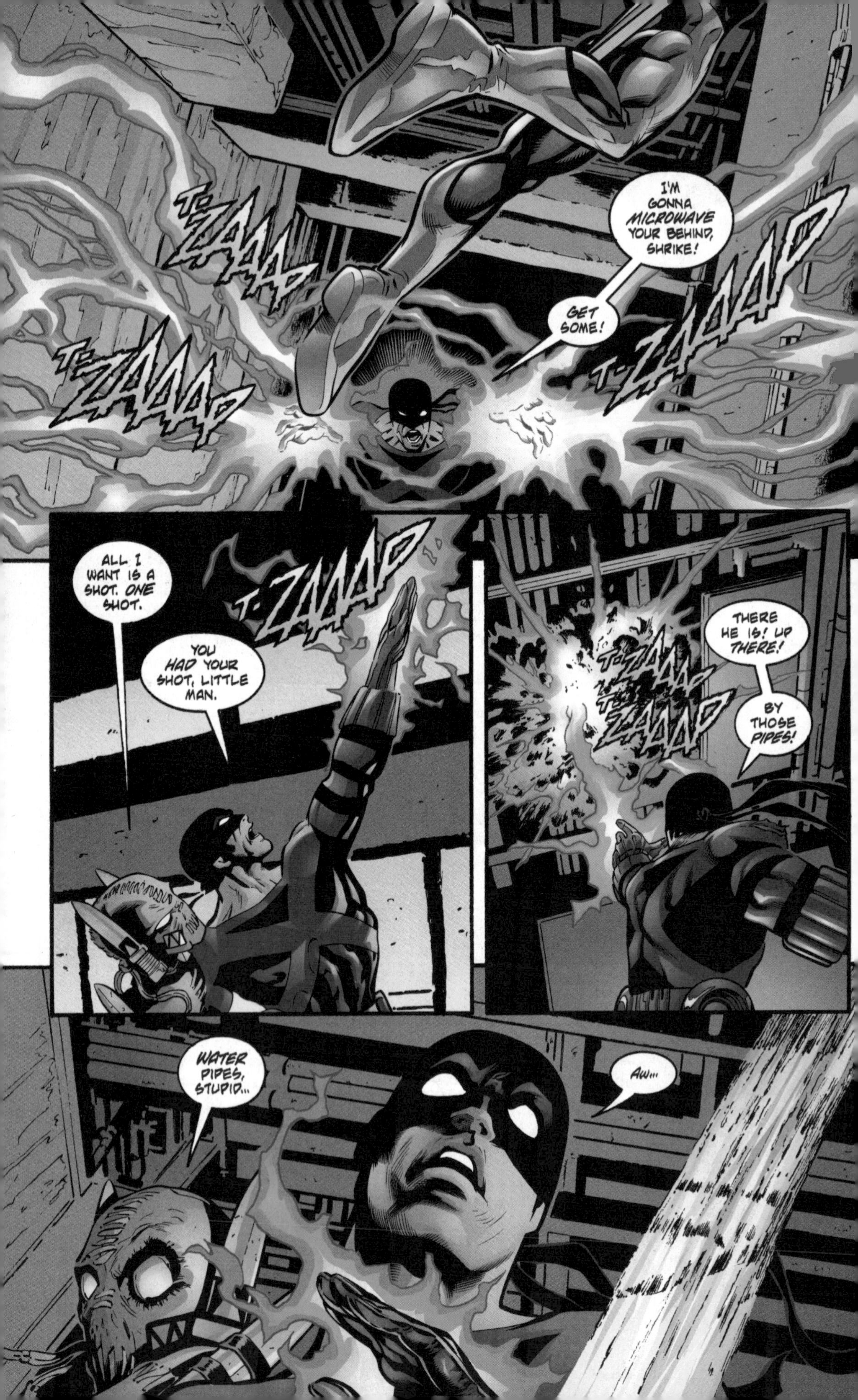
T-ZAAAP
I'M GONNA MICROWAVE YOUR BEHIND, SHRIKE!
GET SOME!
T-ZAAAP
T-ZAAAAP
ALL I WANT IS A SHOT. ONE SHOT.
T-ZAAAP
YOU HAD YOUR SHOT, LITTLE MAN.
T-ZAAAP
T-ZAAAP
THERE HE IS! UP THERE!
BY THOSE PIPES!
WATER PIPES, STUPID...
AW...

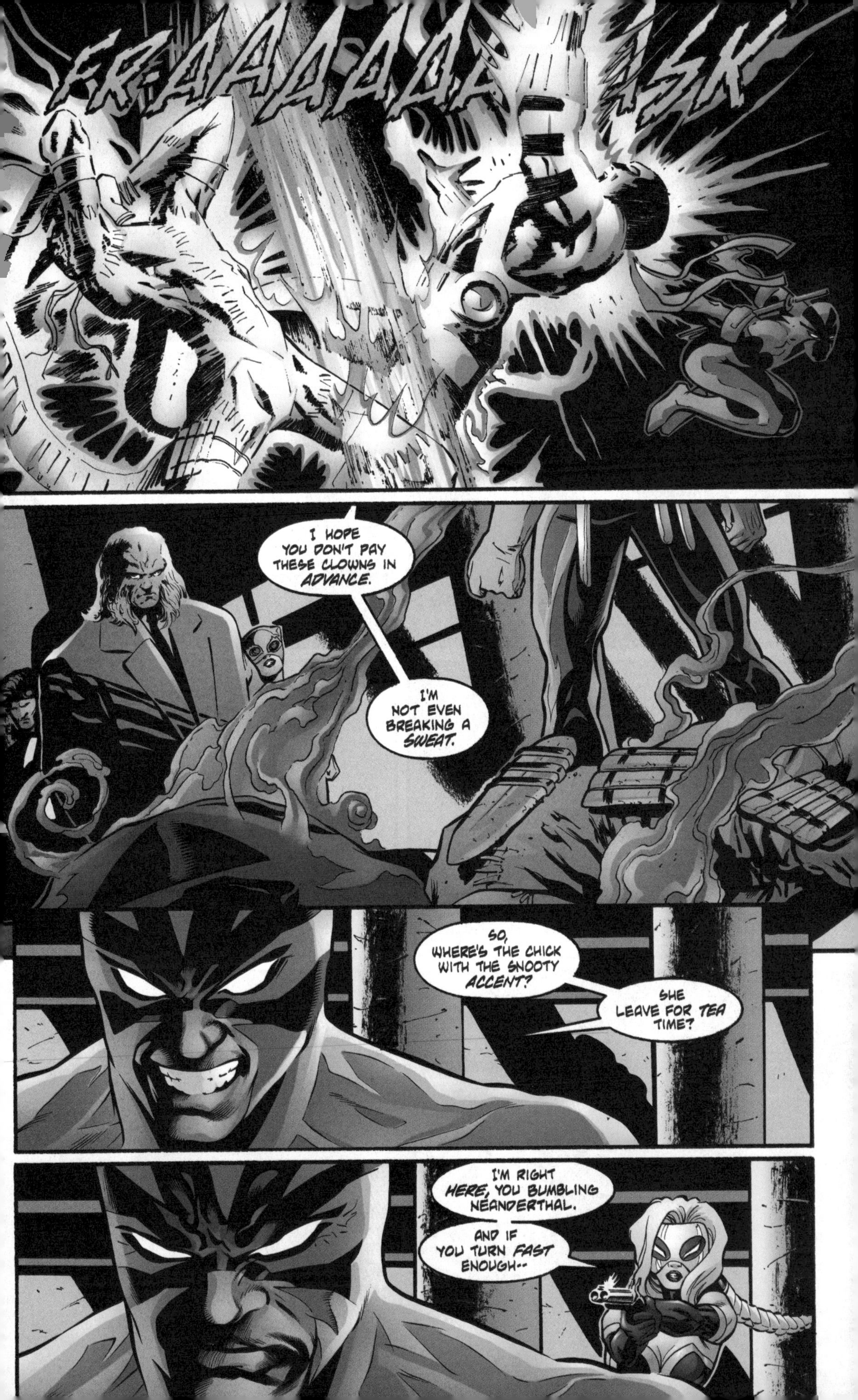
FRAAAAAAASK
I HOPE YOU DON'T PAY THESE CLOWNS IN ADVANCE.
I'M NOT EVEN BREAKING A SWEAT.
SO, WHERE'S THE CHICK WITH THE SNOOTY ACCENT?
SHE LEAVE FOR TEA TIME?
I'M RIGHT HERE, YOU BUMBLING NEANDERTHAL.
AND IF YOU TURN FAST ENOUGH--

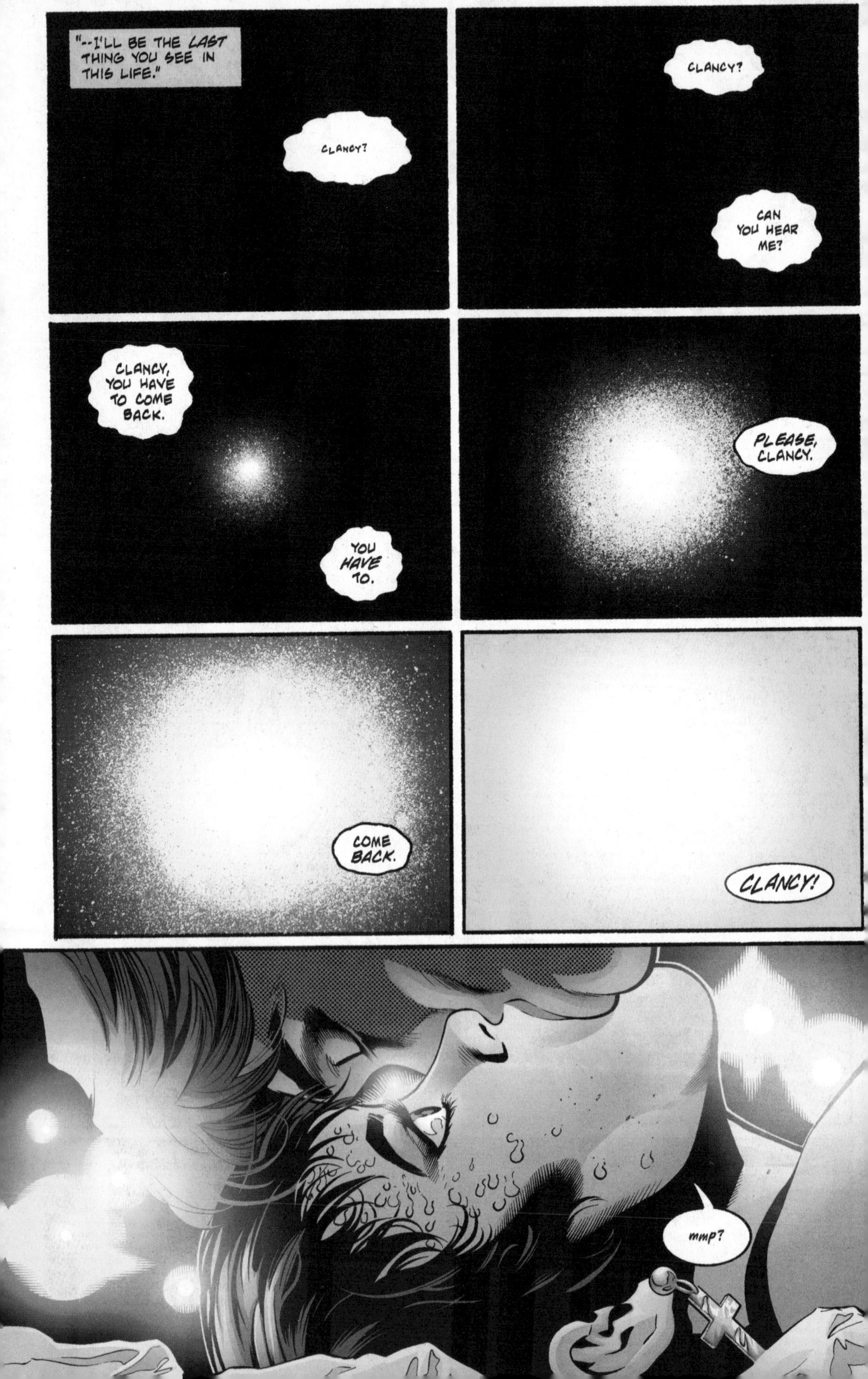
"--I'LL BE THE *LAST* THING YOU SEE IN THIS LIFE."
CLANCY?
CLANCY?
CAN YOU HEAR ME?
CLANCY, YOU HAVE TO COME BACK.
YOU *HAVE* TO.
PLEASE, CLANCY.
COME *BACK.*
CLANCY!
mmp?

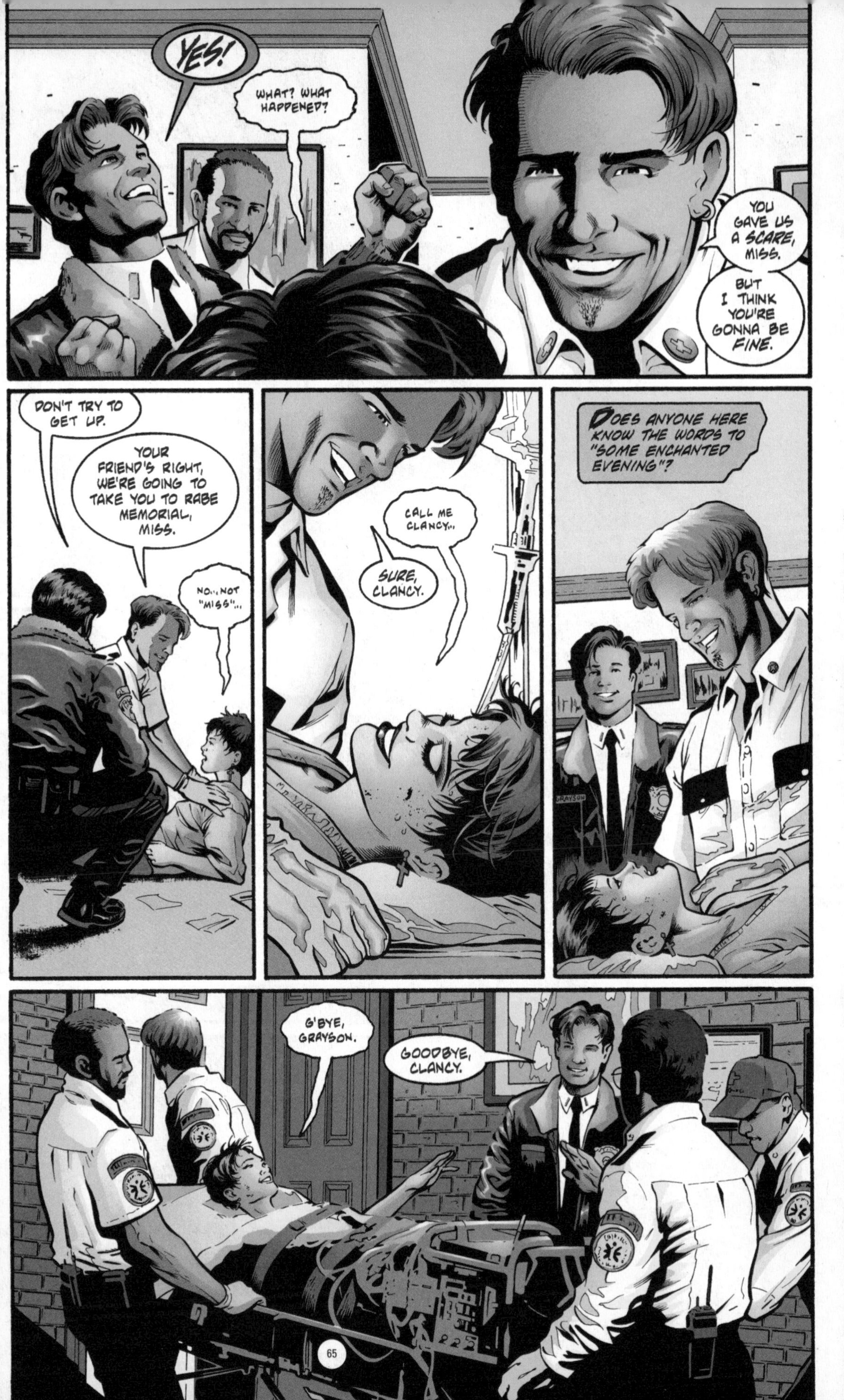
YES!
WHAT? WHAT HAPPENED?
YOU GAVE US A SCARE, MISS.
BUT I THINK YOU'RE GONNA BE FINE.
DON'T TRY TO GET UP.
YOUR FRIEND'S RIGHT, WE'RE GOING TO TAKE YOU TO RABE MEMORIAL, MISS.
NO... NOT "MISS"...
CALL ME CLANCY...
SURE, CLANCY.
DOES ANYONE HERE KNOW THE WORDS TO "SOME ENCHANTED EVENING"?
GRAYSON
G'BYE, GRAYSON.
GOODBYE, CLANCY.

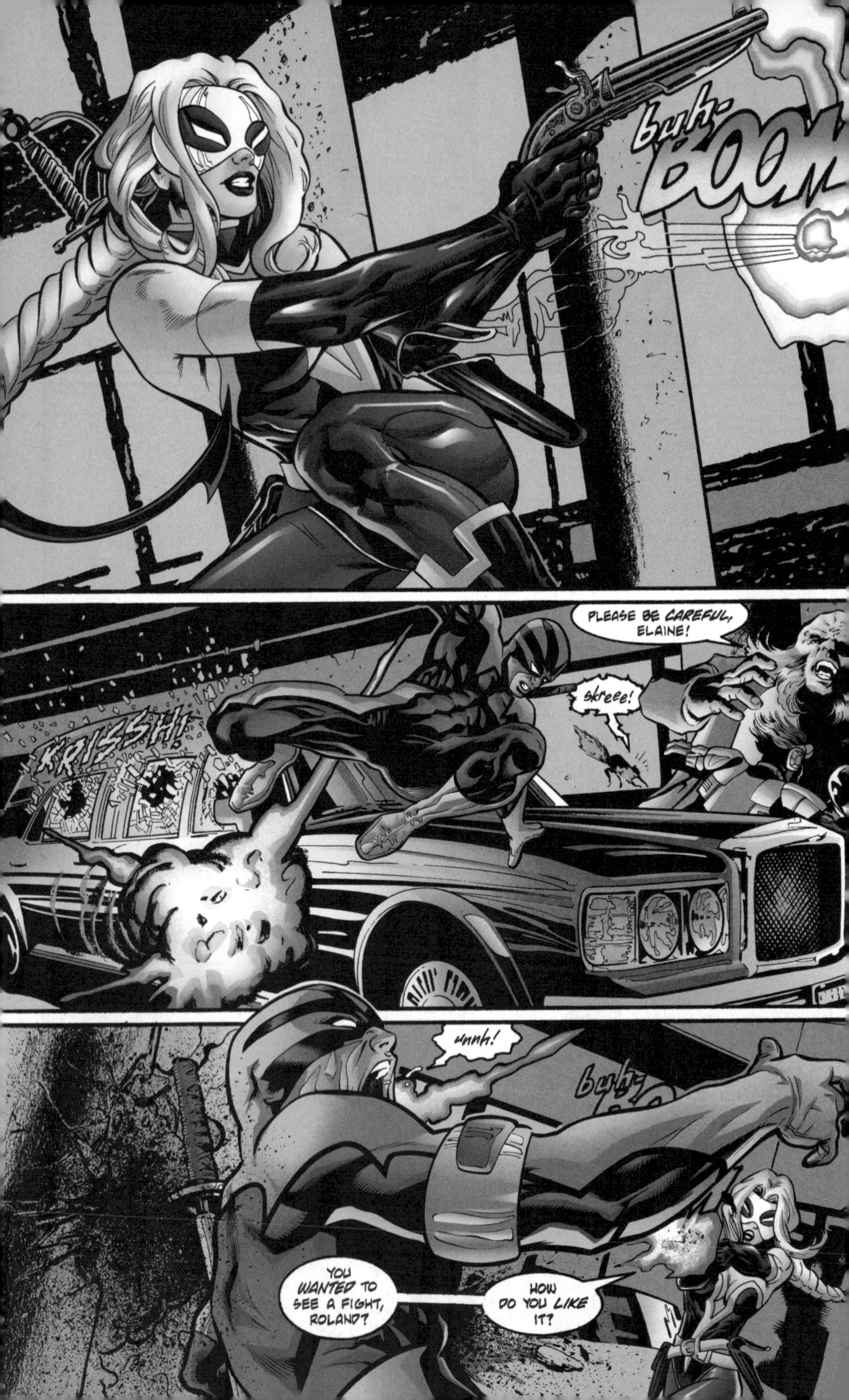
buh-
BOOM
PLEASE BE CAREFUL, ELAINE!
skreee!
KRISSH!
unnh!
YOU WANTED TO SEE A FIGHT, ROLAND?
HOW DO YOU LIKE IT?

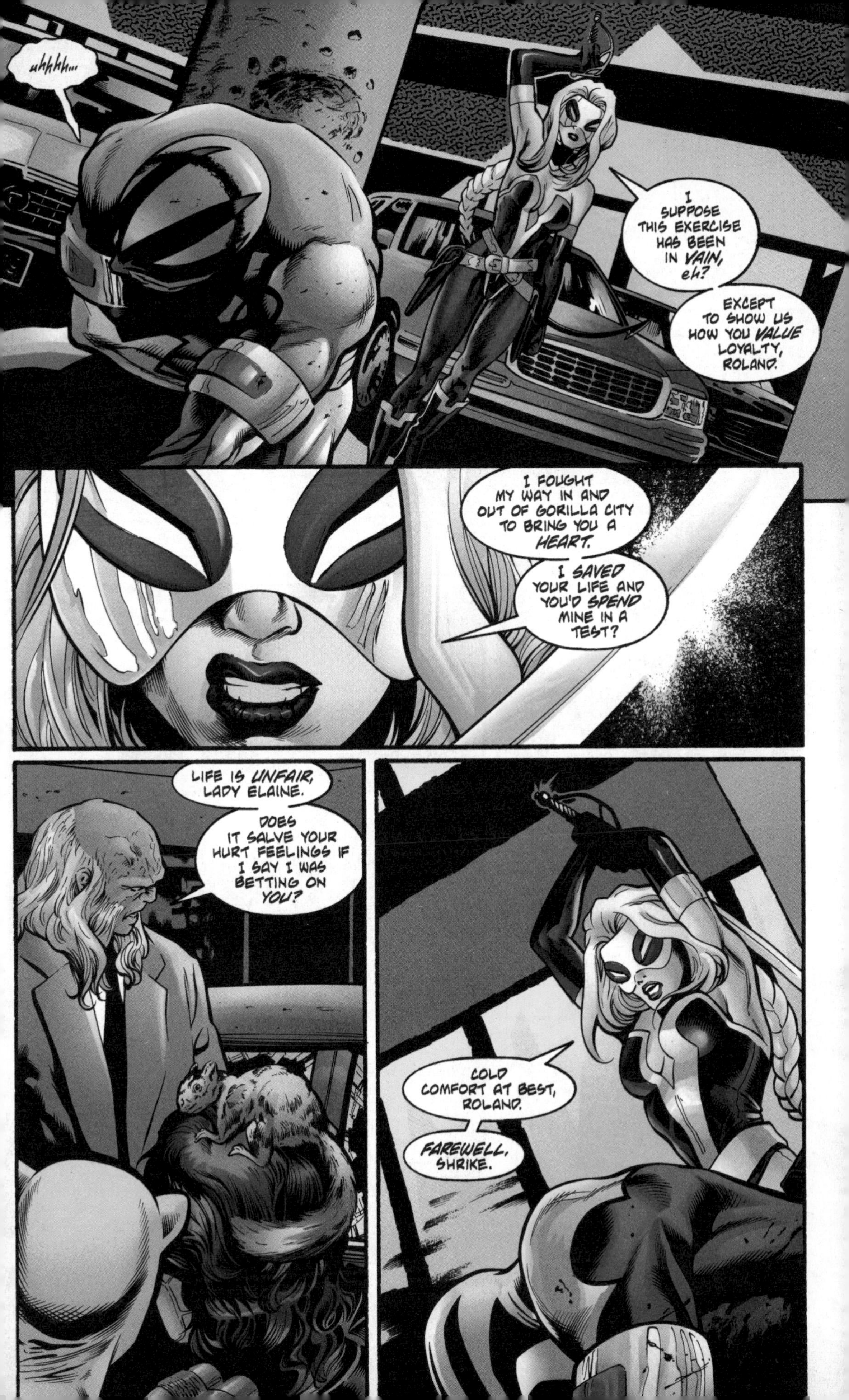
uhhhh...
I SUPPOSE THIS EXERCISE HAS BEEN IN VAIN, eh?
EXCEPT TO SHOW US HOW YOU VALUE LOYALTY, ROLAND.
I FOUGHT MY WAY IN AND OUT OF GORILLA CITY TO BRING YOU A HEART.
I SAVED YOUR LIFE AND YOU'D SPEND MINE IN A TEST?
LIFE IS UNFAIR, LADY ELAINE.
DOES IT SALVE YOUR HURT FEELINGS IF I SAY I WAS BETTING ON YOU?
COLD COMFORT AT BEST, ROLAND.
FAREWELL, SHRIKE.

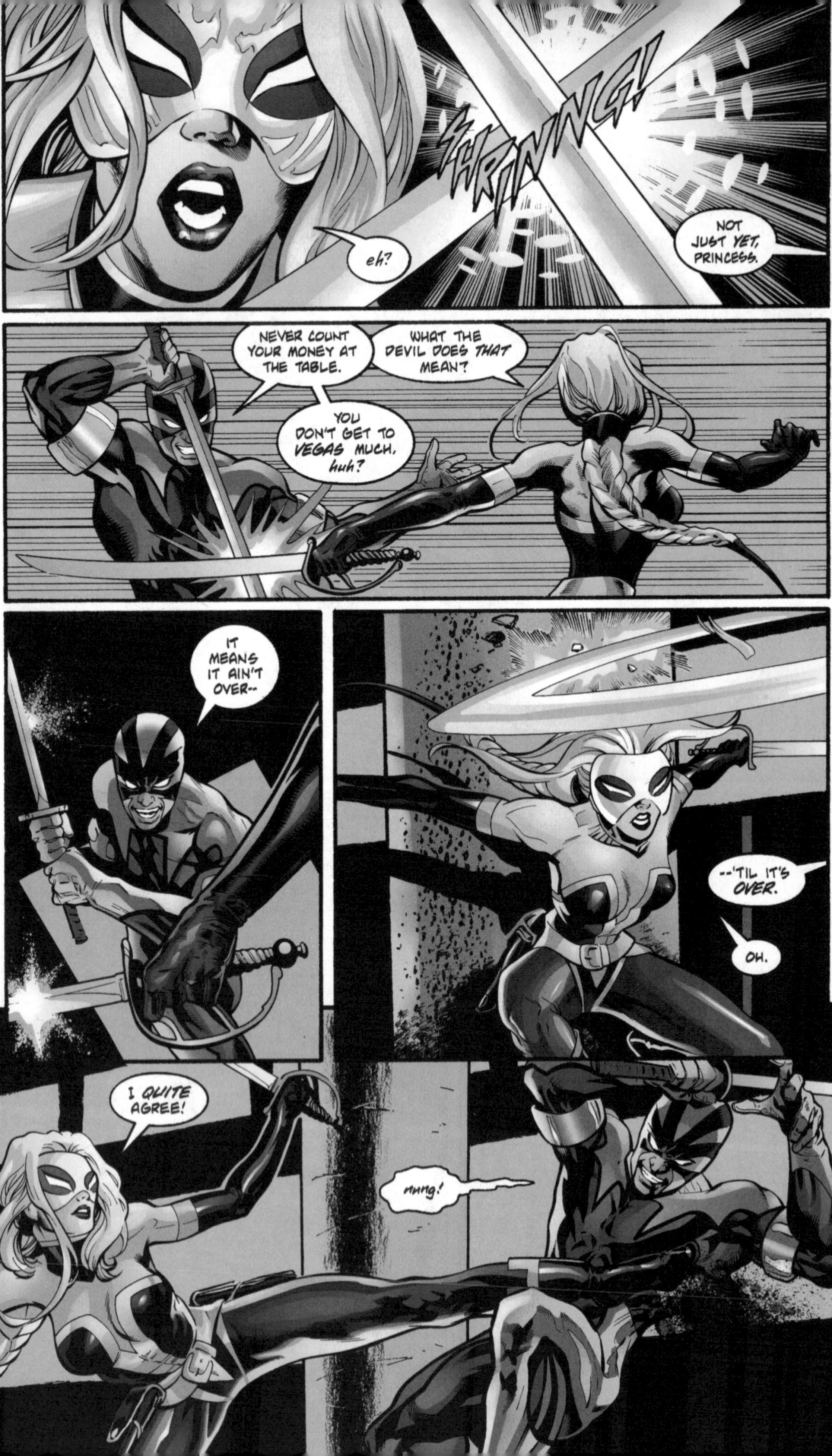
SHRINNNG!
eh?
NOT JUST YET, PRINCESS.
NEVER COUNT YOUR MONEY AT THE TABLE.
WHAT THE DEVIL DOES THAT MEAN?
YOU DON'T GET TO VEGAS MUCH, huh?
IT MEANS IT AIN'T OVER--
--'TIL IT'S OVER.
OH.
I QUITE AGREE!
nnng!

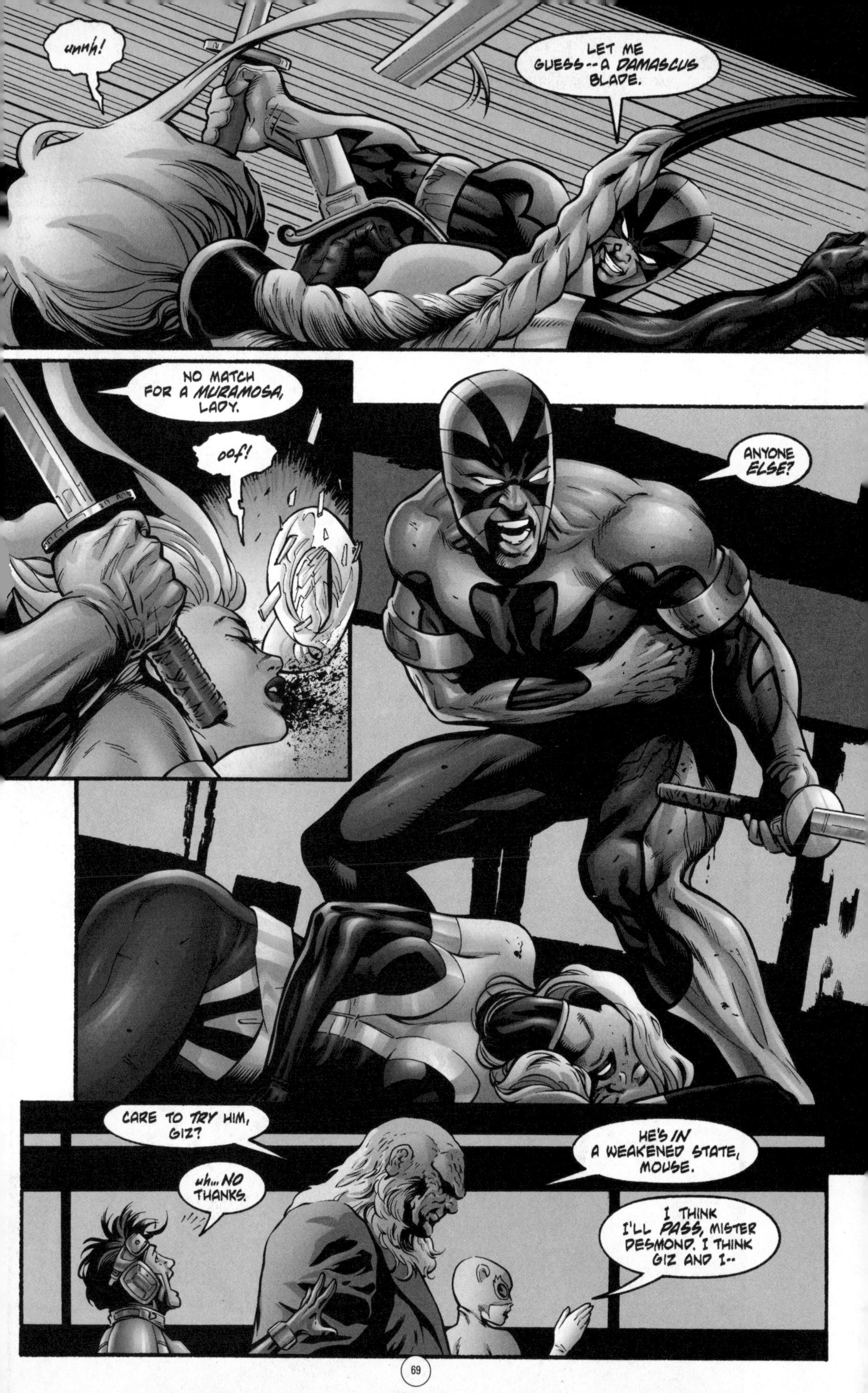
unnh!
LET ME GUESS--A DAMASCUS BLADE.
NO MATCH FOR A MURAMOSA, LADY.
oof!
ANYONE ELSE?
CARE TO TRY HIM, GIZ?
uh...NO THANKS.
HE'S IN A WEAKENED STATE, MOUSE.
I THINK I'LL PASS, MISTER DESMOND. I THINK GIZ AND I--

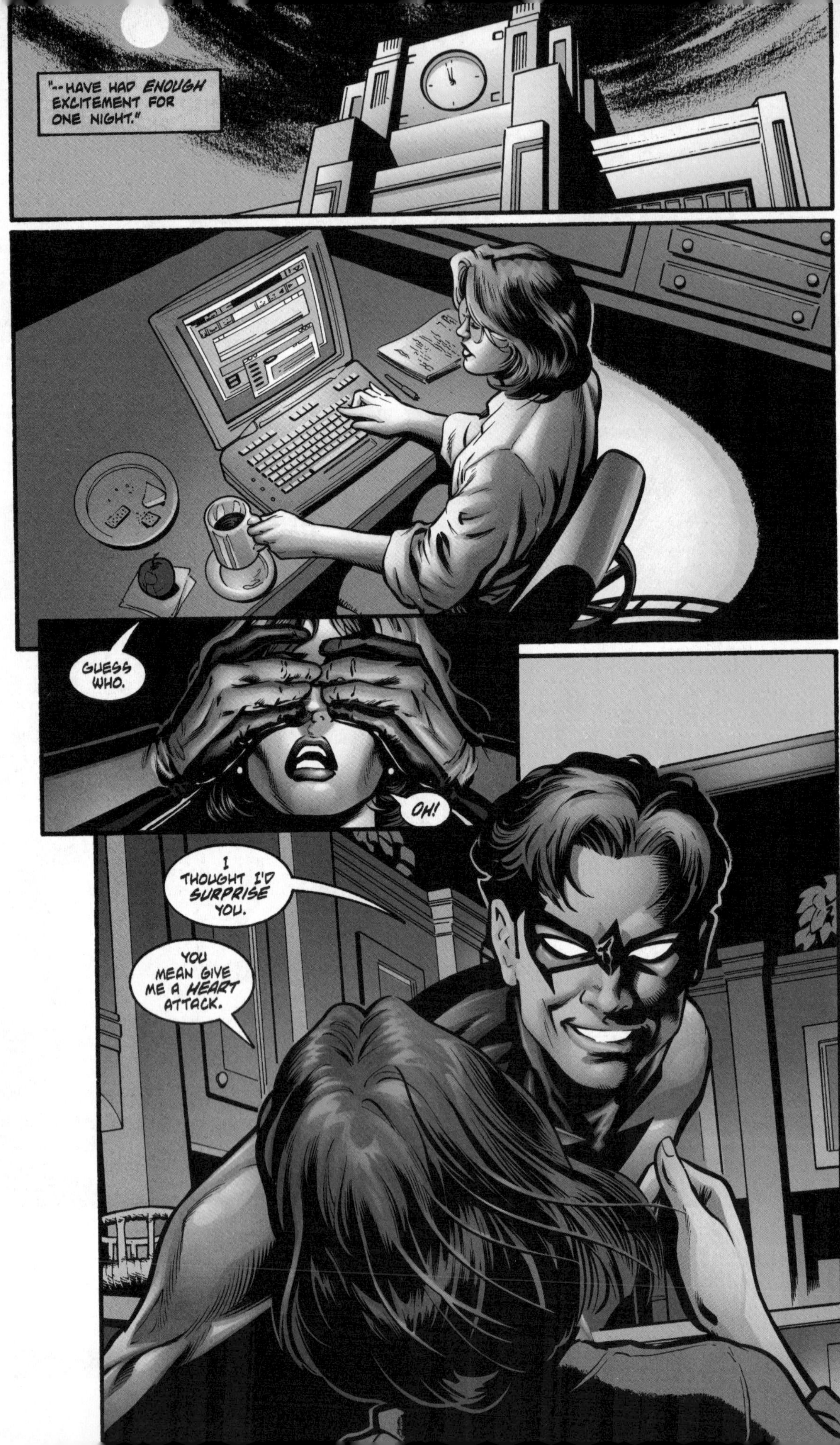
"--HAVE HAD ENOUGH EXCITEMENT FOR ONE NIGHT."
GUESS WHO.
OH!
I THOUGHT I'D SURPRISE YOU.
YOU MEAN GIVE ME A HEART ATTACK.

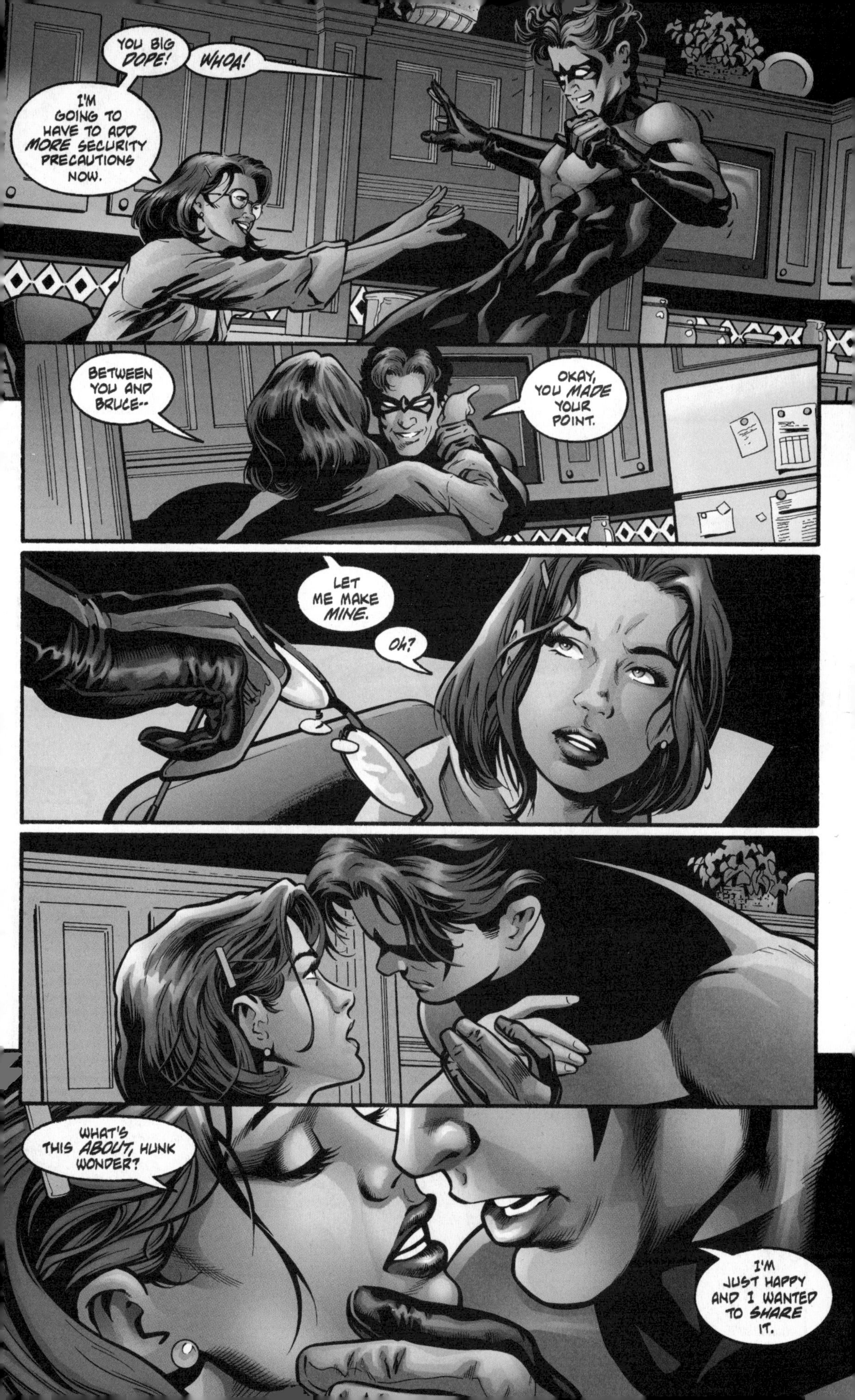

YOU BIG DOPE!
WHOA!
I'M GOING TO HAVE TO ADD MORE SECURITY PRECAUTIONS NOW.
BETWEEN YOU AND BRUCE--
OKAY, YOU MADE YOUR POINT.
LET ME MAKE MINE.
Oh?
WHAT'S THIS ABOUT, HUNK WONDER?
I'M JUST HAPPY AND I WANTED TO SHARE IT.

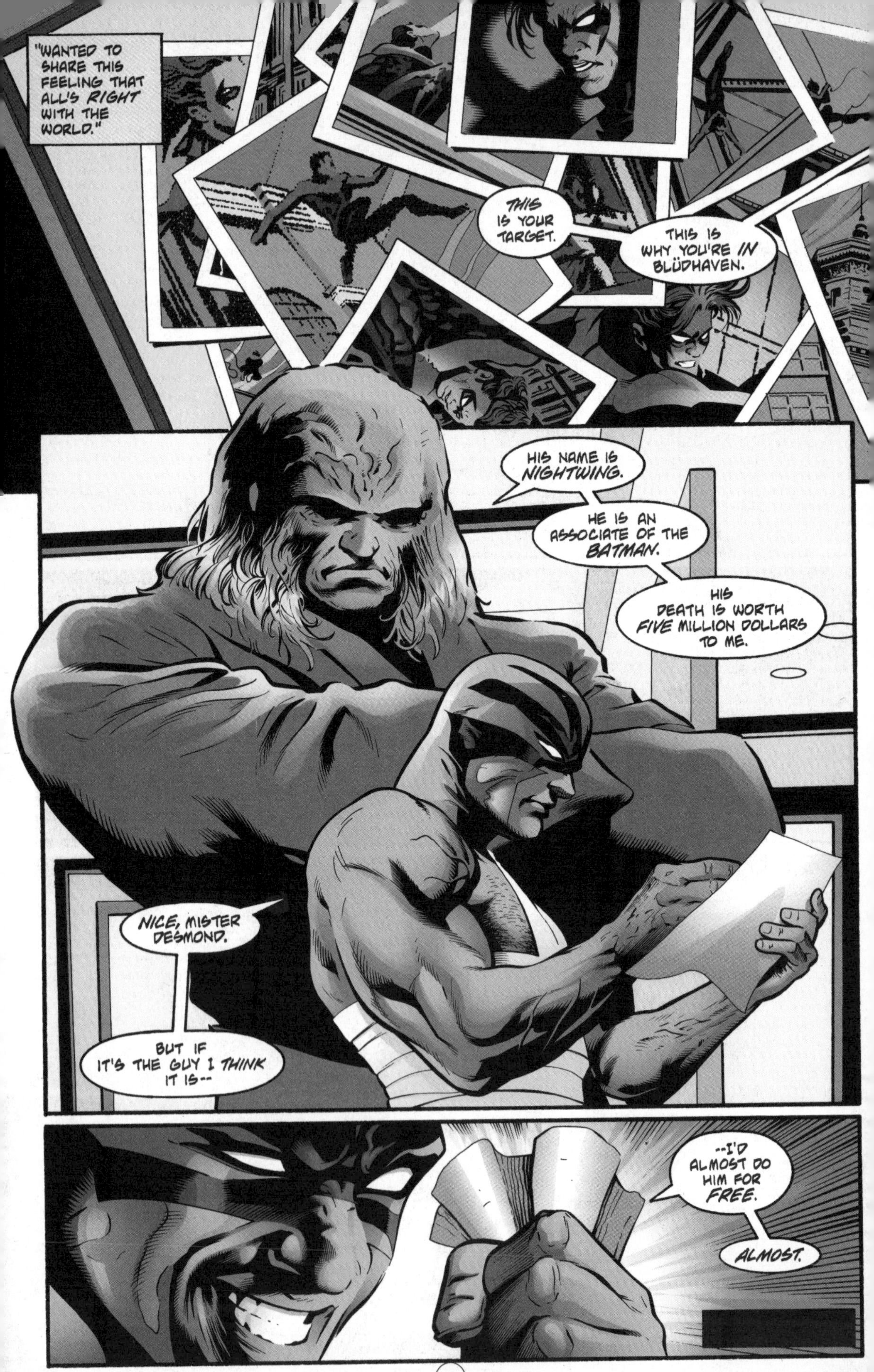
"WANTED TO SHARE THIS FEELING THAT ALL'S *RIGHT* WITH THE WORLD."
THIS IS YOUR TARGET.
THIS IS WHY YOU'RE *IN* BLÜDHAVEN.
HIS NAME IS *NIGHTWING*.
HE IS AN ASSOCIATE OF THE *BATMAN*.
HIS DEATH IS WORTH *FIVE* MILLION DOLLARS TO ME.
NICE, MISTER DESMOND.
BUT IF IT'S THE GUY I *THINK* IT IS--
--I'D ALMOST DO HIM FOR *FREE*.
ALMOST.
[redacted]

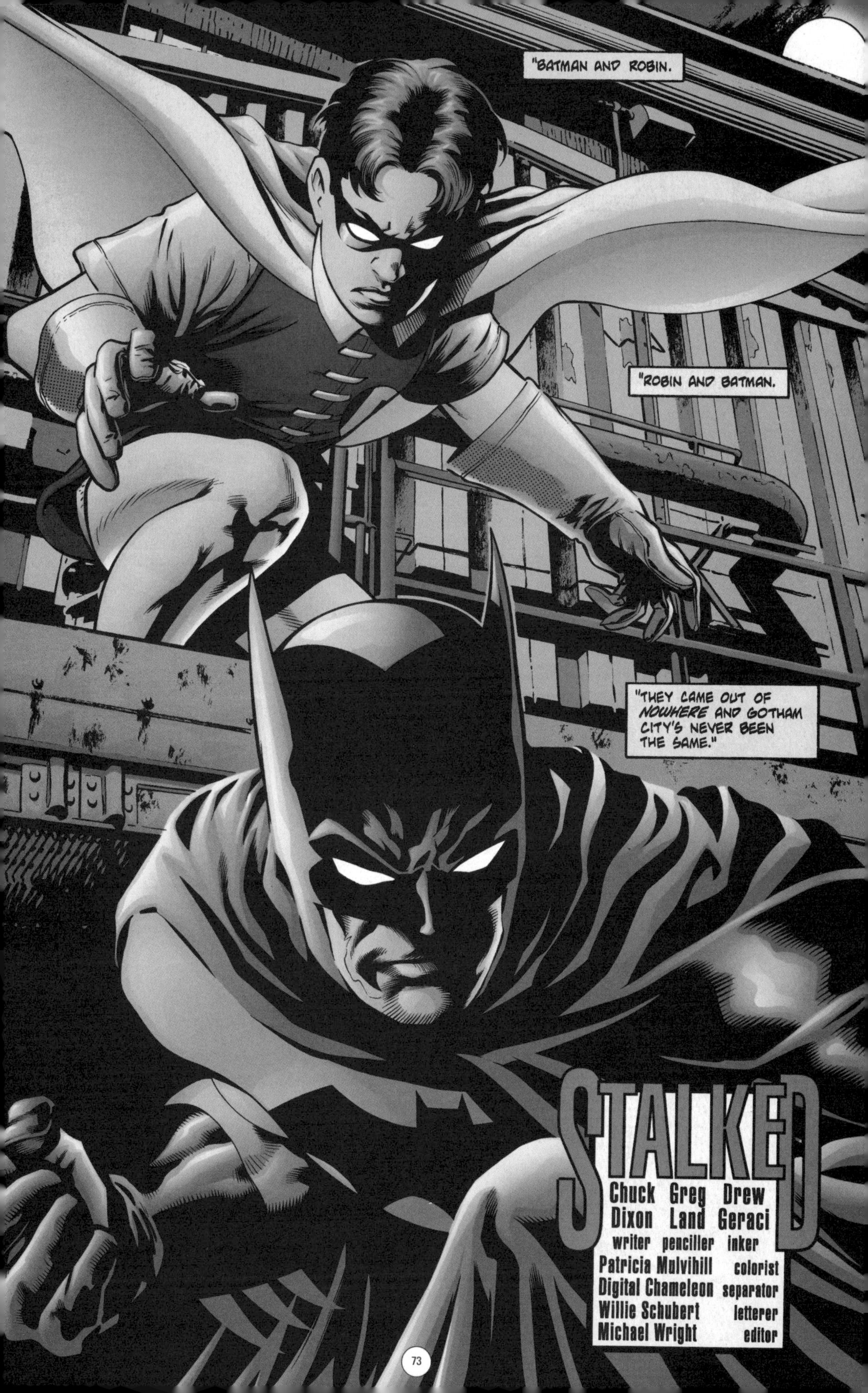
"BATMAN AND ROBIN.
"ROBIN AND BATMAN.
"THEY CAME OUT OF NOWHERE AND GOTHAM CITY'S NEVER BEEN THE SAME."
STALKED
Chuck Dixon writer
Greg Land penciller
Drew Geraci inker
Patricia Mulvihill colorist
Digital Chameleon separator
Willie Schubert letterer
Michael Wright editor

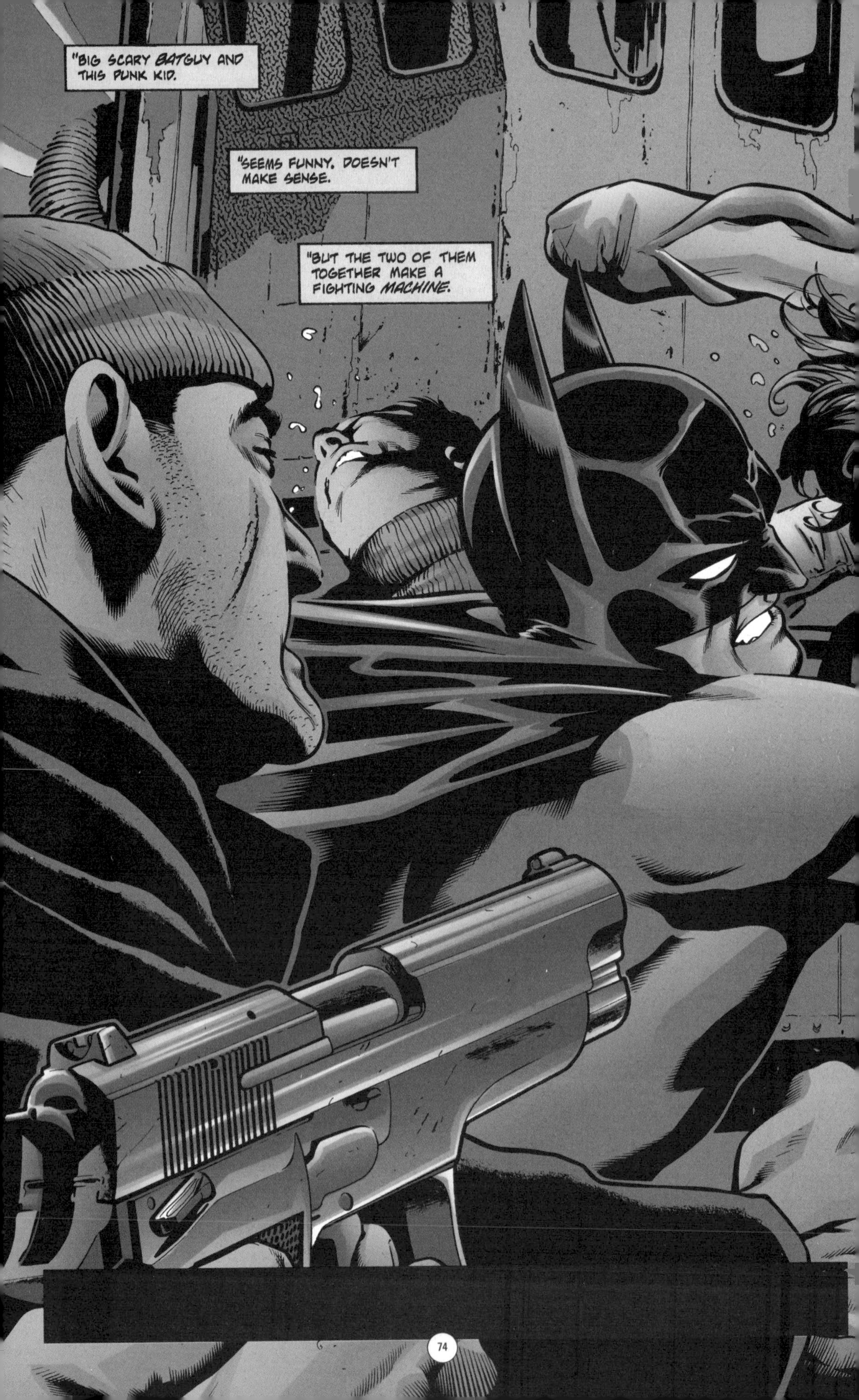
"BIG SCARY BATGUY AND THIS PUNK KID.
"SEEMS FUNNY. DOESN'T MAKE SENSE.
"BUT THE TWO OF THEM TOGETHER MAKE A FIGHTING MACHINE.
[redacted]

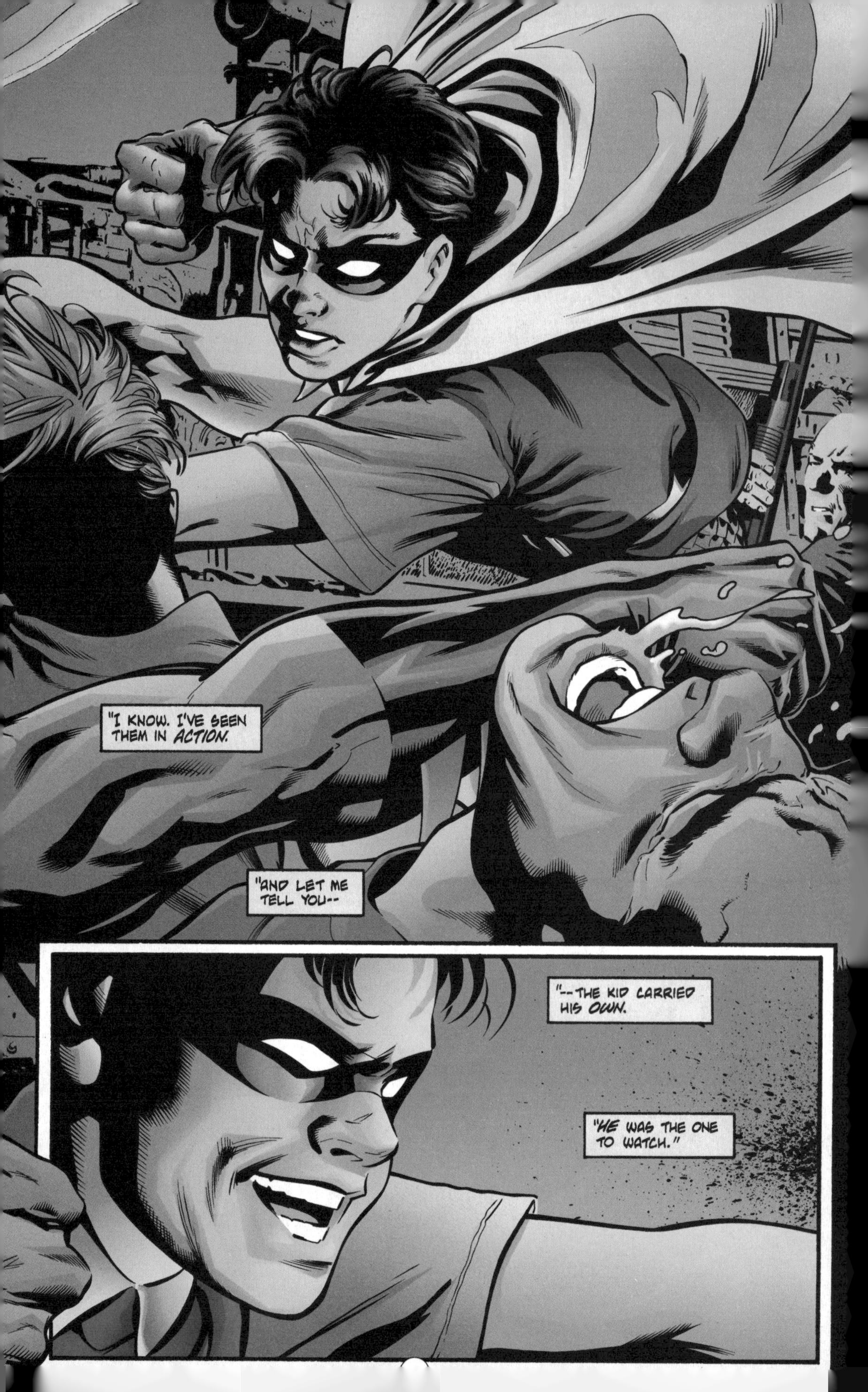
"I KNOW. I'VE SEEN THEM IN ACTION.
"AND LET ME TELL YOU--
"--THE KID CARRIED HIS OWN.
"HE WAS THE ONE TO WATCH."

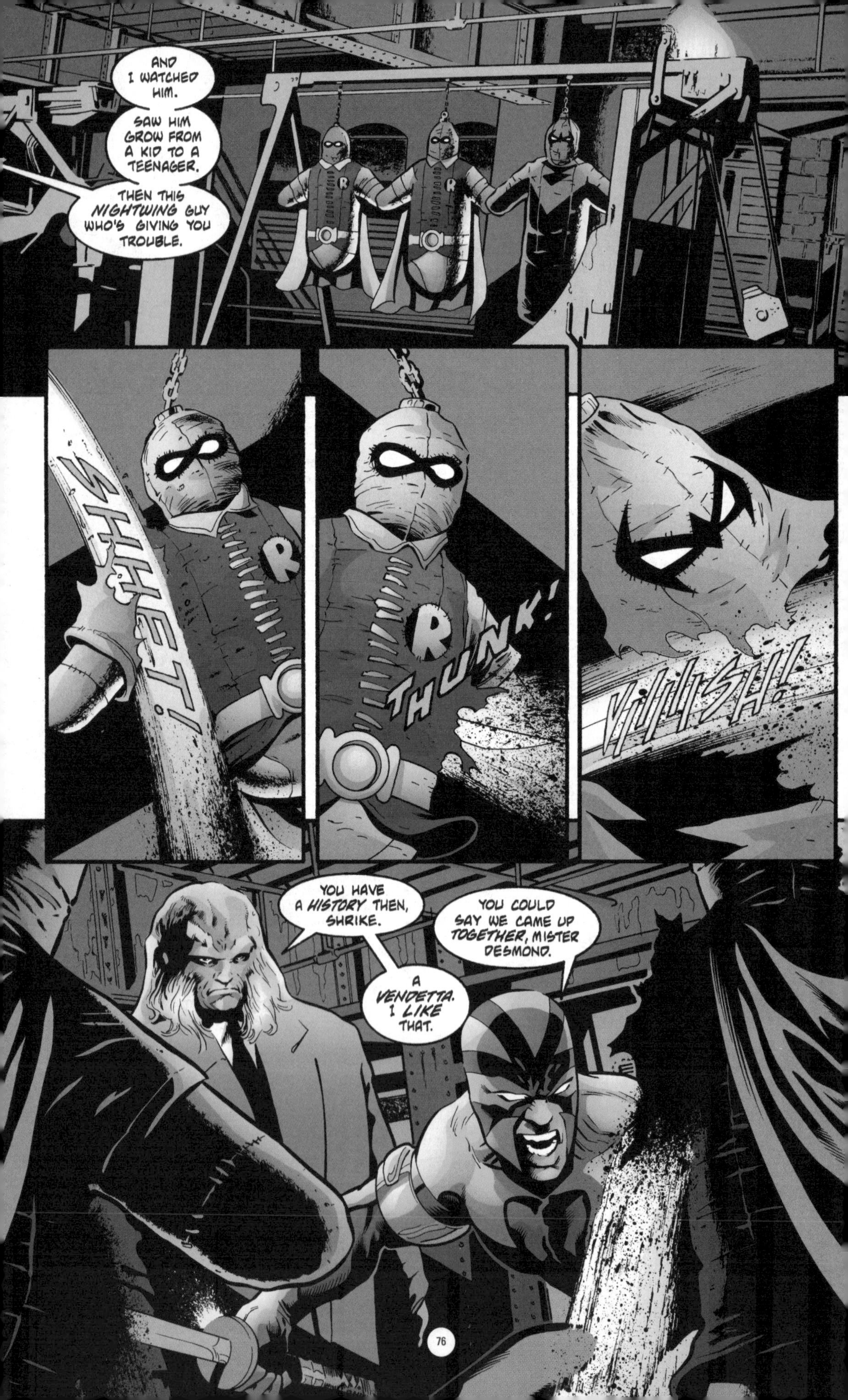

AND I WATCHED HIM.
SAW HIM GROW FROM A KID TO A TEENAGER.
THEN THIS NIGHTWING GUY WHO'S GIVING YOU TROUBLE.
SHHHETT!
THUNK!
VHHHSH!
YOU HAVE A HISTORY THEN, SHRIKE.
A VENDETTA. I LIKE THAT.
YOU COULD SAY WE CAME UP TOGETHER, MISTER DESMOND.

BUSINESS *AND* PLEASURE.

BUT I *STILL* WANT THE FIVE MILL IN CASH.

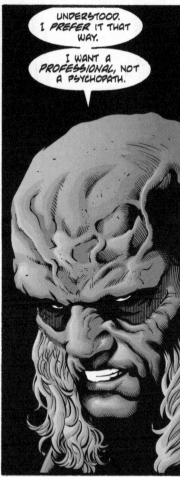

UNDERSTOOD. I *PREFER* IT THAT WAY.

I WANT A *PROFESSIONAL*, NOT A PSYCHOPATH.

YOU SAY HE'S CALLING *BLÜDHAVEN* HOME.

GIVE ME A FEW NIGHTS. I'LL *FIND* HIM. I'LL *STALK* HIM.

"I'LL KNOW EVERYTHING THERE *IS* TO KNOW ABOUT HIM."

DINAH?

oh.

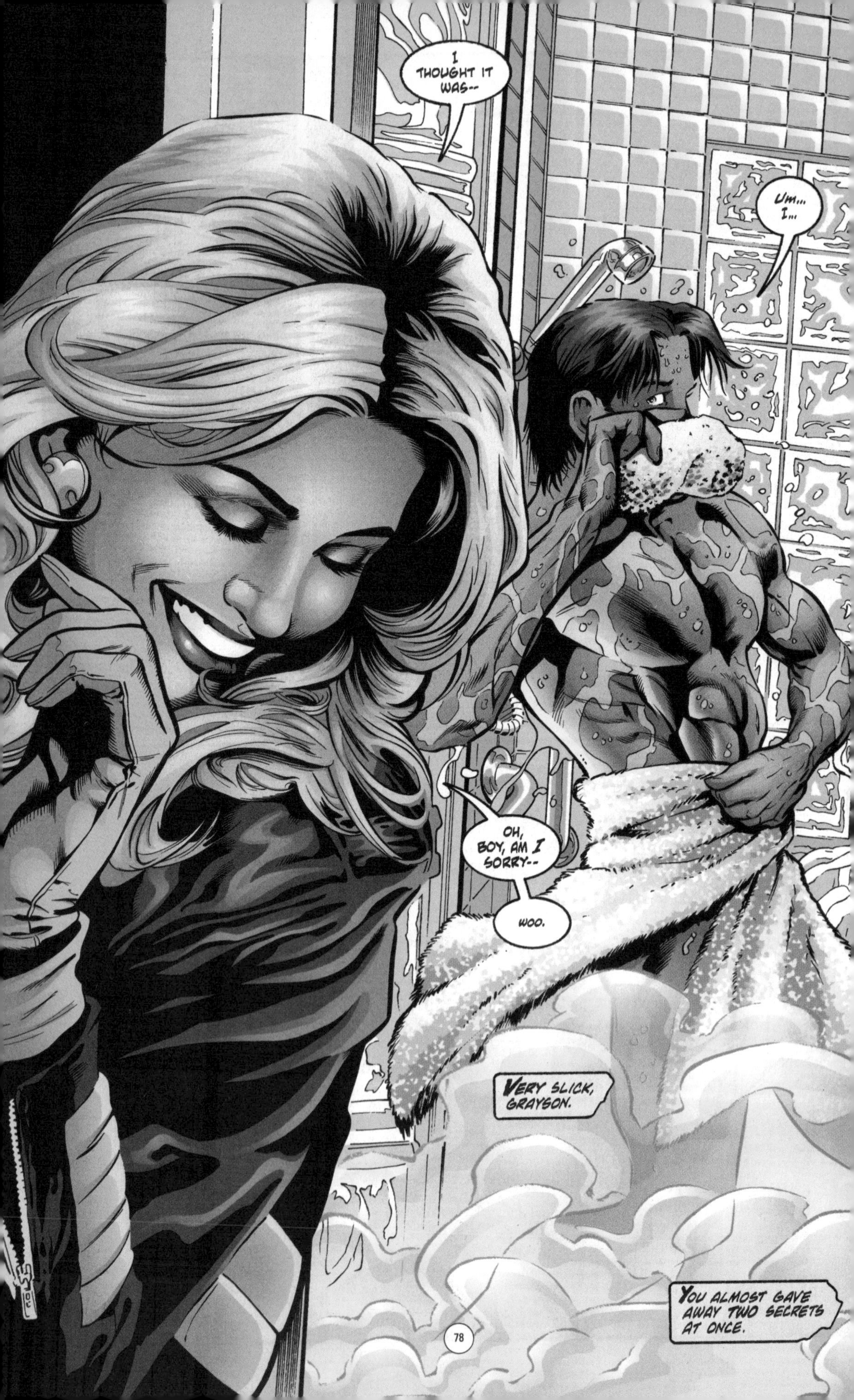
I THOUGHT IT WAS--
UM... I...
OH, BOY, AM I SORRY--
WOO.
VERY SLICK, GRAYSON.
YOU ALMOST GAVE AWAY TWO SECRETS AT ONCE.

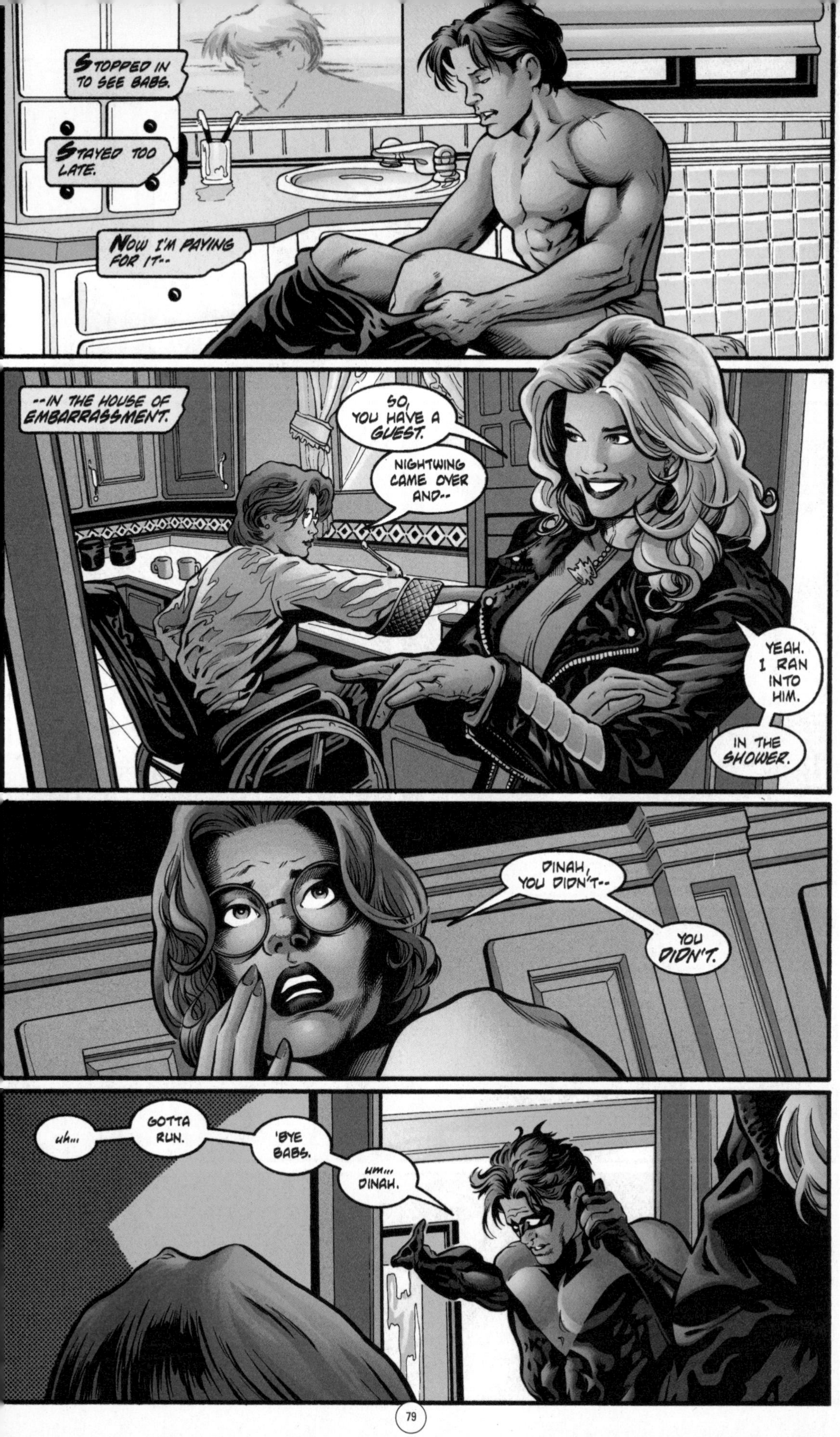

STOPPED IN TO SEE BABS.
STAYED TOO LATE.
NOW I'M PAYING FOR IT--
--IN THE HOUSE OF EMBARRASSMENT.
SO, YOU HAVE A GUEST.
NIGHTWING CAME OVER AND--
YEAH. I RAN INTO HIM.
IN THE SHOWER.
DINAH, YOU DIDN'T--
YOU DIDN'T.
uh...
GOTTA RUN.
'BYE BABS.
um... DINAH.

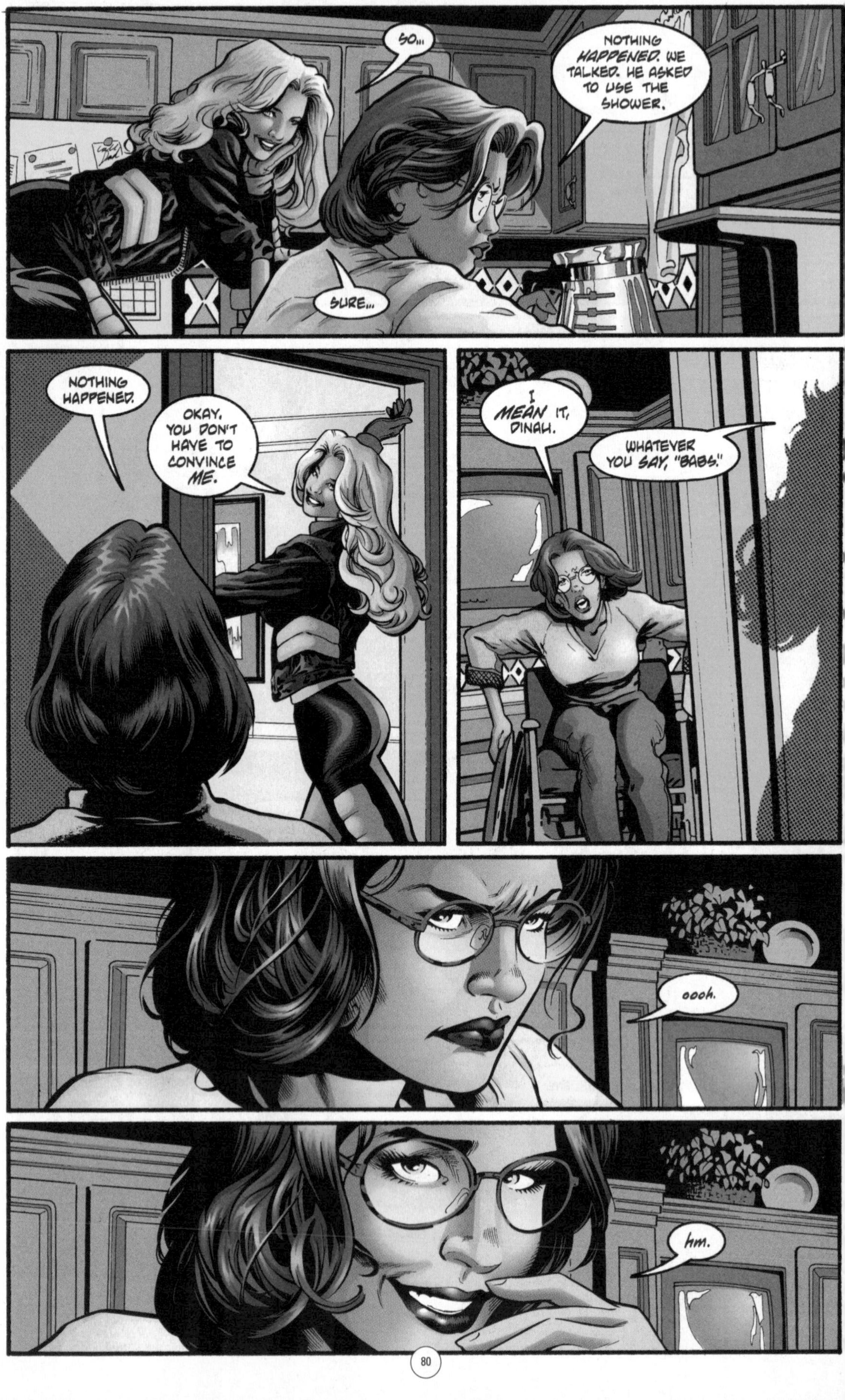
SO...
NOTHING HAPPENED. WE TALKED. HE ASKED TO USE THE SHOWER.
SURE...
NOTHING HAPPENED.
OKAY. YOU DON'T HAVE TO CONVINCE ME.
I MEAN IT, DINAH.
WHATEVER YOU SAY, "BABS."
oooh.
hm.

I KNOW THEY'RE TALKING ABOUT ME RIGHT NOW.

AND GIGGLING.

THAT'LL TEACH ME TO STAY OUT TOO LATE.

Land___ 4 mi. ↑
Gera___ 1 mi. ↑
Dixon A__ 3 mi. ↑

Blüdhaven
INTERSTATE 61 SOUTH 2 MILES ↱

BETTER GET TO BLÜDHAVEN BEFORE THE MORNING RUSH.

OR I'LL BLOW MY CAR'S SECRET IDENTITY TOO.

FORGOT TO OPAQUE THE GLASS.

THAT'S BETTER.

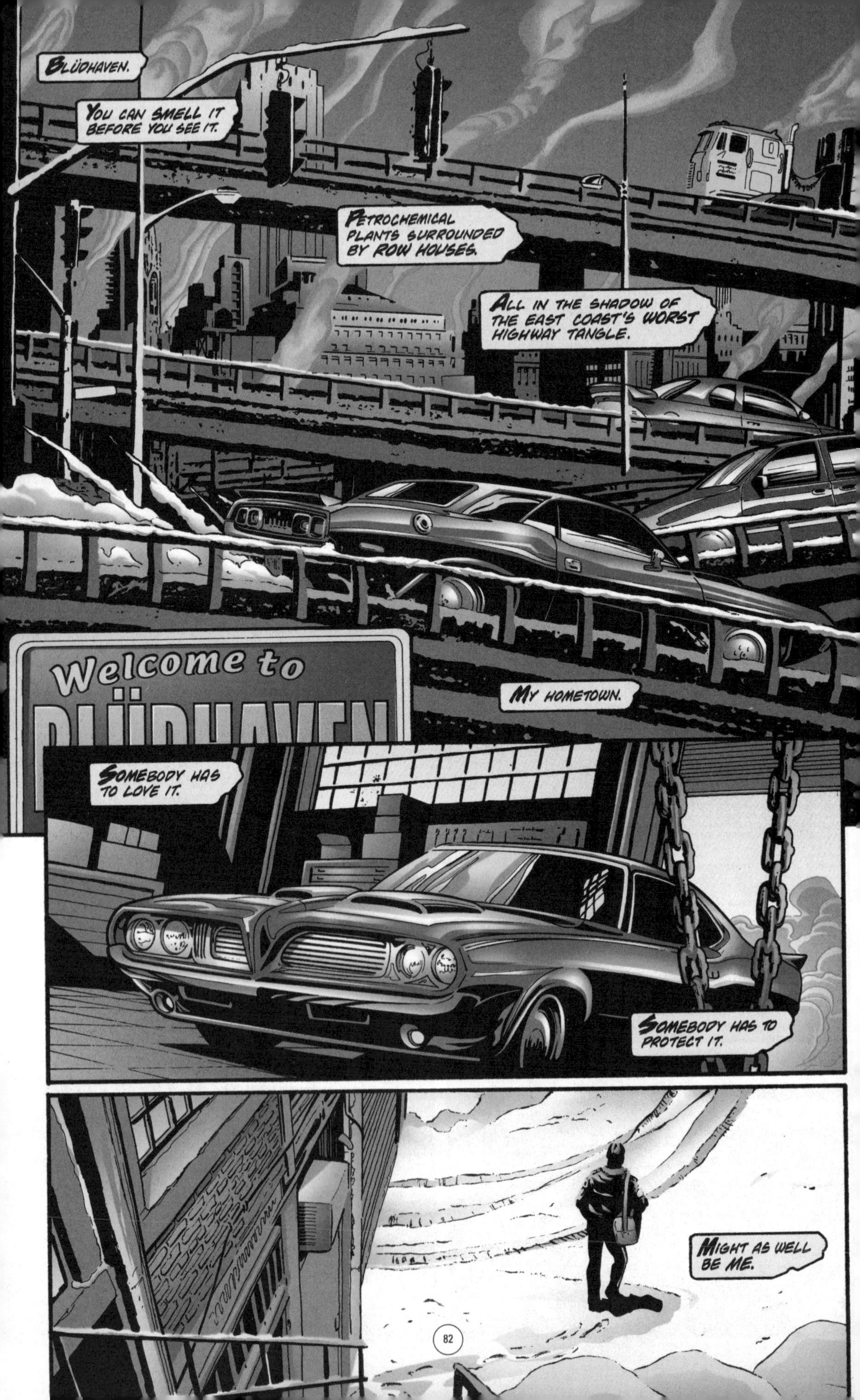
BLÜDHAVEN.
YOU CAN SMELL IT BEFORE YOU SEE IT.
PETROCHEMICAL PLANTS SURROUNDED BY ROW HOUSES.
ALL IN THE SHADOW OF THE EAST COAST'S WORST HIGHWAY TANGLE.
Welcome to
MY HOMETOWN.
SOMEBODY HAS TO LOVE IT.
SOMEBODY HAS TO PROTECT IT.
MIGHT AS WELL BE ME.

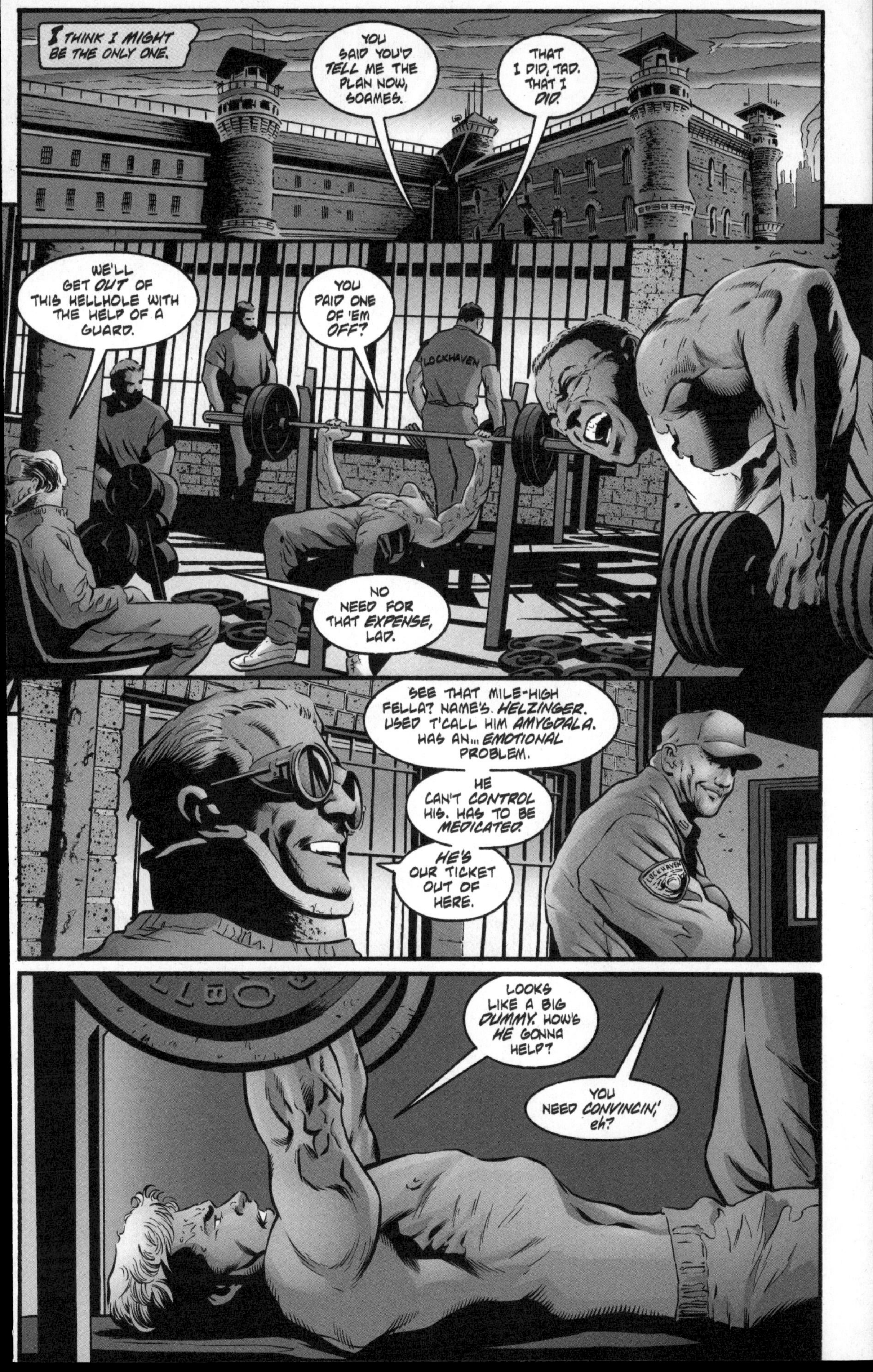
I THINK I MIGHT BE THE ONLY ONE.
YOU SAID YOU'D TELL ME THE PLAN NOW, SOAMES.
THAT I DID, TAD. THAT I DID.
WE'LL GET OUT OF THIS HELLHOLE WITH THE HELP OF A GUARD.
YOU PAID ONE OF 'EM OFF?
LOCKHAVEN
NO NEED FOR THAT EXPENSE, LAD.
SEE THAT MILE-HIGH FELLA? NAME'S HELZINGER. USED T'CALL HIM AMYGDALA. HAS AN... EMOTIONAL PROBLEM.
HE CAN'T CONTROL HIS. HAS TO BE MEDICATED.
HE'S OUR TICKET OUT OF HERE.
LOCKHAVEN
LOOKS LIKE A BIG DUMMY. HOW'S HE GONNA HELP?
YOU NEED CONVINCIN', eh?

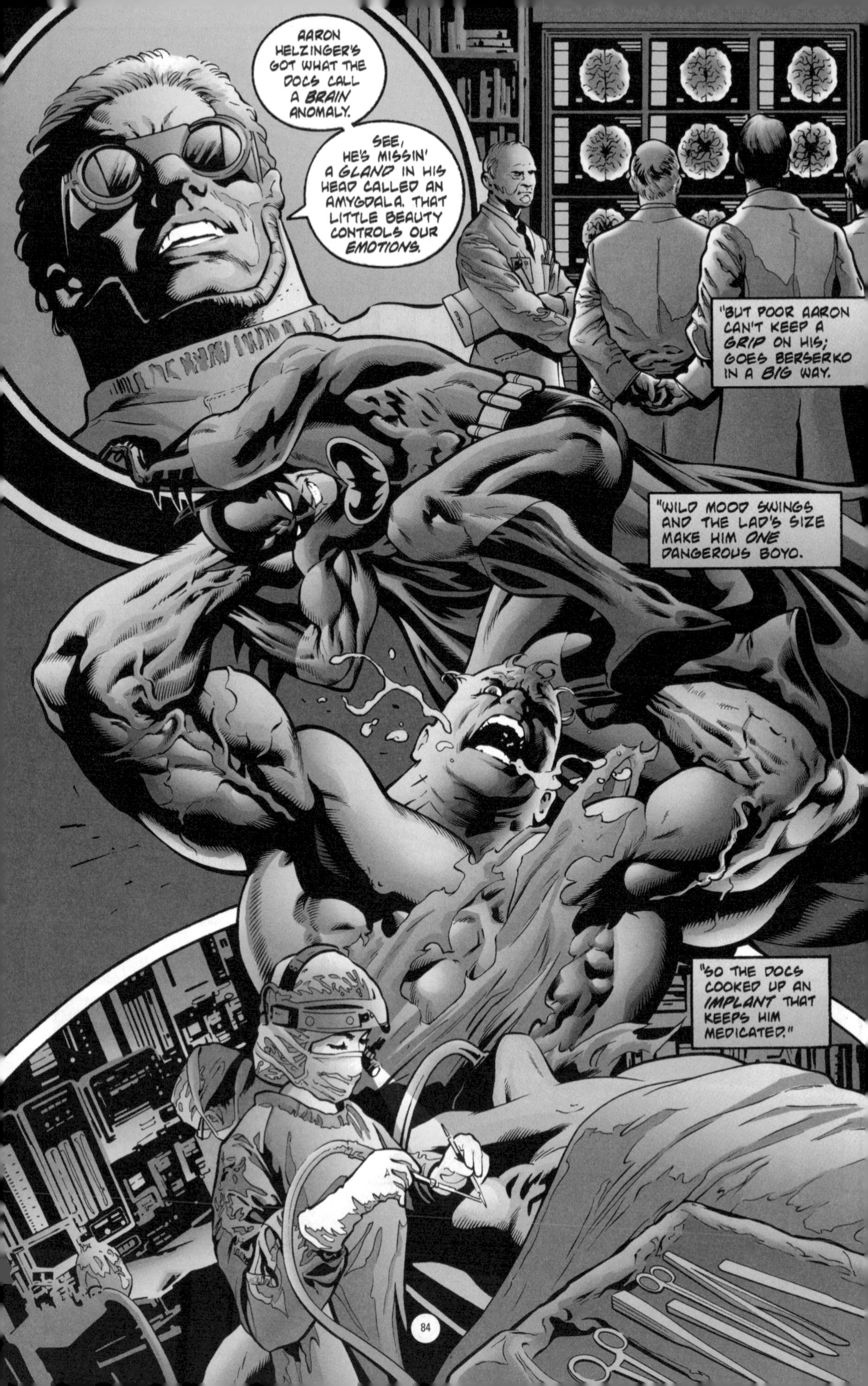
AARON HELZINGER'S GOT WHAT THE DOCS CALL A BRAIN ANOMALY.
SEE, HE'S MISSIN' A GLAND IN HIS HEAD CALLED AN AMYGDALA. THAT LITTLE BEAUTY CONTROLS OUR EMOTIONS.
"BUT POOR AARON CAN'T KEEP A GRIP ON HIS; GOES BERSERKO IN A BIG WAY.
"WILD MOOD SWINGS AND THE LAD'S SIZE MAKE HIM ONE DANGEROUS BOYO.
"SO THE DOCS COOKED UP AN IMPLANT THAT KEEPS HIM MEDICATED."

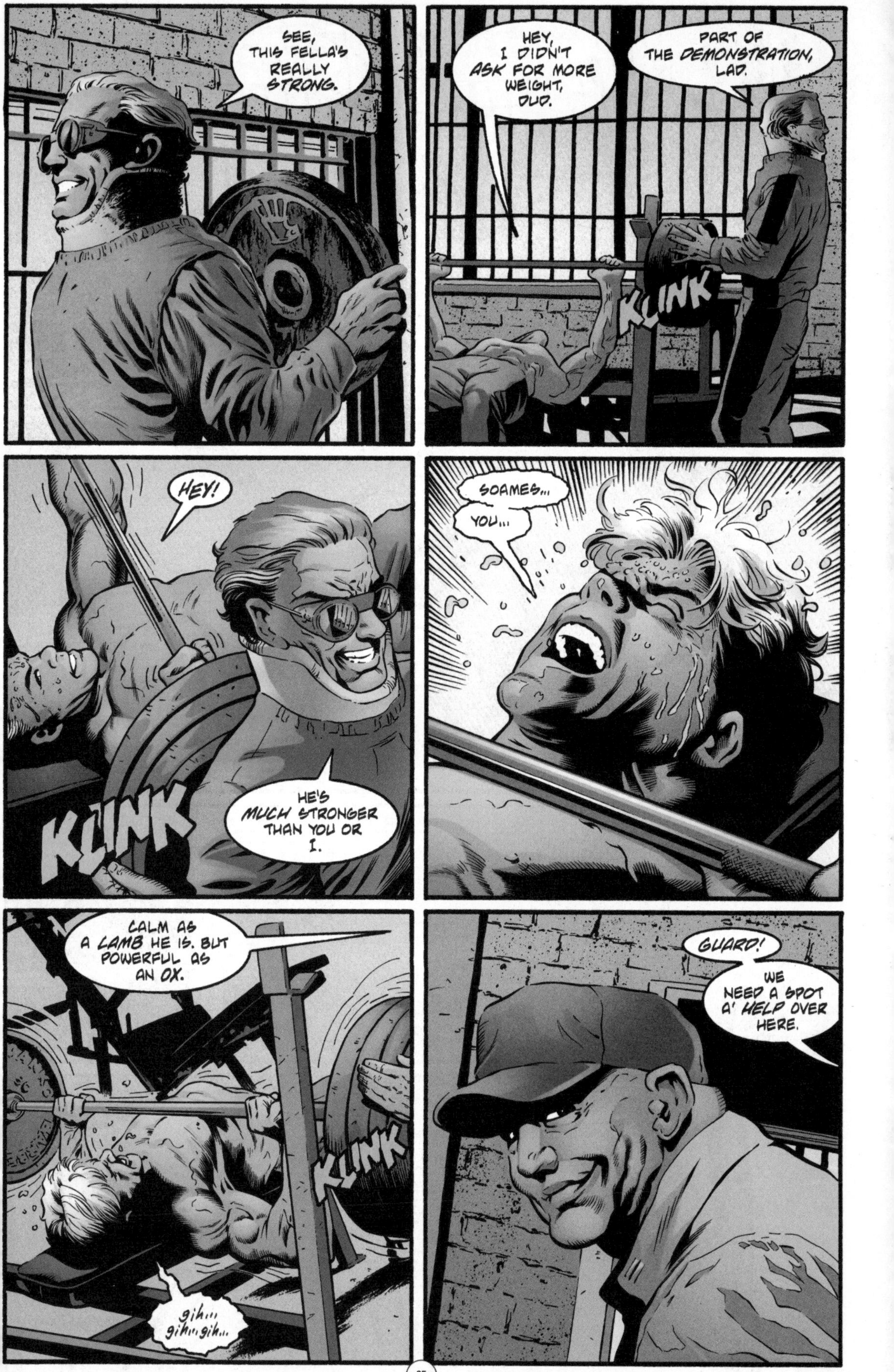
SEE, THIS FELLA'S REALLY STRONG.
HEY, I DIDN'T ASK FOR MORE WEIGHT, DUD.
PART OF THE DEMONSTRATION, LAD.
KLINK
HEY!
HE'S MUCH STRONGER THAN YOU OR I.
KLINK
SOAMES...
YOU...
CALM AS A LAMB HE IS. BUT POWERFUL AS AN OX.
KLINK
gih... gih... gih...
GUARD!
WE NEED A SPOT A' HELP OVER HERE.

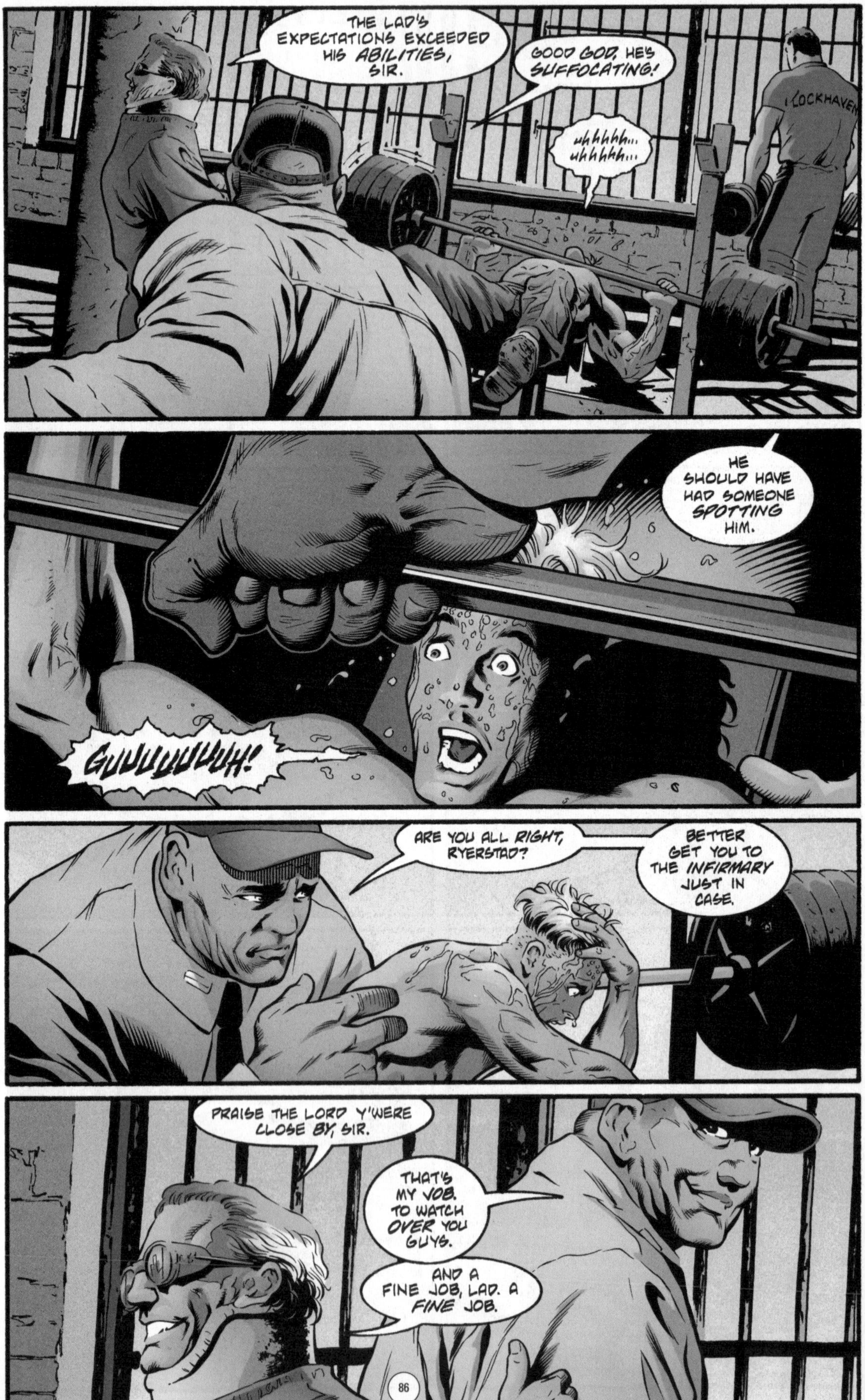
THE LAD'S EXPECTATIONS EXCEEDED HIS ABILITIES, SIR.
GOOD GOD, HE'S SUFFOCATING!
uhhhhh... uhhhhh...
LOCKHAVEN
HE SHOULD HAVE HAD SOMEONE SPOTTING HIM.
GUUUUUUUH!
ARE YOU ALL RIGHT, RYERSTAD?
BETTER GET YOU TO THE INFIRMARY JUST IN CASE.
PRAISE THE LORD Y'WERE CLOSE BY, SIR.
THAT'S MY JOB. TO WATCH OVER YOU GUYS.
AND A FINE JOB, LAD. A FINE JOB.

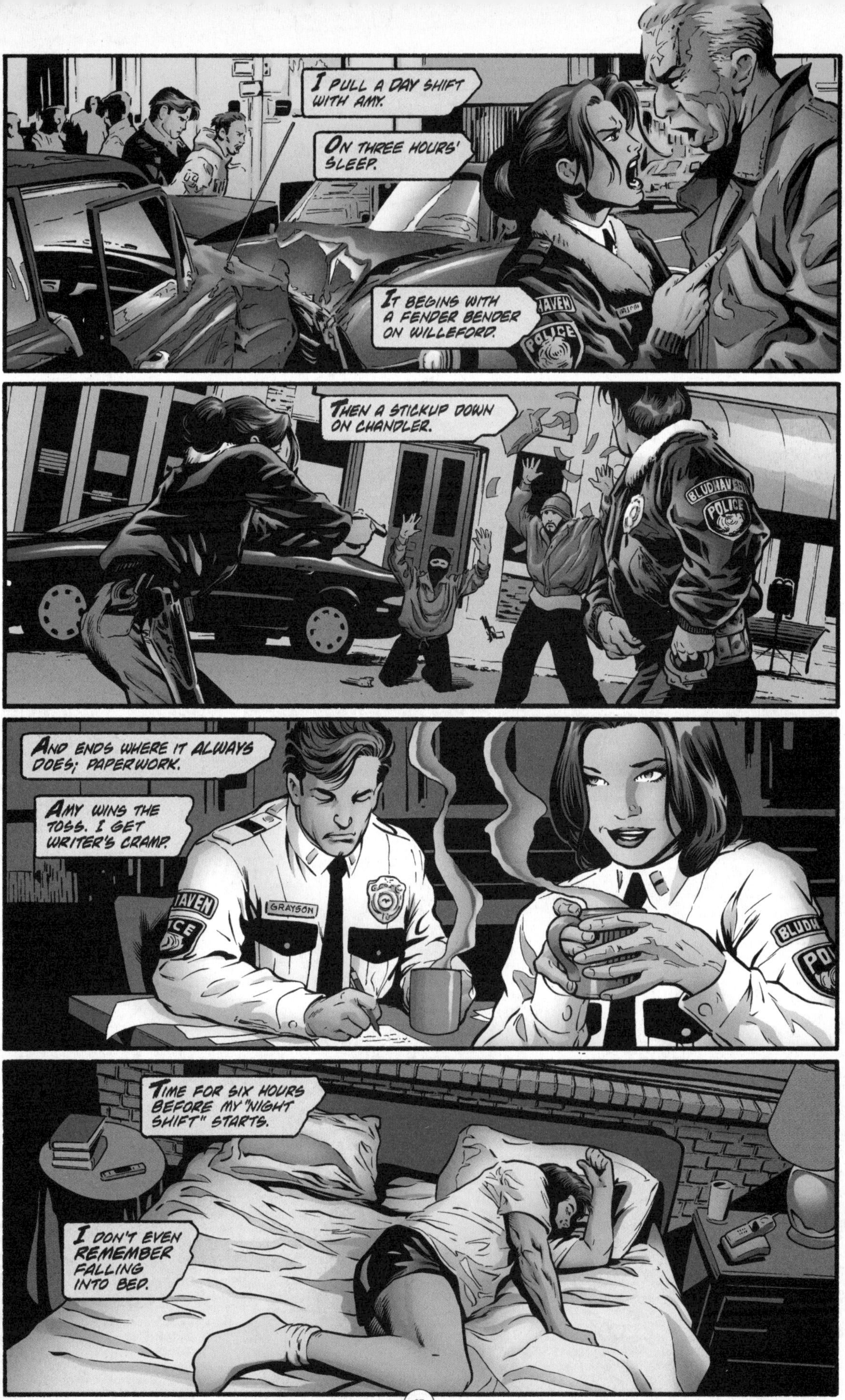
I PULL A DAY SHIFT WITH AMY.
ON THREE HOURS' SLEEP.
IT BEGINS WITH A FENDER BENDER ON WILLEFORD.
THEN A STICKUP DOWN ON CHANDLER.
AND ENDS WHERE IT ALWAYS DOES; PAPERWORK.
AMY WINS THE TOSS. I GET WRITER'S CRAMP.
TIME FOR SIX HOURS BEFORE MY "NIGHT SHIFT" STARTS.
I DON'T EVEN REMEMBER FALLING INTO BED.

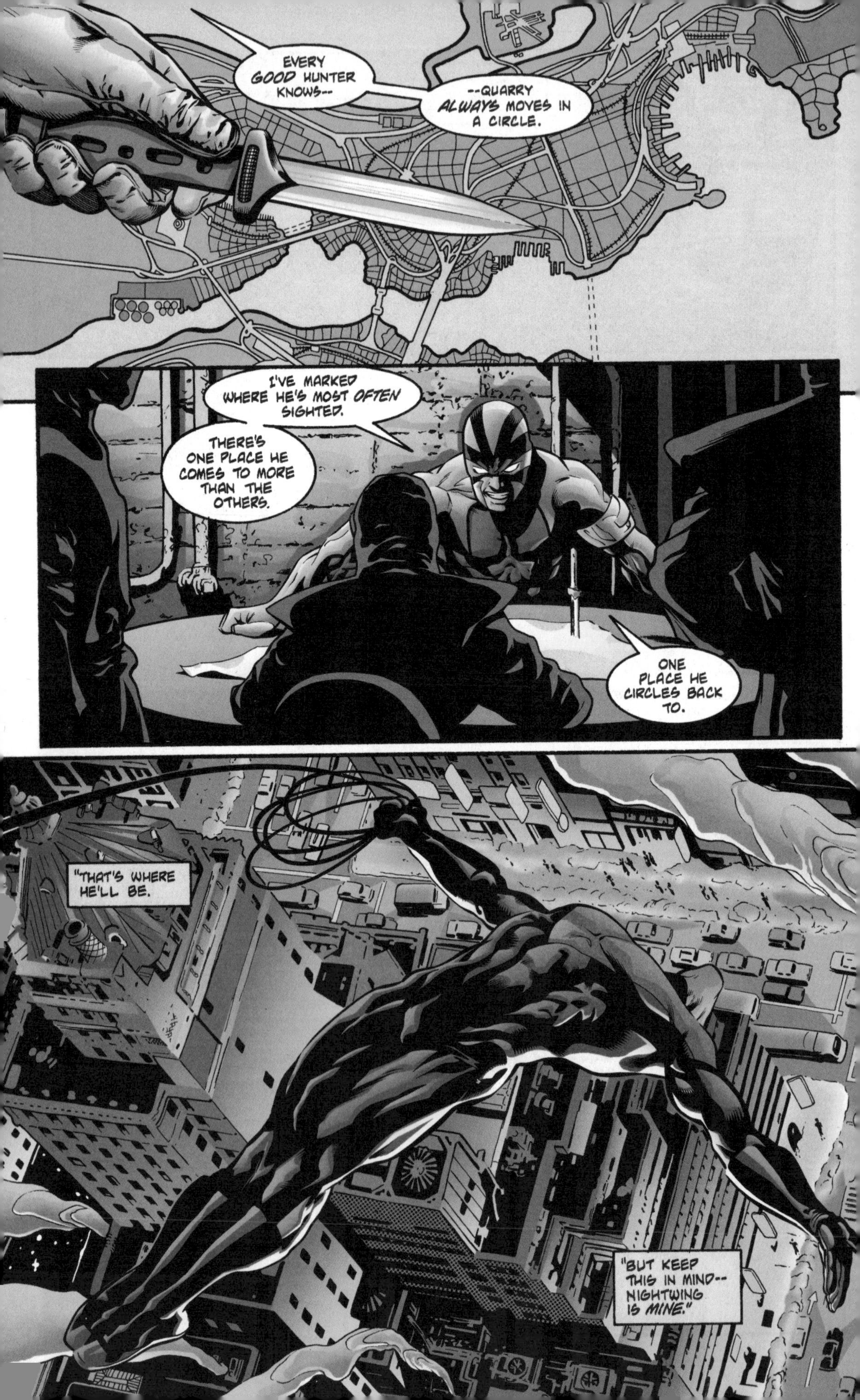
EVERY GOOD HUNTER KNOWS--
--QUARRY ALWAYS MOVES IN A CIRCLE.
I'VE MARKED WHERE HE'S MOST OFTEN SIGHTED.
THERE'S ONE PLACE HE COMES TO MORE THAN THE OTHERS.
ONE PLACE HE CIRCLES BACK TO.
"THAT'S WHERE HE'LL BE.
"BUT KEEP THIS IN MIND-- NIGHTWING IS MINE."

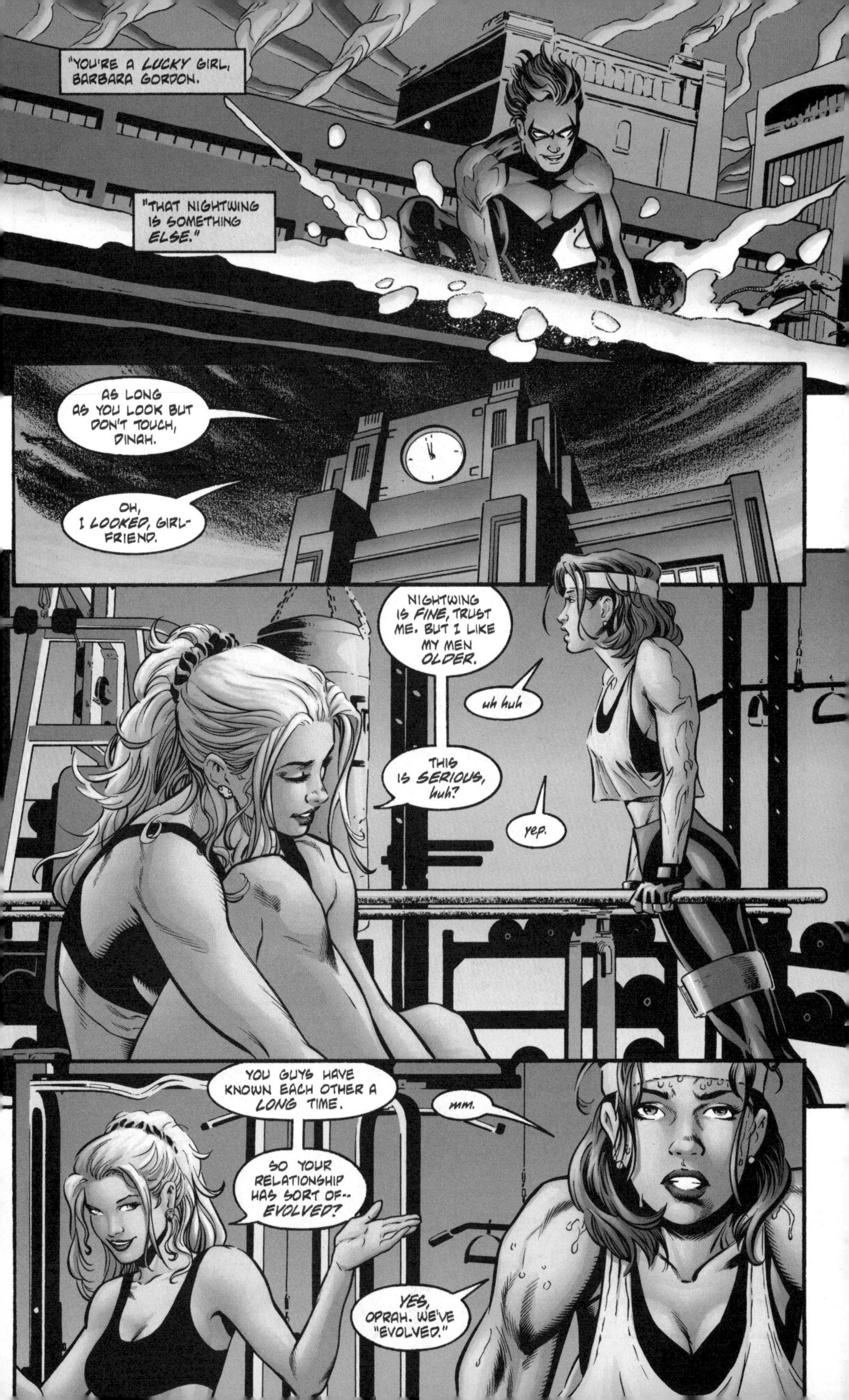
"YOU'RE A LUCKY GIRL, BARBARA GORDON.
"THAT NIGHTWING IS SOMETHING ELSE."
AS LONG AS YOU LOOK BUT DON'T TOUCH, DINAH.
OH, I LOOKED, GIRL-FRIEND.
NIGHTWING IS FINE, TRUST ME. BUT I LIKE MY MEN OLDER.
uh huh
THIS IS SERIOUS, huh?
yep.
YOU GUYS HAVE KNOWN EACH OTHER A LONG TIME.
mm.
SO YOUR RELATIONSHIP HAS SORT OF-- EVOLVED?
YES, OPRAH. WE'VE "EVOLVED."

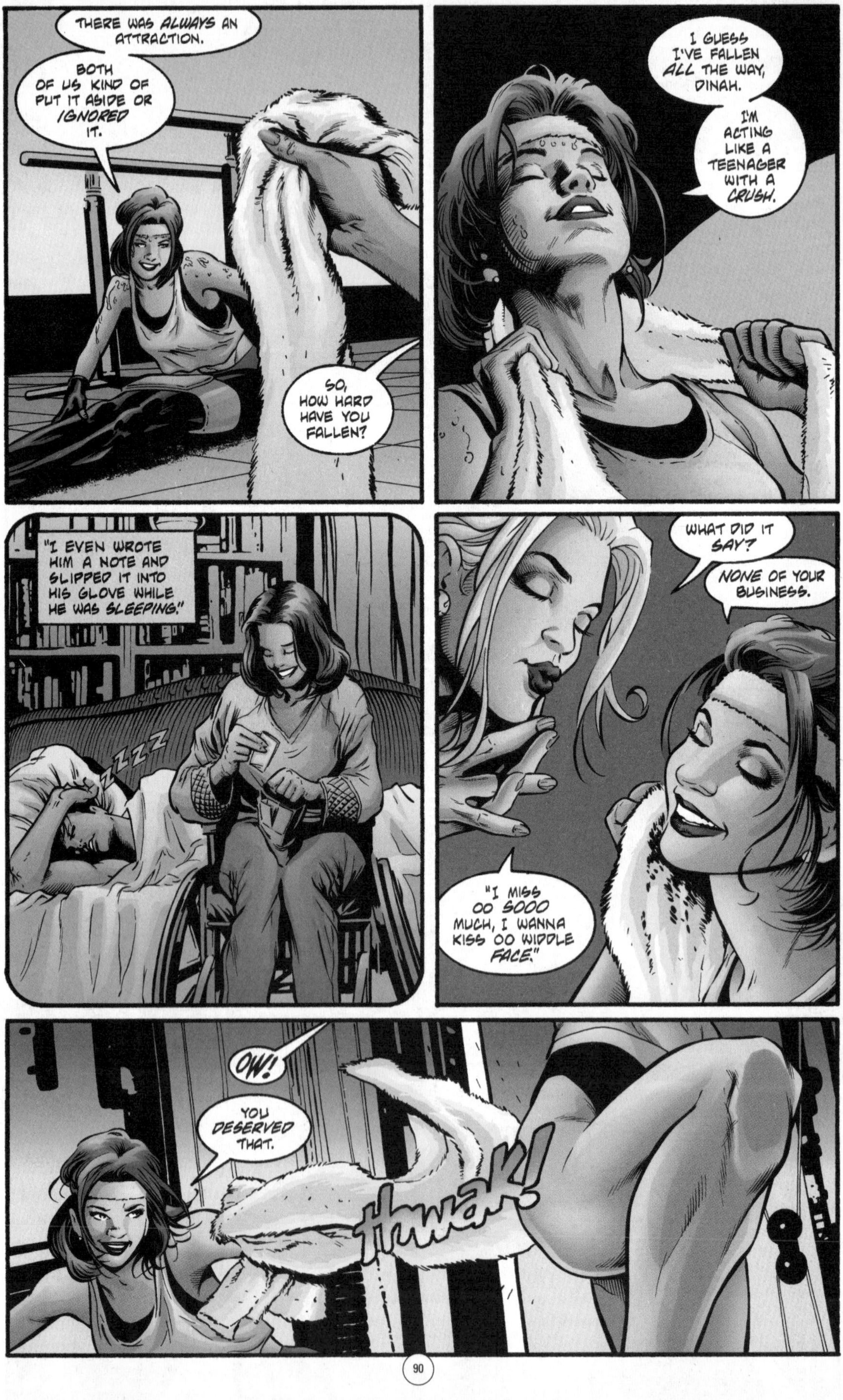
THERE WAS ALWAYS AN ATTRACTION.
BOTH OF US KIND OF PUT IT ASIDE OR IGNORED IT.
SO, HOW HARD HAVE YOU FALLEN?
I GUESS I'VE FALLEN ALL THE WAY, DINAH.
I'M ACTING LIKE A TEENAGER WITH A CRUSH.
"I EVEN WROTE HIM A NOTE AND SLIPPED IT INTO HIS GLOVE WHILE HE WAS SLEEPING."
ZZZZ
WHAT DID IT SAY?
NONE OF YOUR BUSINESS.
"I MISS OO SOOO MUCH, I WANNA KISS OO WIDDLE FACE."
OW!
YOU DESERVED THAT.
THWAK!

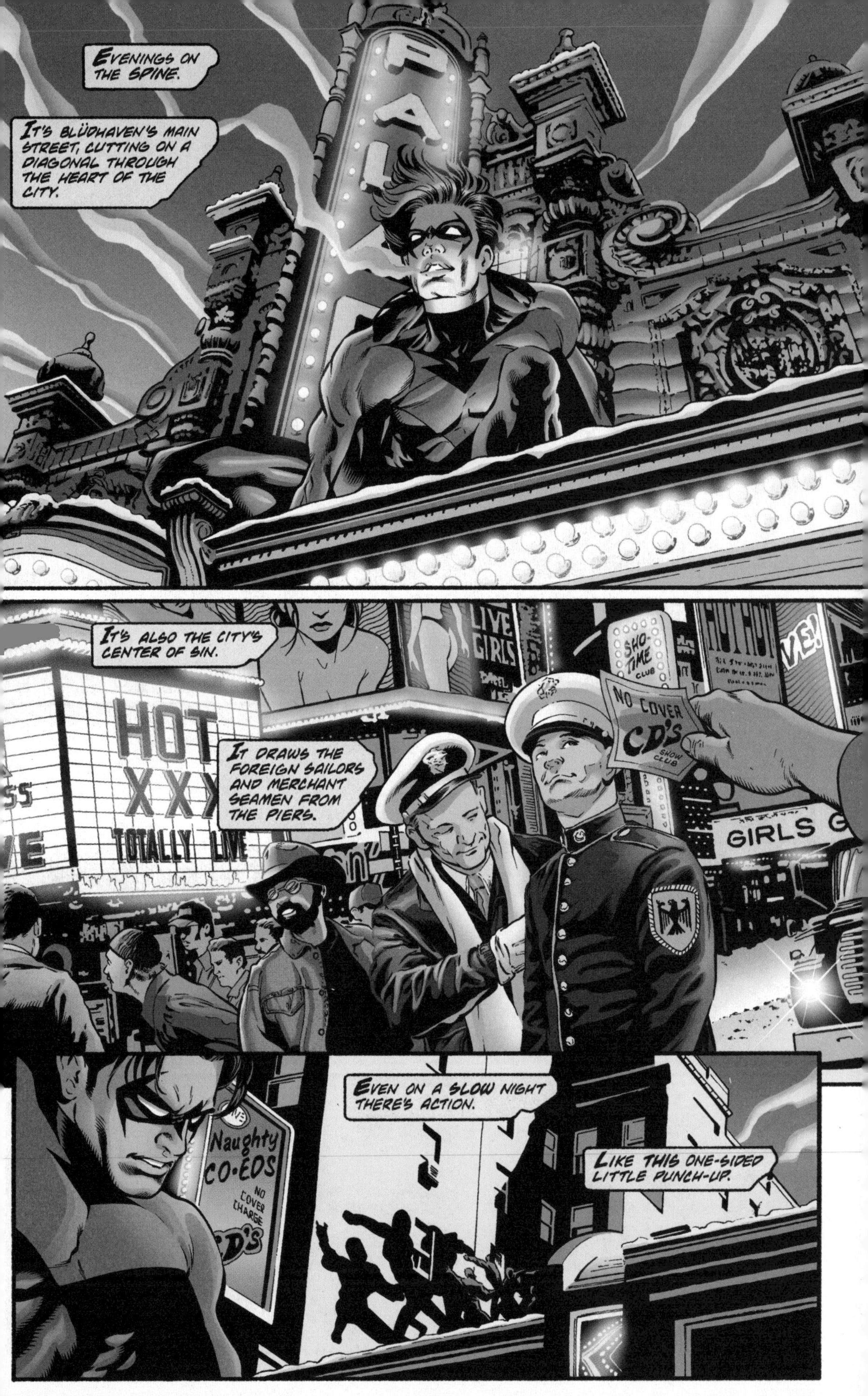
EVENINGS ON THE SPINE.
IT'S BLÜDHAVEN'S MAIN STREET, CUTTING ON A DIAGONAL THROUGH THE HEART OF THE CITY.
IT'S ALSO THE CITY'S CENTER OF SIN.
LIVE GIRLS
SHO-TIME CLUB
HOT XXX TOTALLY LIVE
NO COVER CD's SHOW CLUB
IT DRAWS THE FOREIGN SAILORS AND MERCHANT SEAMEN FROM THE PIERS.
GIRLS
Naughty CO-EDS NO COVER CHARGE
EVEN ON A SLOW NIGHT THERE'S ACTION.
LIKE THIS ONE-SIDED LITTLE PUNCH-UP.

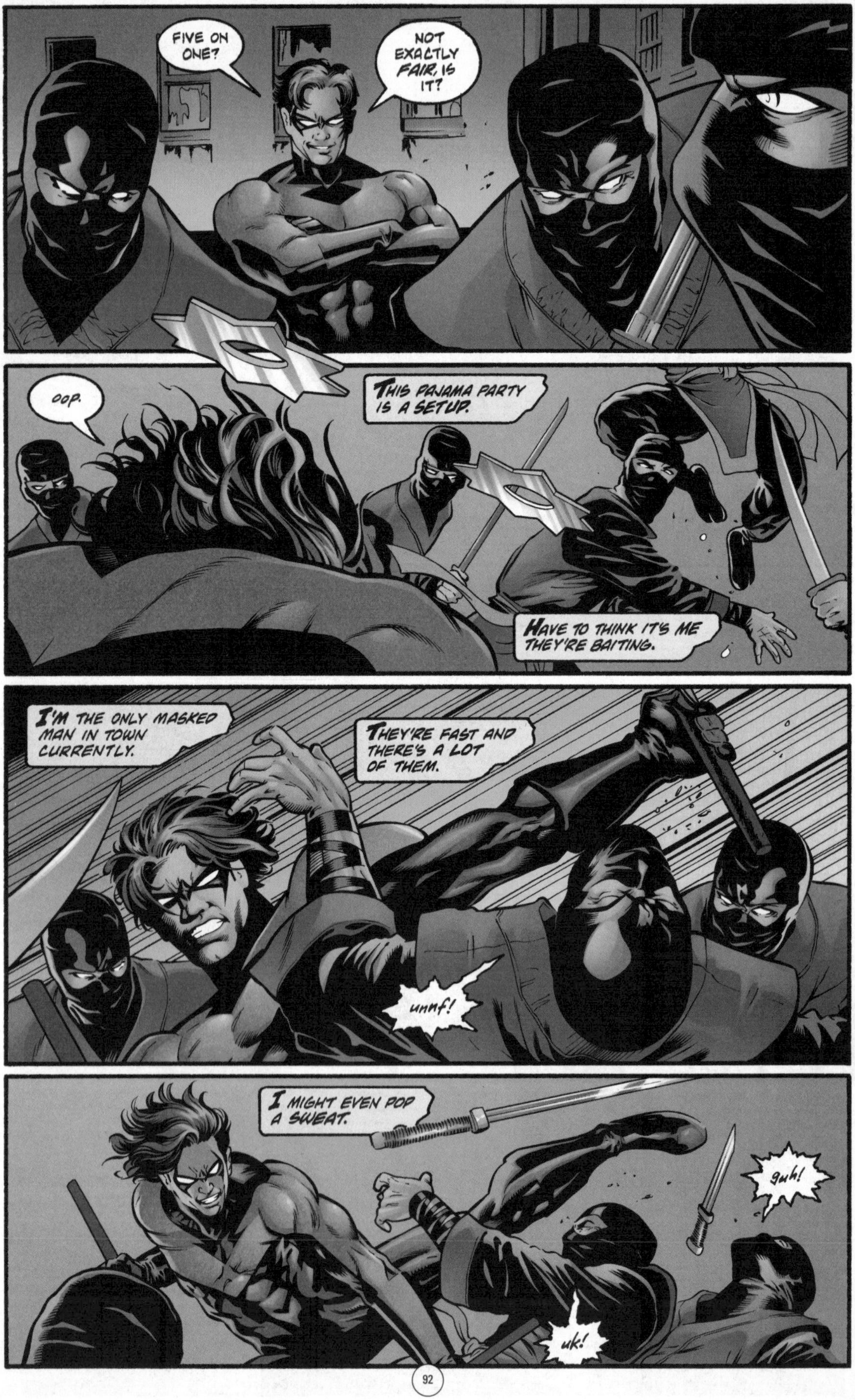
FIVE ON ONE?
NOT EXACTLY FAIR, IS IT?
oop.
THIS PAJAMA PARTY IS A SETUP.
HAVE TO THINK IT'S ME THEY'RE BAITING.
I'M THE ONLY MASKED MAN IN TOWN CURRENTLY.
THEY'RE FAST AND THERE'S A LOT OF THEM.
unnf!
I MIGHT EVEN POP A SWEAT.
guh!
uk!

THEY'RE RUNNING.

IN THE HEAT OF THIS I FORGET A COMMON PRACTICE OF A TRAP--

--THEY USUALLY HAVE TWO COMPONENTS.

THE LURE.

AND THE SNARE.

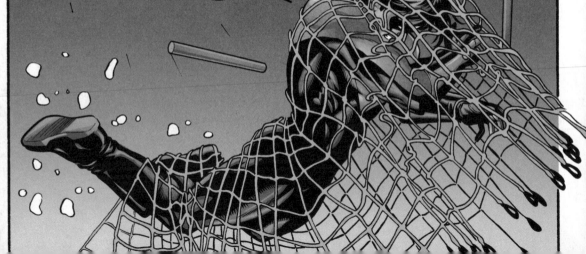

uh?

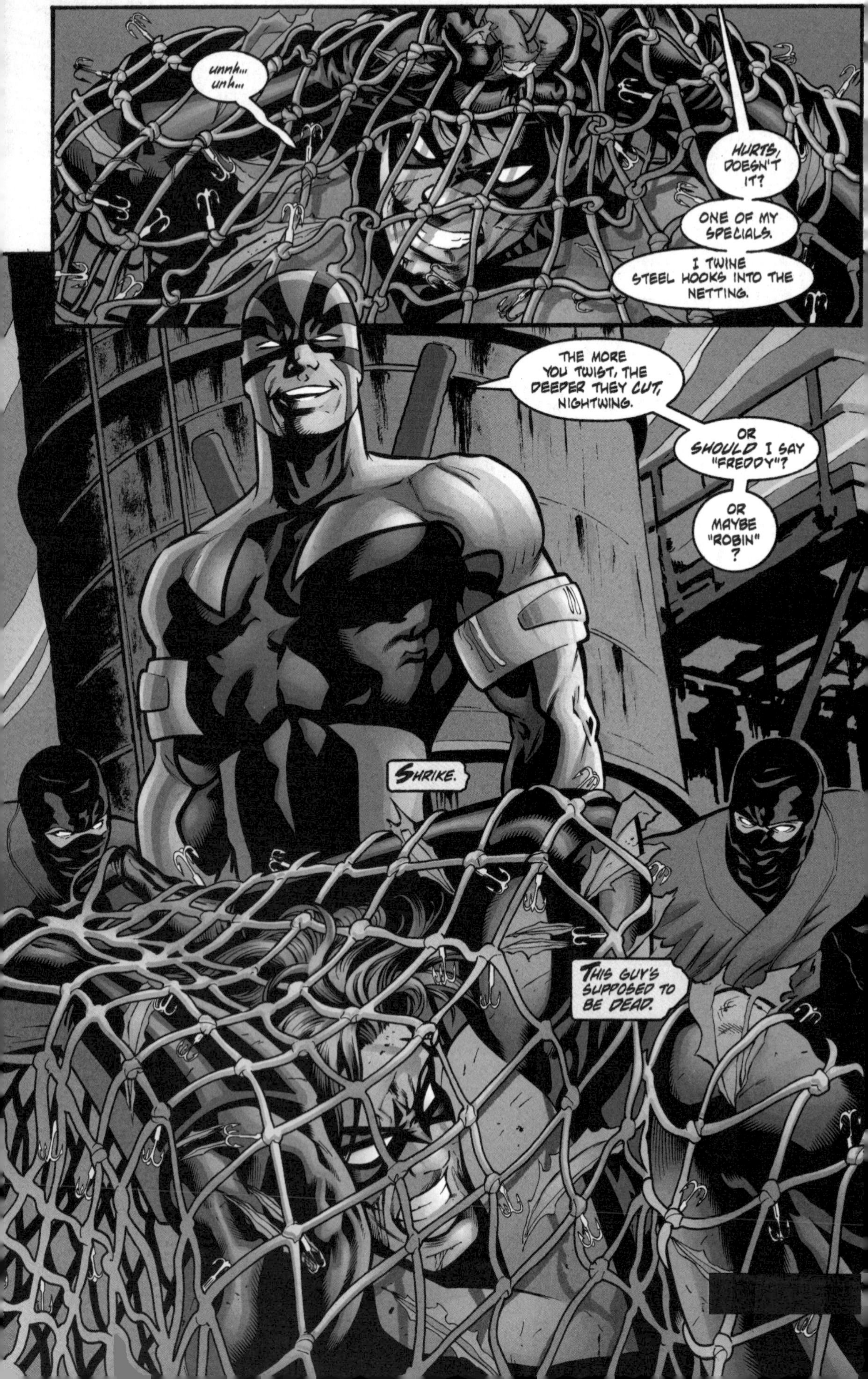
unnh... unh...
HURTS, DOESN'T IT?
ONE OF MY SPECIALS.
I TWINE STEEL HOOKS INTO THE NETTING.
THE MORE YOU TWIST, THE DEEPER THEY CUT, NIGHTWING.
OR SHOULD I SAY "FREDDY"?
OR MAYBE "ROBIN"?
SHRIKE.
THIS GUY'S SUPPOSED TO BE DEAD.

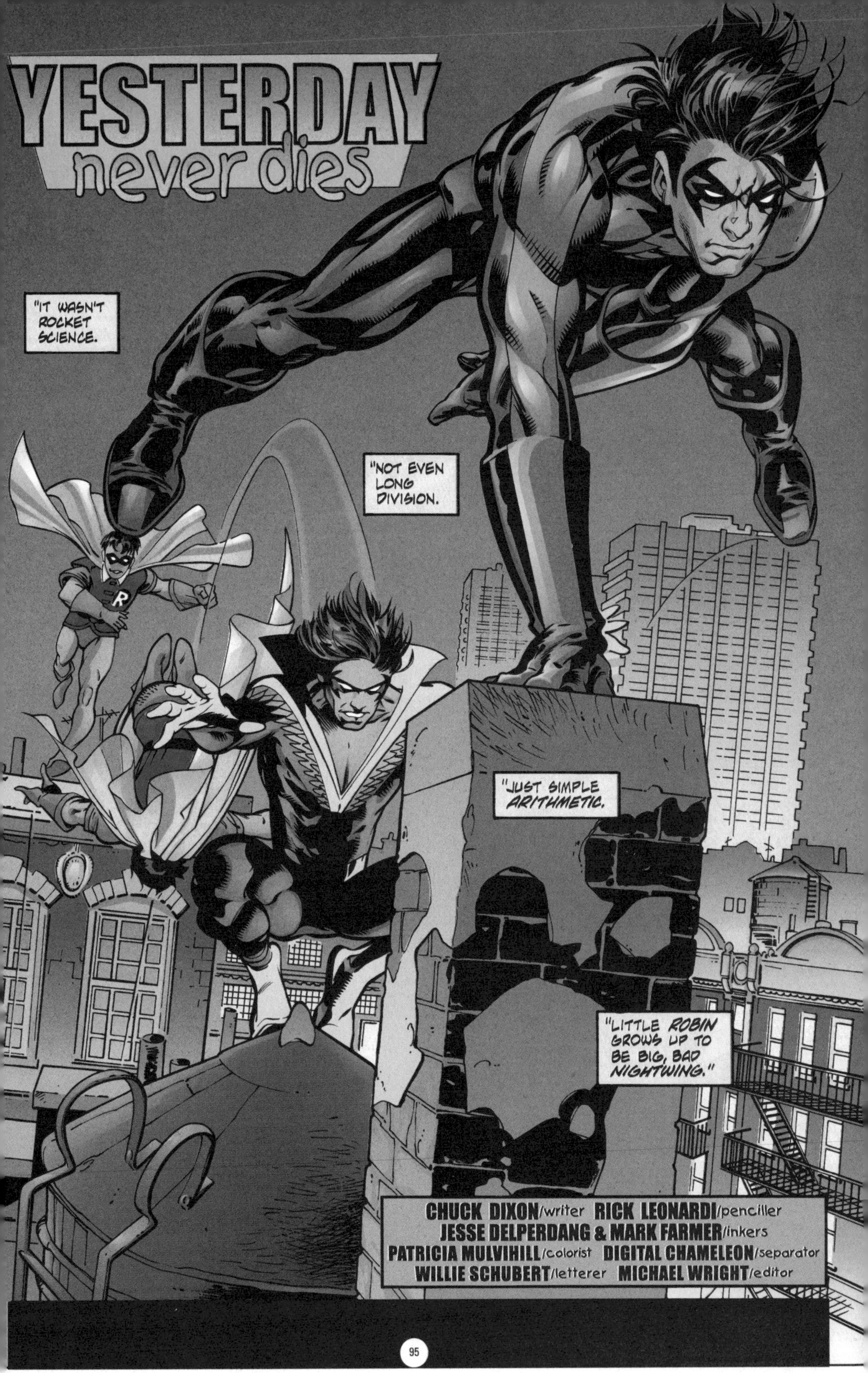

YESTERDAY
never dies
"IT WASN'T ROCKET SCIENCE.
"NOT EVEN LONG DIVISION.
"JUST SIMPLE ARITHMETIC.
"LITTLE ROBIN GROWS UP TO BE BIG, BAD NIGHTWING."
CHUCK DIXON/writer RICK LEONARDI/penciller
JESSE DELPERDANG & MARK FARMER/inkers
PATRICIA MULVIHILL/colorist DIGITAL CHAMELEON/separator
WILLIE SCHUBERT/letterer MICHAEL WRIGHT/editor

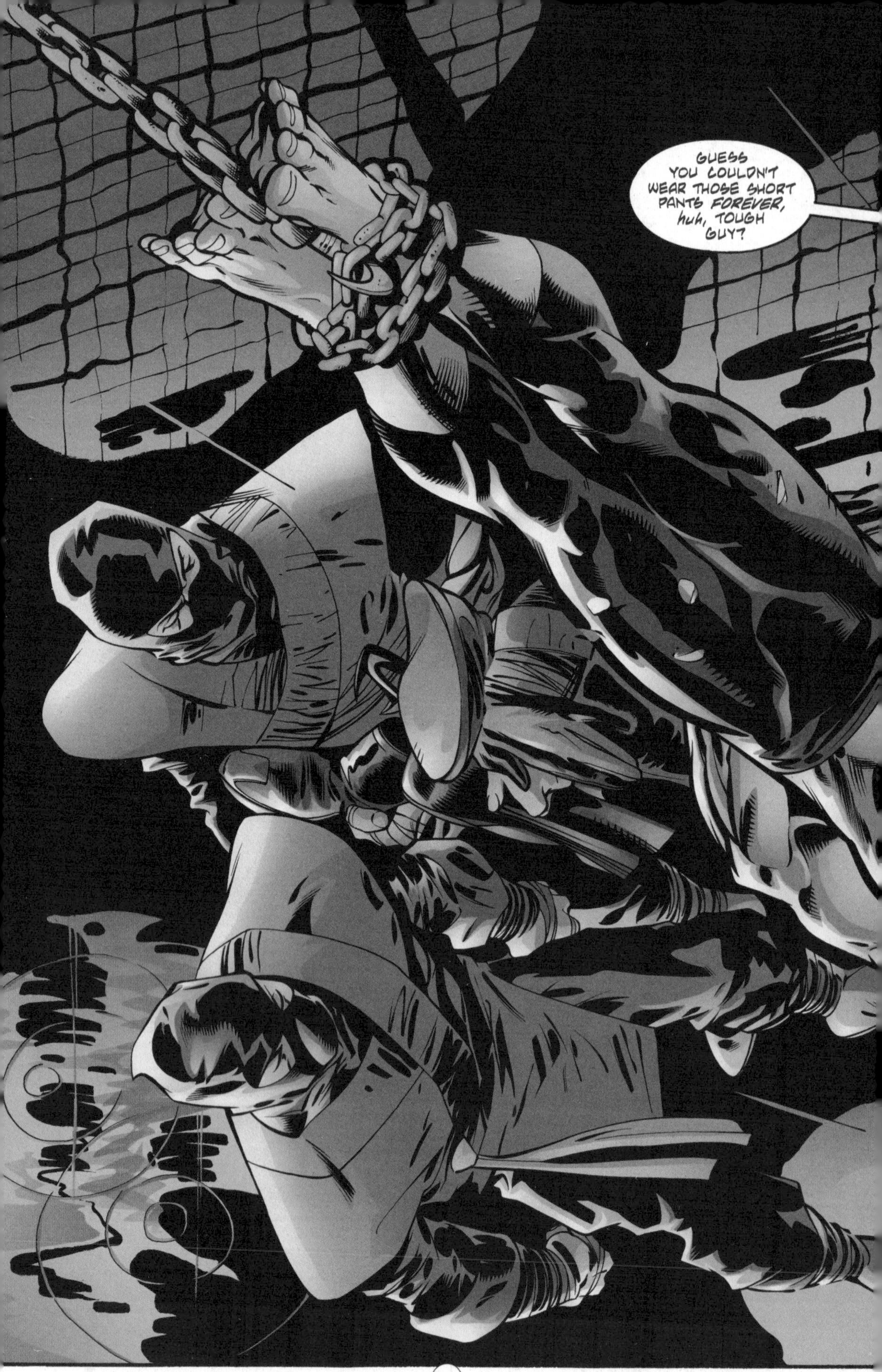
GUESS YOU COULDN'T WEAR THOSE SHORT PANTS FOREVER, huh, TOUGH GUY?

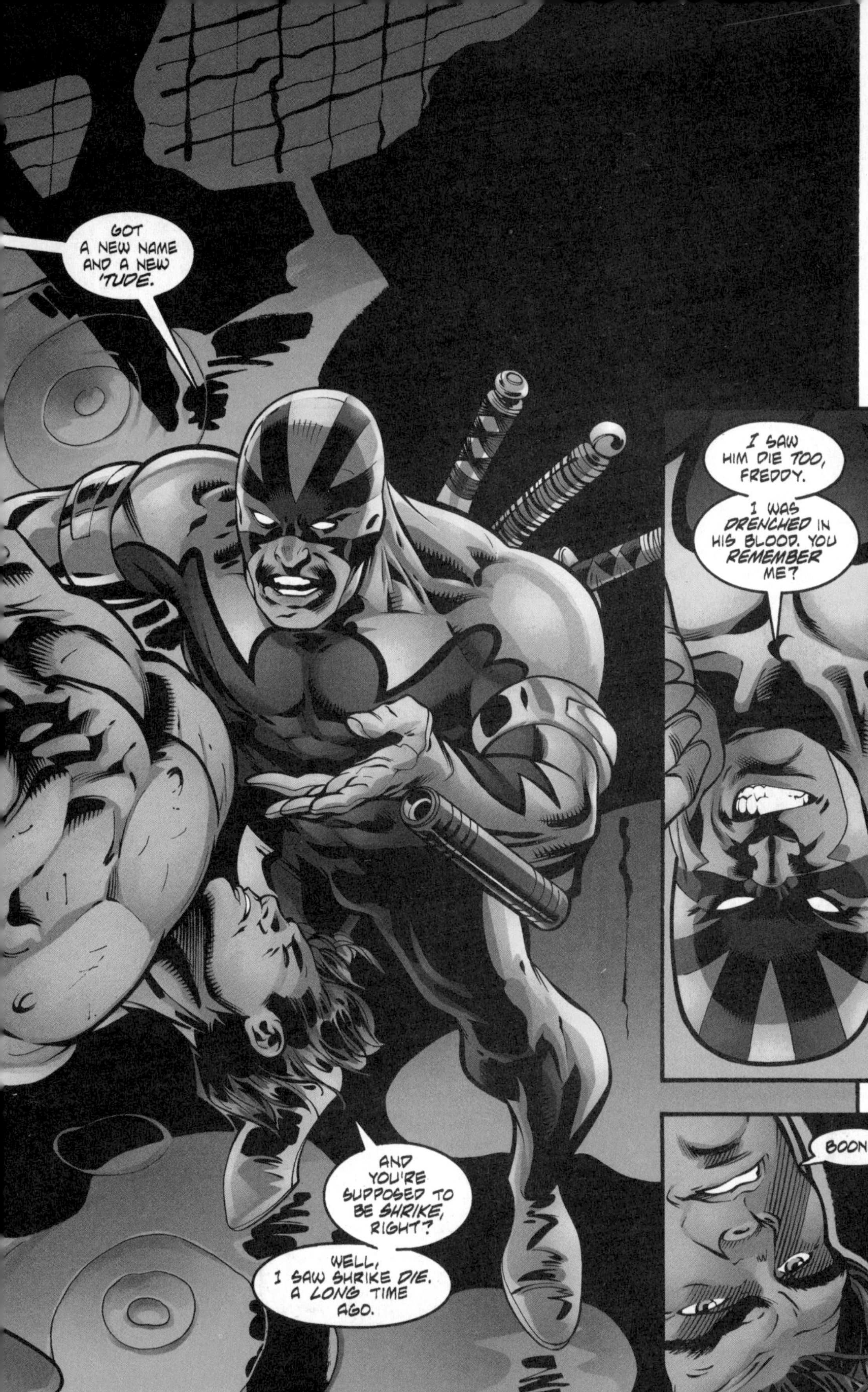
GOT A NEW NAME AND A NEW 'TUDE.
AND YOU'RE SUPPOSED TO BE SHRIKE, RIGHT?
WELL, I SAW SHRIKE DIE. A LONG TIME AGO.
I SAW HIM DIE TOO, FREDDY.
I WAS DRENCHED IN HIS BLOOD. YOU REMEMBER ME?
BOONE...
[redacted]

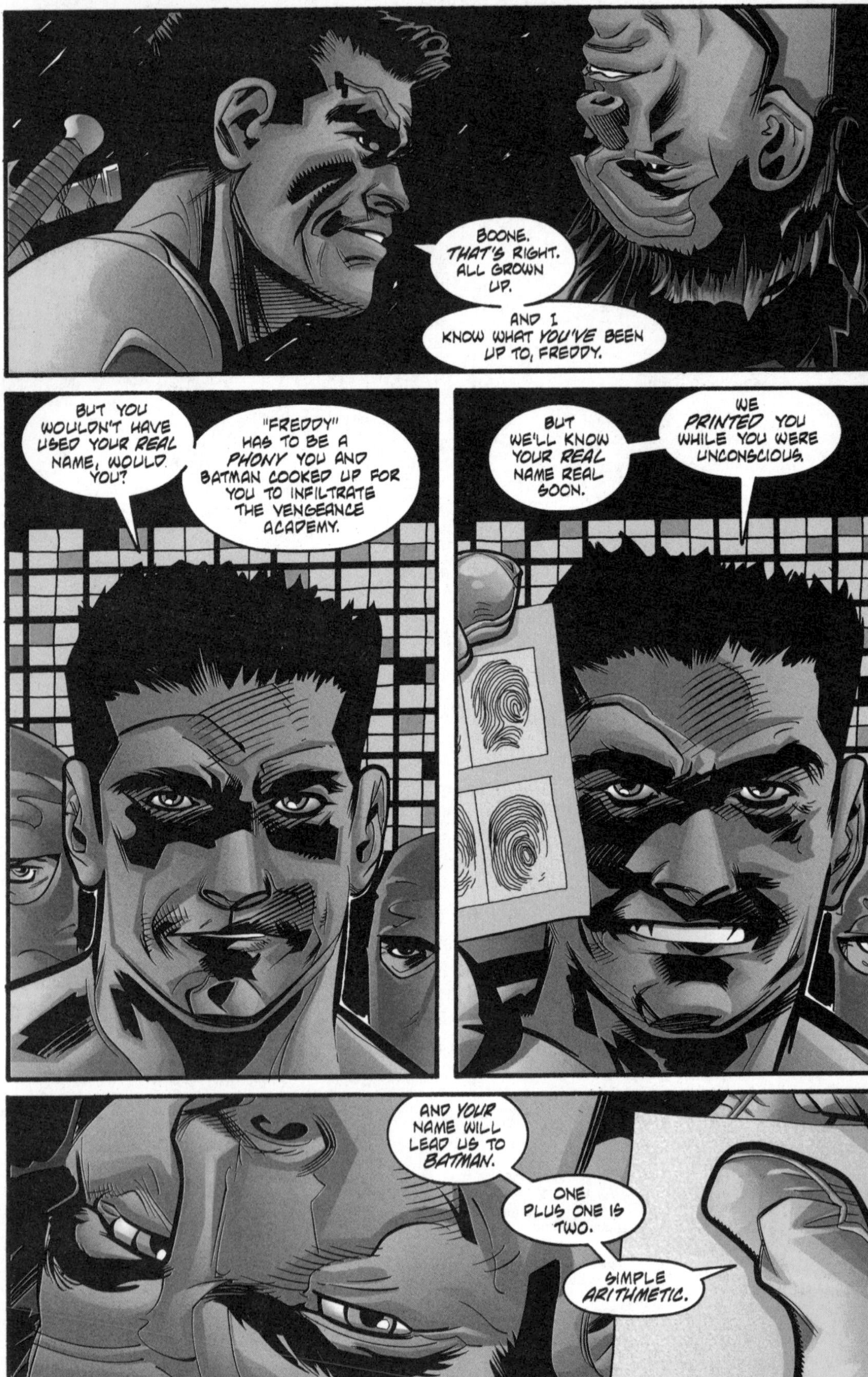

BOONE. THAT'S RIGHT. ALL GROWN UP.
AND I KNOW WHAT YOU'VE BEEN UP TO, FREDDY.
BUT YOU WOULDN'T HAVE USED YOUR REAL NAME, WOULD YOU?
"FREDDY" HAS TO BE A PHONY YOU AND BATMAN COOKED UP FOR YOU TO INFILTRATE THE VENGEANCE ACADEMY.
WE PRINTED YOU WHILE YOU WERE UNCONSCIOUS.
BUT WE'LL KNOW YOUR REAL NAME REAL SOON.
AND YOUR NAME WILL LEAD US TO BATMAN.
ONE PLUS ONE IS TWO.
SIMPLE ARITHMETIC.

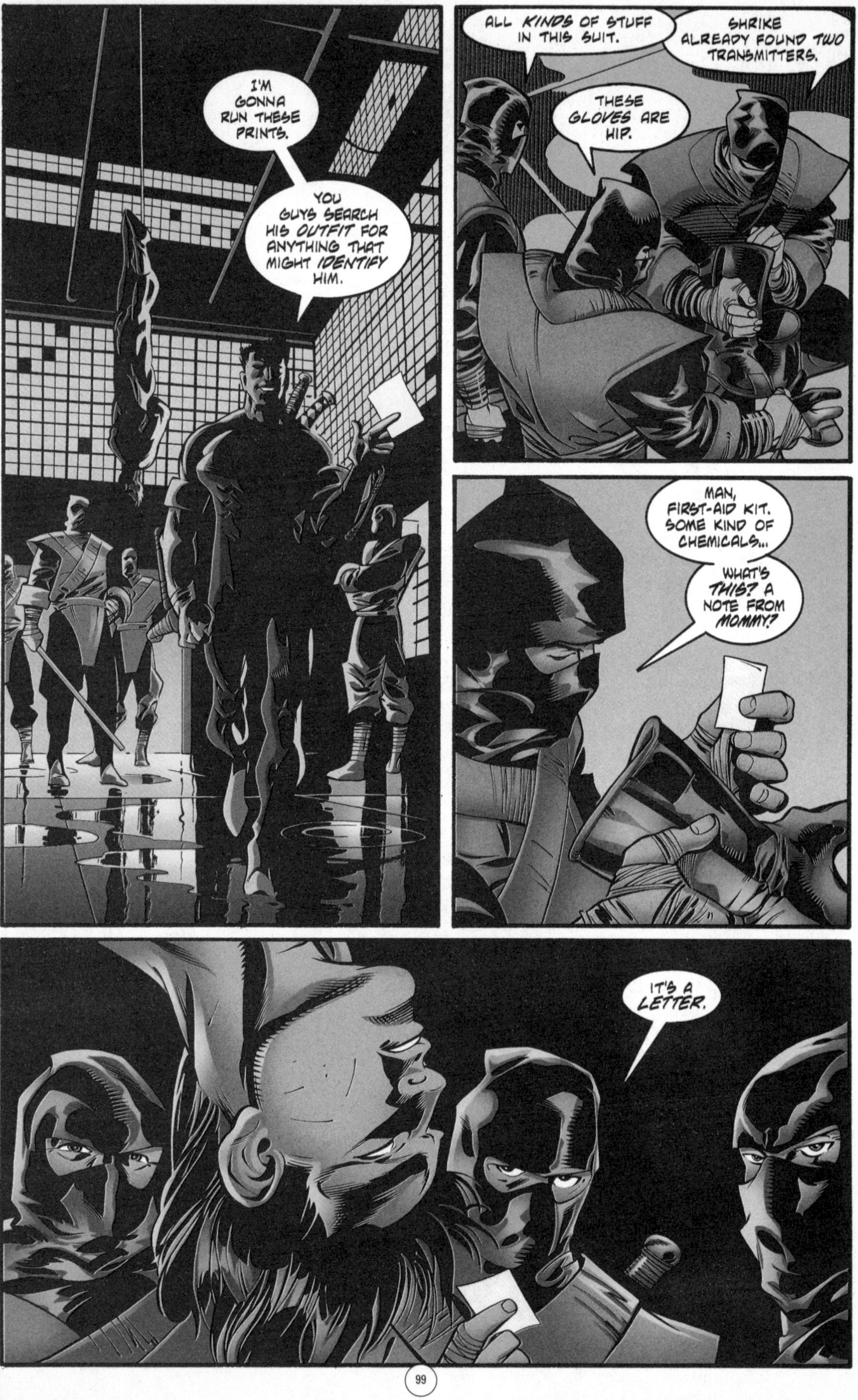
I'M GONNA RUN THESE PRINTS.
YOU GUYS SEARCH HIS OUTFIT FOR ANYTHING THAT MIGHT IDENTIFY HIM.
ALL KINDS OF STUFF IN THIS SUIT.
SHRIKE ALREADY FOUND TWO TRANSMITTERS.
THESE GLOVES ARE HIP.
MAN, FIRST-AID KIT. SOME KIND OF CHEMICALS...
WHAT'S THIS? A NOTE FROM MOMMY?
IT'S A LETTER.

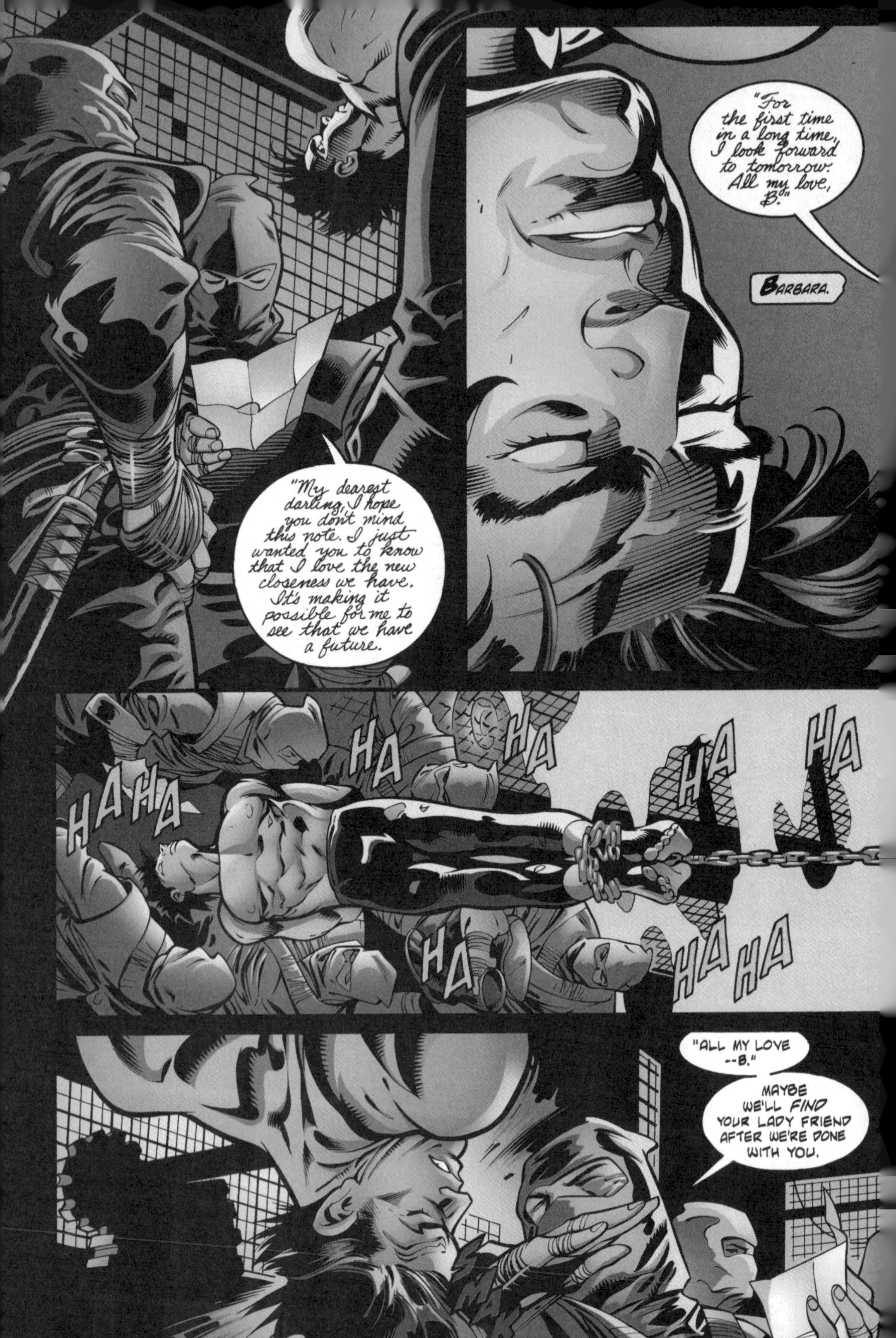
"For the first time in a long time, I look forward to tomorrow. All my love, B."
BARBARA.
"My dearest darling, I hope you don't mind this note. I just wanted you to know that I love the new closeness we have. It's making it possible for me to see that we have a future.
HAHA
HA
HA
HA
HA
HA
HAHA
HA
"ALL MY LOVE --B."
MAYBE WE'LL FIND YOUR LADY FRIEND AFTER WE'RE DONE WITH YOU.

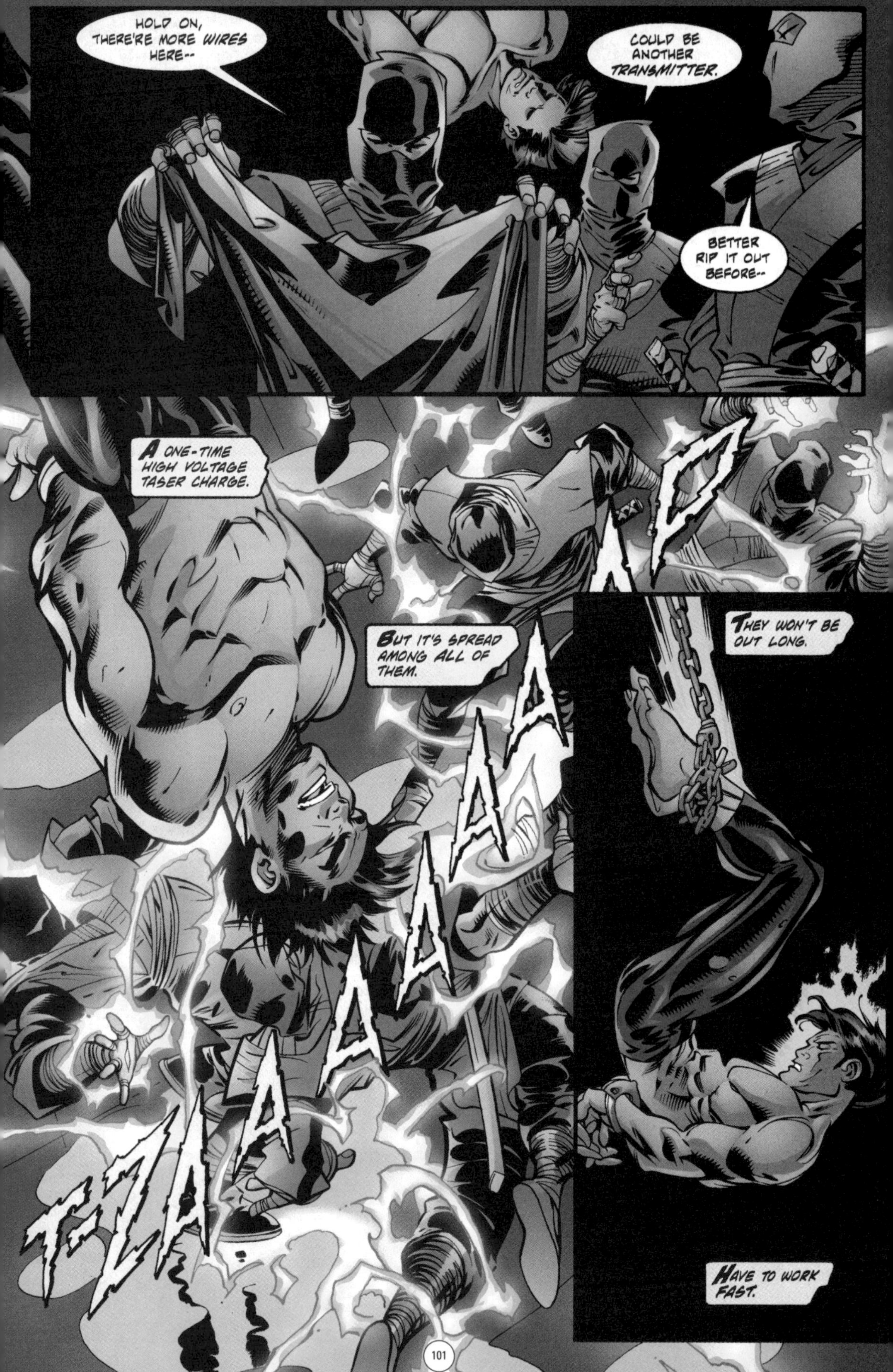
HOLD ON, THERE'RE MORE WIRES HERE--
COULD BE ANOTHER TRANSMITTER.
BETTER RIP IT OUT BEFORE--
A ONE-TIME HIGH VOLTAGE TASER CHARGE.
BUT IT'S SPREAD AMONG ALL OF THEM.
T-ZAAAAAAAAP
THEY WON'T BE OUT LONG.
HAVE TO WORK FAST.

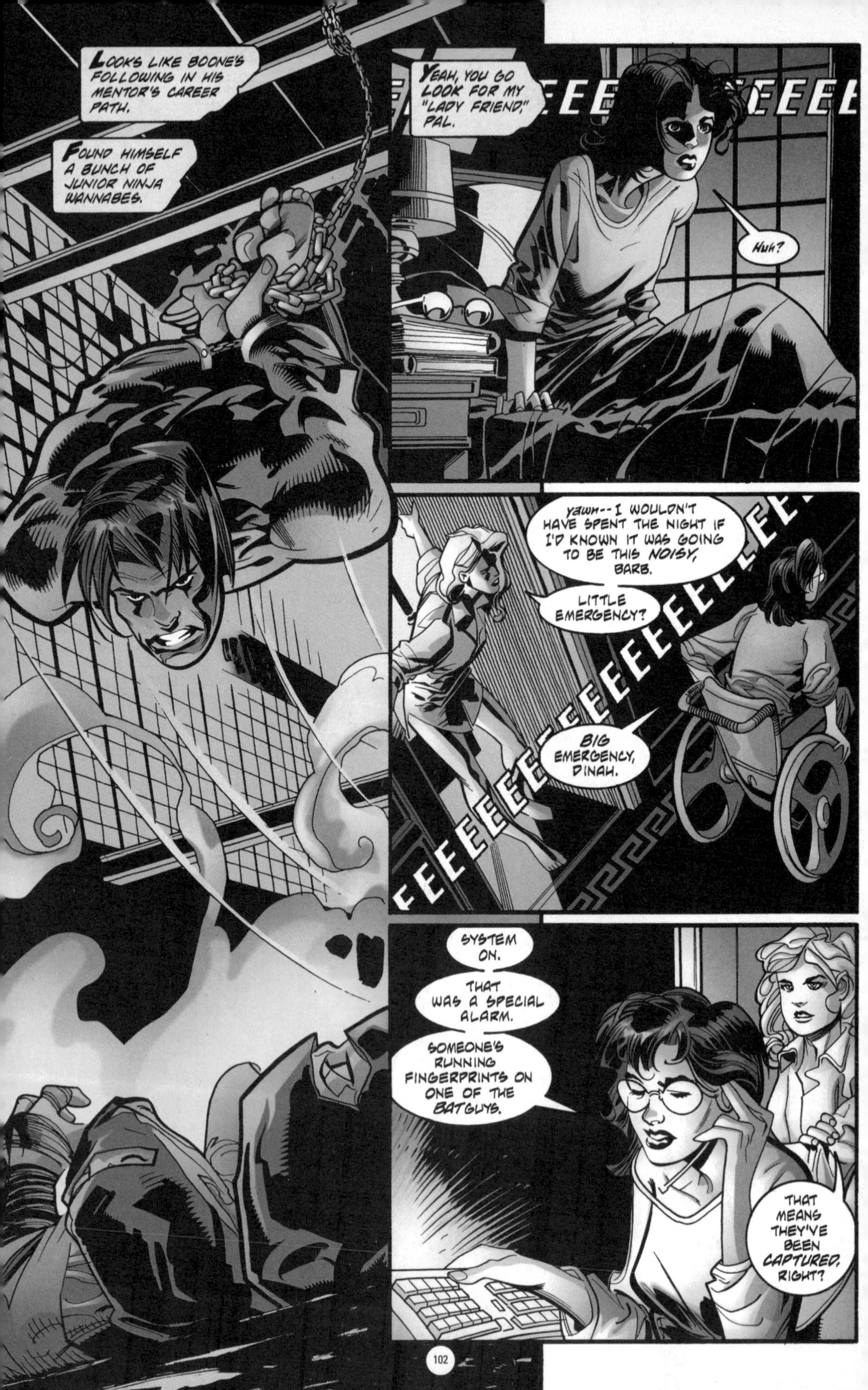
LOOKS LIKE BOONE'S FOLLOWING IN HIS MENTOR'S CAREER PATH.
FOUND HIMSELF A BUNCH OF JUNIOR NINJA WANNABES.
YEAH, YOU GO LOOK FOR MY "LADY FRIEND," PAL.
EEEEEEE
HUH?
YAWN-- I WOULDN'T HAVE SPENT THE NIGHT IF I'D KNOWN IT WAS GOING TO BE THIS NOISY, BARB.
LITTLE EMERGENCY?
BIG EMERGENCY, DINAH.
EEEEEEEEEEEEEEE
SYSTEM ON.
THAT WAS A SPECIAL ALARM.
SOMEONE'S RUNNING FINGERPRINTS ON ONE OF THE BATGUYS.
THAT MEANS THEY'VE BEEN CAPTURED, RIGHT?

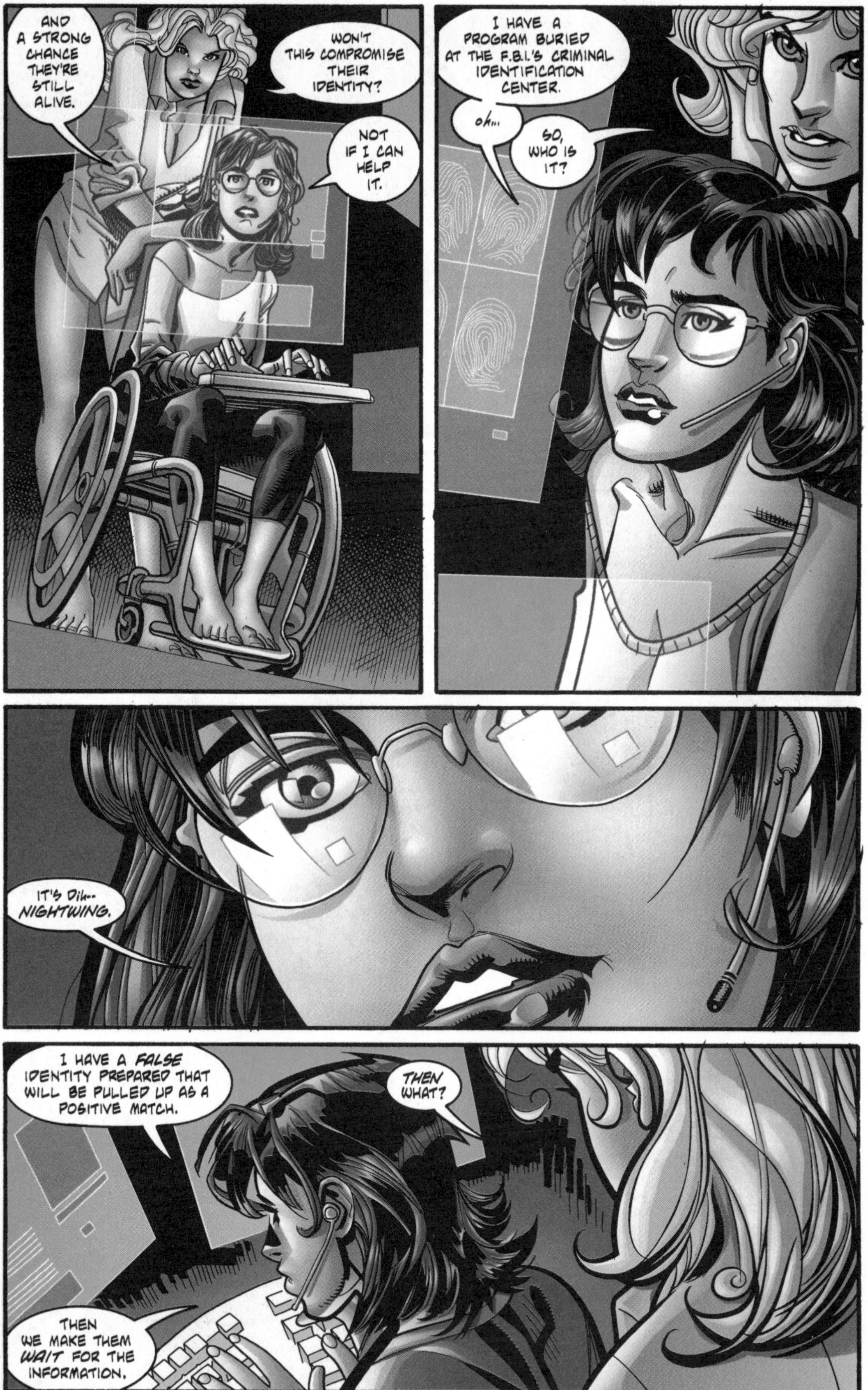
AND A STRONG CHANCE THEY'RE STILL ALIVE.
WON'T THIS COMPROMISE THEIR IDENTITY?
NOT IF I CAN HELP IT.
I HAVE A PROGRAM BURIED AT THE F.B.I.'S CRIMINAL IDENTIFICATION CENTER.
oh...
SO, WHO IS IT?
IT'S Dik-- NIGHTWING.
I HAVE A FALSE IDENTITY PREPARED THAT WILL BE PULLED UP AS A POSITIVE MATCH.
THEN WHAT?
THEN WE MAKE THEM WAIT FOR THE INFORMATION.

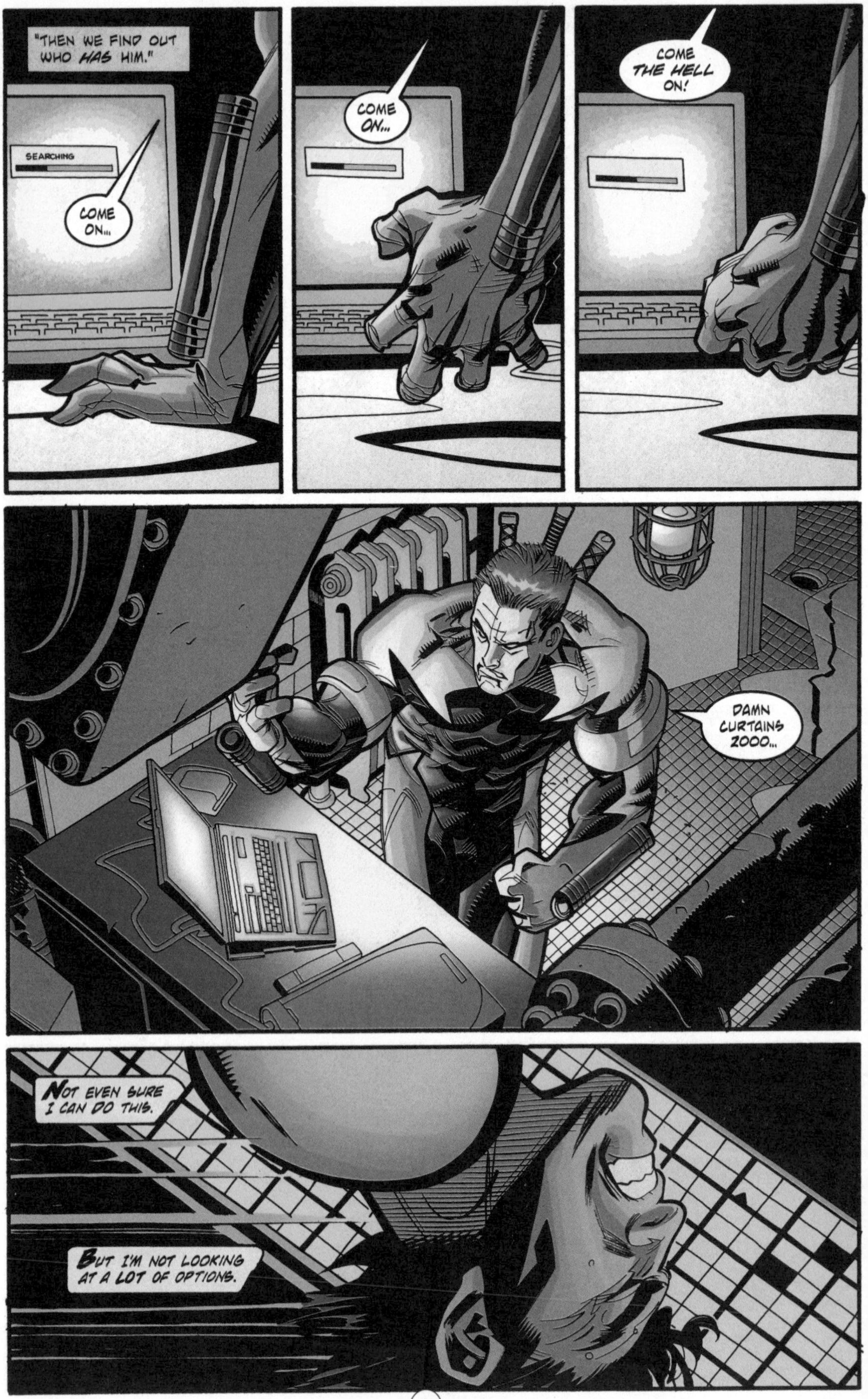
"THEN WE FIND OUT WHO HAS HIM."
SEARCHING
COME ON...
COME ON...
COME THE HELL ON!
DAMN CURTAINS 2000...
NOT EVEN SURE I CAN DO THIS.
BUT I'M NOT LOOKING AT A LOT OF OPTIONS.

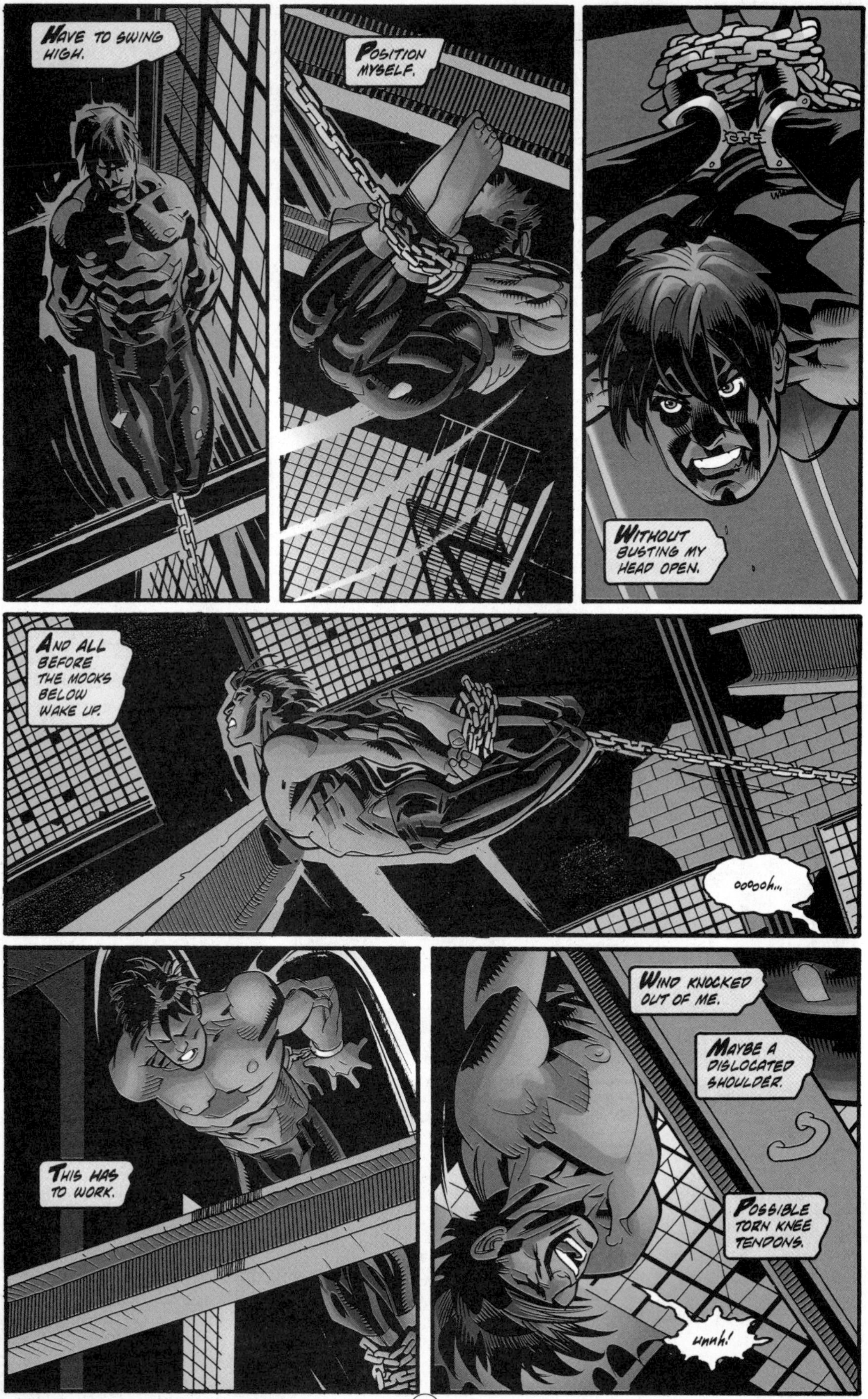
HAVE TO SWING HIGH.
POSITION MYSELF.
WITHOUT BUSTING MY HEAD OPEN.
AND ALL BEFORE THE MOOKS BELOW WAKE UP.
ooooh...
THIS HAS TO WORK.
WIND KNOCKED OUT OF ME.
MAYBE A DISLOCATED SHOULDER.
POSSIBLE TORN KNEE TENDONS.
unnh!

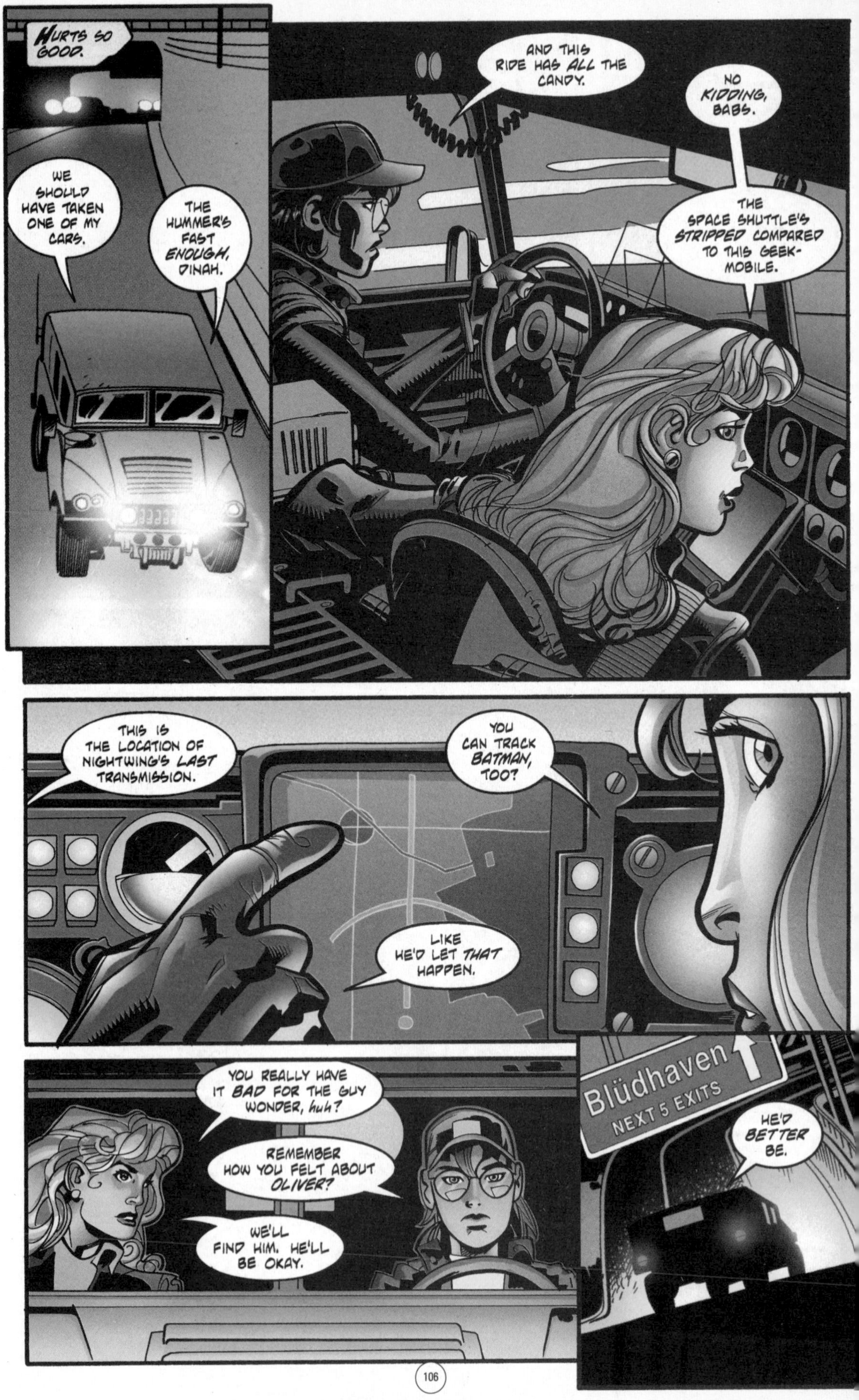
HURTS SO GOOD.
WE SHOULD HAVE TAKEN ONE OF MY CARS.
THE HUMMER'S FAST ENOUGH, DINAH.
AND THIS RIDE HAS ALL THE CANDY.
NO KIDDING, BABS.
THE SPACE SHUTTLE'S STRIPPED COMPARED TO THIS GEEK-MOBILE.
THIS IS THE LOCATION OF NIGHTWING'S LAST TRANSMISSION.
YOU CAN TRACK BATMAN, TOO?
LIKE HE'D LET THAT HAPPEN.
YOU REALLY HAVE IT BAD FOR THE GUY WONDER, huh?
REMEMBER HOW YOU FELT ABOUT OLIVER?
WE'LL FIND HIM. HE'LL BE OKAY.
Blüdhaven
NEXT 5 EXITS
HE'D BETTER BE.

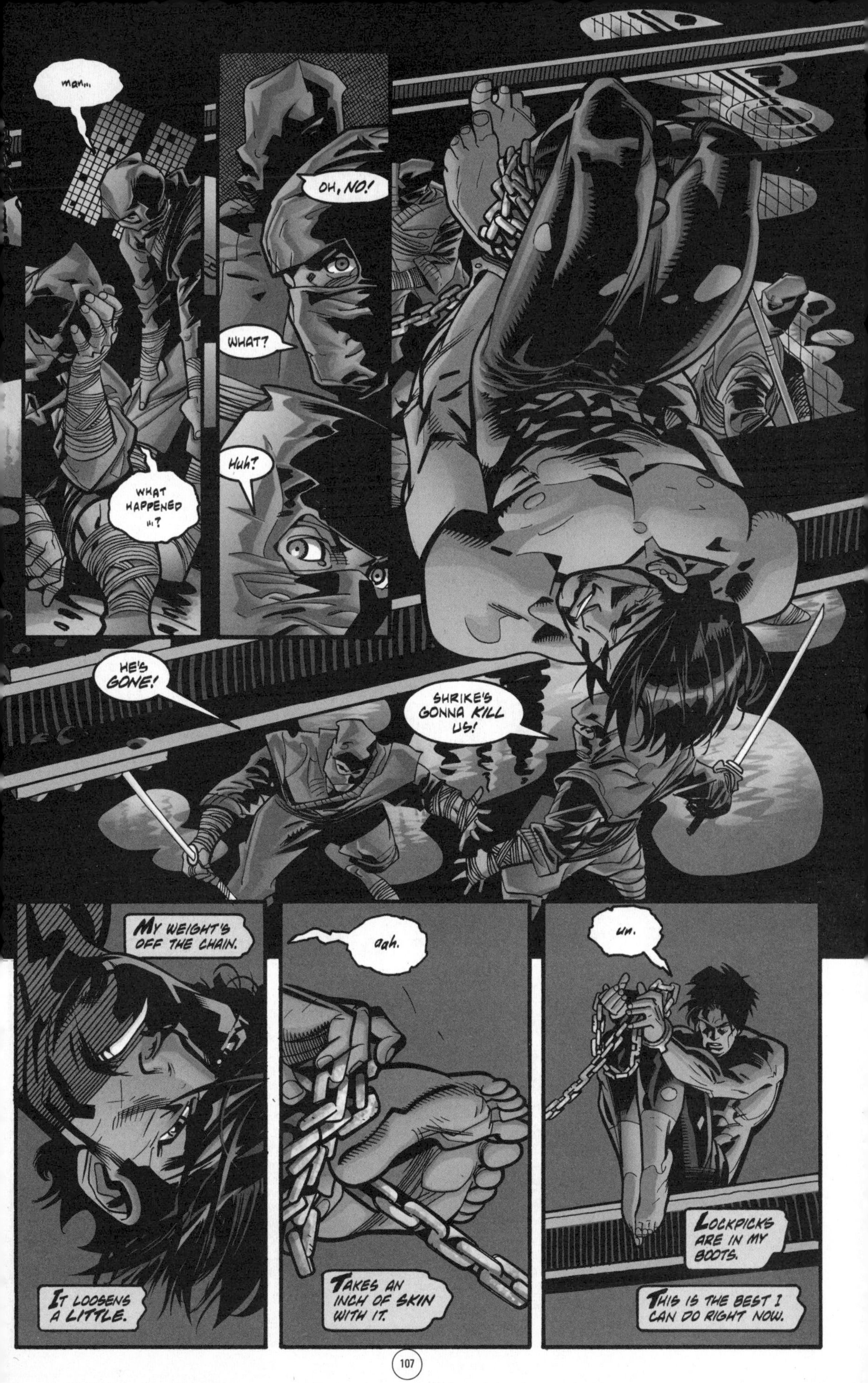
man...
OH, NO!
WHAT?
Huh?
WHAT HAPPENED ...?
HE'S GONE!
SHRIKE'S GONNA KILL US!
MY WEIGHT'S OFF THE CHAIN.
IT LOOSENS A LITTLE.
aah.
TAKES AN INCH OF SKIN WITH IT.
un.
LOCKPICKS ARE IN MY BOOTS.
THIS IS THE BEST I CAN DO RIGHT NOW.

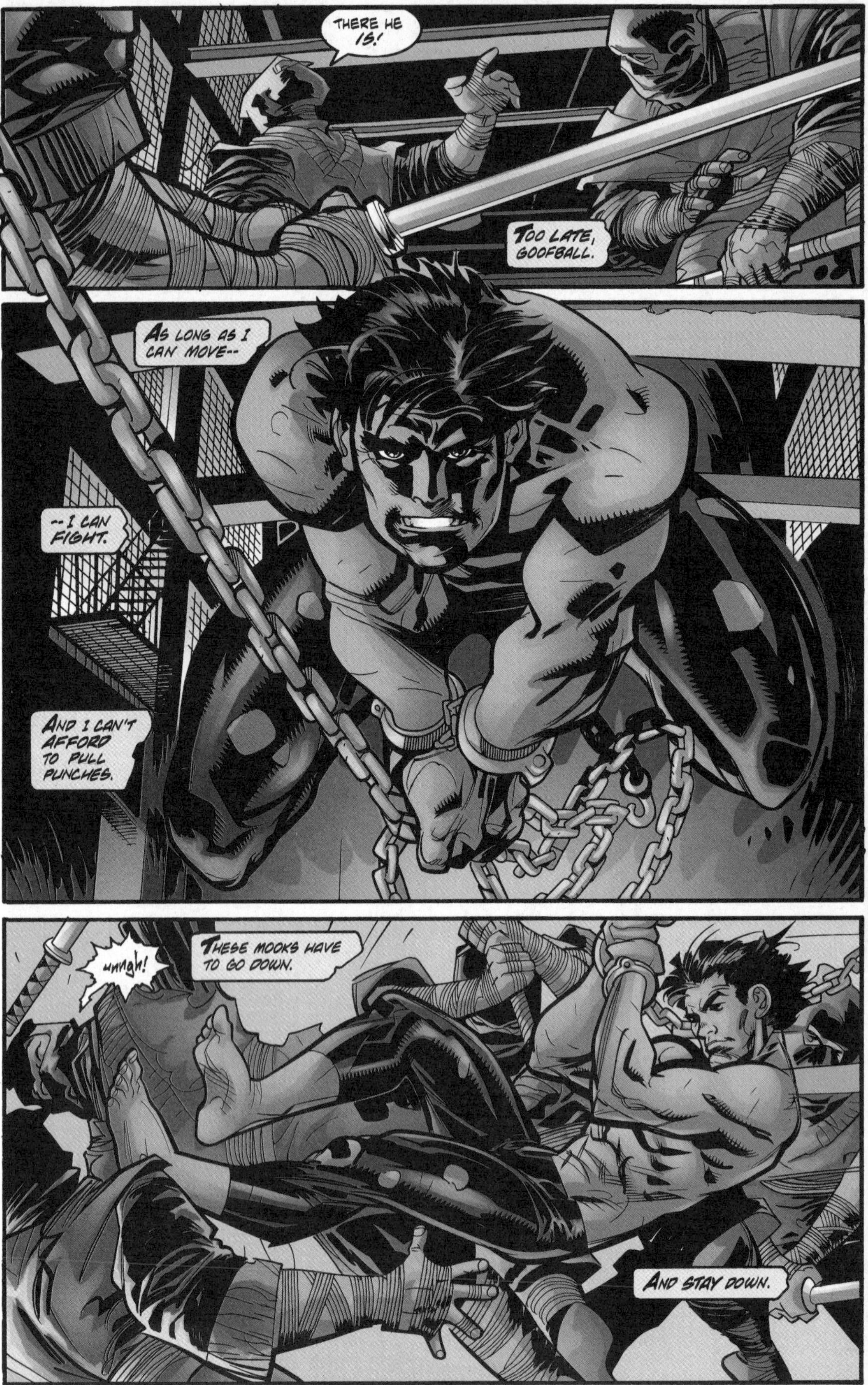
THERE HE IS!
TOO LATE, GOOFBALL.
AS LONG AS I CAN MOVE--
--I CAN FIGHT.
AND I CAN'T AFFORD TO PULL PUNCHES.
unngh!
THESE MOOKS HAVE TO GO DOWN.
AND STAY DOWN.

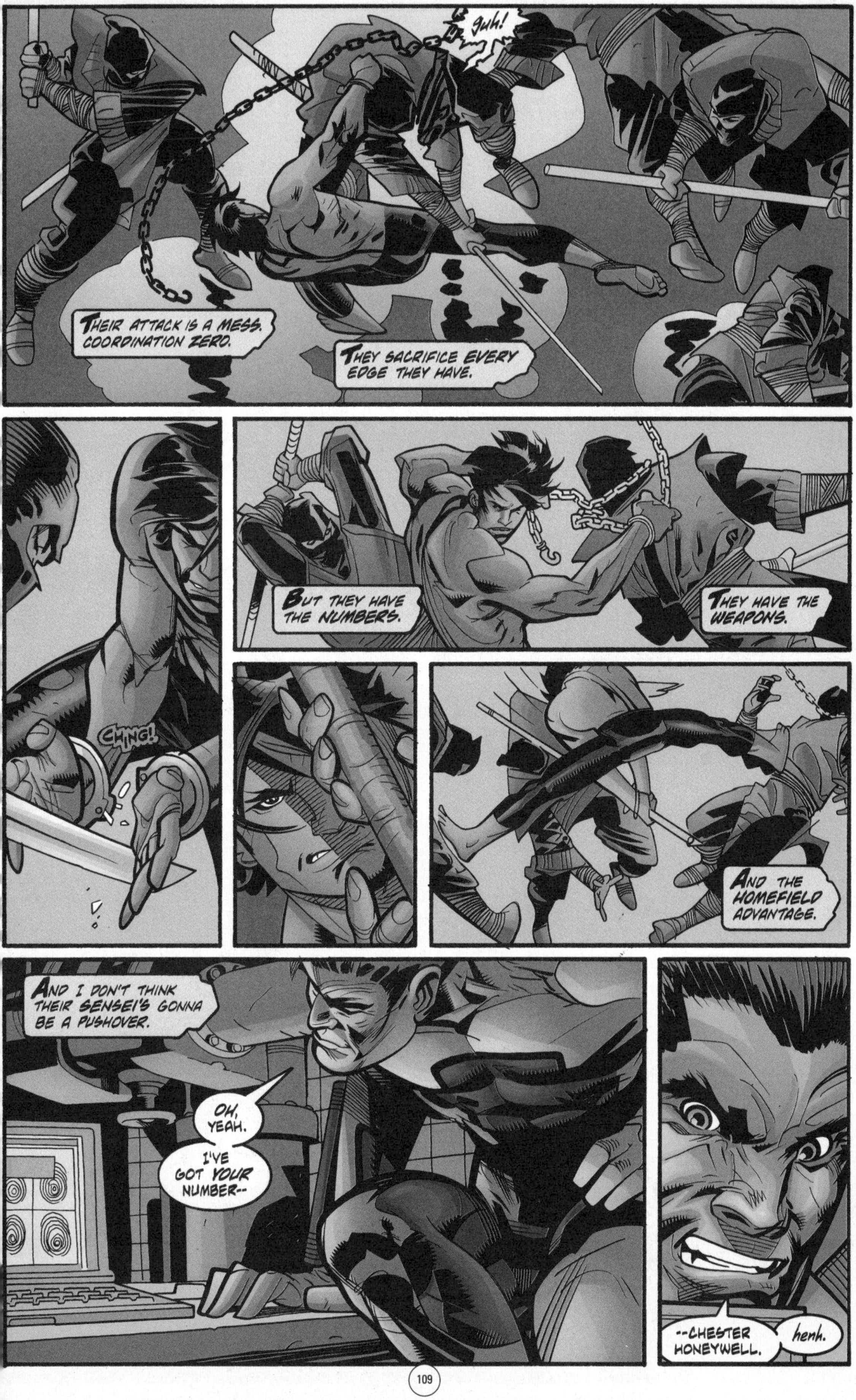
guh!
THEIR ATTACK IS A MESS. COORDINATION ZERO.
THEY SACRIFICE EVERY EDGE THEY HAVE.
BUT THEY HAVE THE NUMBERS.
THEY HAVE THE WEAPONS.
CHING!
AND THE HOMEFIELD ADVANTAGE.
AND I DON'T THINK THEIR SENSEI'S GONNA BE A PUSHOVER.
OH, YEAH.
I'VE GOT YOUR NUMBER--
--CHESTER HONEYWELL.
henh.

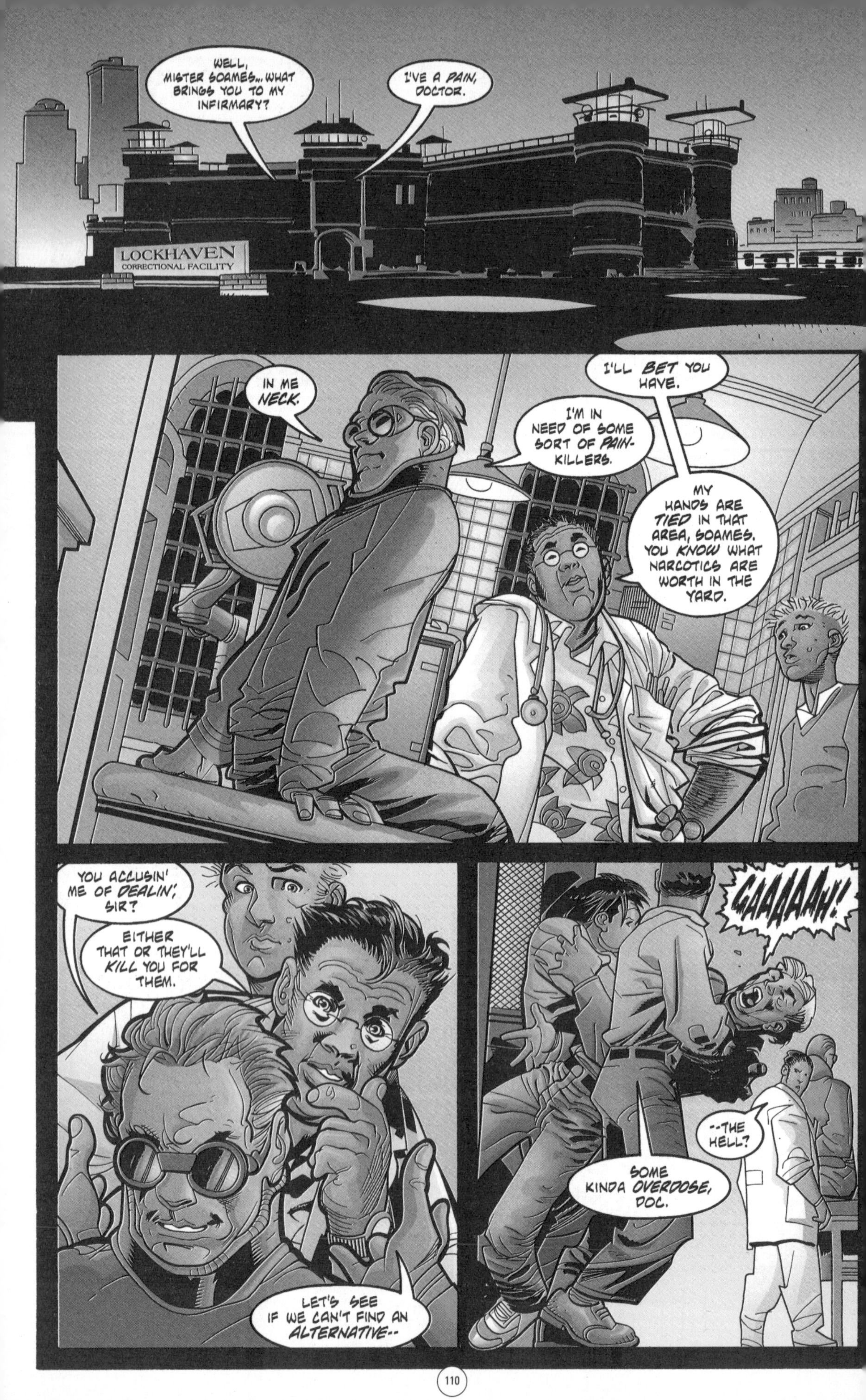
WELL, MISTER SOAMES... WHAT BRINGS YOU TO MY INFIRMARY?
I'VE A PAIN, DOCTOR.
LOCKHAVEN
CORRECTIONAL FACILITY
IN ME NECK.
I'M IN NEED OF SOME SORT OF PAIN-KILLERS.
I'LL BET YOU HAVE.
MY HANDS ARE TIED IN THAT AREA, SOAMES. YOU KNOW WHAT NARCOTICS ARE WORTH IN THE YARD.
YOU ACCUSIN' ME OF DEALIN', SIR?
EITHER THAT OR THEY'LL KILL YOU FOR THEM.
LET'S SEE IF WE CAN'T FIND AN ALTERNATIVE--
GAAAAAH!
--THE HELL?
SOME KINDA OVERDOSE, DOC.

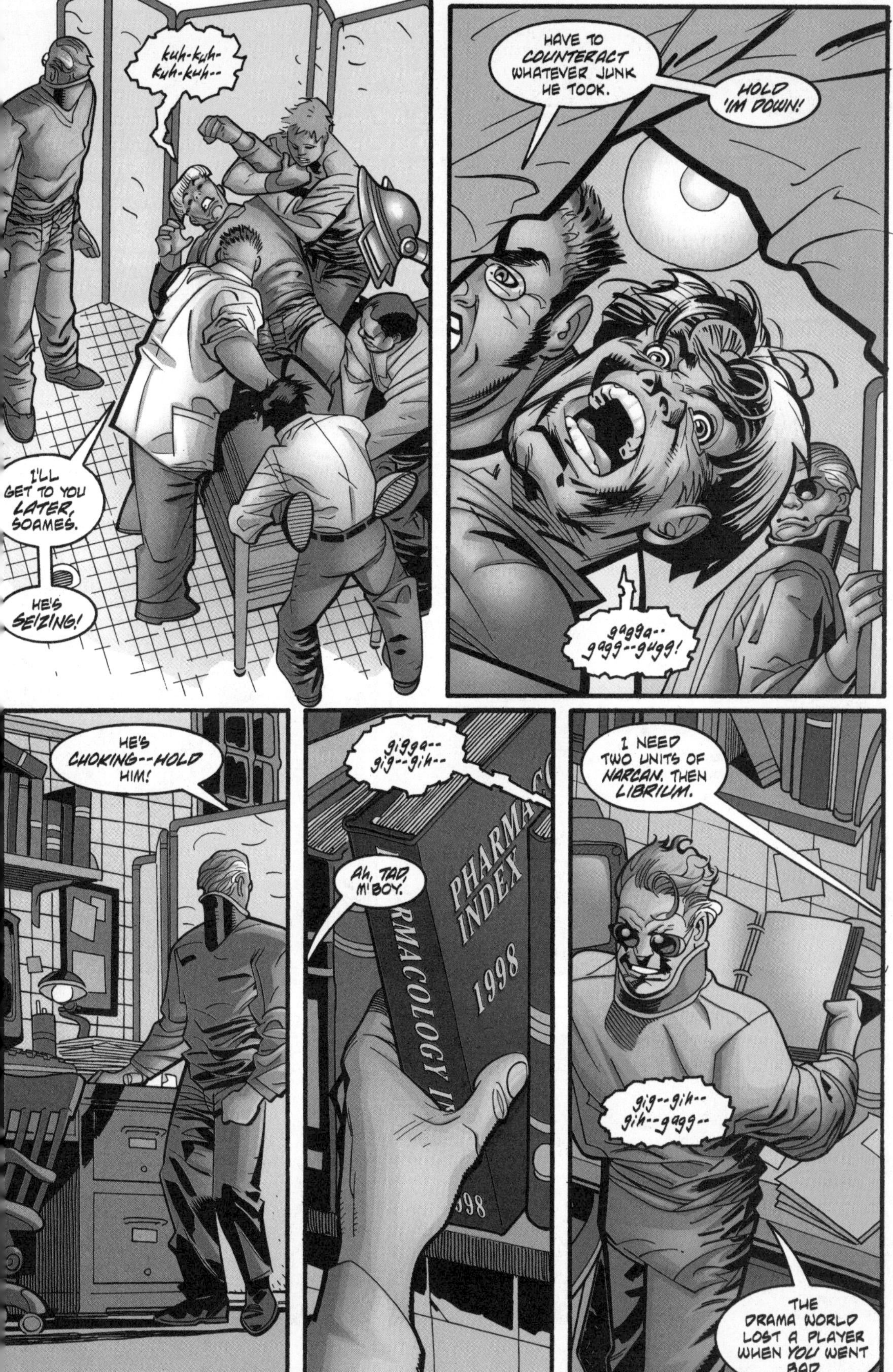
kuh-kuh-
kuh-kuh--
I'LL GET TO YOU LATER, SOAMES.
HE'S SEIZING!
HAVE TO COUNTERACT WHATEVER JUNK HE TOOK.
HOLD 'IM DOWN!
gagga--
gagg--gugg!
HE'S CHOKING--HOLD HIM!
gigga--
gig--gih--
Ah, TAD, M'BOY.
PHARMA INDEX
PHARMACOLOGY IN
1998
I NEED TWO UNITS OF NARCAN. THEN LIBRIUM.
gig--gih--
gih--gagg--
THE DRAMA WORLD LOST A PLAYER WHEN YOU WENT BAD.

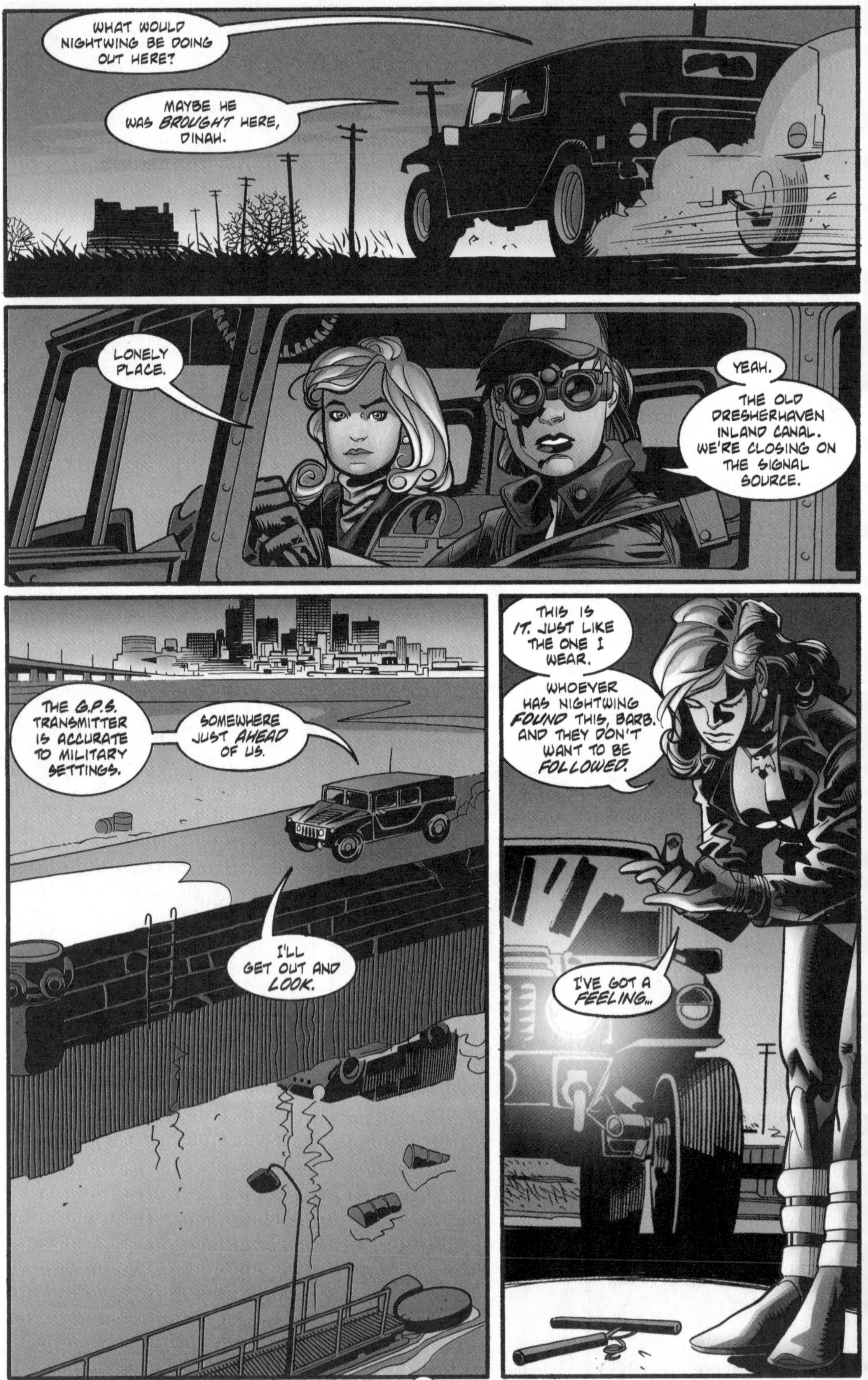
WHAT WOULD NIGHTWING BE DOING OUT HERE?
MAYBE HE WAS *BROUGHT* HERE, DINAH.
LONELY PLACE.
YEAH.
THE OLD DRESHERHAVEN INLAND CANAL. WE'RE CLOSING ON THE SIGNAL SOURCE.
THE G.P.S. TRANSMITTER IS ACCURATE TO MILITARY SETTINGS.
SOMEWHERE JUST *AHEAD* OF US.
I'LL GET OUT AND *LOOK*.
THIS IS *IT*. JUST LIKE THE ONE I WEAR.
WHOEVER HAS NIGHTWING *FOUND* THIS, BARB. AND THEY DON'T WANT TO BE *FOLLOWED*.
I'VE GOT A *FEELING*...

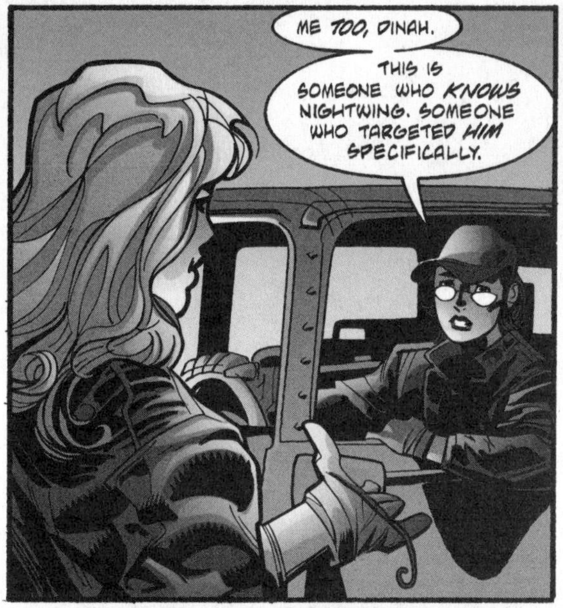
ME TOO, DINAH.
THIS IS SOMEONE WHO KNOWS NIGHTWING. SOMEONE WHO TARGETED HIM SPECIFICALLY.

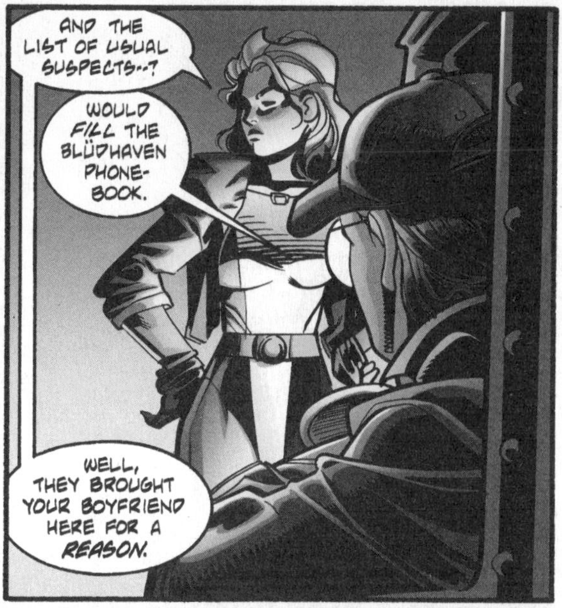
AND THE LIST OF USUAL SUSPECTS--?
WOULD FILL THE BLÜDHAVEN PHONE-BOOK.
WELL, THEY BROUGHT YOUR BOYFRIEND HERE FOR A REASON.

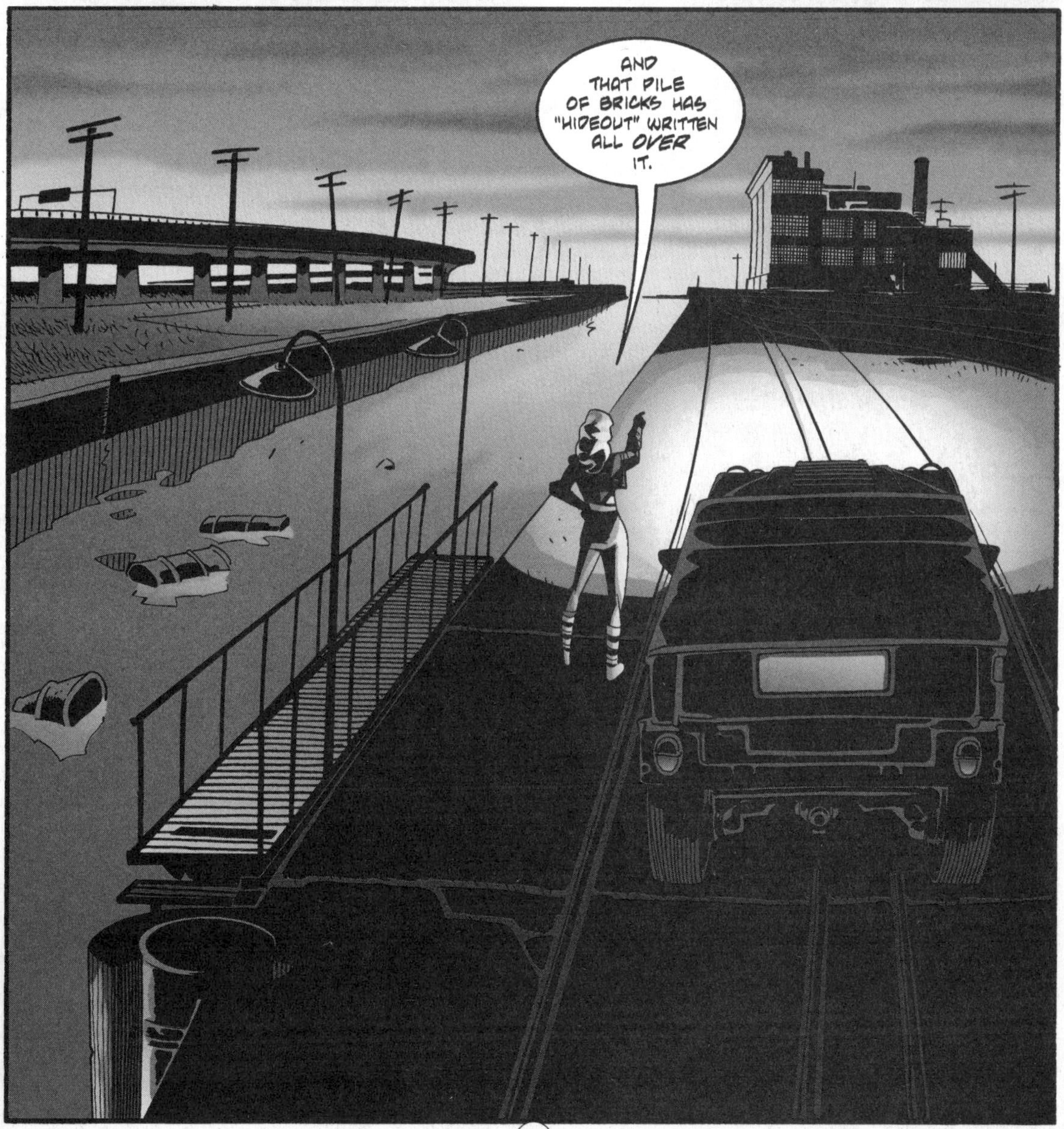
AND THAT PILE OF BRICKS HAS "HIDEOUT" WRITTEN ALL OVER IT.

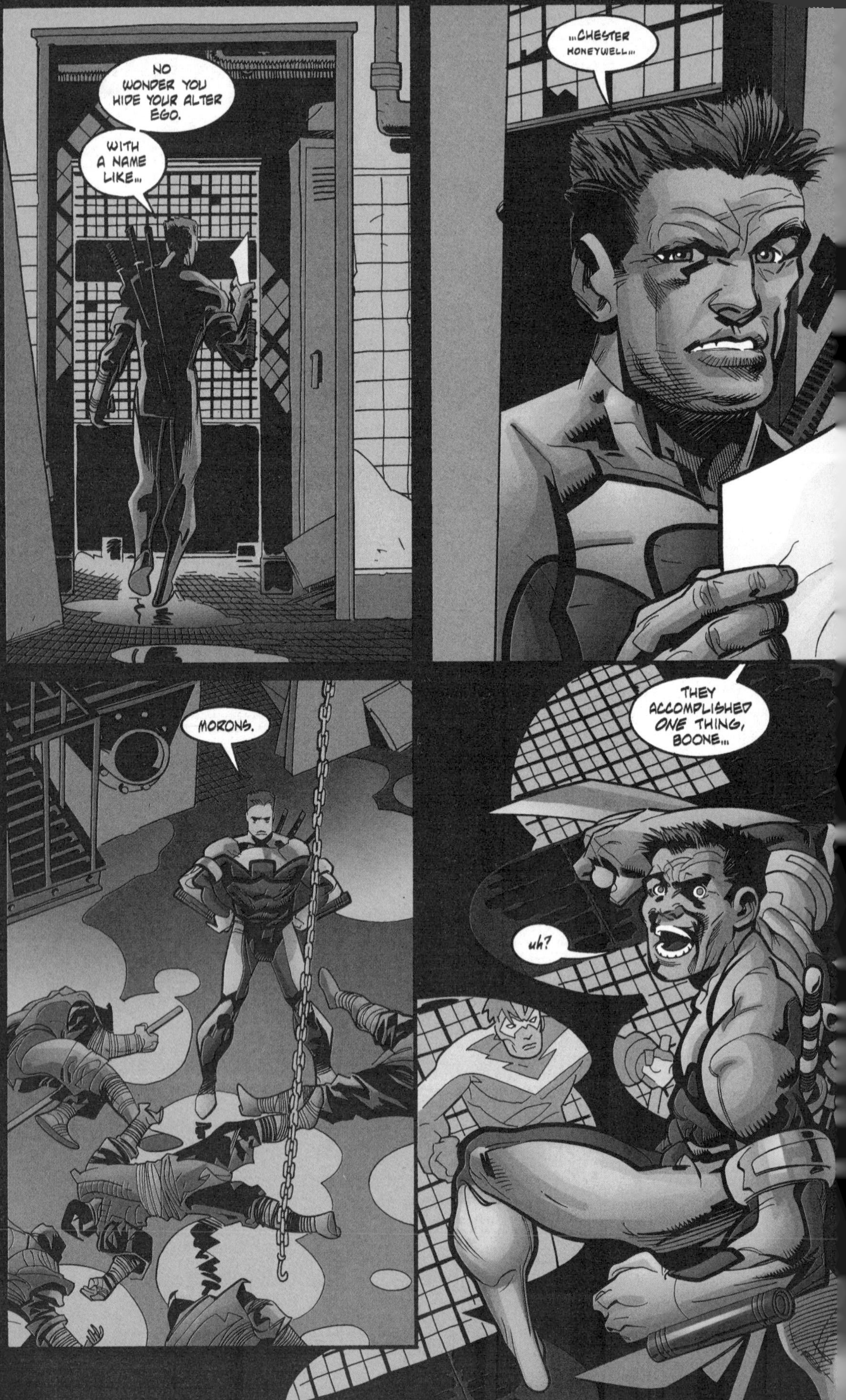
NO WONDER YOU HIDE YOUR ALTER EGO.
WITH A NAME LIKE...
...CHESTER HONEYWELL...
MORONS.
THEY ACCOMPLISHED ONE THING, BOONE...
uh?

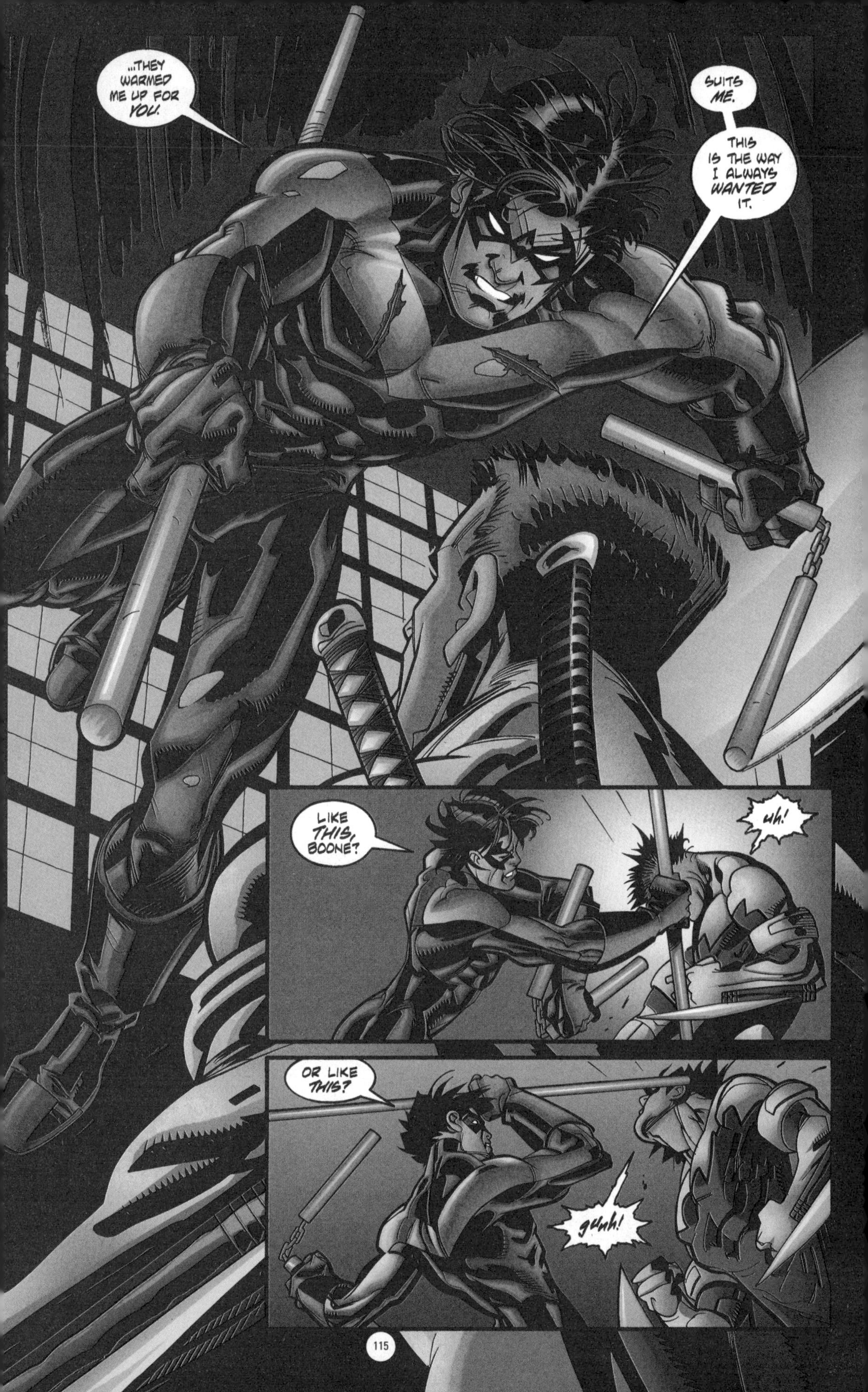
...THEY WARMED ME UP FOR YOU.
SUITS ME.
THIS IS THE WAY I ALWAYS WANTED IT.
LIKE THIS, BOONE?
uh!
OR LIKE THIS?
gunh!

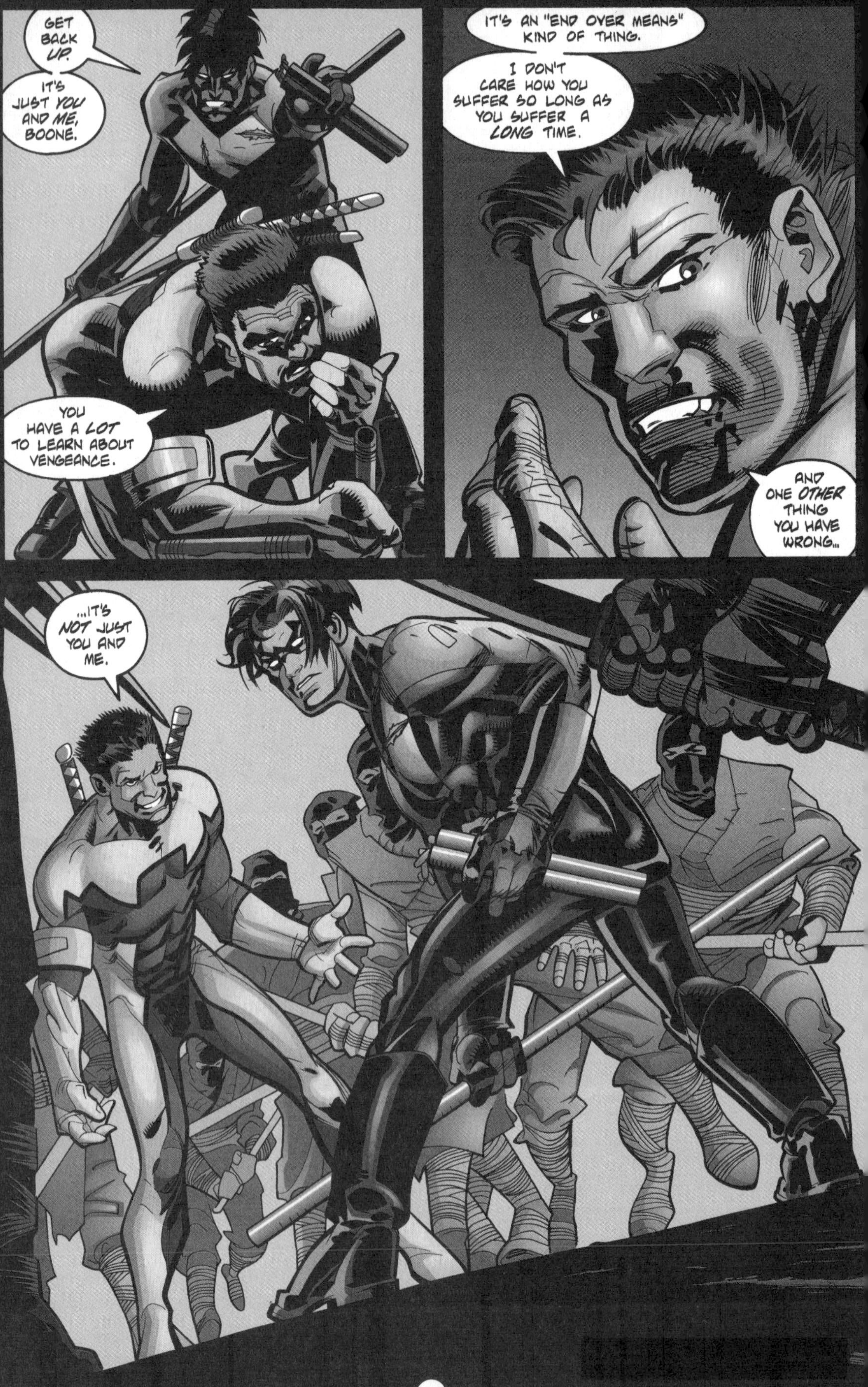
GET BACK UP.
IT'S JUST YOU AND ME, BOONE.
YOU HAVE A LOT TO LEARN ABOUT VENGEANCE.
IT'S AN "END OVER MEANS" KIND OF THING.
I DON'T CARE HOW YOU SUFFER SO LONG AS YOU SUFFER A LONG TIME.
AND ONE OTHER THING YOU HAVE WRONG...
...IT'S NOT JUST YOU AND ME.

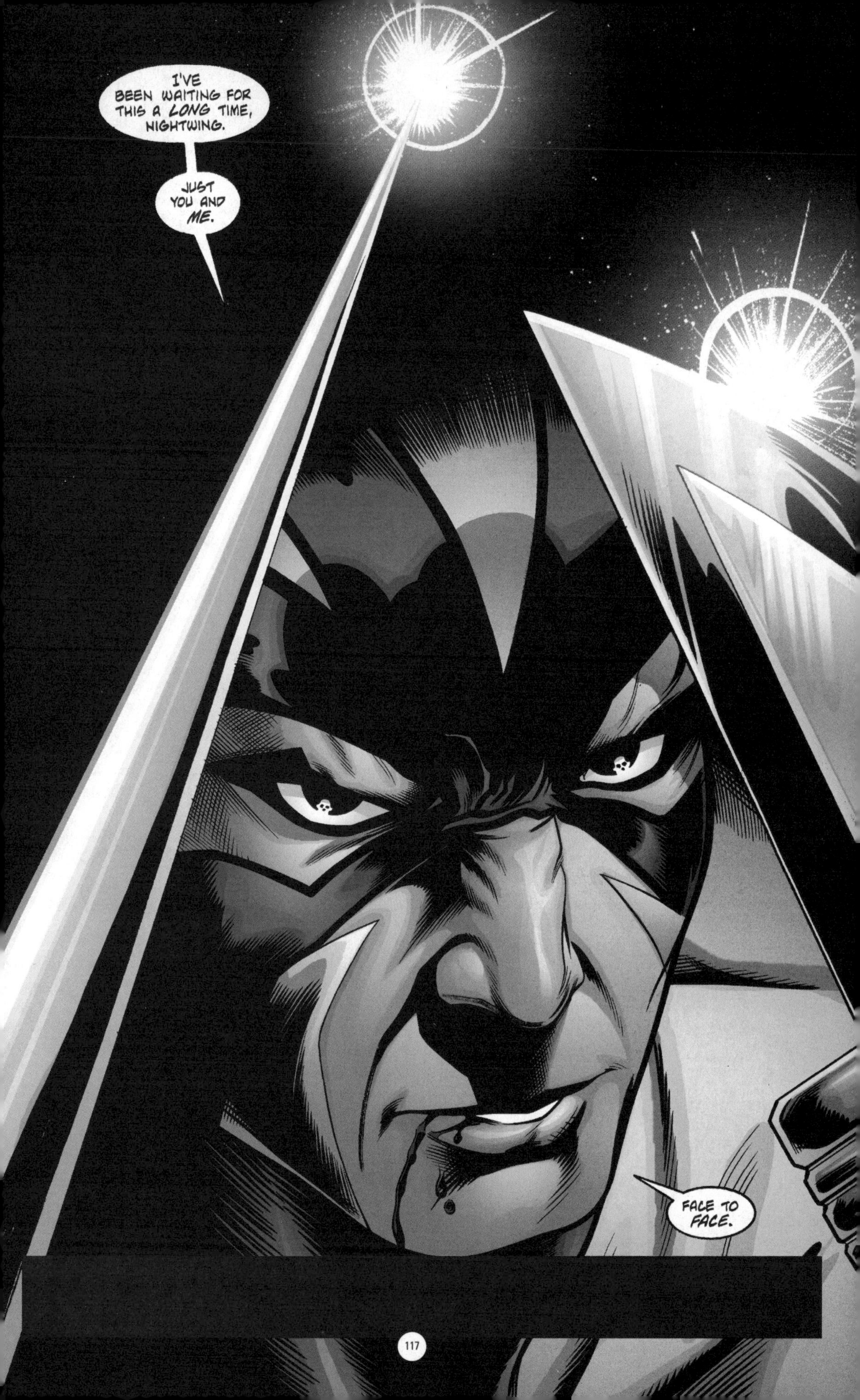

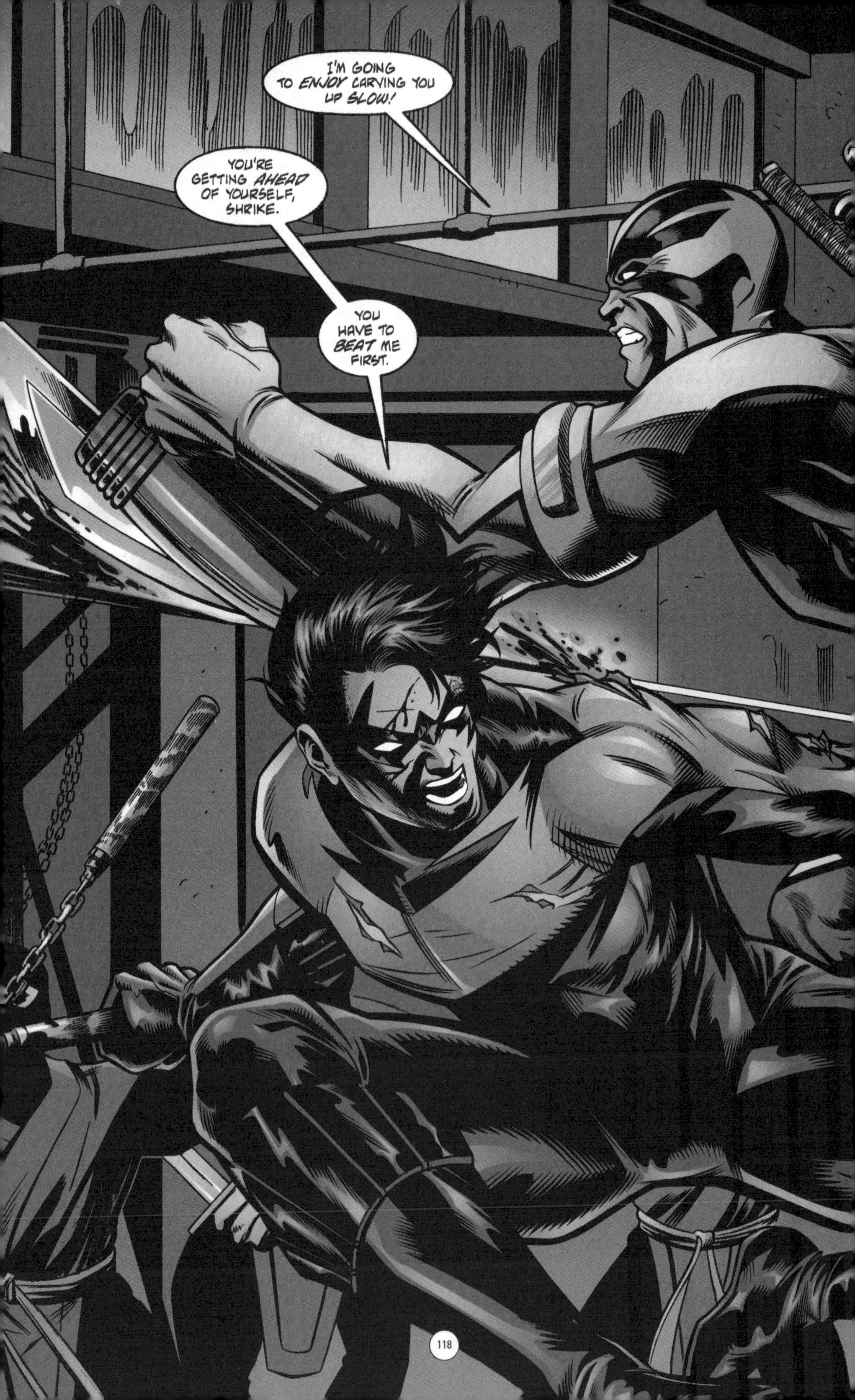
I'M GOING TO ENJOY CARVING YOU UP SLOW!
YOU'RE GETTING AHEAD OF YOURSELF, SHRIKE.
YOU HAVE TO BEAT ME FIRST.

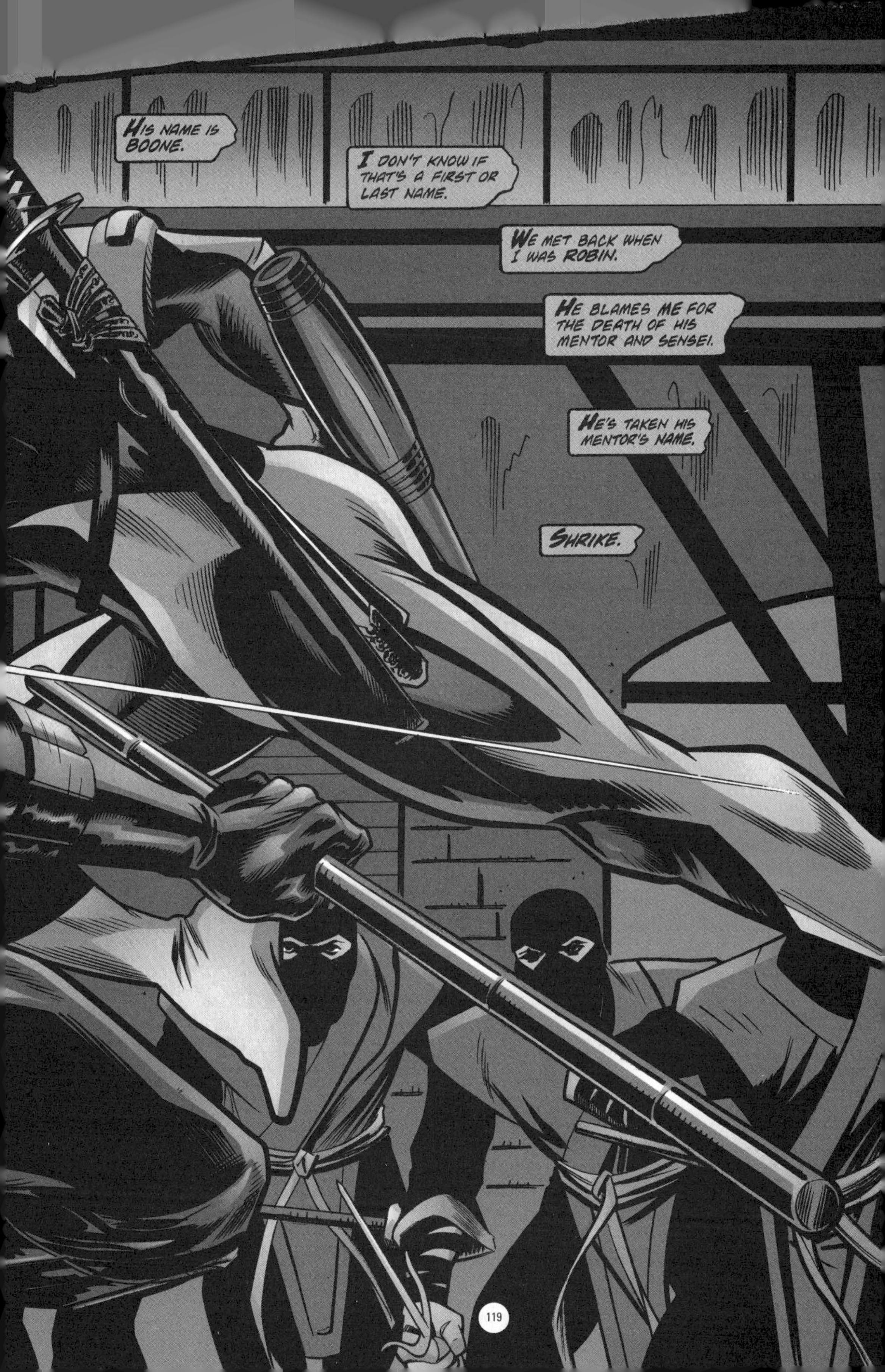
HIS NAME IS BOONE.
I DON'T KNOW IF THAT'S A FIRST OR LAST NAME.
WE MET BACK WHEN I WAS ROBIN.
HE BLAMES ME FOR THE DEATH OF HIS MENTOR AND SENSEI.
HE'S TAKEN HIS MENTOR'S NAME.
SHRIKE.

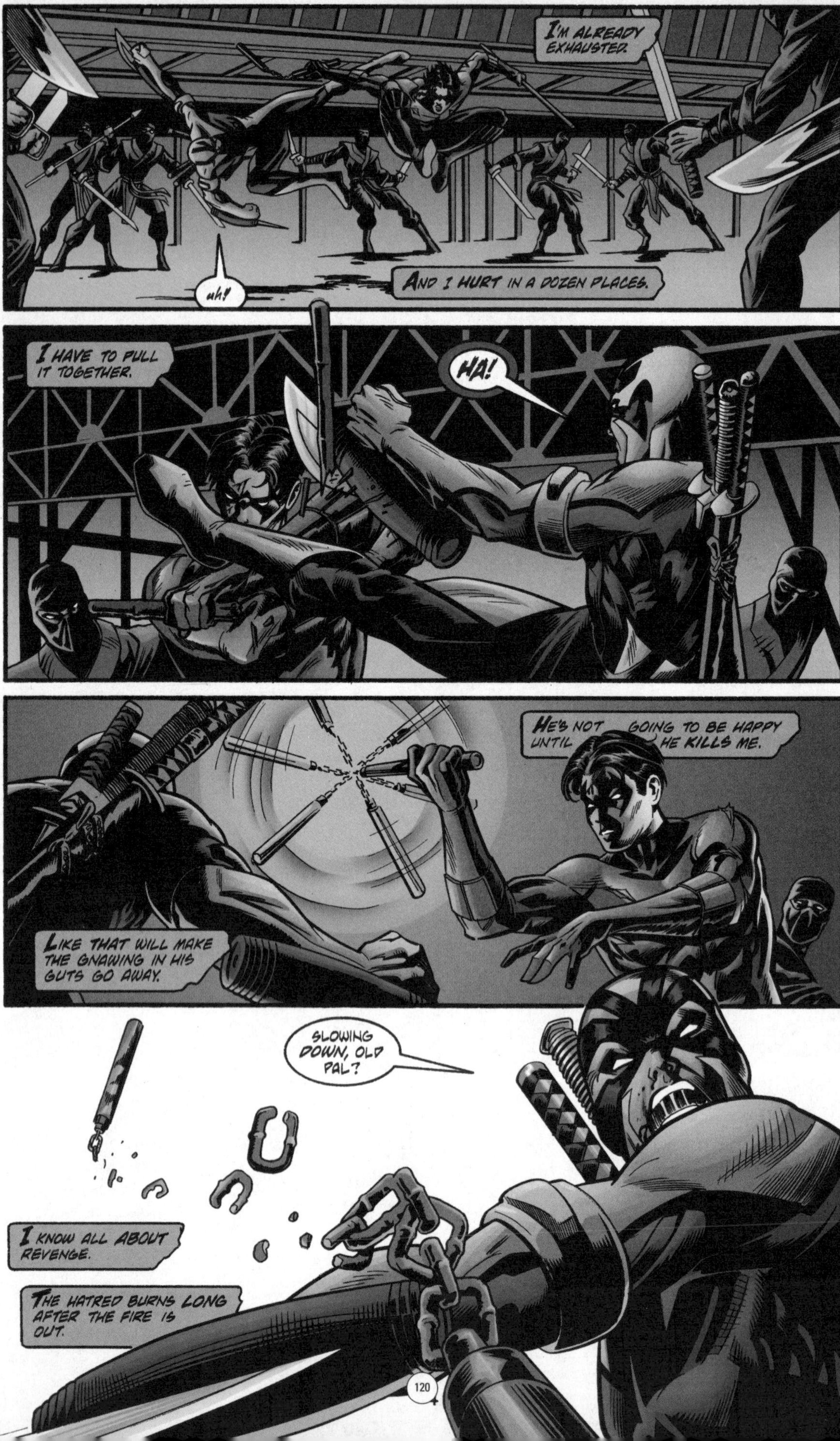

I'M ALREADY EXHAUSTED.
uh!
AND I HURT IN A DOZEN PLACES.
I HAVE TO PULL IT TOGETHER.
HA!
HE'S NOT GOING TO BE HAPPY UNTIL HE KILLS ME.
LIKE THAT WILL MAKE THE GNAWING IN HIS GUTS GO AWAY.
SLOWING DOWN, OLD PAL?
I KNOW ALL ABOUT REVENGE.
THE HATRED BURNS LONG AFTER THE FIRE IS OUT.

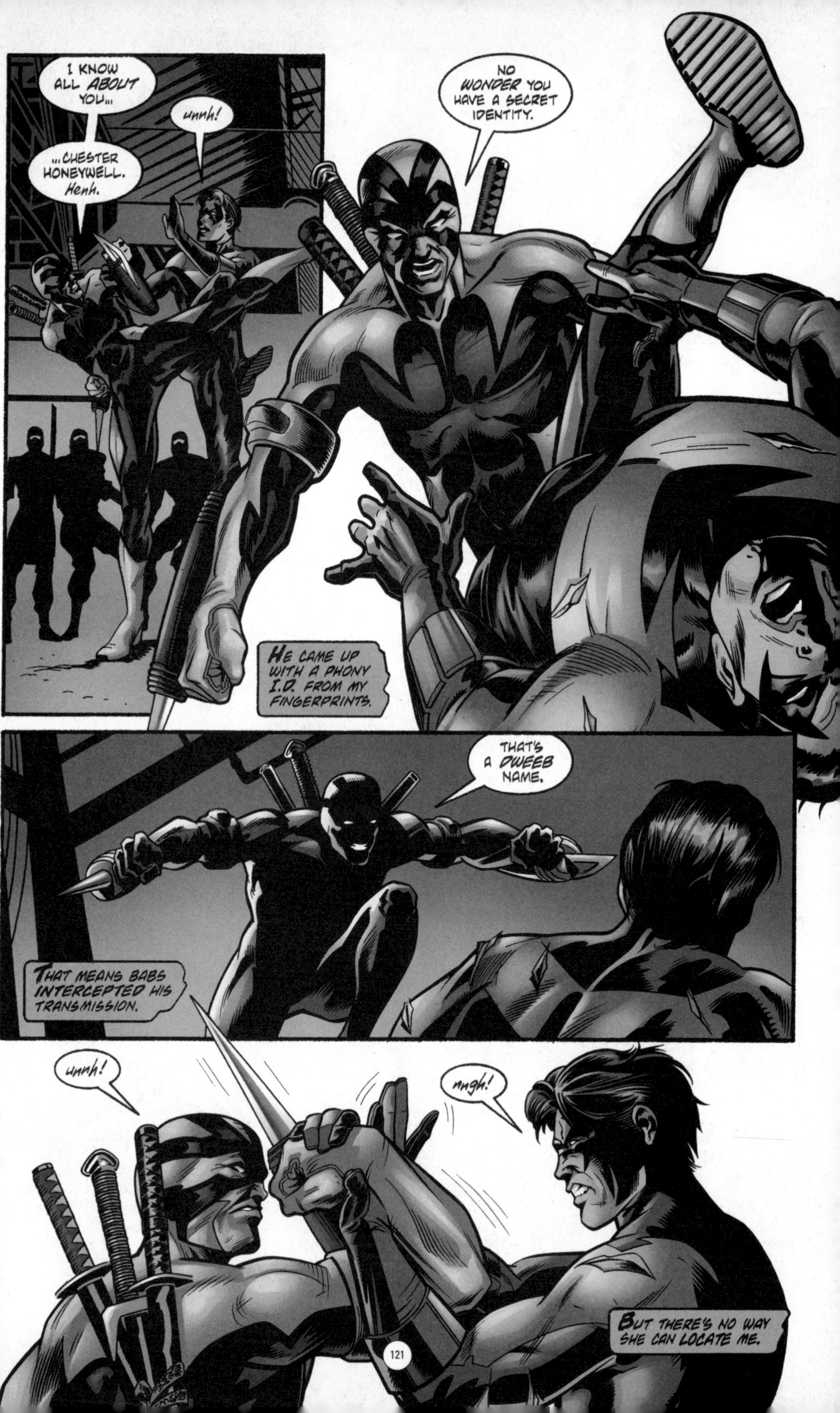

I KNOW ALL ABOUT YOU...
unnh!
...CHESTER HONEYWELL. Henh.
NO WONDER YOU HAVE A SECRET IDENTITY.
HE CAME UP WITH A PHONY I.D. FROM MY FINGERPRINTS.
THAT'S A DWEEB NAME.
THAT MEANS BABS INTERCEPTED HIS TRANSMISSION.
unnh!
nngh!
BUT THERE'S NO WAY SHE CAN LOCATE ME.

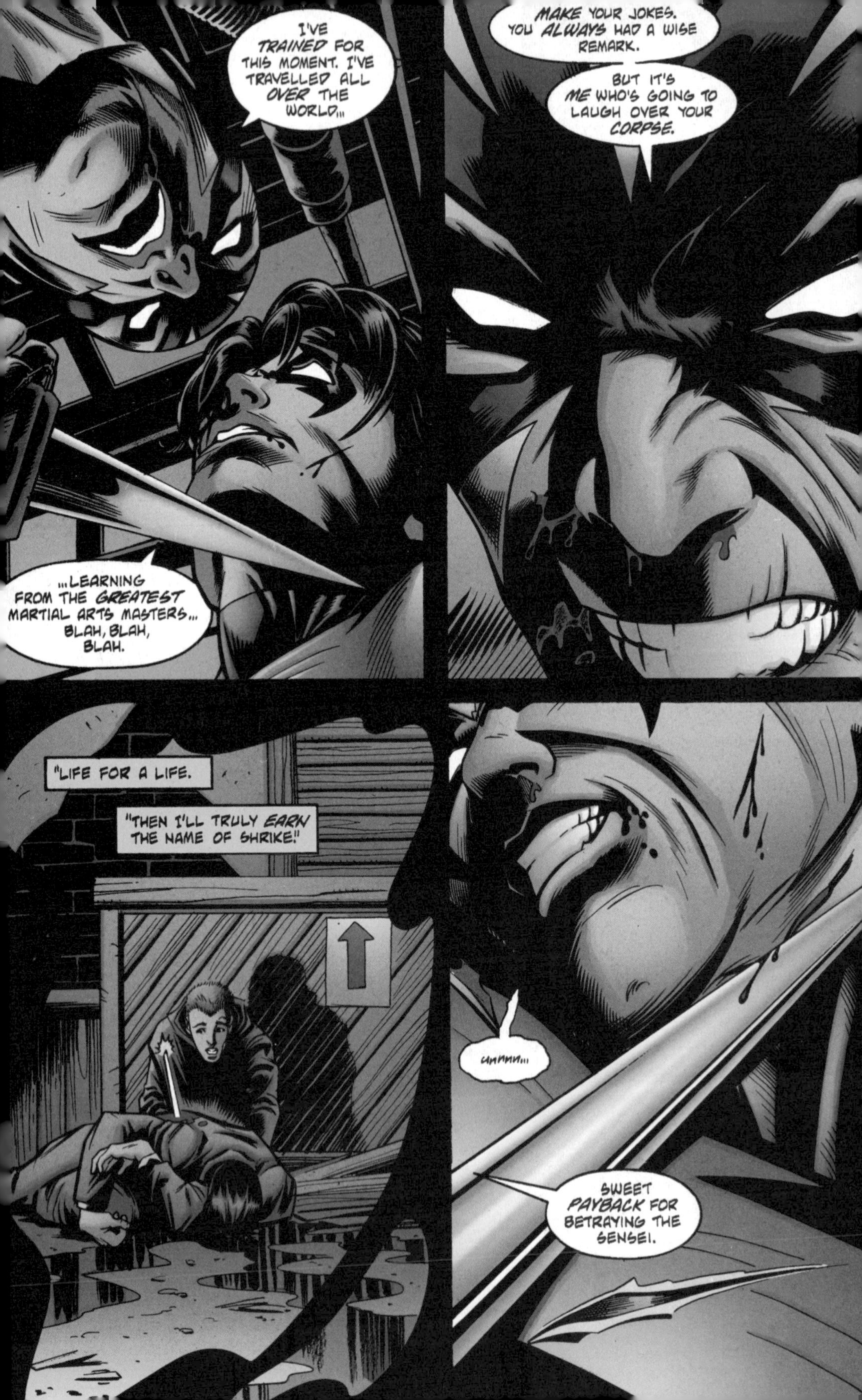
I'VE TRAINED FOR THIS MOMENT. I'VE TRAVELLED ALL OVER THE WORLD...
...LEARNING FROM THE GREATEST MARTIAL ARTS MASTERS... BLAH, BLAH, BLAH.
MAKE YOUR JOKES. YOU ALWAYS HAD A WISE REMARK.
BUT IT'S ME WHO'S GOING TO LAUGH OVER YOUR CORPSE.
"LIFE FOR A LIFE.
"THEN I'LL TRULY EARN THE NAME OF SHRIKE."
UNNNN...
SWEET PAYBACK FOR BETRAYING THE SENSEI.

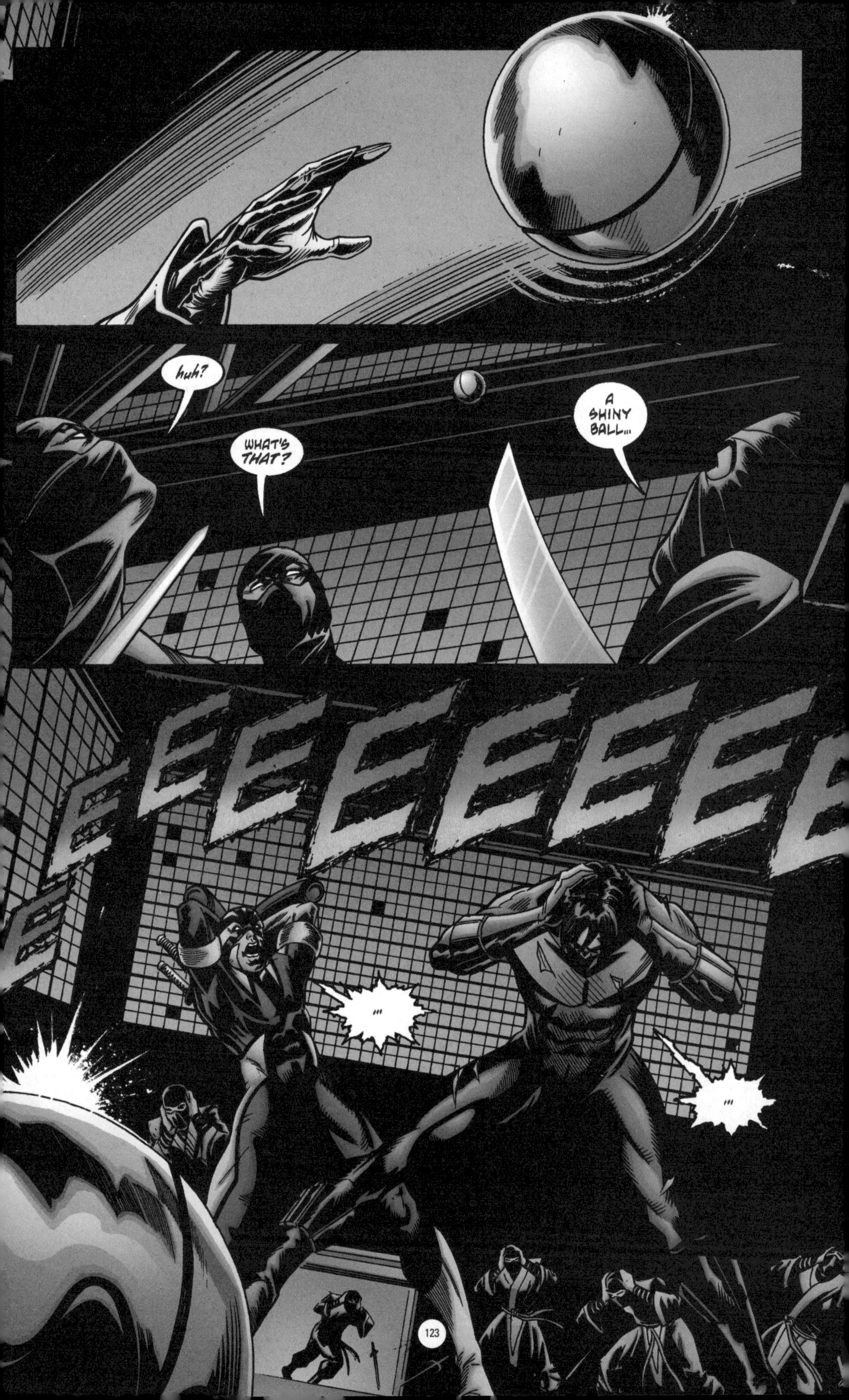
huh?
WHAT'S THAT?
A SHINY BALL...
EEEEEEEE

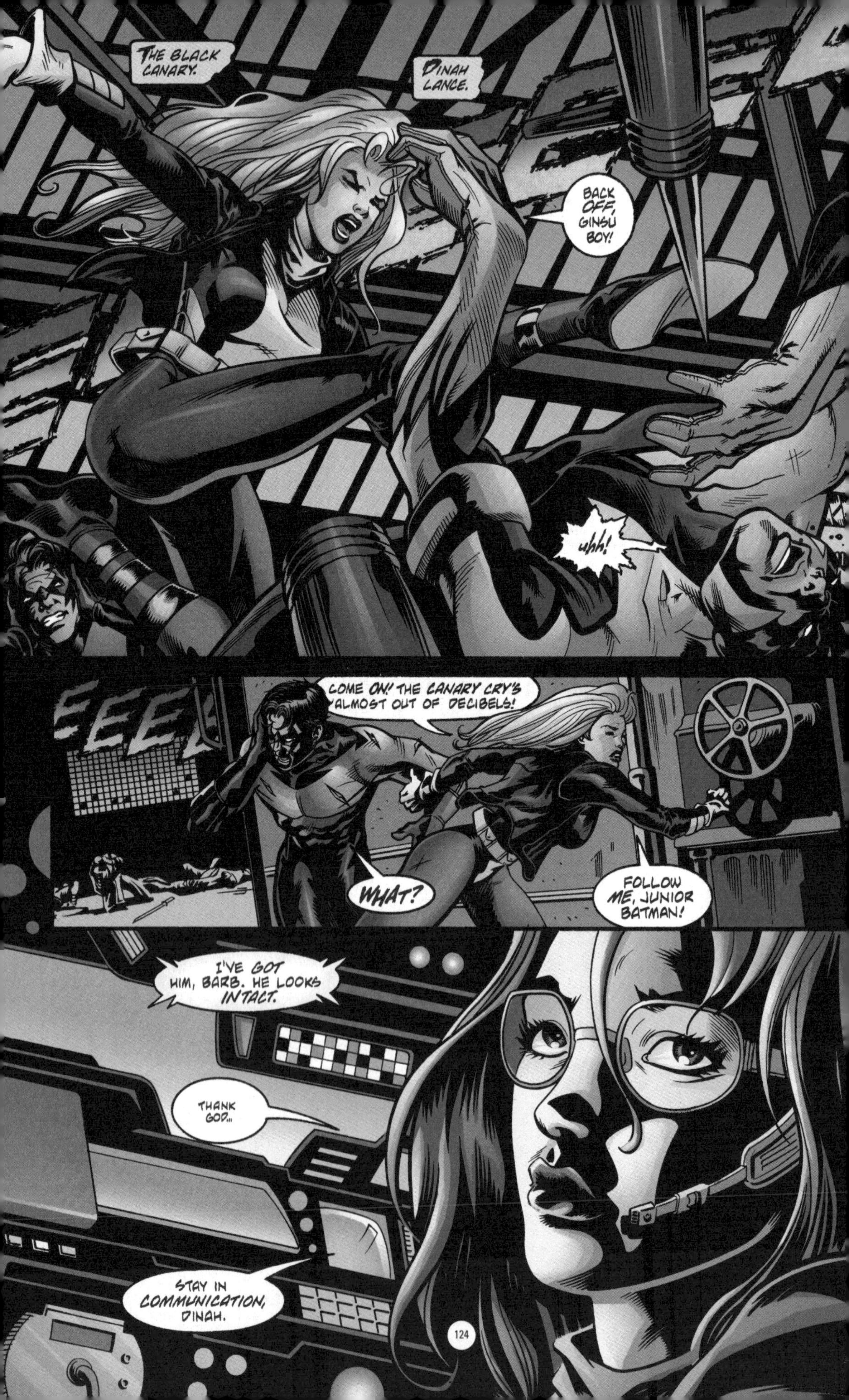
THE BLACK CANARY.
DINAH LANCE.
BACK OFF, GINSU BOY!
uhh!
COME ON! THE CANARY CRY'S ALMOST OUT OF DECIBELS!
WHAT?
FOLLOW ME, JUNIOR BATMAN!
I'VE GOT HIM, BARB. HE LOOKS INTACT.
THANK GOD...
STAY IN COMMUNICATION, DINAH.

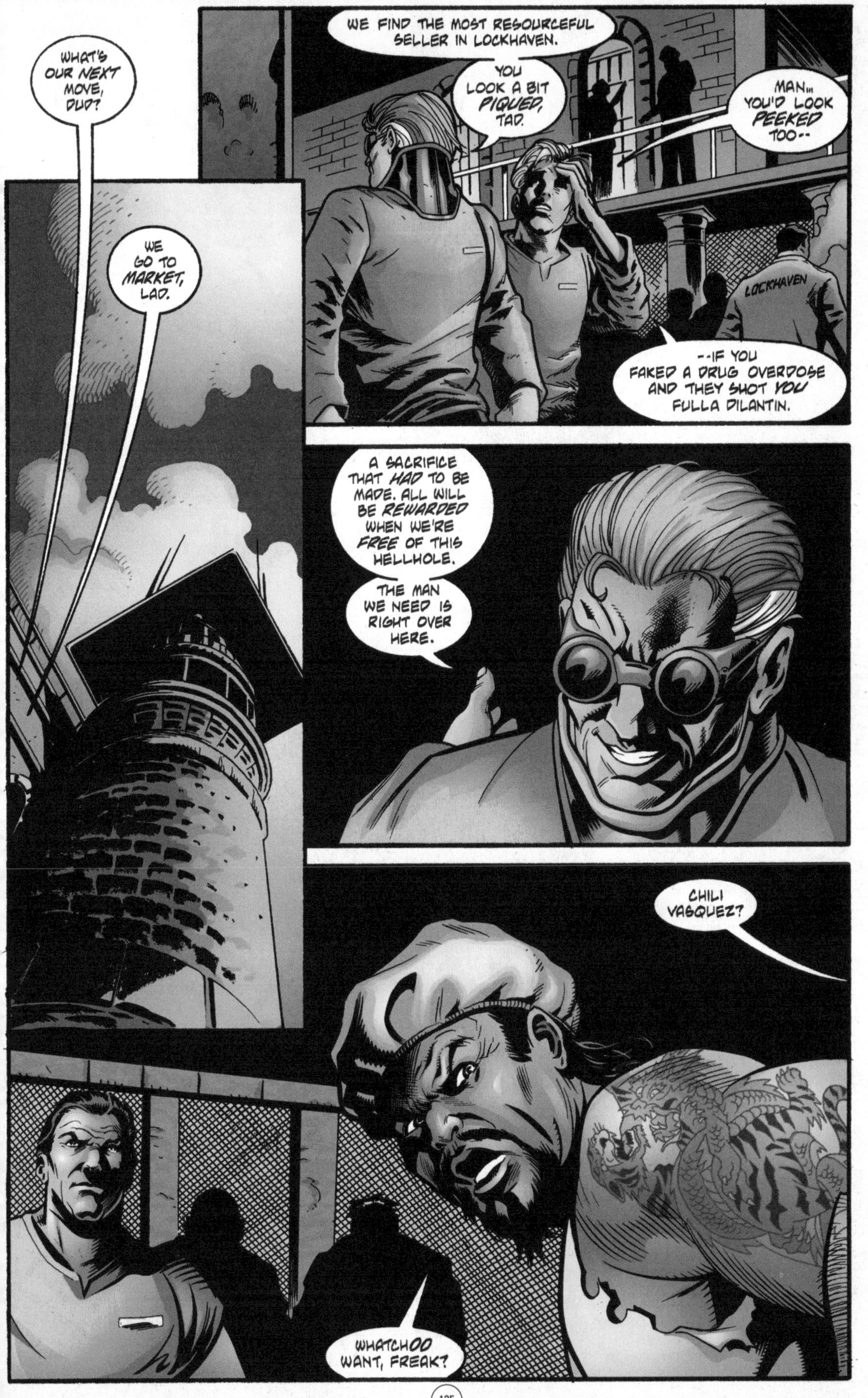

WHAT'S OUR NEXT MOVE, DUD?
WE GO TO MARKET, LAD.
WE FIND THE MOST RESOURCEFUL SELLER IN LOCKHAVEN.
YOU LOOK A BIT PIQUED, TAD.
MAN... YOU'D LOOK PEEKED TOO--
LOCKHAVEN
--IF YOU FAKED A DRUG OVERDOSE AND THEY SHOT YOU FULLA DILANTIN.
A SACRIFICE THAT HAD TO BE MADE. ALL WILL BE REWARDED WHEN WE'RE FREE OF THIS HELLHOLE.
THE MAN WE NEED IS RIGHT OVER HERE.
CHILI VASQUEZ?
WHATCHOO WANT, FREAK?

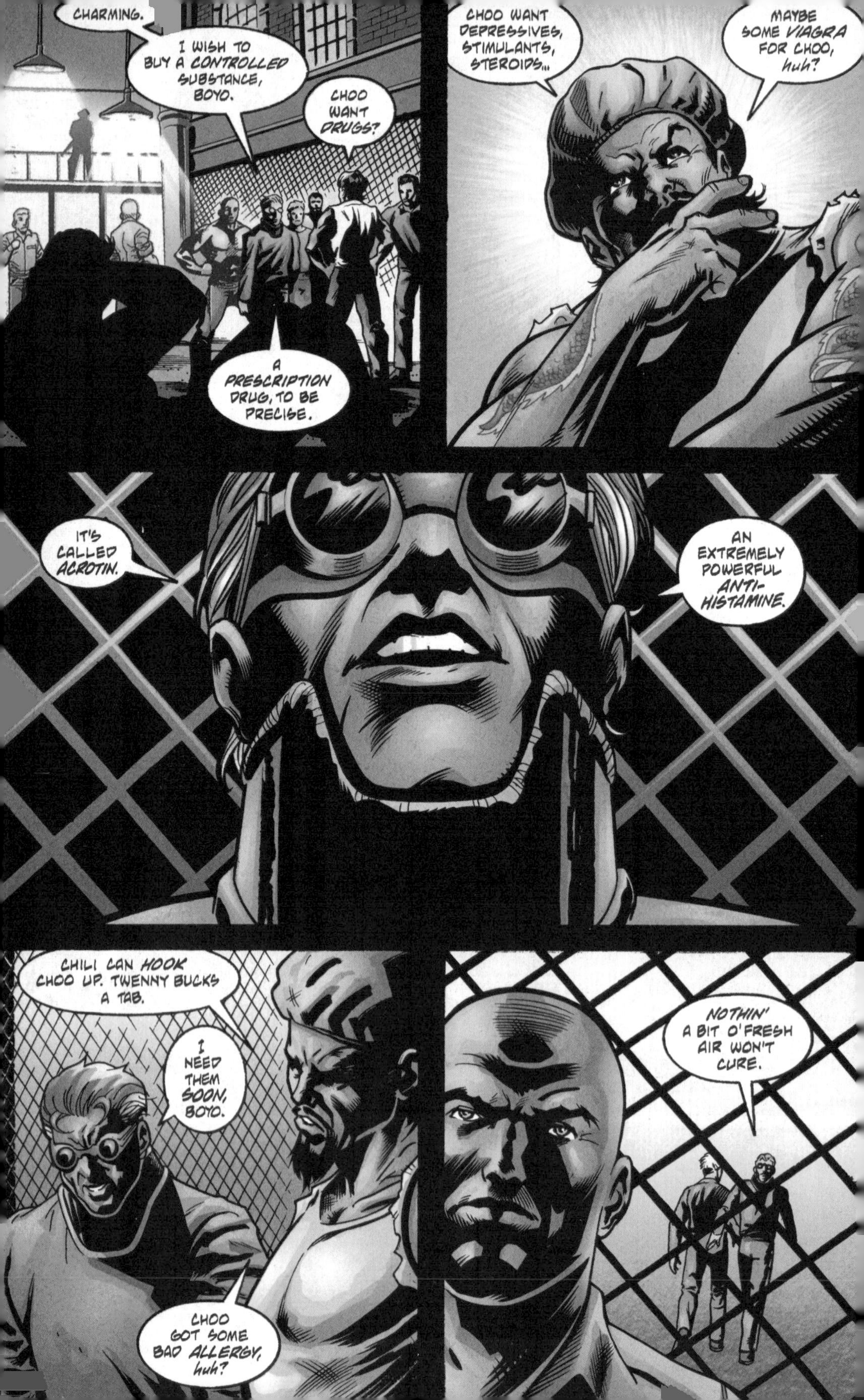
CHARMING.
I WISH TO BUY A CONTROLLED SUBSTANCE, BOYO.
CHOO WANT DRUGS?
A PRESCRIPTION DRUG, TO BE PRECISE.
CHOO WANT DEPRESSIVES, STIMULANTS, STEROIDS...
MAYBE SOME VIAGRA FOR CHOO, huh?
IT'S CALLED ACROTIN.
AN EXTREMELY POWERFUL ANTI-HISTAMINE.
CHILI CAN HOOK CHOO UP. TWENNY BUCKS A TAB.
I NEED THEM SOON, BOYO.
CHOO GOT SOME BAD ALLERGY, huh?
NOTHIN' A BIT O'FRESH AIR WON'T CURE.

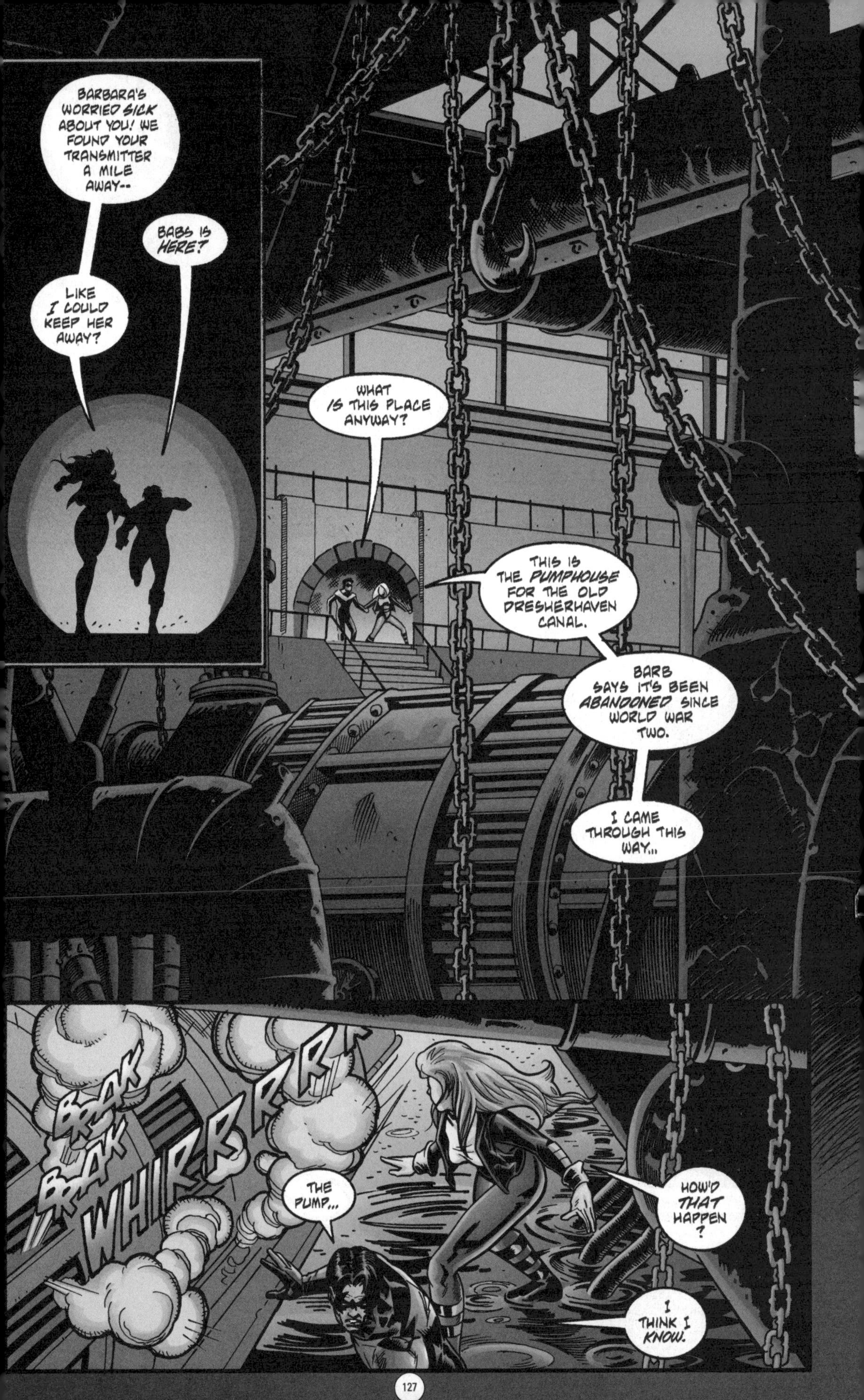
BARBARA'S WORRIED SICK ABOUT YOU! WE FOUND YOUR TRANSMITTER A MILE AWAY--
BABS IS HERE?
LIKE I COULD KEEP HER AWAY?
WHAT IS THIS PLACE ANYWAY?
THIS IS THE PUMPHOUSE FOR THE OLD DRESHERHAVEN CANAL.
BARB SAYS IT'S BEEN ABANDONED SINCE WORLD WAR TWO.
I CAME THROUGH THIS WAY...
BRAK
BRAK
WHIRRRRT
THE PUMP...
HOW'D THAT HAPPEN?
I THINK I KNOW.

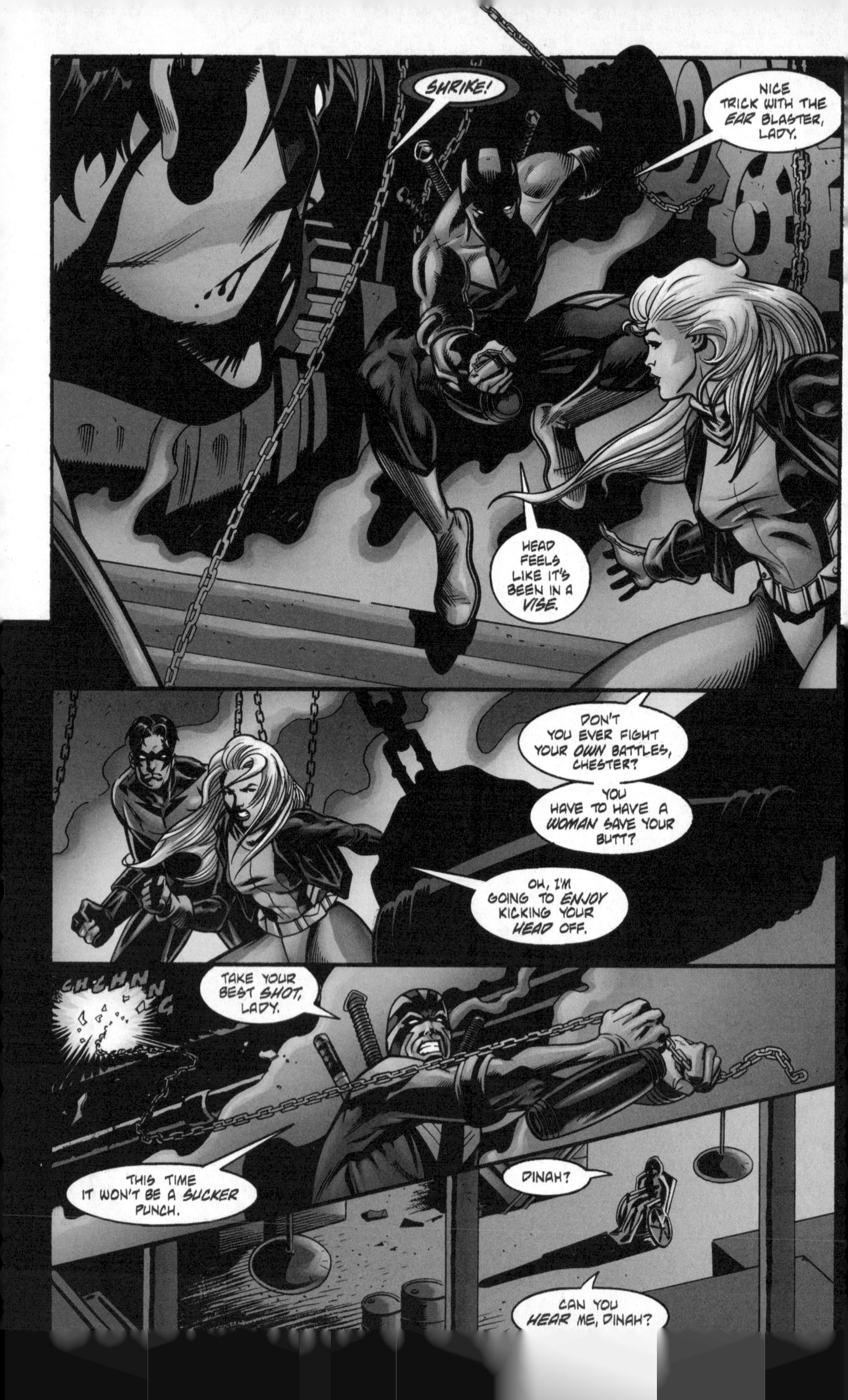
SHRIKE!
NICE TRICK WITH THE EAR BLASTER, LADY.
HEAD FEELS LIKE IT'S BEEN IN A VISE.
DON'T YOU EVER FIGHT YOUR OWN BATTLES, CHESTER?
YOU HAVE TO HAVE A WOMAN SAVE YOUR BUTT?
OH, I'M GOING TO ENJOY KICKING YOUR HEAD OFF.
CH-CHNNNG
TAKE YOUR BEST SHOT, LADY.
THIS TIME IT WON'T BE A SUCKER PUNCH.
DINAH?
CAN YOU HEAR ME, DINAH?

BATMAN *FIRE* YOU, CHESTER?

YOU *SCREW* UP SO BAD YOU GOTTA PARTNER WITH *BARBIE* HERE?

STAY *BACK.* THIS GUY'S *ALL--*

agkh!

CANARY!

CANARY, *huh?*

LET'S *HEAR* HER SING *NOW!*

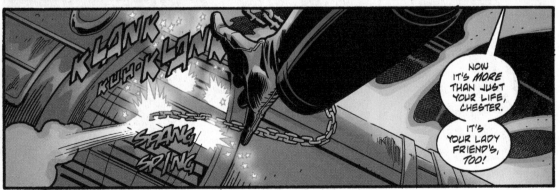

KLANK

KLIHKLANK

SPANG SPING

NOW IT'S *MORE* THAN JUST YOUR *LIFE,* CHESTER.

IT'S YOUR *LADY FRIEND'S,* TOO!

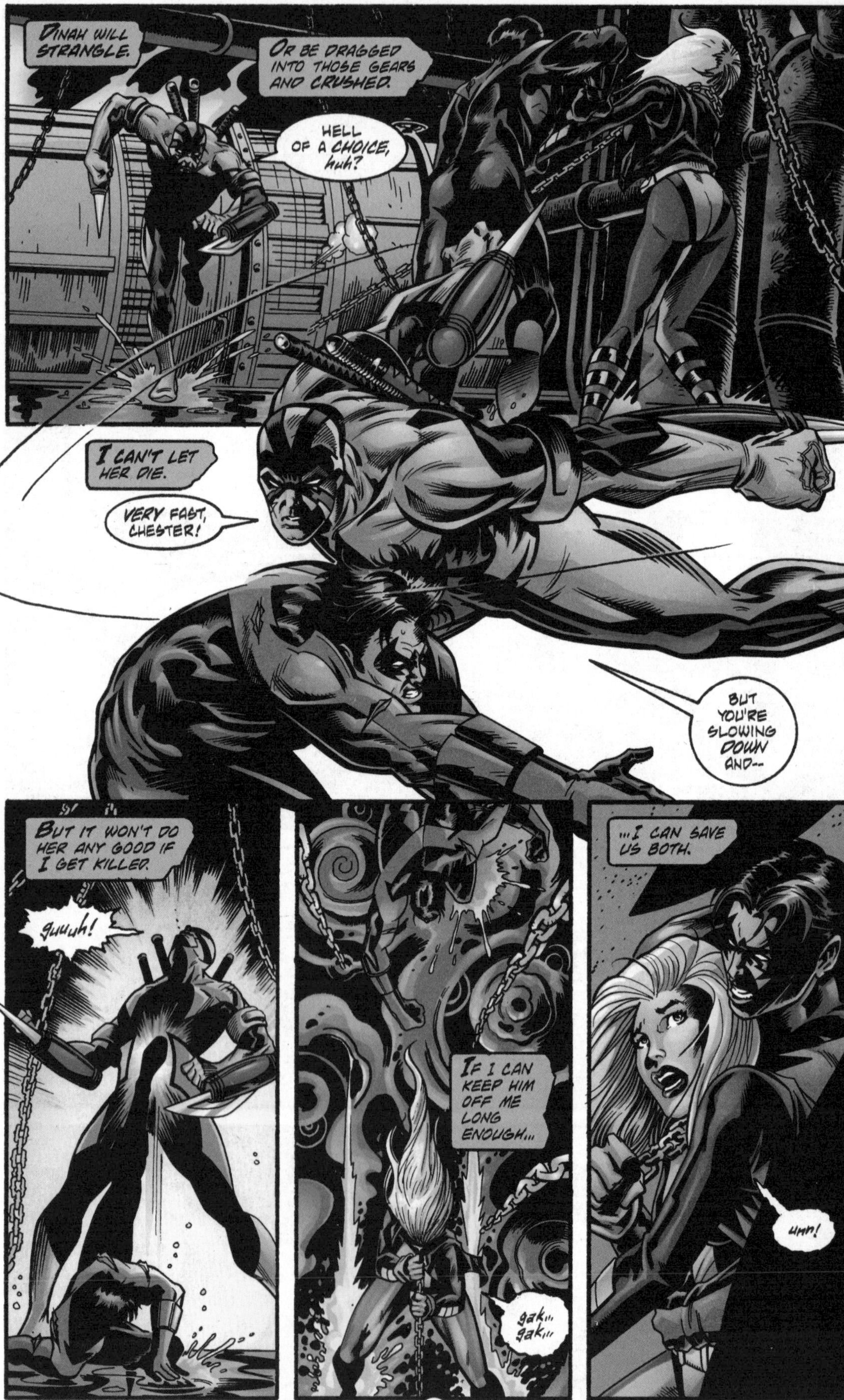

DINAH WILL STRANGLE.
OR BE DRAGGED INTO THOSE GEARS AND CRUSHED.
HELL OF A CHOICE, huh?
I CAN'T LET HER DIE.
VERY FAST, CHESTER!
BUT YOU'RE SLOWING DOWN AND--
BUT IT WON'T DO HER ANY GOOD IF I GET KILLED.
guuuh!
IF I CAN KEEP HIM OFF ME LONG ENOUGH...
gak... gak...
...I CAN SAVE US BOTH.
unn!

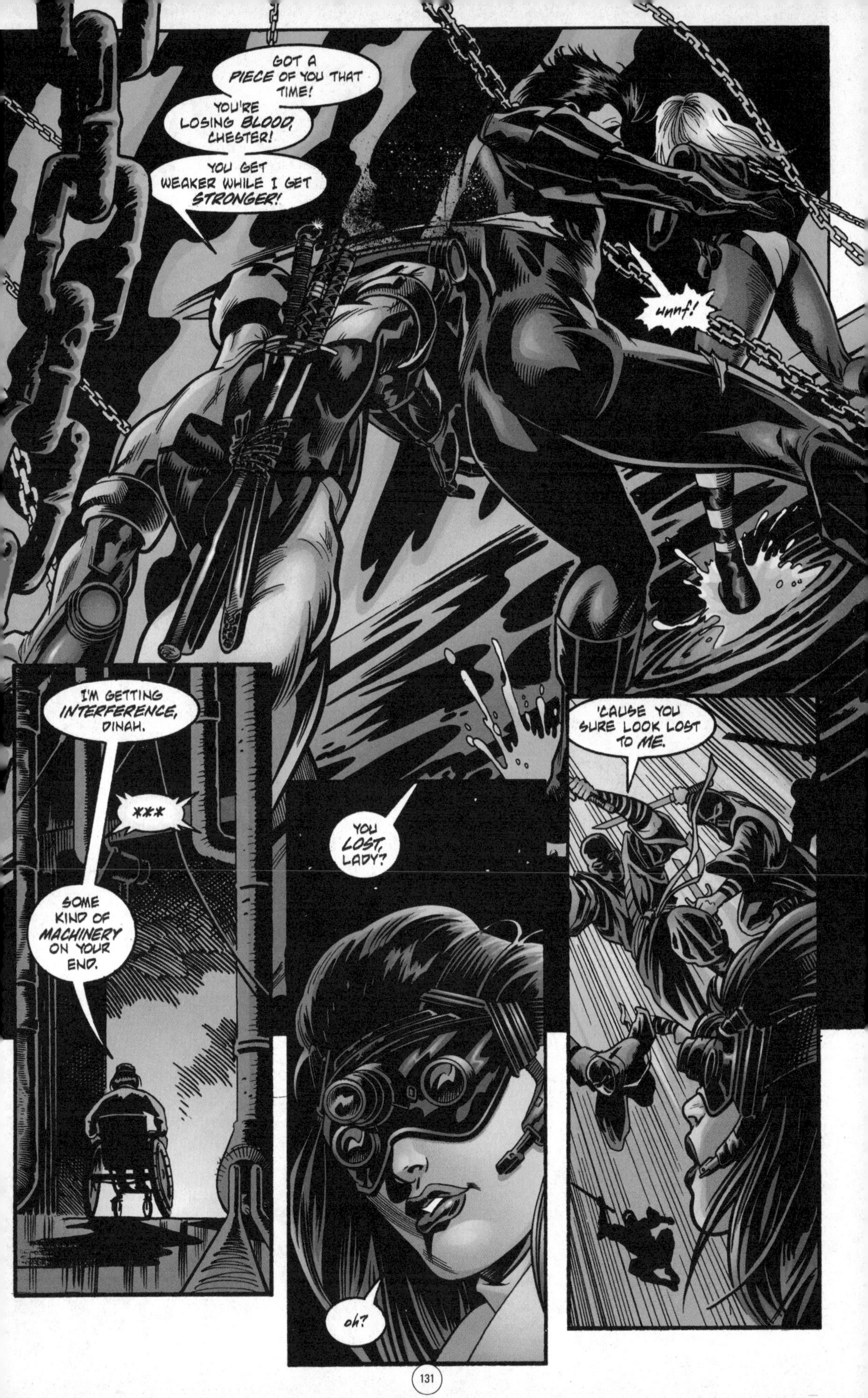
GOT A PIECE OF YOU THAT TIME!
YOU'RE LOSING BLOOD, CHESTER!
YOU GET WEAKER WHILE I GET STRONGER!
unnf!
I'M GETTING INTERFERENCE, DINAH.
***
SOME KIND OF MACHINERY ON YOUR END.
YOU LOST, LADY?
oh?
'CAUSE YOU SURE LOOK LOST TO ME.

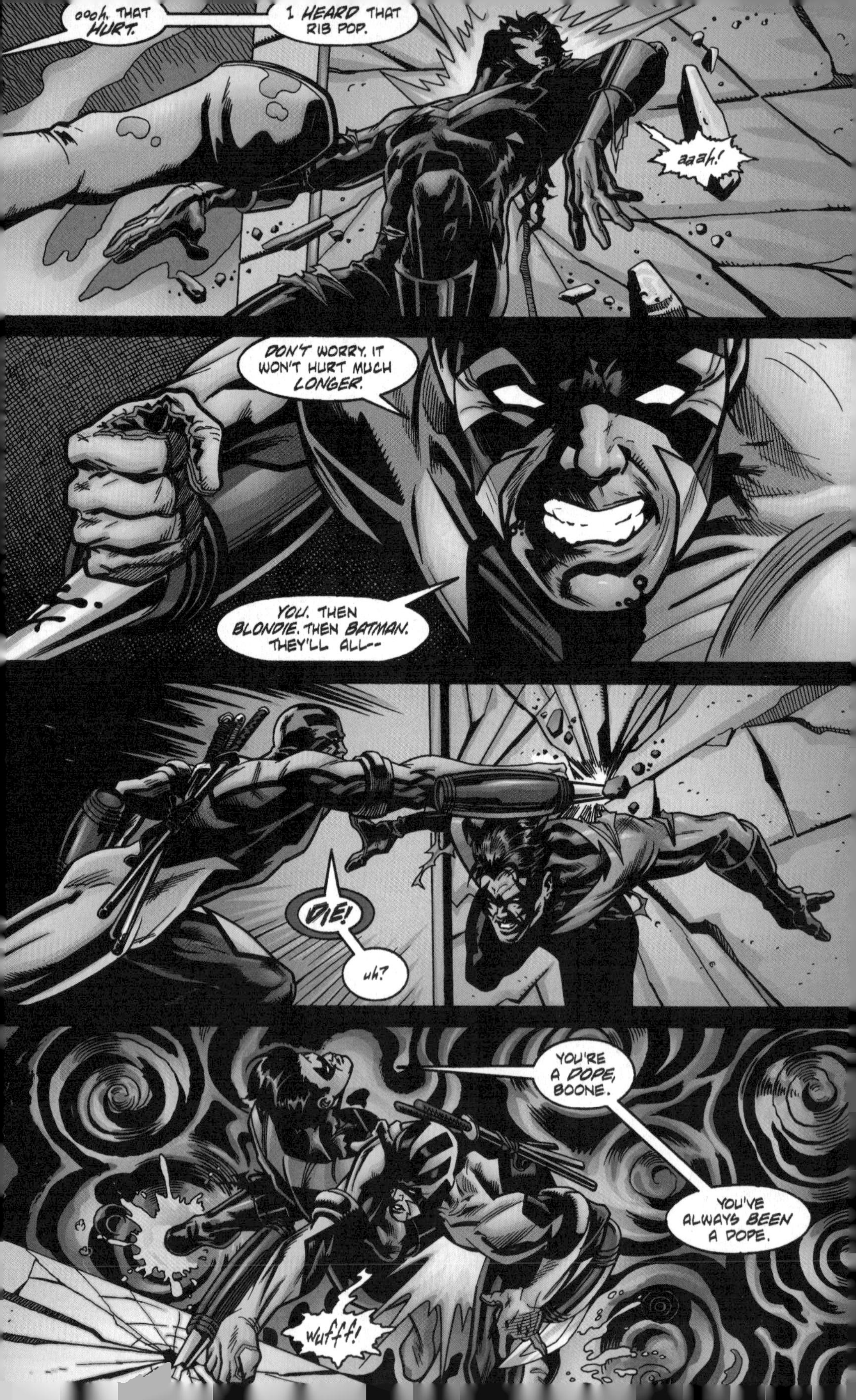
oooh. THAT HURT.
I HEARD THAT RIB POP.
aaah!
DON'T WORRY. IT WON'T HURT MUCH LONGER.
YOU. THEN BLONDIE. THEN BATMAN. THEY'LL ALL--
DIE!
uh?
YOU'RE A DOPE, BOONE.
YOU'VE ALWAYS BEEN A DOPE.
wufff!

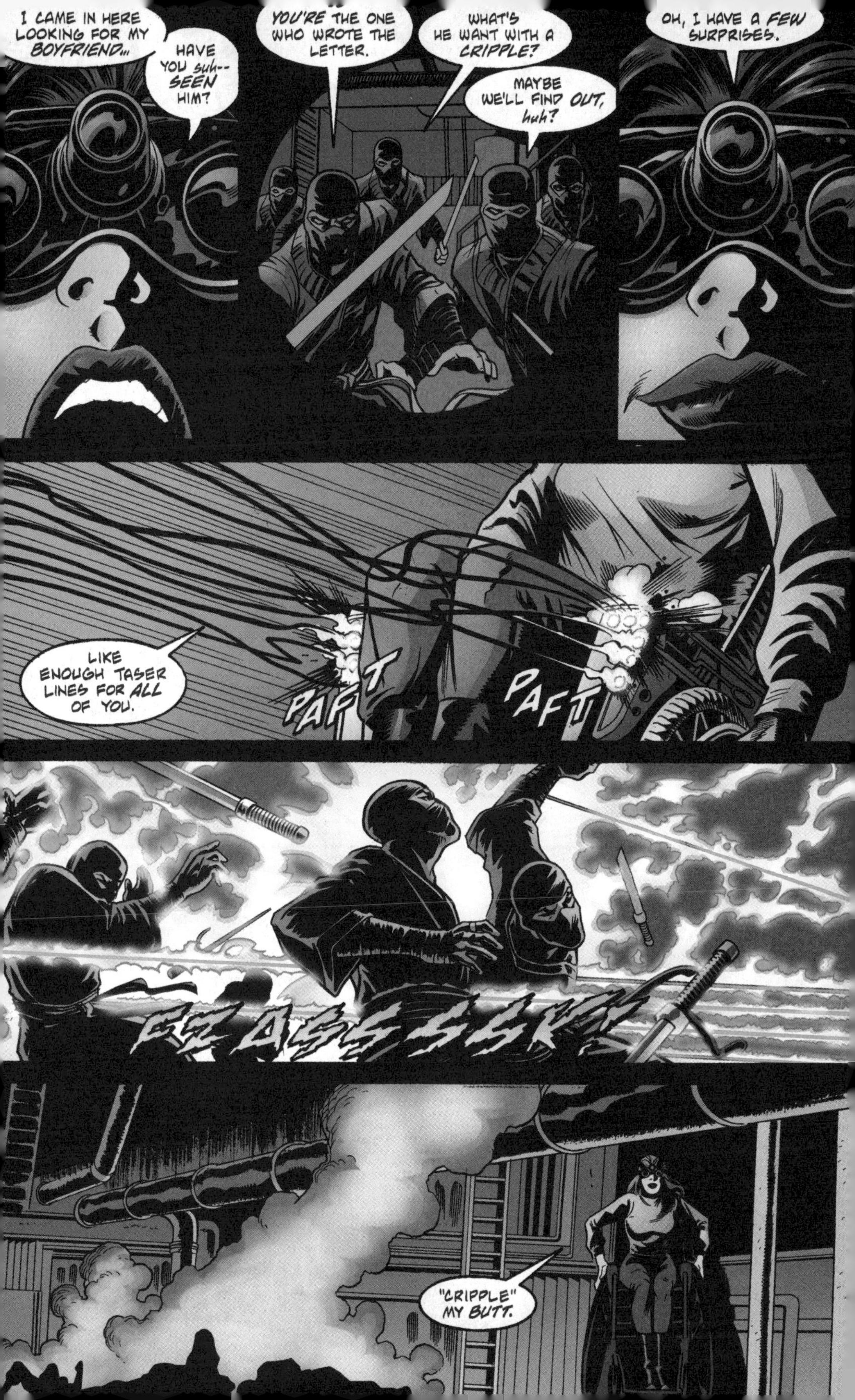
I CAME IN HERE LOOKING FOR MY BOYFRIEND...
HAVE YOU suh-- SEEN HIM?
YOU'RE THE ONE WHO WROTE THE LETTER.
WHAT'S HE WANT WITH A CRIPPLE?
MAYBE WE'LL FIND OUT, huh?
OH, I HAVE A FEW SURPRISES.
LIKE ENOUGH TASER LINES FOR ALL OF YOU.
PAFT
PAFT
"CRIPPLE" MY BUTT.

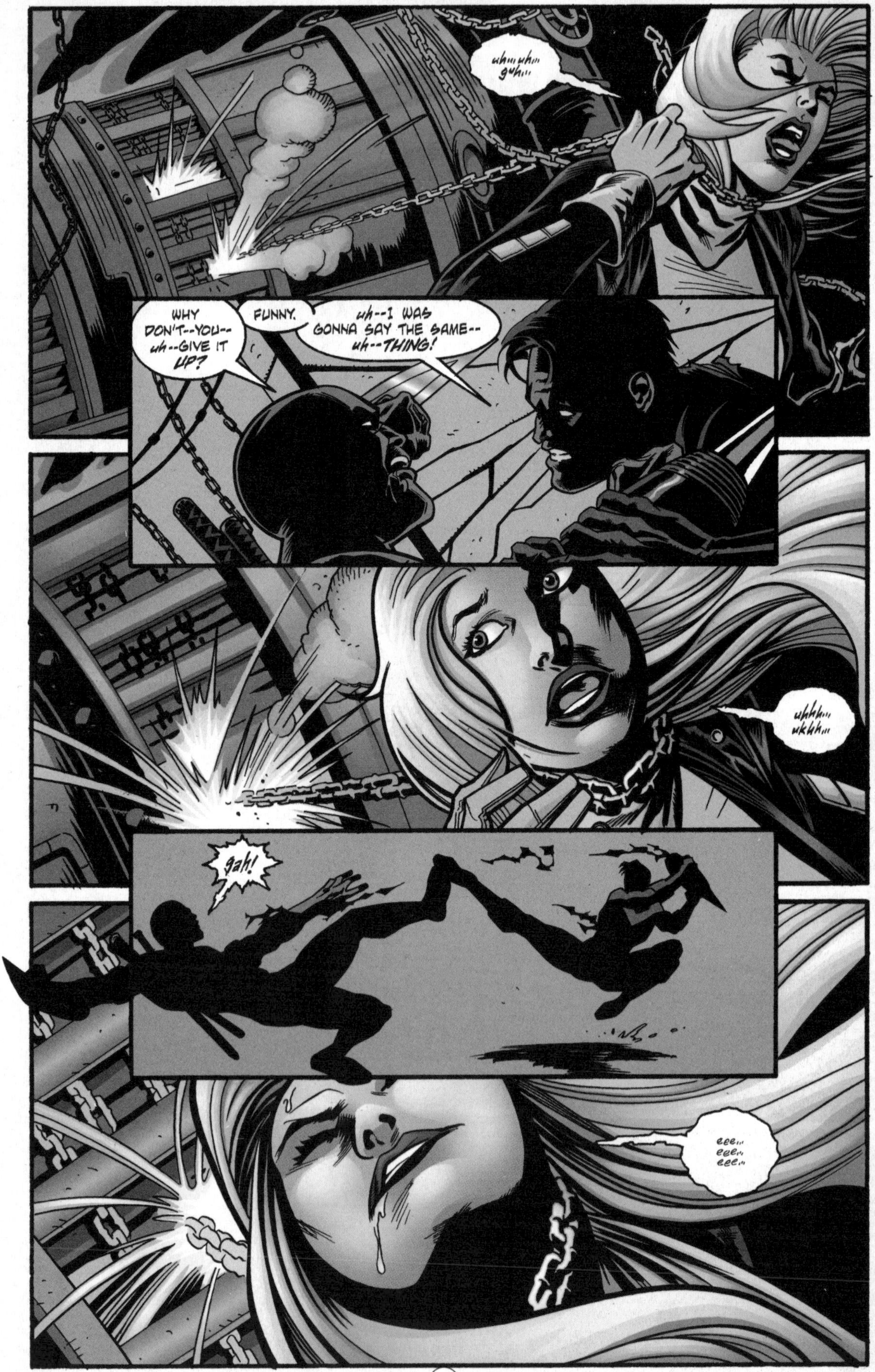
uh... uh... guh...
WHY DON'T--YOU--uh--GIVE IT UP?
FUNNY.
uh--I WAS GONNA SAY THE SAME--uh--THING!
uhhh... ukhh...
gah!
eee... eee... eee...

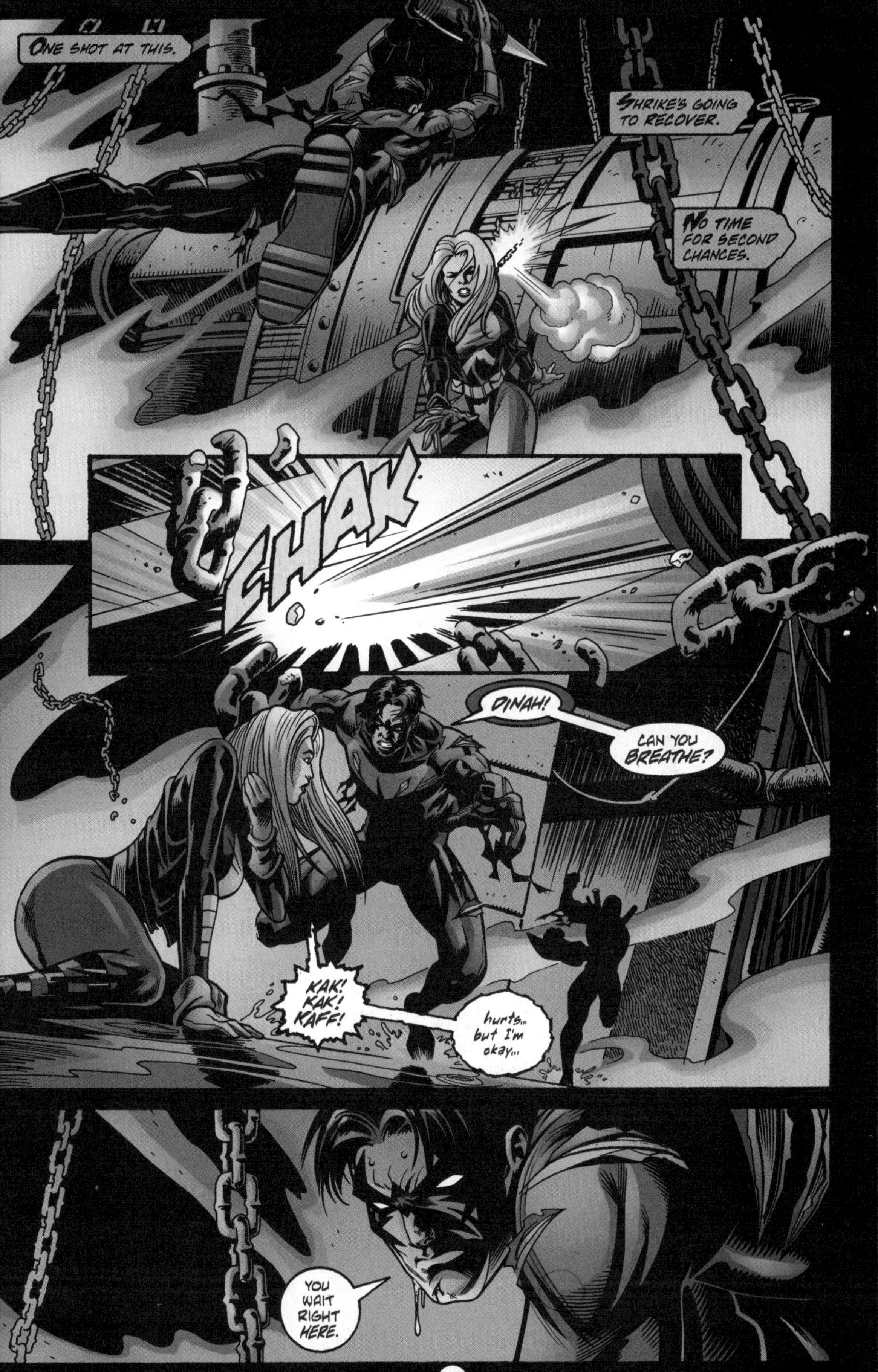

ONE SHOT AT THIS.
SHRIKE'S GOING TO RECOVER.
NO TIME FOR SECOND CHANCES.
CHAK
DINAH!
CAN YOU BREATHE?
KAK! KAK! KAFE!
hurts... but I'm okay...
YOU WAIT RIGHT HERE.

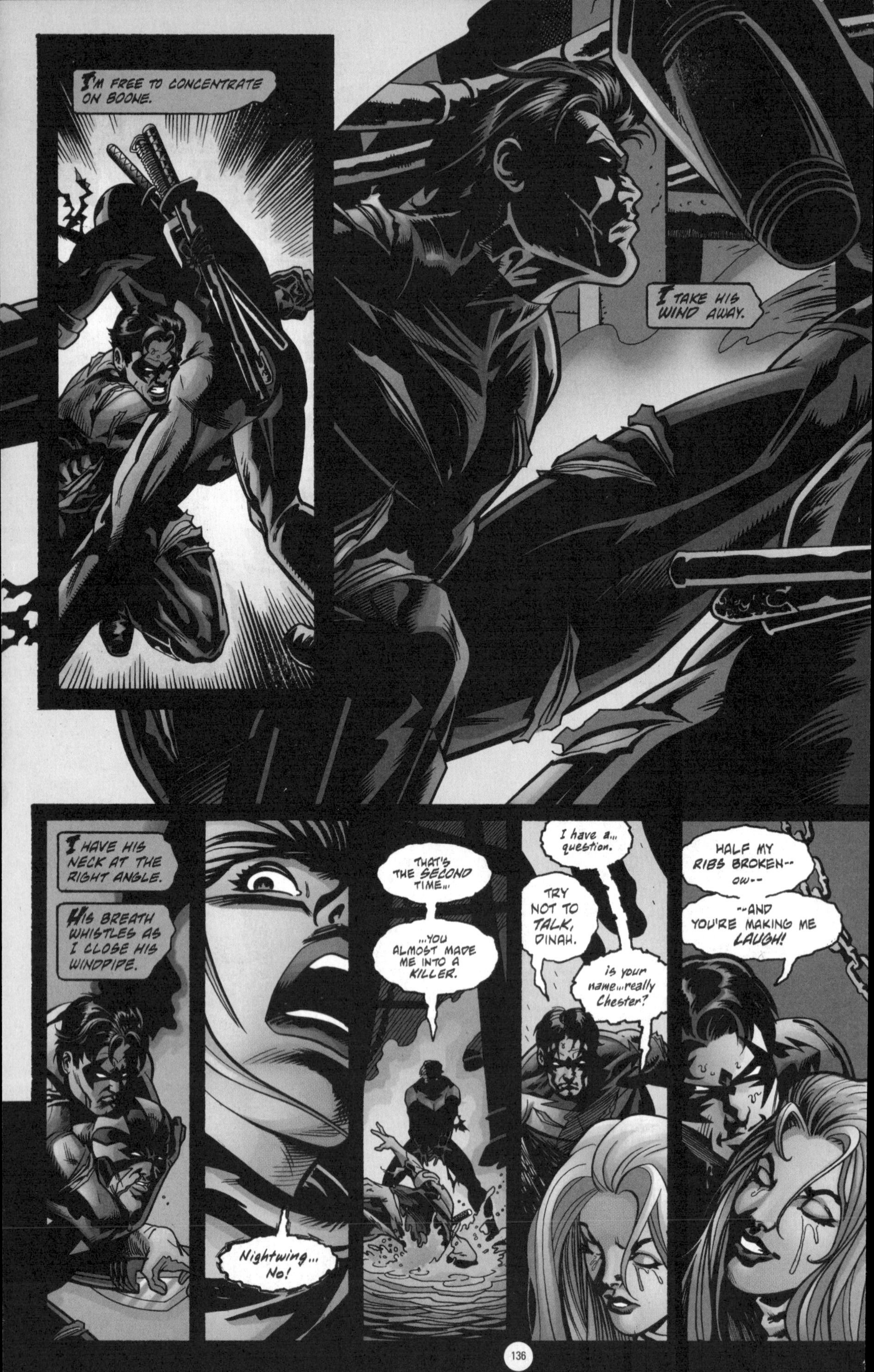
I'M FREE TO CONCENTRATE ON BOONE.
I TAKE HIS WIND AWAY.
I HAVE HIS NECK AT THE RIGHT ANGLE.
HIS BREATH WHISTLES AS I CLOSE HIS WINDPIPE.
Nightwing... No!
THAT'S THE SECOND TIME...
...YOU ALMOST MADE ME INTO A KILLER.
I have a... question.
TRY NOT TO TALK, DINAH.
is your name...really Chester?
HALF MY RIBS BROKEN-- OW--
--AND YOU'RE MAKING ME LAUGH!

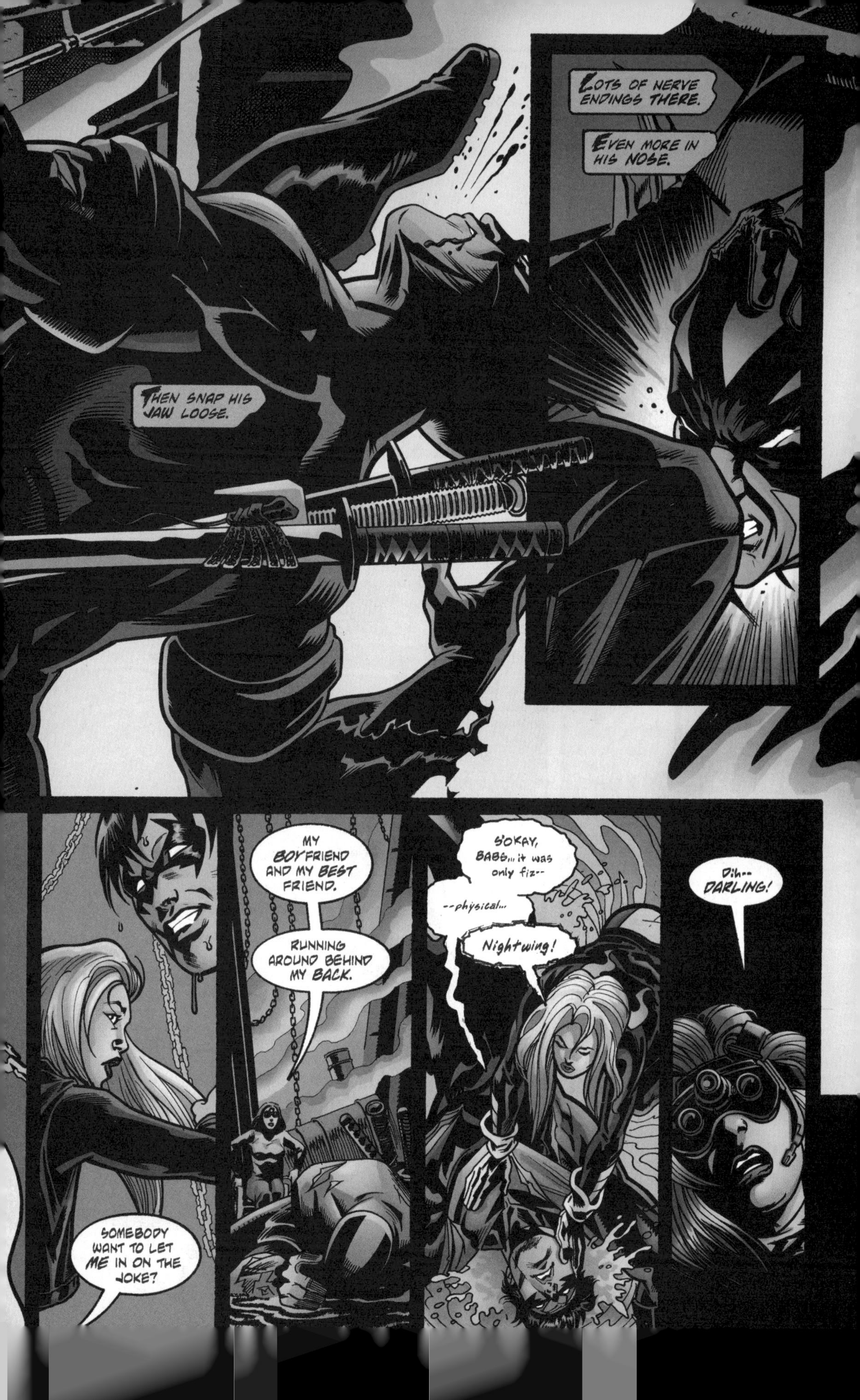

LOTS OF NERVE ENDINGS THERE.
EVEN MORE IN HIS NOSE.
THEN SNAP HIS JAW LOOSE.
SOMEBODY WANT TO LET ME IN ON THE JOKE?
MY BOYFRIEND AND MY BEST FRIEND.
RUNNING AROUND BEHIND MY BACK.
S'OKAY, BABS... it was only fiz--
--physical...
Nightwing!
Dih-- DARLING!

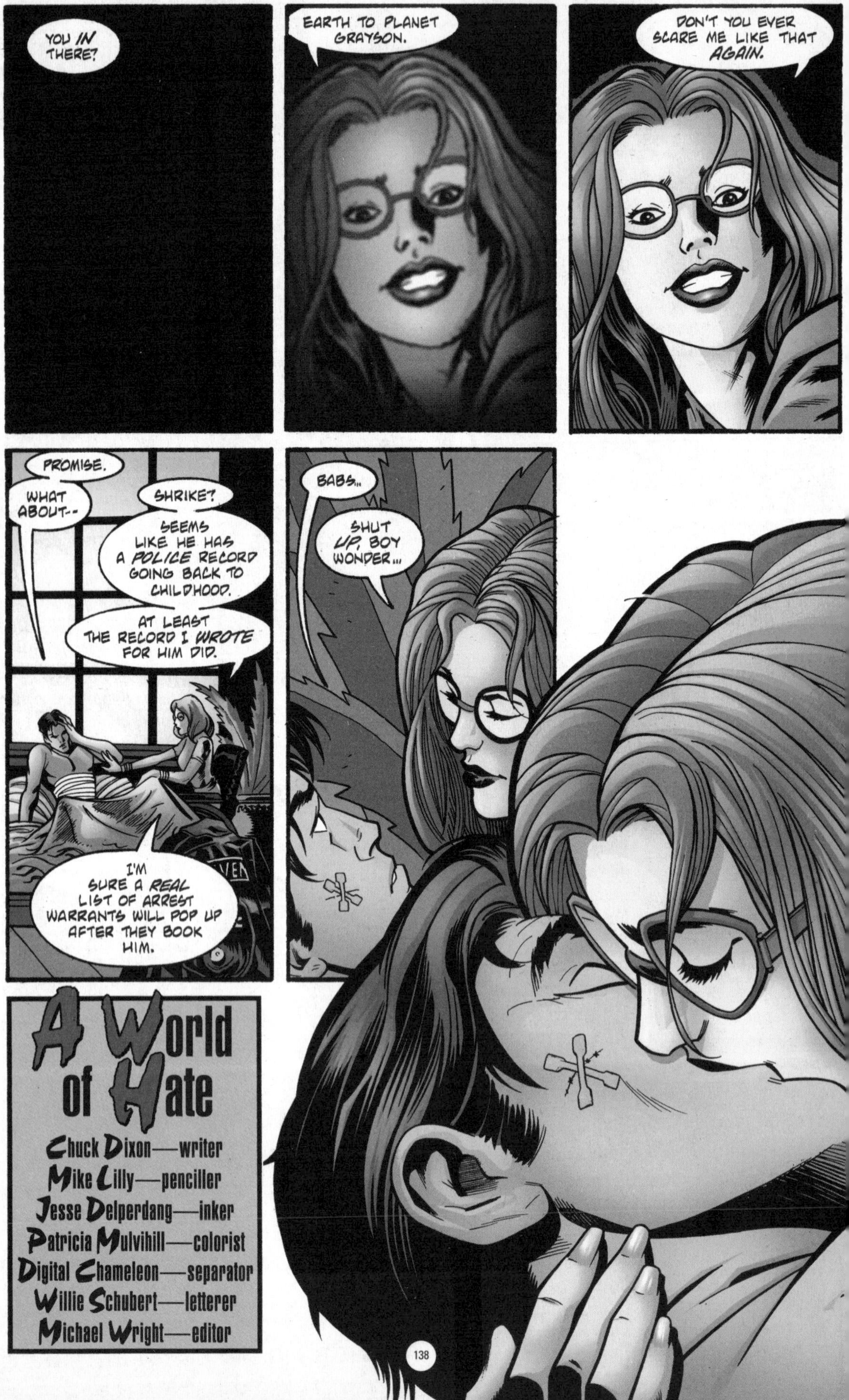

YOU IN THERE?
EARTH TO PLANET GRAYSON.
DON'T YOU EVER SCARE ME LIKE THAT AGAIN.
PROMISE.
WHAT ABOUT--
SHRIKE?
SEEMS LIKE HE HAS A POLICE RECORD GOING BACK TO CHILDHOOD.
AT LEAST THE RECORD I WROTE FOR HIM DID.
I'M SURE A REAL LIST OF ARREST WARRANTS WILL POP UP AFTER THEY BOOK HIM.
BABS...
SHUT UP, BOY WONDER...
A World of Hate
Chuck Dixon—writer
Mike Lilly—penciller
Jesse Delperdang—inker
Patricia Mulvihill—colorist
Digital Chameleon—separator
Willie Schubert—letterer
Michael Wright—editor

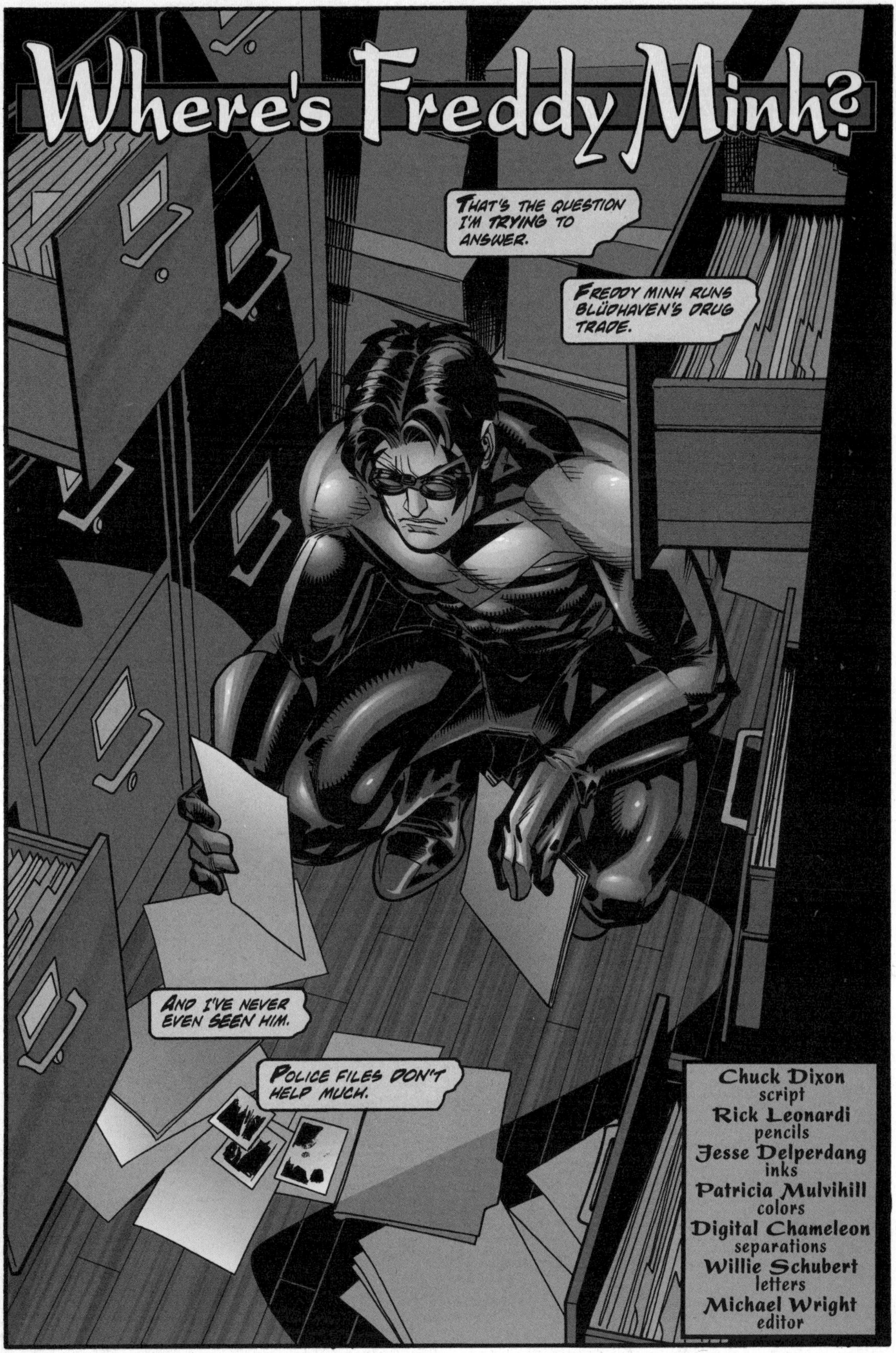
Where's Freddy Minh?
THAT'S THE QUESTION I'M TRYING TO ANSWER.
FREDDY MINH RUNS BLÜDHAVEN'S DRUG TRADE.
AND I'VE NEVER EVEN SEEN HIM.
POLICE FILES DON'T HELP MUCH.
Chuck Dixon script
Rick Leonardi pencils
Jesse Delperdang inks
Patricia Mulvihill colors
Digital Chameleon separations
Willie Schubert letters
Michael Wright editor

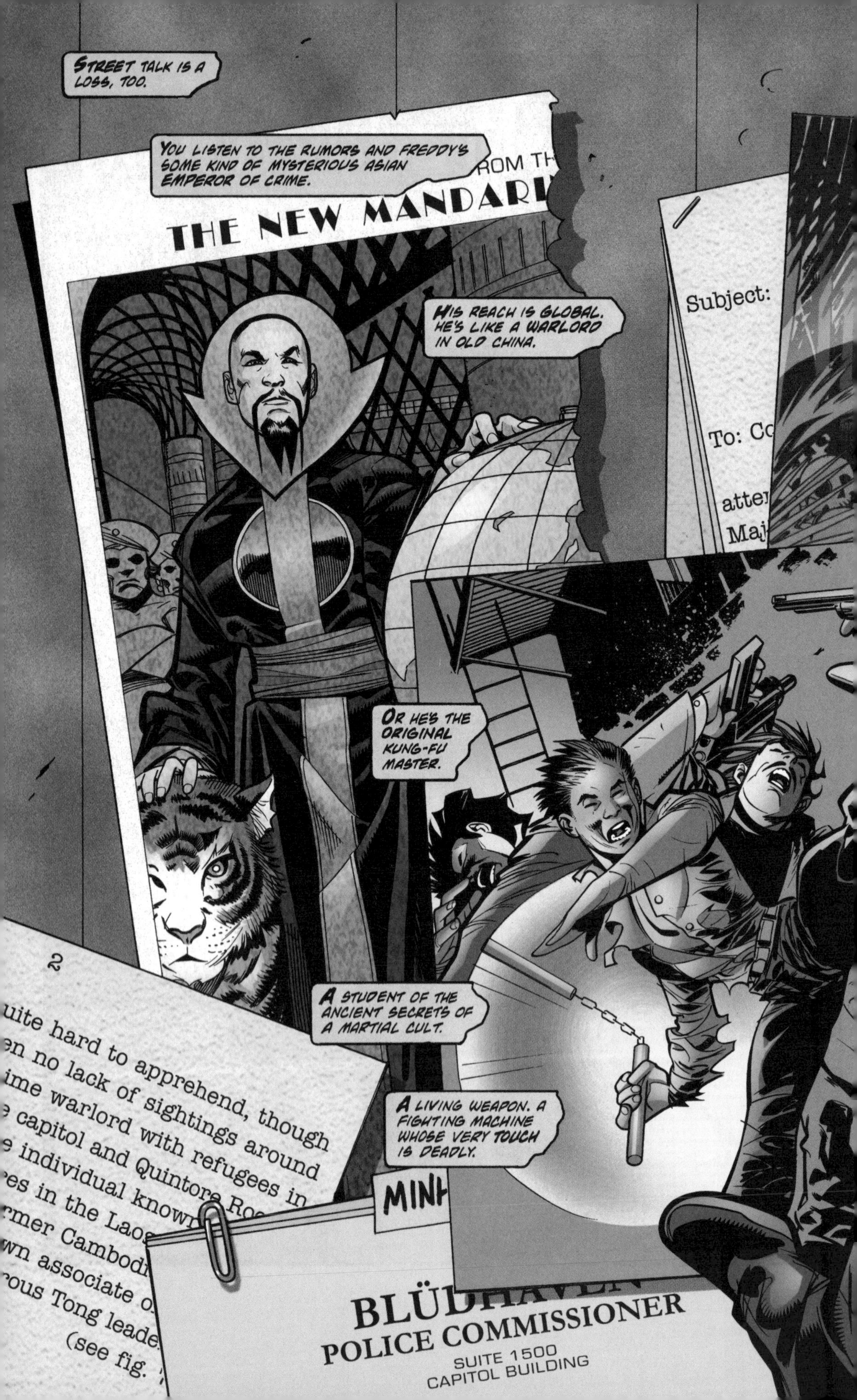
STREET TALK IS A LOSS, TOO.
YOU LISTEN TO THE RUMORS AND FREDDY'S SOME KIND OF MYSTERIOUS ASIAN EMPEROR OF CRIME.
ROM TH
THE NEW MANDARI
HIS REACH IS GLOBAL. HE'S LIKE A WARLORD IN OLD CHINA.
Subject:
To: Co
atter
Maj
OR HE'S THE ORIGINAL KUNG-FU MASTER.
2
A STUDENT OF THE ANCIENT SECRETS OF A MARTIAL CULT.
uite hard to apprehend, though
en no lack of sightings around
ime warlord with refugees in
e capitol and Quintore Ro
e individual known
es in the Lao
rmer Cambod
wn associate o
ous Tong leade
(see fig.
A LIVING WEAPON. A FIGHTING MACHINE WHOSE VERY TOUCH IS DEADLY.
MINH
BLÜDHAVEN
POLICE COMMISSIONER
SUITE 1500
CAPITOL BUILDING

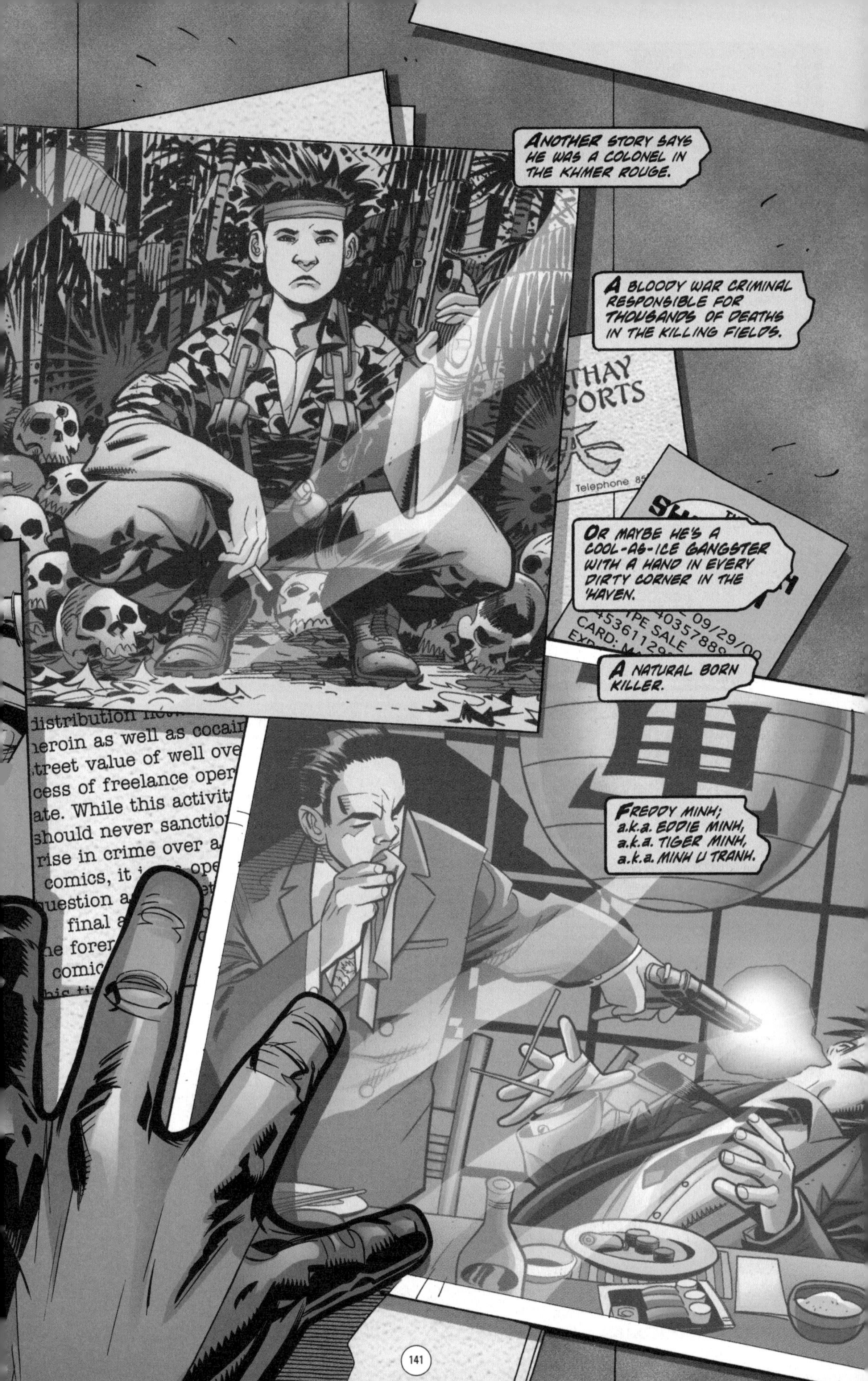
ANOTHER STORY SAYS HE WAS A COLONEL IN THE KHMER ROUGE.
A BLOODY WAR CRIMINAL RESPONSIBLE FOR THOUSANDS OF DEATHS IN THE KILLING FIELDS.
OR MAYBE HE'S A COOL-AS-ICE GANGSTER WITH A HAND IN EVERY DIRTY CORNER IN THE 'HAVEN.
A NATURAL BORN KILLER.
FREDDY MINH; a.k.a. EDDIE MINH, a.k.a. TIGER MINH, a.k.a. MINH U TRANH.

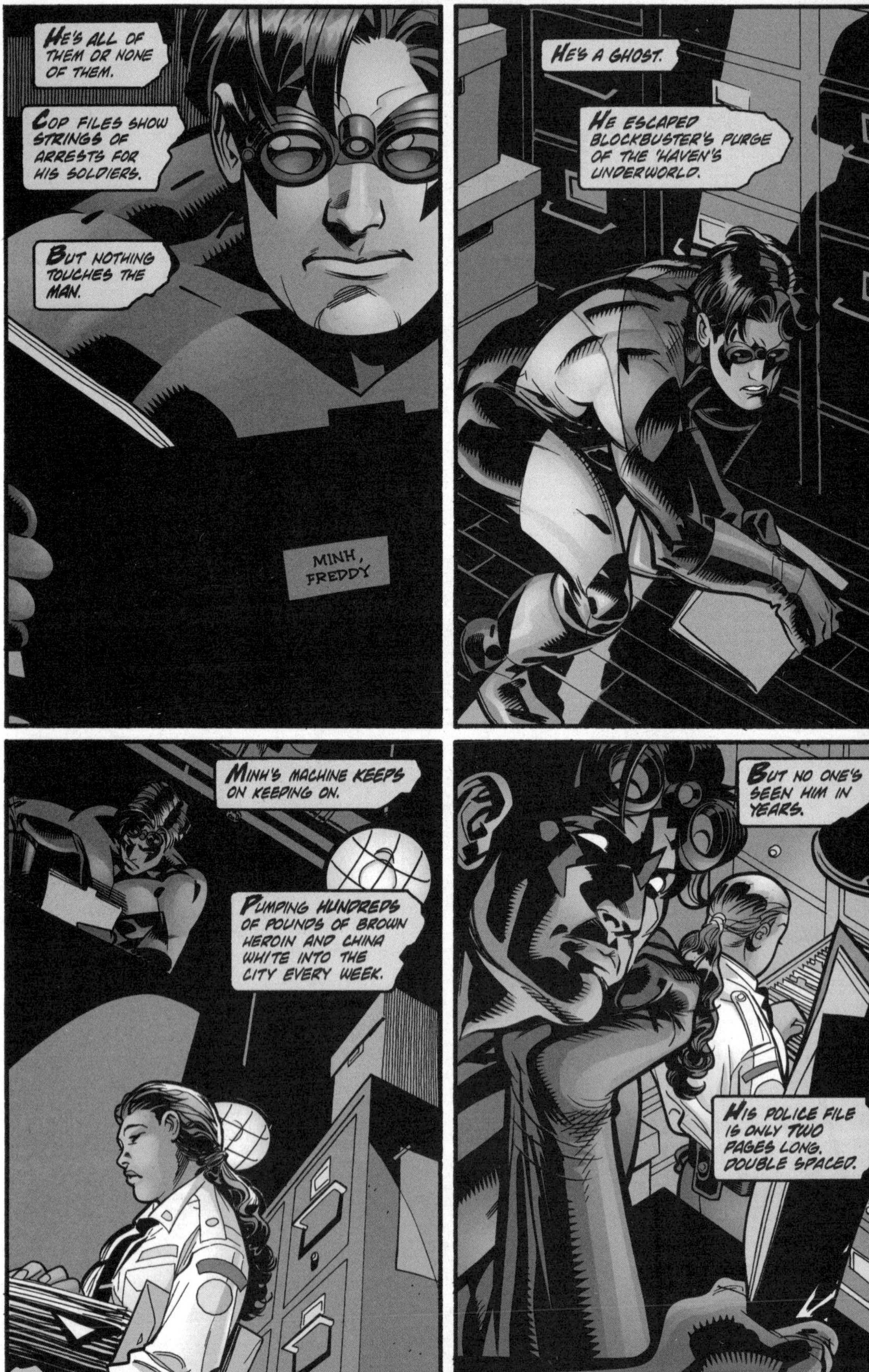
HE'S ALL OF THEM OR NONE OF THEM.
COP FILES SHOW STRINGS OF ARRESTS FOR HIS SOLDIERS.
BUT NOTHING TOUCHES THE MAN.
MINH, FREDDY
HE'S A GHOST.
HE ESCAPED BLOCKBUSTER'S PURGE OF THE 'HAVEN'S UNDERWORLD.
MINH'S MACHINE KEEPS ON KEEPING ON.
PUMPING HUNDREDS OF POUNDS OF BROWN HEROIN AND CHINA WHITE INTO THE CITY EVERY WEEK.
BUT NO ONE'S SEEN HIM IN YEARS.
HIS POLICE FILE IS ONLY TWO PAGES LONG. DOUBLE SPACED.
I'M GOING TO HAVE TO LOOK ELSEWHERE.

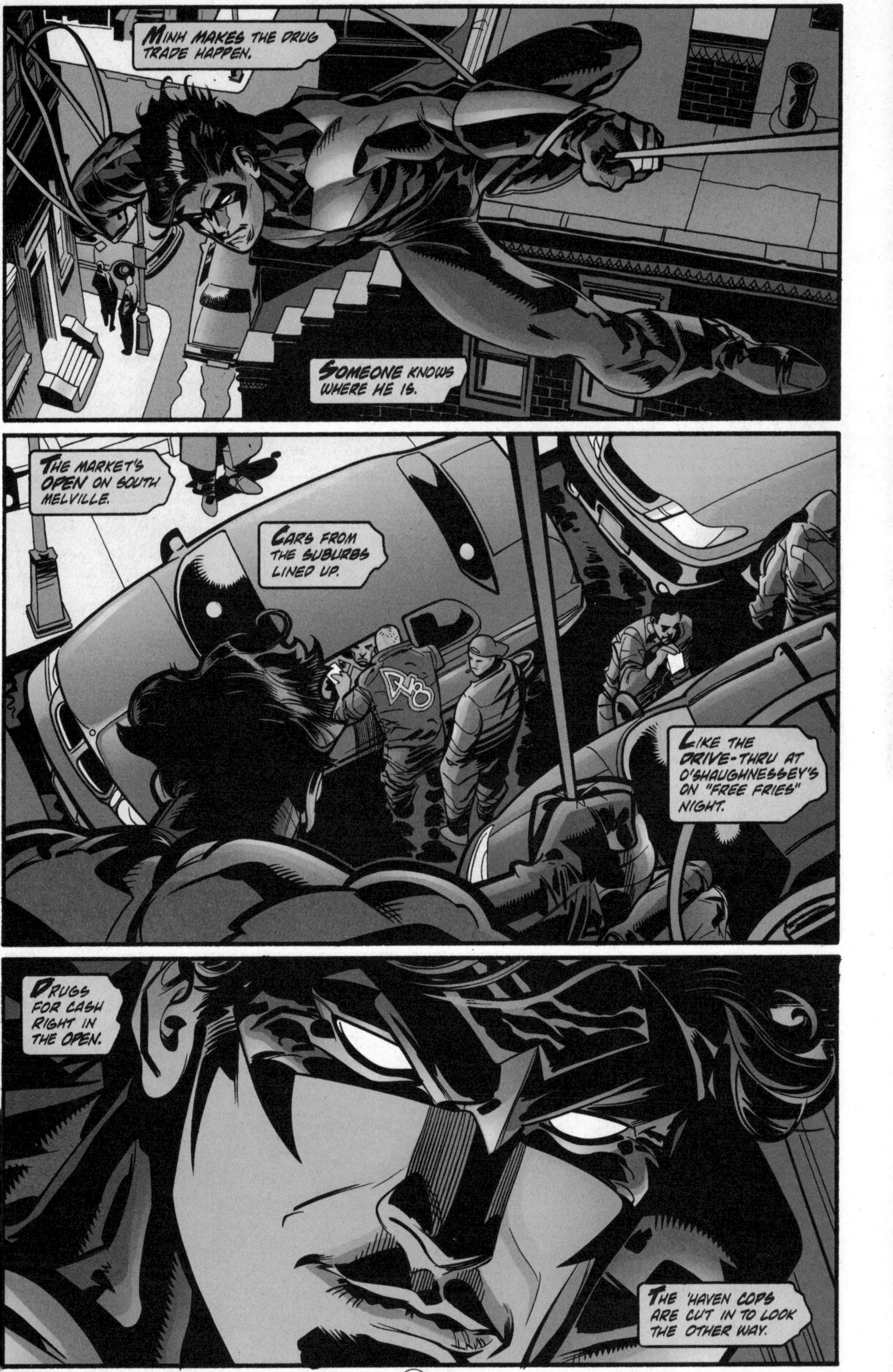
MINH MAKES THE DRUG TRADE HAPPEN.
SOMEONE KNOWS WHERE HE IS.
THE MARKET'S OPEN ON SOUTH MELVILLE.
CARS FROM THE SUBURBS LINED UP.
LIKE THE DRIVE-THRU AT O'SHAUGHNESSEY'S ON "FREE FRIES" NIGHT.
DRUGS FOR CASH RIGHT IN THE OPEN.
THE 'HAVEN COPS ARE CUT IN TO LOOK THE OTHER WAY.

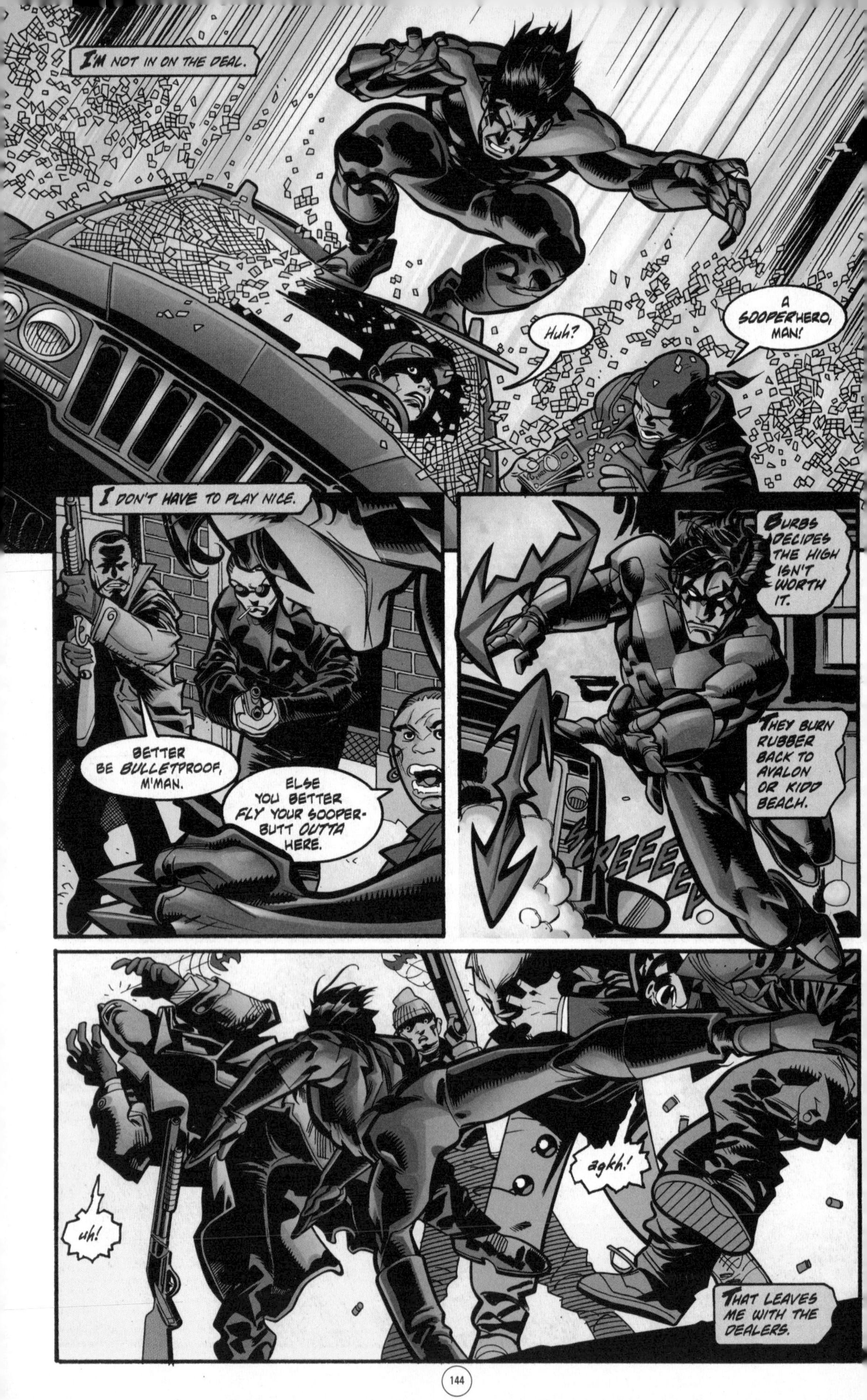
I'M NOT IN ON THE DEAL.
Huh?
A SOOPERHERO, MAN!
I DON'T HAVE TO PLAY NICE.
BETTER BE BULLETPROOF, M'MAN.
ELSE YOU BETTER FLY YOUR SOOPER-BUTT OUTTA HERE.
BURBS DECIDES THE HIGH ISN'T WORTH IT.
THEY BURN RUBBER BACK TO AVALON OR KIDD BEACH.
SCREEEEEP
uh!
agkh!
THAT LEAVES ME WITH THE DEALERS.

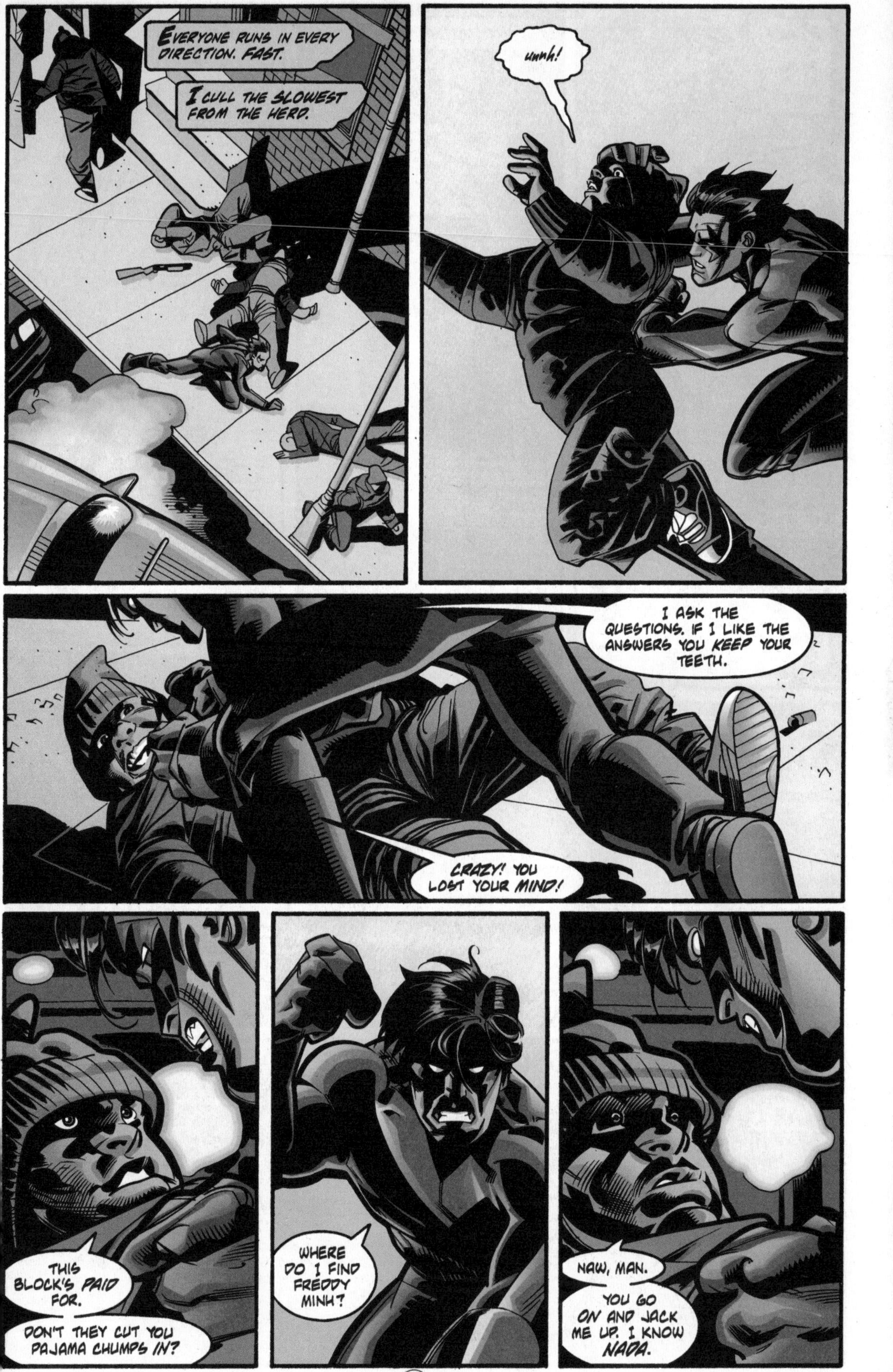

EVERYONE RUNS IN EVERY DIRECTION. FAST.
I CULL THE SLOWEST FROM THE HERD.
unnh!
I ASK THE QUESTIONS. IF I LIKE THE ANSWERS YOU KEEP YOUR TEETH.
CRAZY! YOU LOST YOUR MIND!
THIS BLOCK'S PAID FOR.
DON'T THEY CUT YOU PAJAMA CHUMPS IN?
WHERE DO I FIND FREDDY MINH?
NAW, MAN.
YOU GO ON AND JACK ME UP. I KNOW NADA.

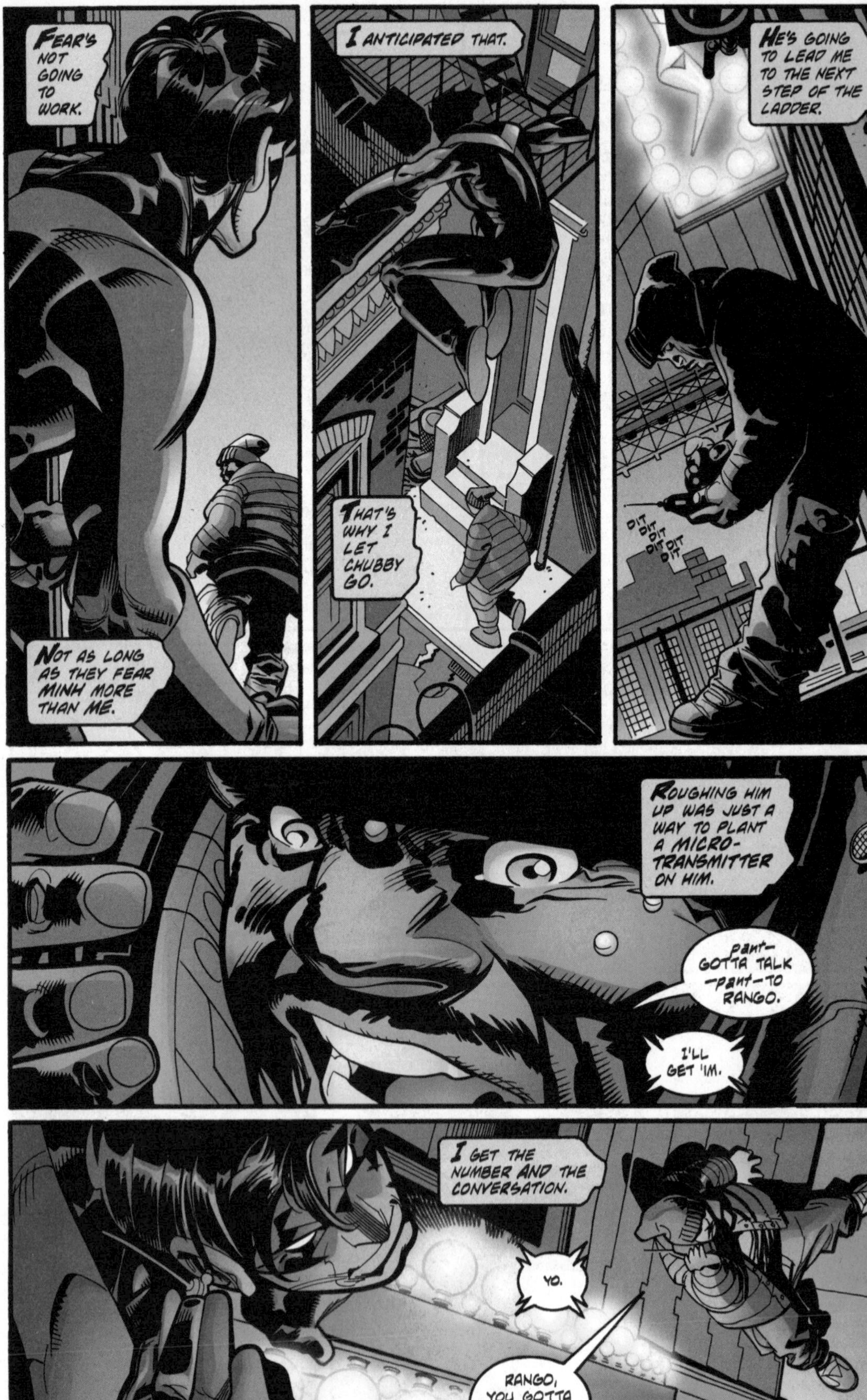
FEAR'S NOT GOING TO WORK.
NOT AS LONG AS THEY FEAR MINH MORE THAN ME.
I ANTICIPATED THAT.
THAT'S WHY I LET CHUBBY GO.
HE'S GOING TO LEAD ME TO THE NEXT STEP OF THE LADDER.
DIT DIT DIT DIT DIT DIT
ROUGHING HIM UP WAS JUST A WAY TO PLANT A MICRO-TRANSMITTER ON HIM.
-pant- GOTTA TALK -pant- TO RANGO.
I'LL GET 'IM.
I GET THE NUMBER AND THE CONVERSATION.
YO.
RANGO, YOU GOTTA LISTEN T'ME--

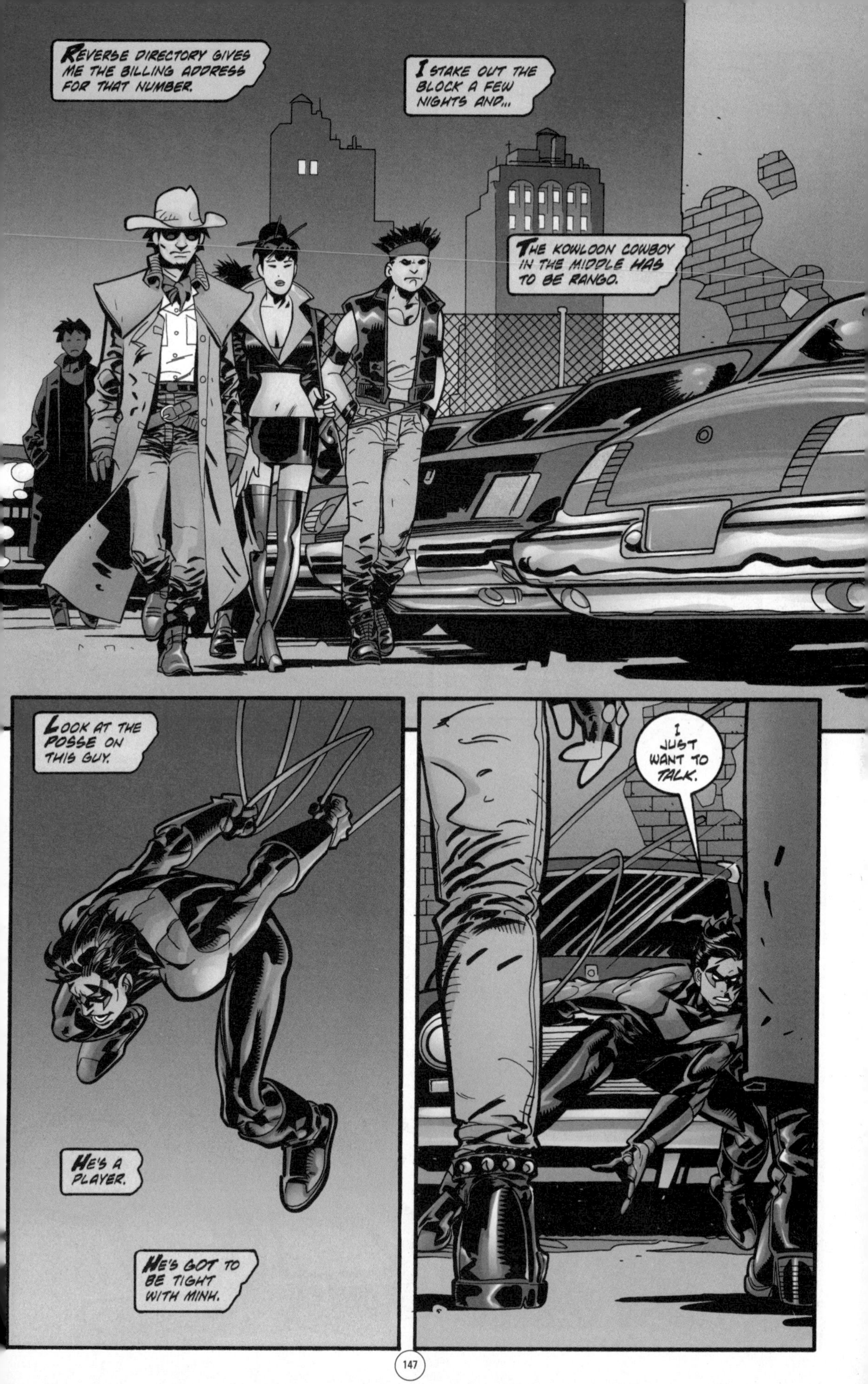
REVERSE DIRECTORY GIVES ME THE BILLING ADDRESS FOR THAT NUMBER.
I STAKE OUT THE BLOCK A FEW NIGHTS AND...
THE KOWLOON COWBOY IN THE MIDDLE HAS TO BE RANGO.
LOOK AT THE POSSE ON THIS GUY.
HE'S A PLAYER.
HE'S GOT TO BE TIGHT WITH MINH.
I JUST WANT TO TALK.

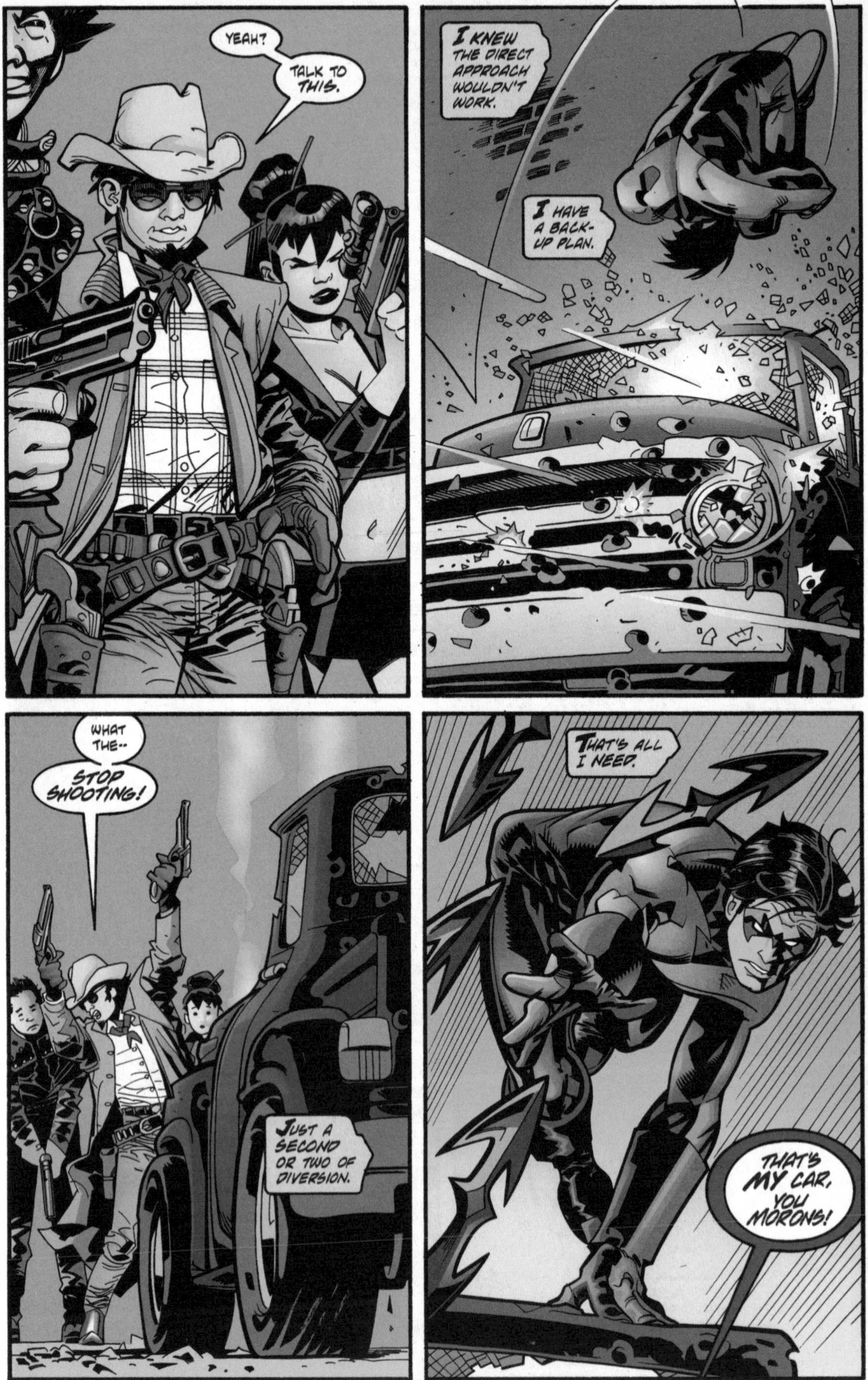
YEAH?
TALK TO THIS.
I KNEW THE DIRECT APPROACH WOULDN'T WORK.
I HAVE A BACK-UP PLAN.
WHAT THE--
STOP SHOOTING!
JUST A SECOND OR TWO OF DIVERSION.
THAT'S ALL I NEED.
THAT'S MY CAR, YOU MORONS!

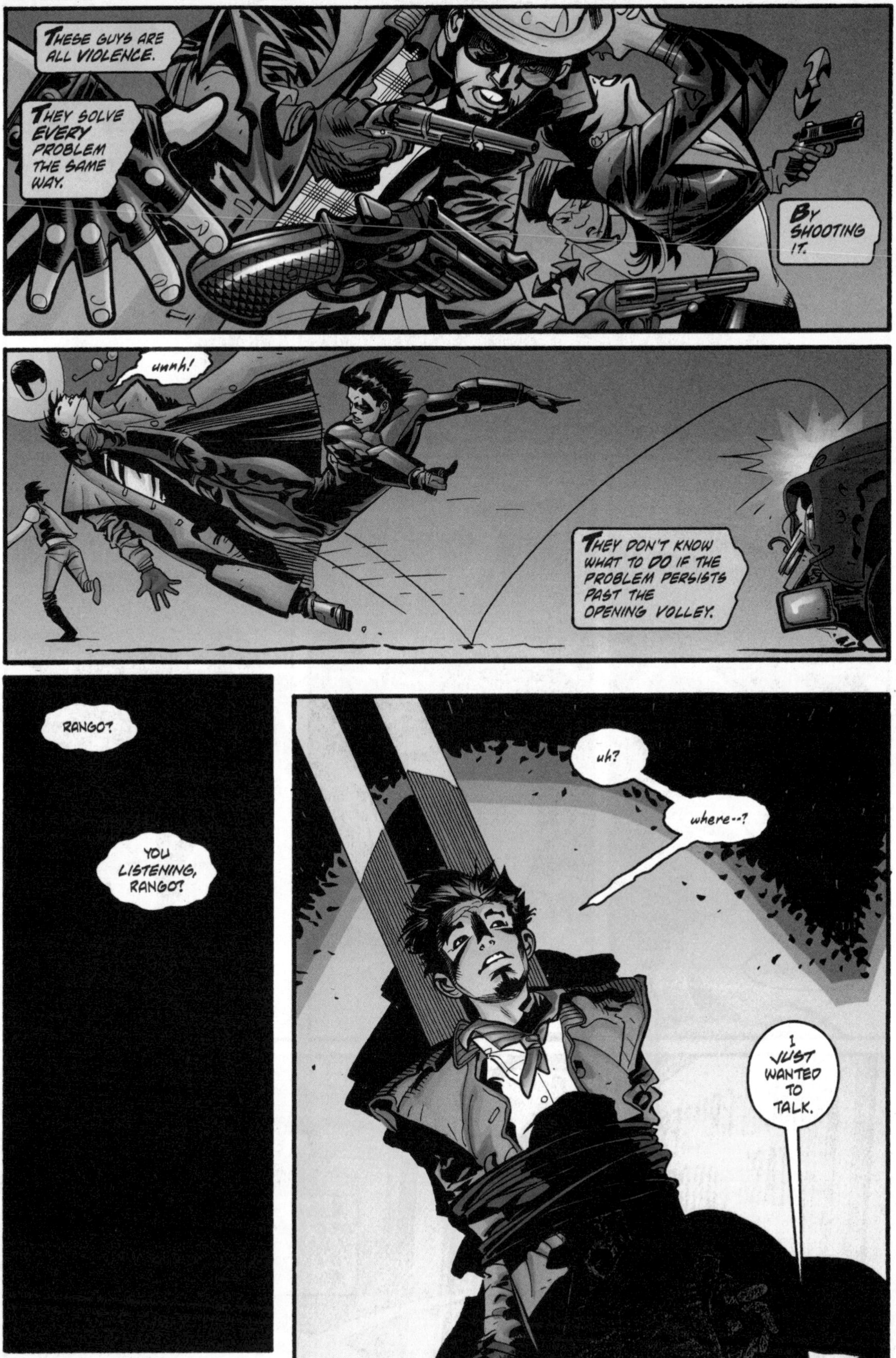
THESE GUYS ARE ALL VIOLENCE.
THEY SOLVE EVERY PROBLEM THE SAME WAY.
BY SHOOTING IT.
unnh!
THEY DON'T KNOW WHAT TO DO IF THE PROBLEM PERSISTS PAST THE OPENING VOLLEY.
RANGO?
YOU LISTENING, RANGO?
uh?
where--?
I JUST WANTED TO TALK.

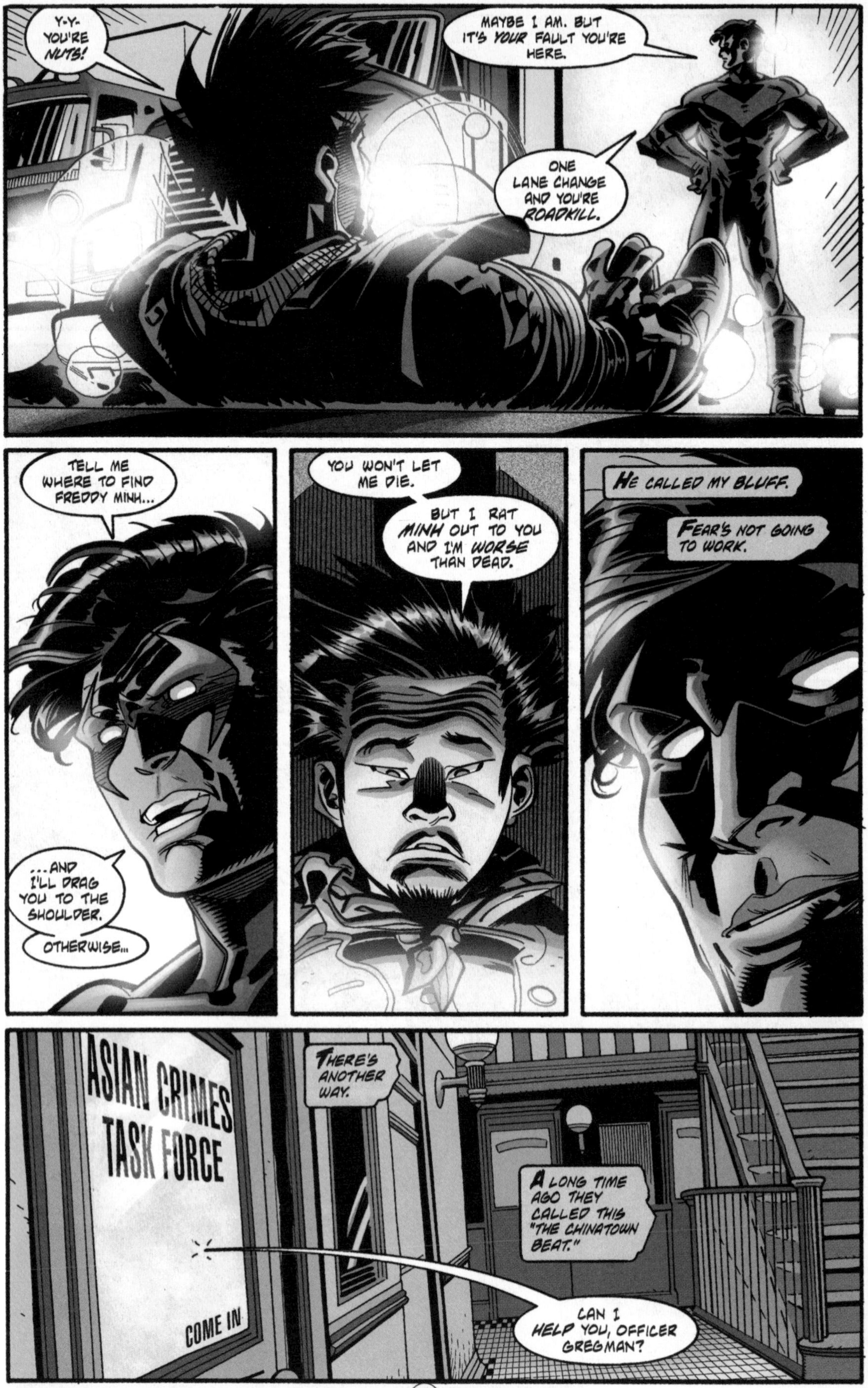
Y-Y-YOU'RE NUTS!
MAYBE I AM. BUT IT'S YOUR FAULT YOU'RE HERE.
ONE LANE CHANGE AND YOU'RE ROADKILL.
TELL ME WHERE TO FIND FREDDY MINH...
...AND I'LL DRAG YOU TO THE SHOULDER.
OTHERWISE...
YOU WON'T LET ME DIE.
BUT I RAT MINH OUT TO YOU AND I'M WORSE THAN DEAD.
HE CALLED MY BLUFF.
FEAR'S NOT GOING TO WORK.
ASIAN CRIMES TASK FORCE
COME IN
THERE'S ANOTHER WAY.
A LONG TIME AGO THEY CALLED THIS "THE CHINATOWN BEAT."
CAN I HELP YOU, OFFICER GREGMAN?

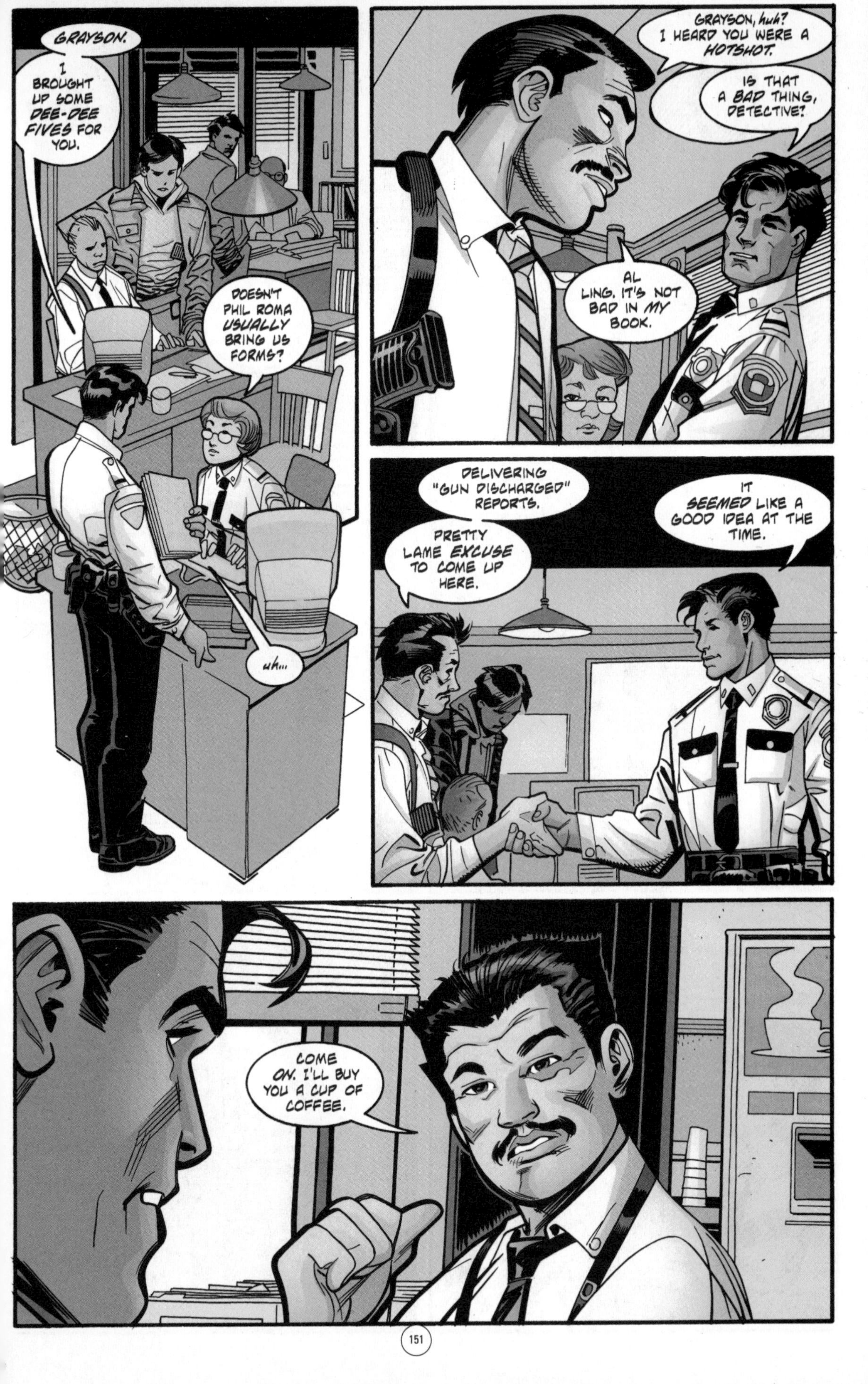
GRAYSON.
I BROUGHT UP SOME DEE-DEE FIVES FOR YOU.
DOESN'T PHIL ROMA USUALLY BRING US FORMS?
uh...
GRAYSON, huh? I HEARD YOU WERE A HOTSHOT.
IS THAT A BAD THING, DETECTIVE?
AL LING. IT'S NOT BAD IN MY BOOK.
DELIVERING "GUN DISCHARGED" REPORTS.
PRETTY LAME EXCUSE TO COME UP HERE.
IT SEEMED LIKE A GOOD IDEA AT THE TIME.
COME ON. I'LL BUY YOU A CUP OF COFFEE.

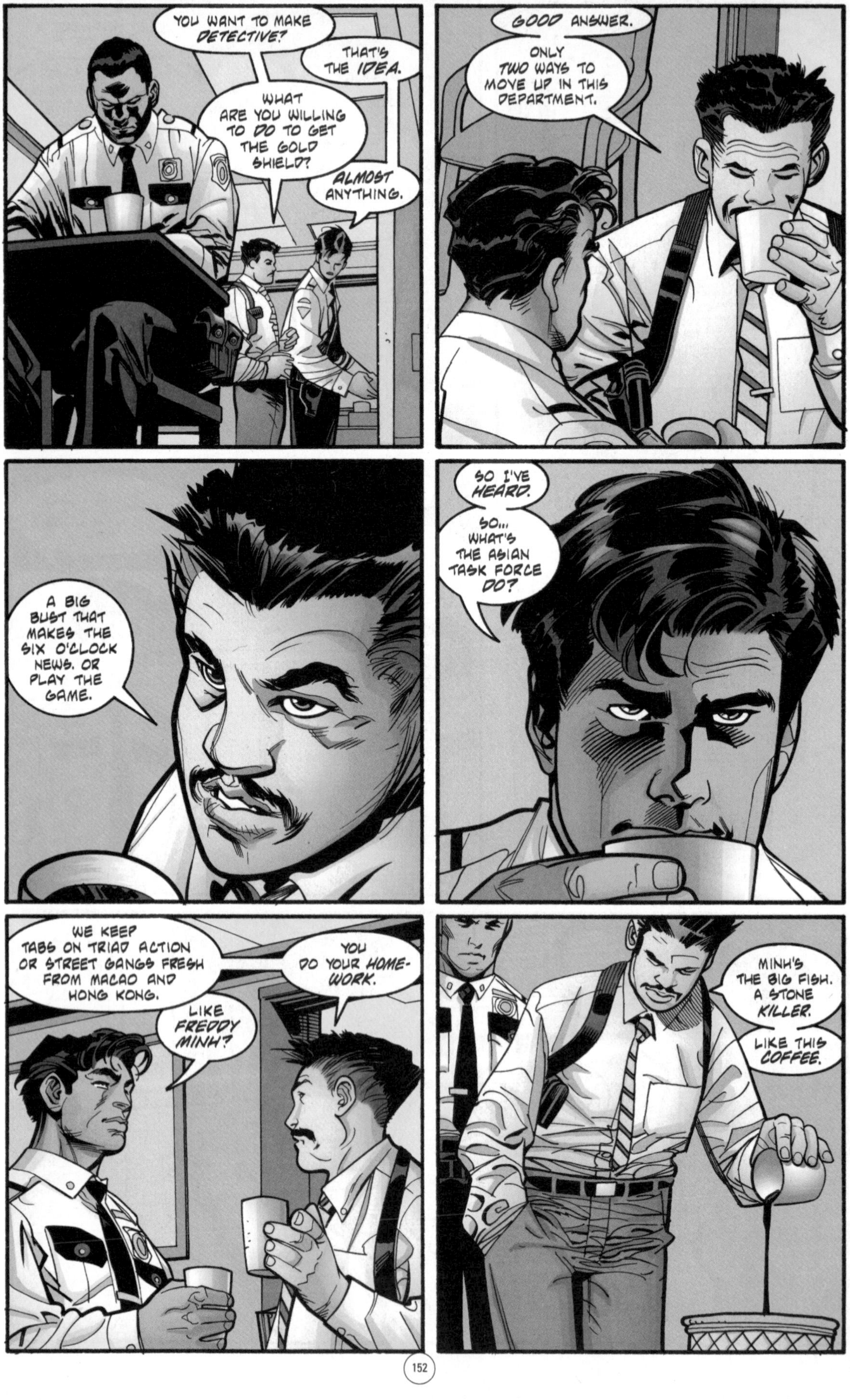
YOU WANT TO MAKE DETECTIVE?
THAT'S THE IDEA.
WHAT ARE YOU WILLING TO DO TO GET THE GOLD SHIELD?
ALMOST ANYTHING.
GOOD ANSWER.
ONLY TWO WAYS TO MOVE UP IN THIS DEPARTMENT.
A BIG BUST THAT MAKES THE SIX O'CLOCK NEWS. OR PLAY THE GAME.
SO I'VE HEARD.
SO... WHAT'S THE ASIAN TASK FORCE DO?
WE KEEP TABS ON TRIAD ACTION OR STREET GANGS FRESH FROM MACAO AND HONG KONG.
LIKE FREDDY MINH?
YOU DO YOUR HOMEWORK.
MINH'S THE BIG FISH. A STONE KILLER.
LIKE THIS COFFEE.

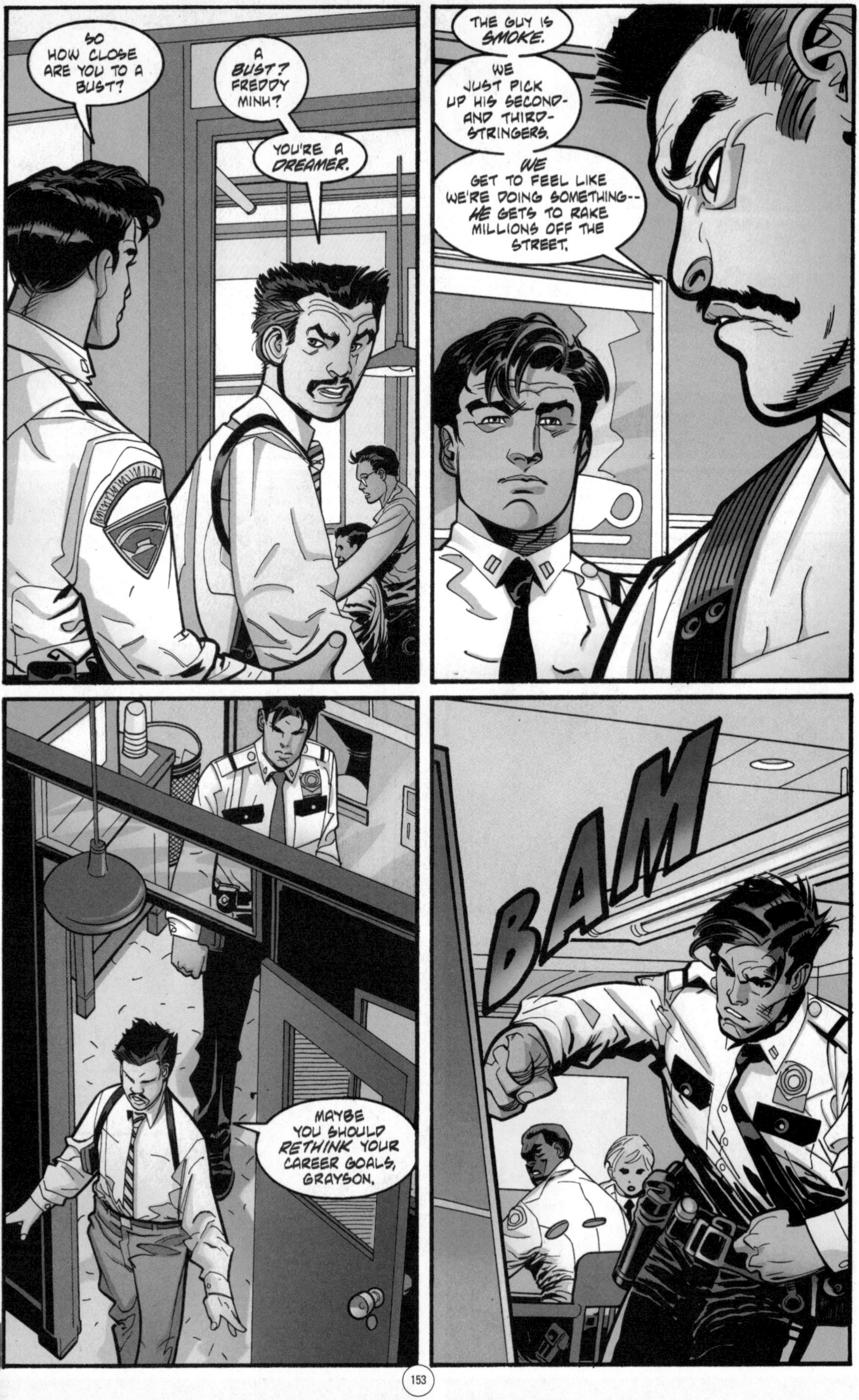
SO HOW CLOSE ARE YOU TO A BUST?
A BUST? FREDDY MINH?
YOU'RE A DREAMER.
THE GUY IS SMOKE.
WE JUST PICK UP HIS SECOND- AND THIRD-STRINGERS.
WE GET TO FEEL LIKE WE'RE DOING SOMETHING-- HE GETS TO RAKE MILLIONS OFF THE STREET.
MAYBE YOU SHOULD RETHINK YOUR CAREER GOALS, GRAYSON.
BAM

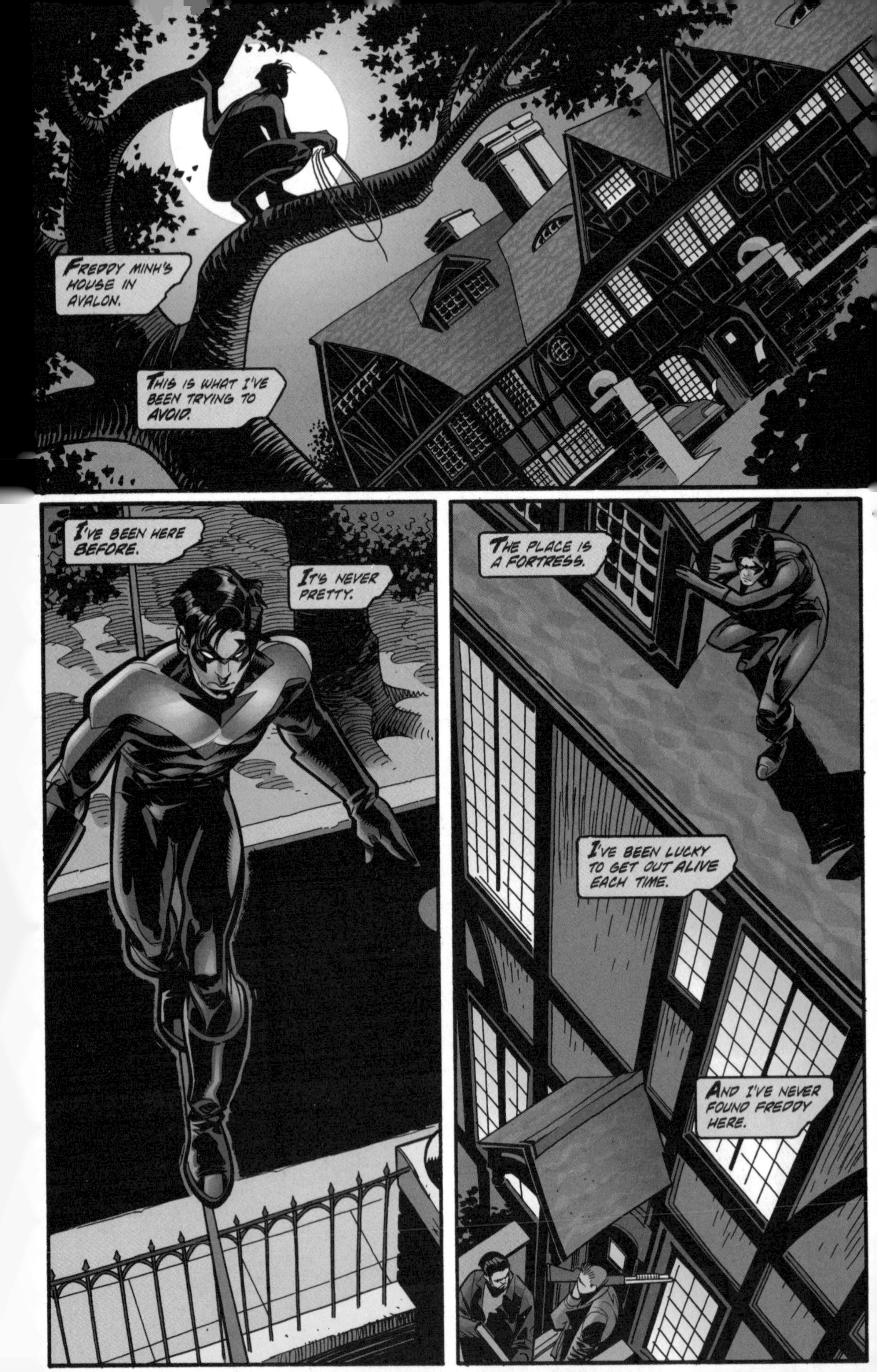
FREDDY MINH'S HOUSE IN AVALON.
THIS IS WHAT I'VE BEEN TRYING TO AVOID.
I'VE BEEN HERE BEFORE.
IT'S NEVER PRETTY.
THE PLACE IS A FORTRESS.
I'VE BEEN LUCKY TO GET OUT ALIVE EACH TIME.
AND I'VE NEVER FOUND FREDDY HERE.

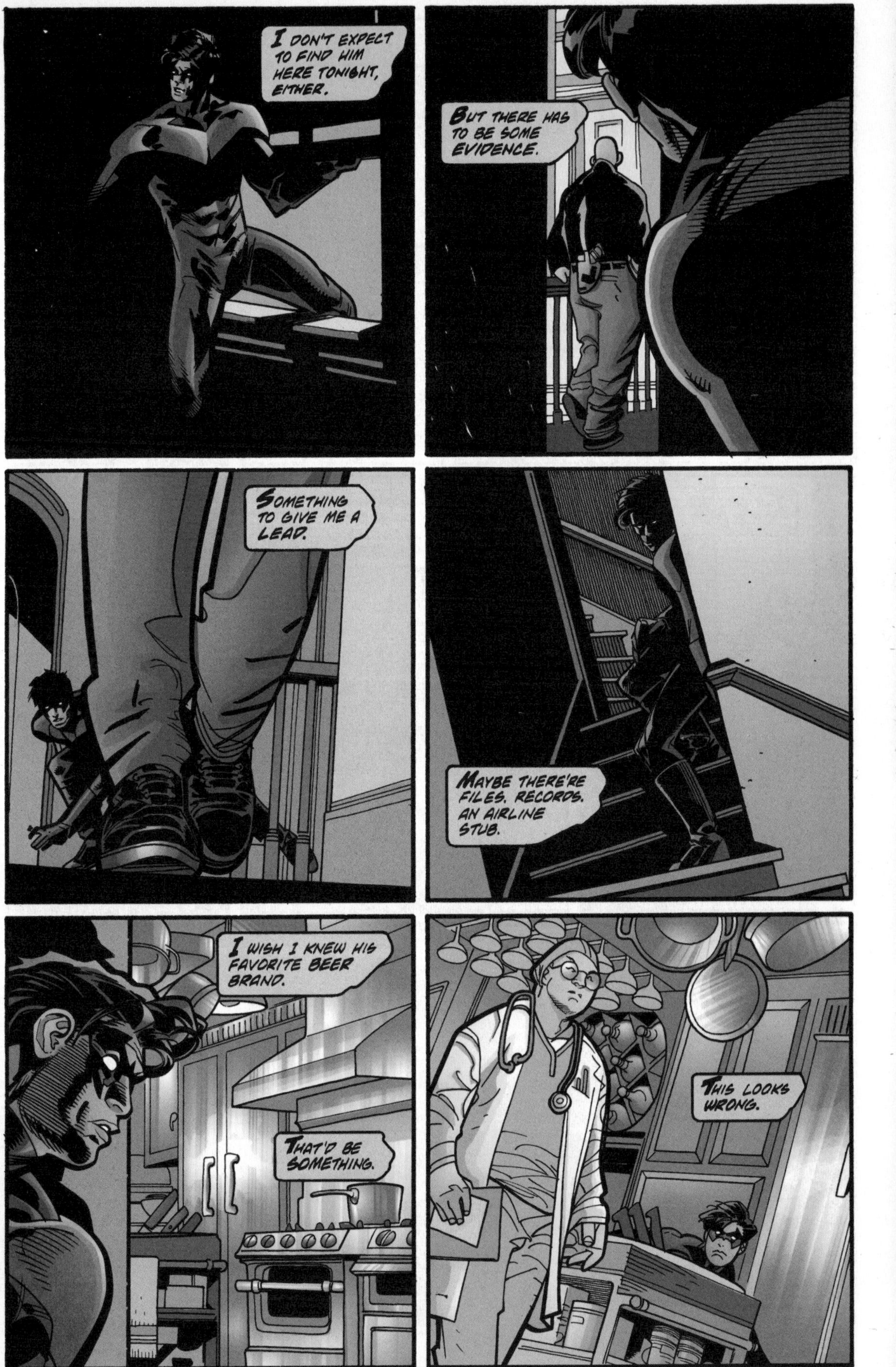
I DON'T EXPECT TO FIND HIM HERE TONIGHT, EITHER.
BUT THERE HAS TO BE SOME EVIDENCE.
SOMETHING TO GIVE ME A LEAD.
MAYBE THERE'RE FILES. RECORDS. AN AIRLINE STUB.
I WISH I KNEW HIS FAVORITE BEER BRAND.
THAT'D BE SOMETHING.
THIS LOOKS WRONG.

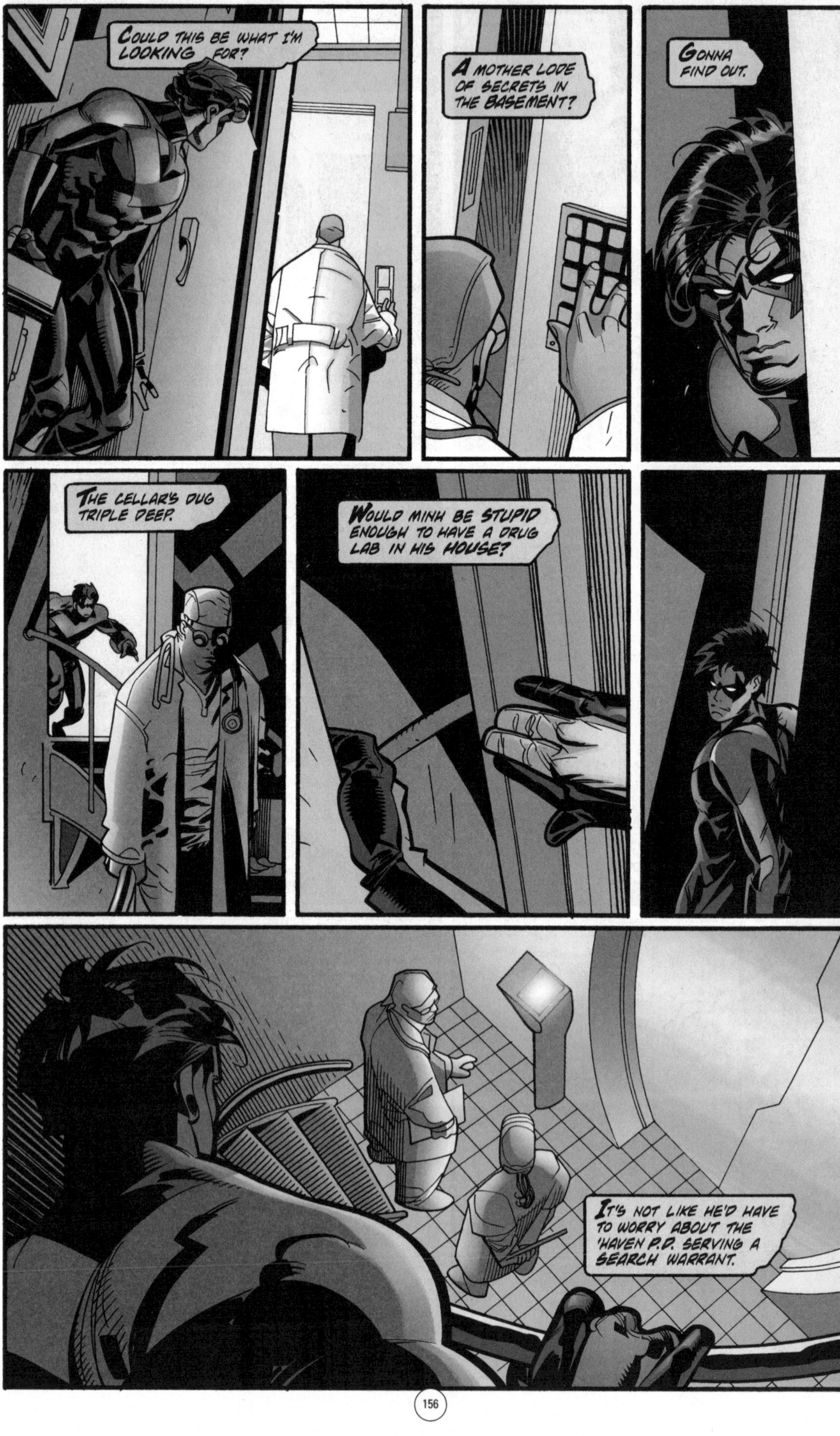
COULD THIS BE WHAT I'M LOOKING FOR?
A MOTHER LODE OF SECRETS IN THE BASEMENT?
GONNA FIND OUT.
THE CELLAR'S DUG TRIPLE DEEP.
WOULD MINH BE STUPID ENOUGH TO HAVE A DRUG LAB IN HIS HOUSE?
IT'S NOT LIKE HE'D HAVE TO WORRY ABOUT THE 'HAVEN P.D. SERVING A SEARCH WARRANT.

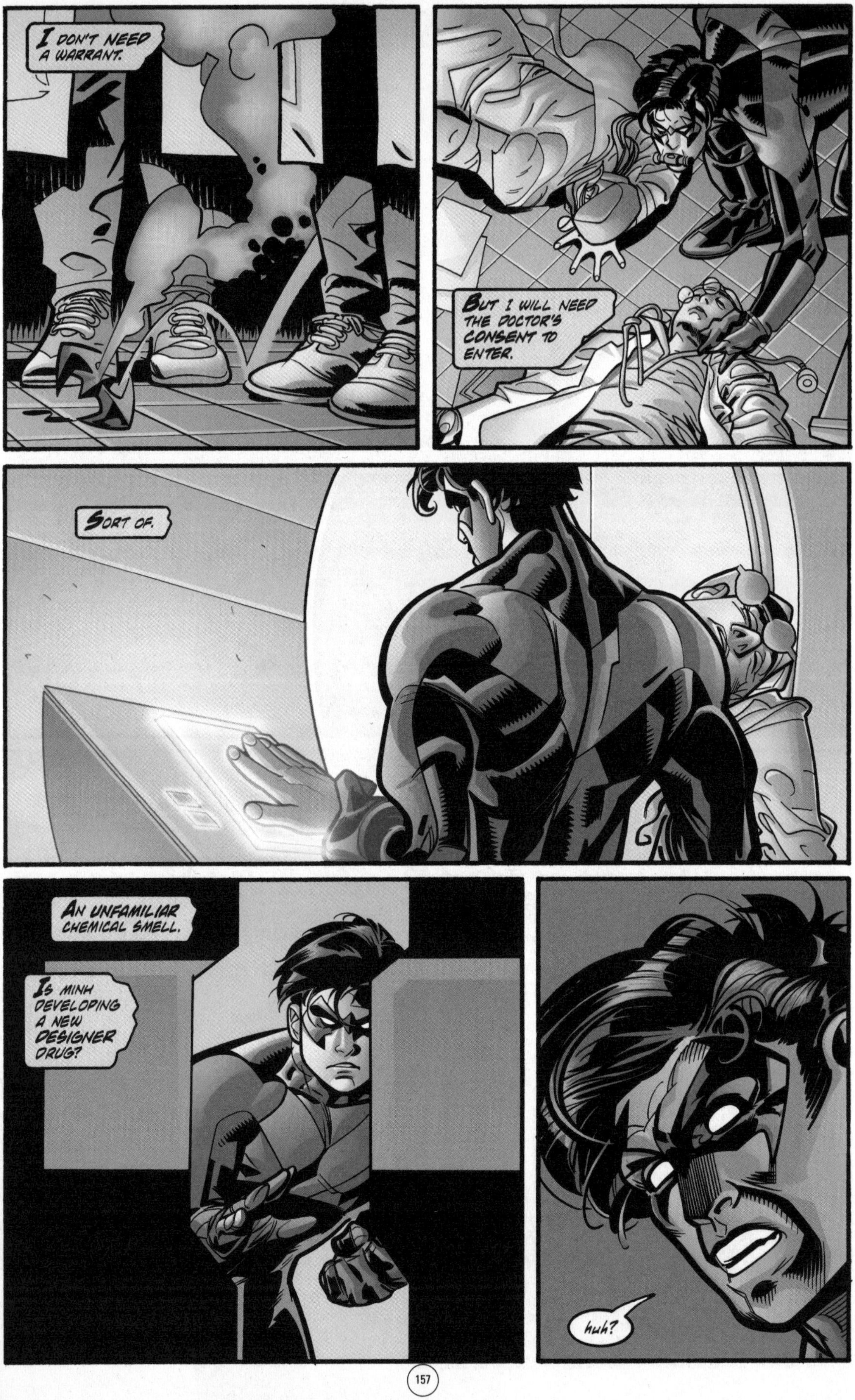
I DON'T NEED A WARRANT.
BUT I WILL NEED THE DOCTOR'S CONSENT TO ENTER.
SORT OF.
AN UNFAMILIAR CHEMICAL SMELL.
IS MINH DEVELOPING A NEW DESIGNER DRUG?
huh?

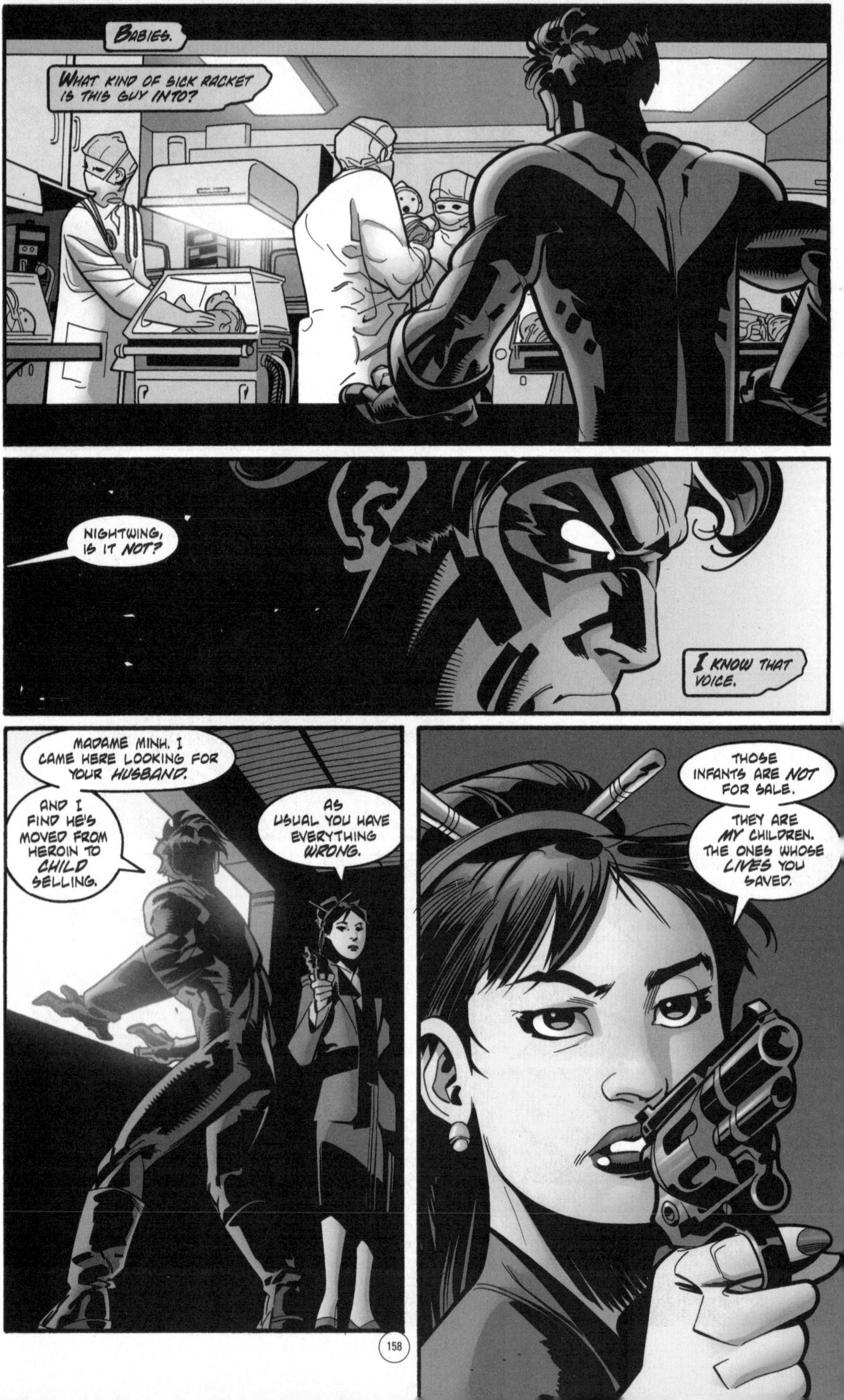
BABIES.
WHAT KIND OF SICK RACKET IS THIS GUY INTO?
NIGHTWING, IS IT NOT?
I KNOW THAT VOICE.
MADAME MINH. I CAME HERE LOOKING FOR YOUR HUSBAND.
AND I FIND HE'S MOVED FROM HEROIN TO CHILD SELLING.
AS USUAL YOU HAVE EVERYTHING WRONG.
THOSE INFANTS ARE NOT FOR SALE.
THEY ARE MY CHILDREN. THE ONES WHOSE LIVES YOU SAVED.

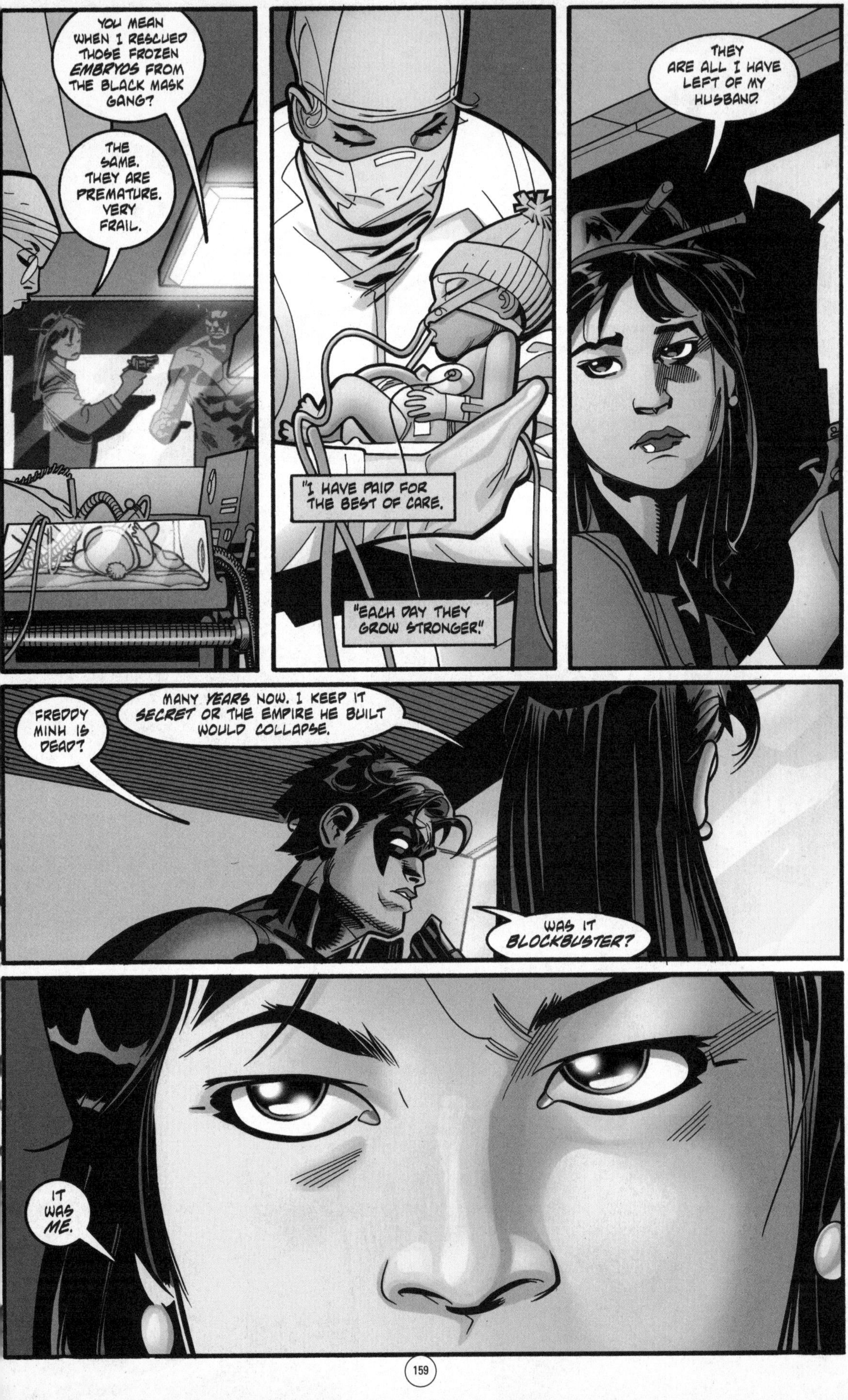
YOU MEAN WHEN I RESCUED THOSE FROZEN EMBRYOS FROM THE BLACK MASK GANG?
THE SAME. THEY ARE PREMATURE. VERY FRAIL.
"I HAVE PAID FOR THE BEST OF CARE.
"EACH DAY THEY GROW STRONGER."
THEY ARE ALL I HAVE LEFT OF MY HUSBAND.
FREDDY MINH IS DEAD?
MANY YEARS NOW. I KEEP IT SECRET OR THE EMPIRE HE BUILT WOULD COLLAPSE.
WAS IT BLOCKBUSTER?
IT WAS ME.

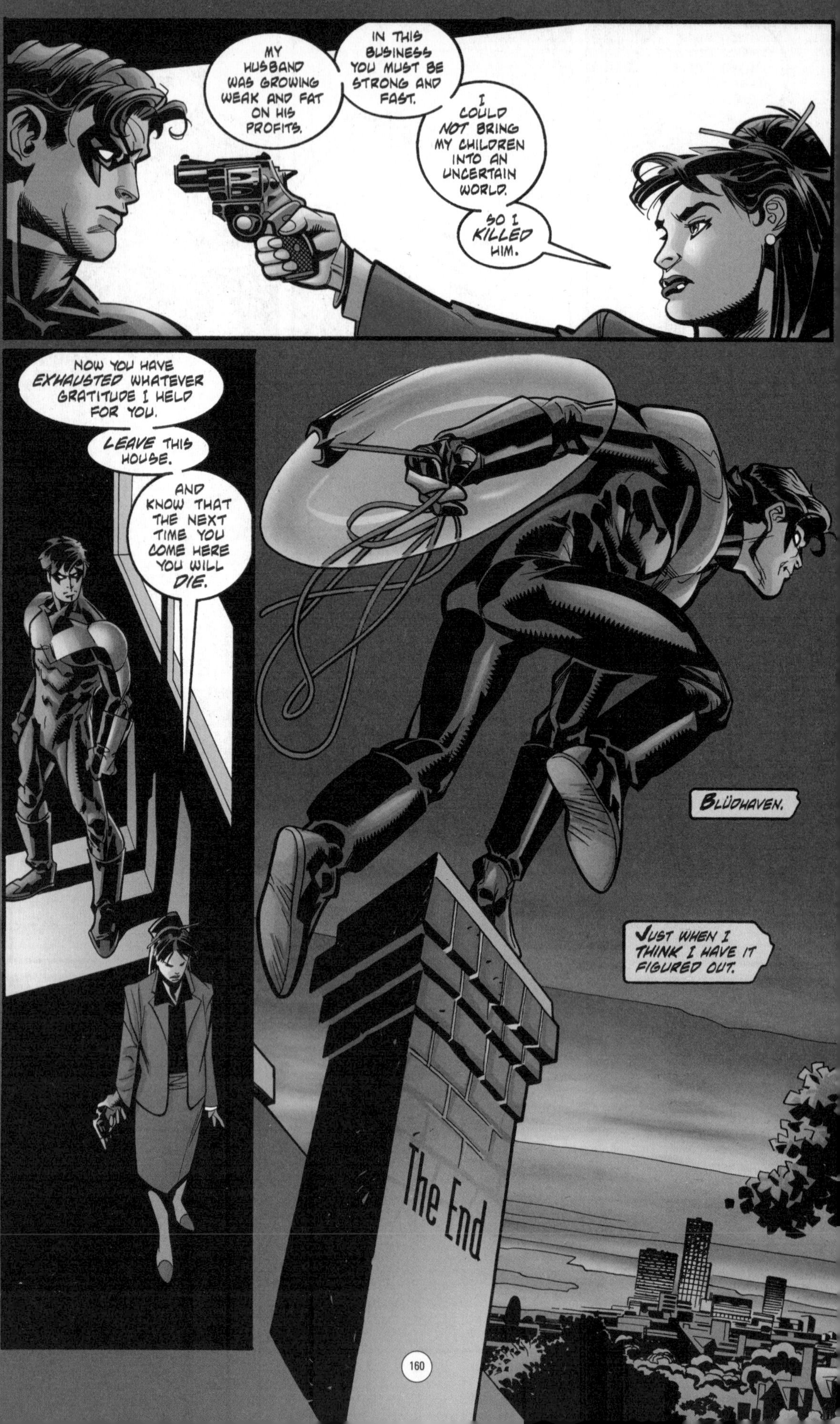

MY HUSBAND WAS GROWING WEAK AND FAT ON HIS PROFITS.
IN THIS BUSINESS YOU MUST BE STRONG AND FAST.
I COULD NOT BRING MY CHILDREN INTO AN UNCERTAIN WORLD.
SO I KILLED HIM.
NOW YOU HAVE EXHAUSTED WHATEVER GRATITUDE I HELD FOR YOU.
LEAVE THIS HOUSE.
AND KNOW THAT THE NEXT TIME YOU COME HERE YOU WILL DIE.
BLÜDHAVEN.
JUST WHEN I THINK I HAVE IT FIGURED OUT.
The End

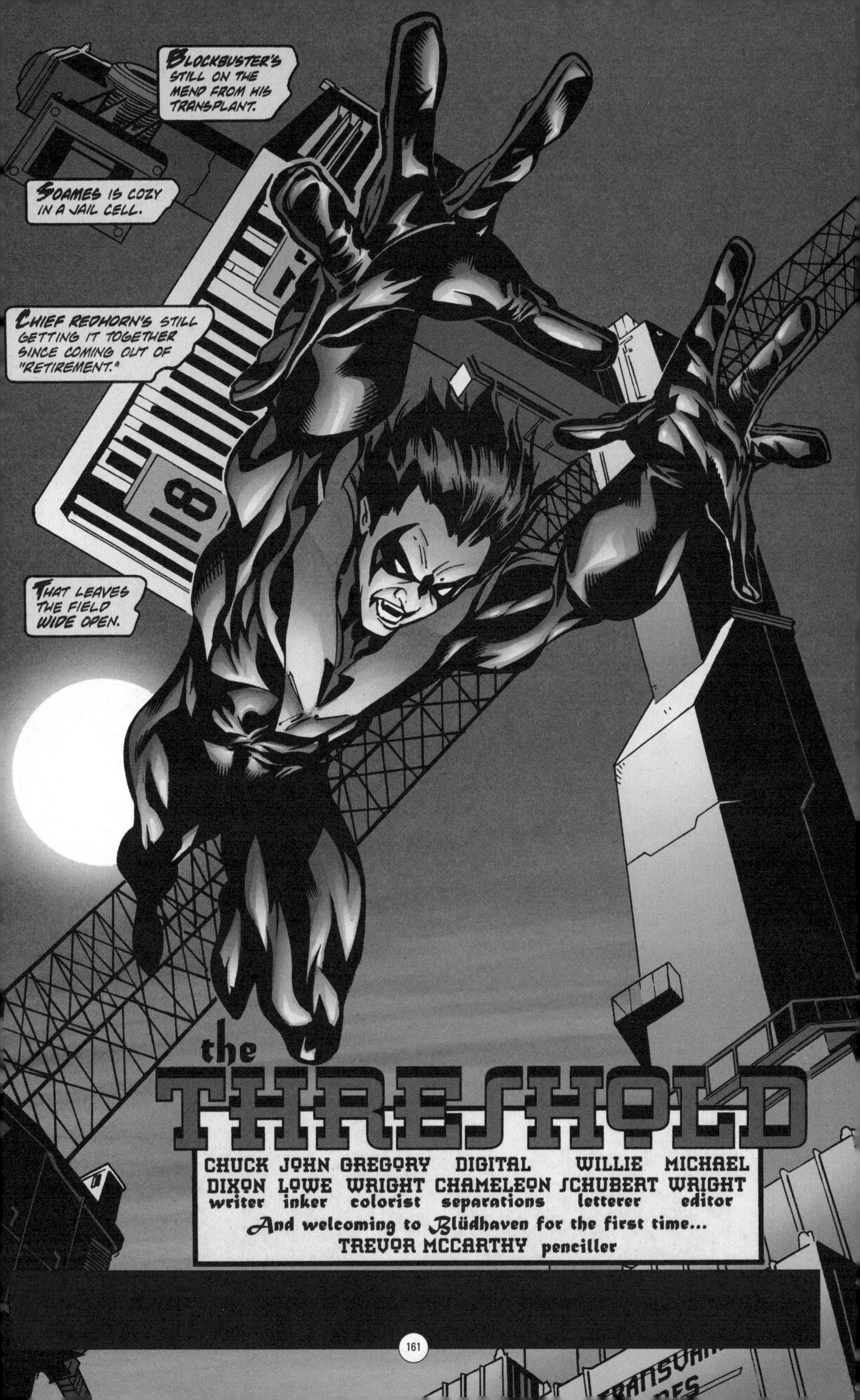
BLOCKBUSTER'S STILL ON THE MEND FROM HIS TRANSPLANT.
SOAMES IS COZY IN A JAIL CELL.
CHIEF REDHORN'S STILL GETTING IT TOGETHER SINCE COMING OUT OF "RETIREMENT."
THAT LEAVES THE FIELD WIDE OPEN.
the THRESHOLD
CHUCK DIXON writer
JOHN LOWE inker
GREGORY WRIGHT colorist
DIGITAL CHAMELEON separations
WILLIE SCHUBERT letterer
MICHAEL WRIGHT editor
And welcoming to Blüdhaven for the first time...
TREVOR McCARTHY penciller

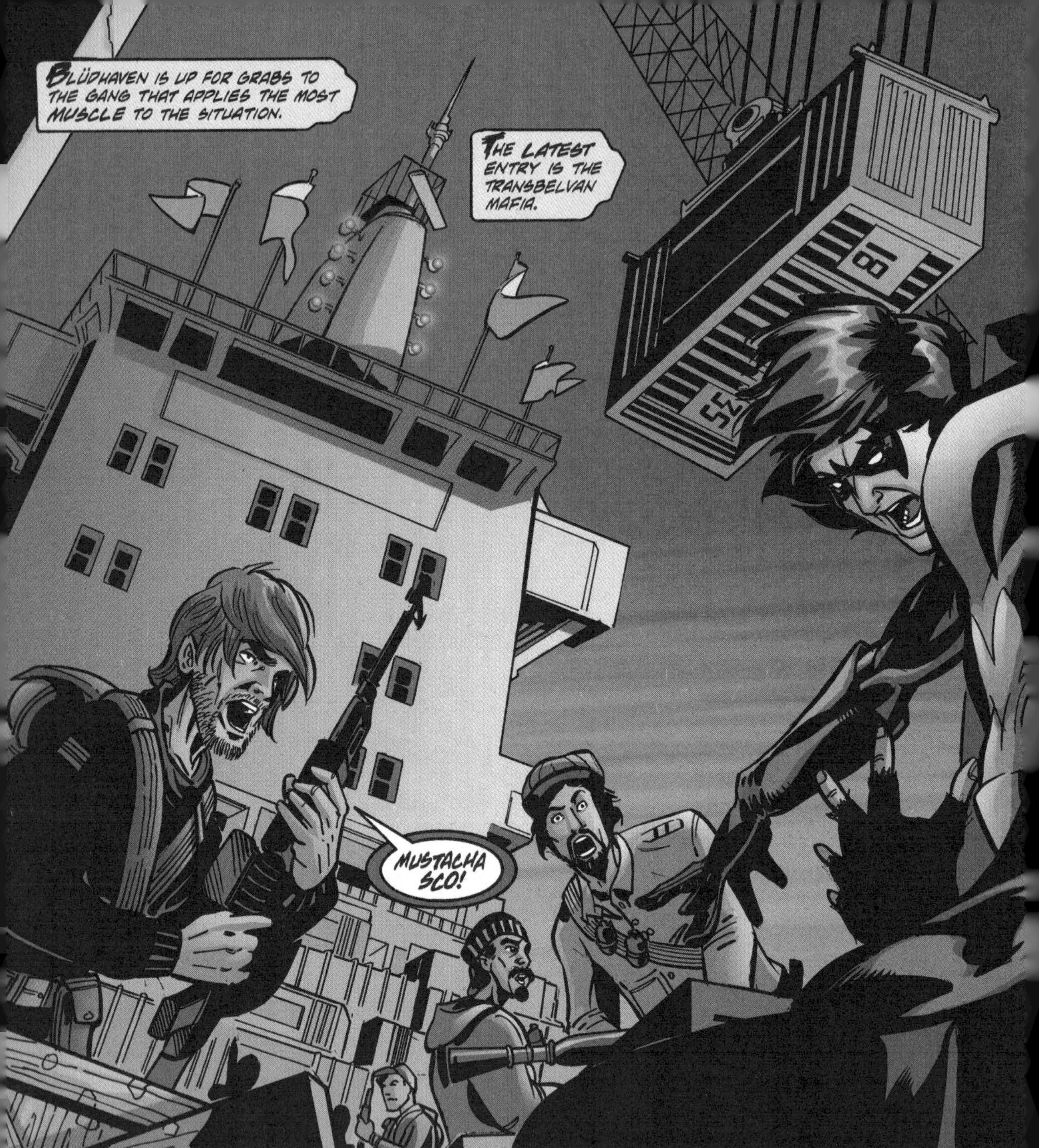
BLÜDHAVEN IS UP FOR GRABS TO THE GANG THAT APPLIES THE MOST MUSCLE TO THE SITUATION.
THE LATEST ENTRY IS THE TRANSBELVAN MAFIA.
MUSTACHA SCO!

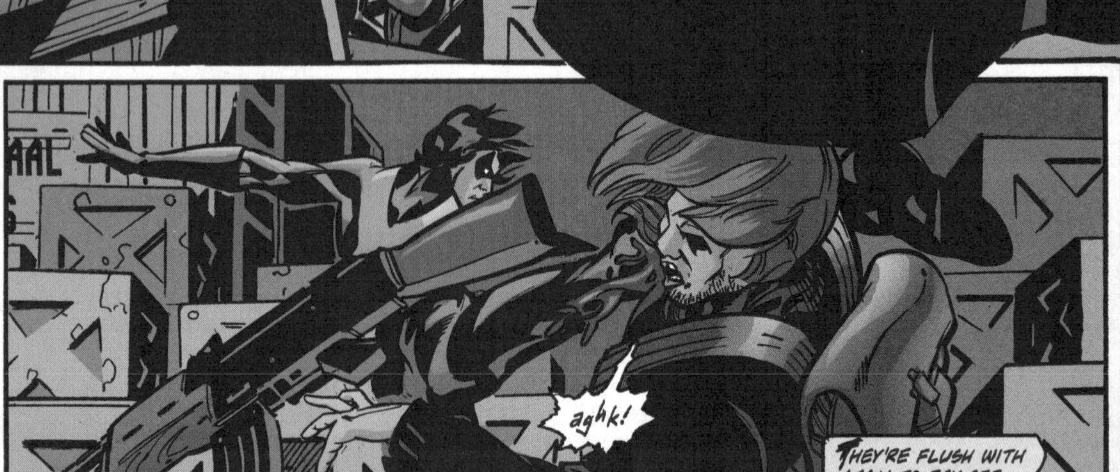
aghk!
THEY'RE FLUSH WITH CASH TO PAY OFF THE HARBOR COPS.

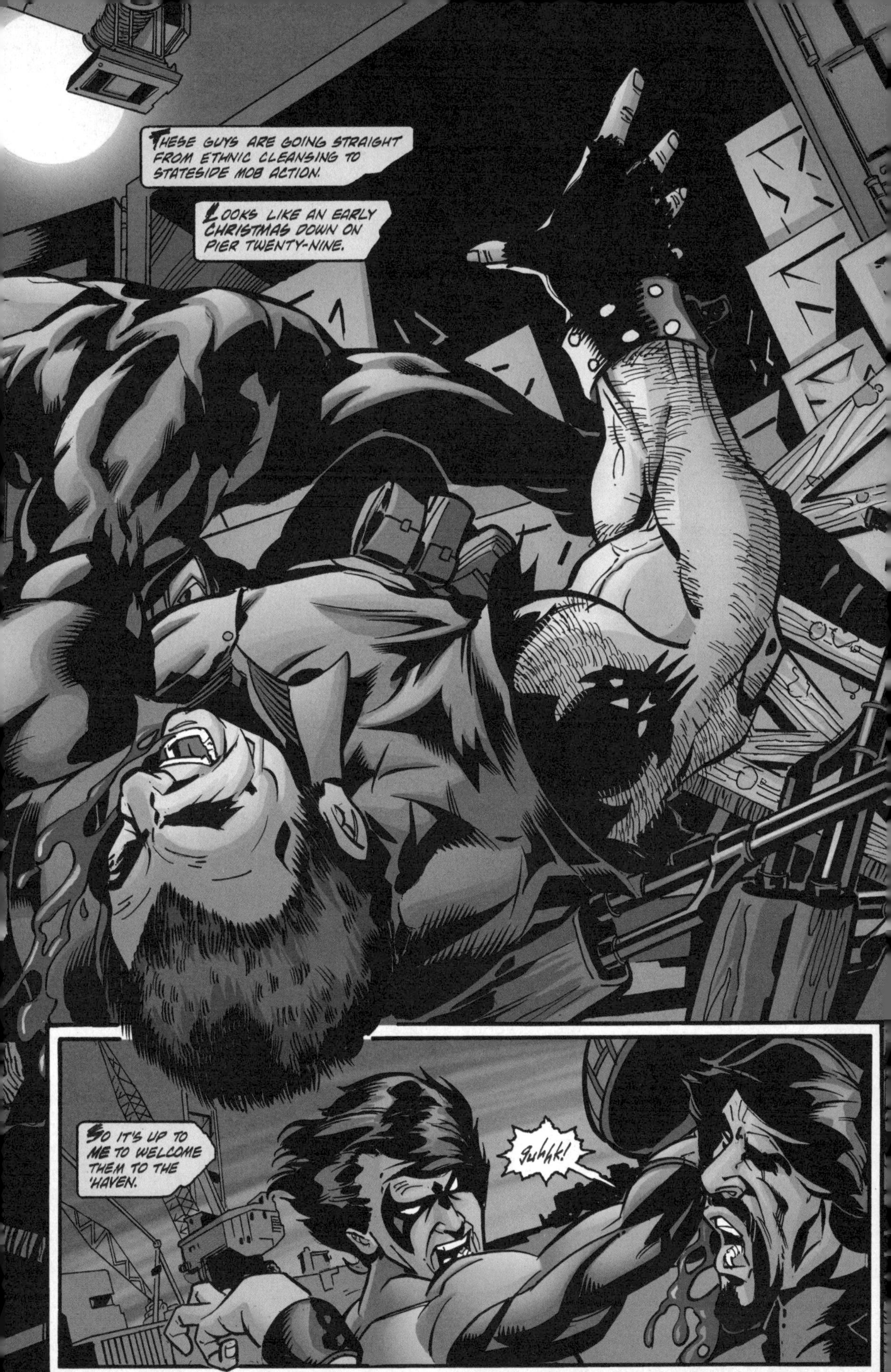
THESE GUYS ARE GOING STRAIGHT FROM ETHNIC CLEANSING TO STATESIDE MOB ACTION.
LOOKS LIKE AN EARLY CHRISTMAS DOWN ON PIER TWENTY-NINE.
SO IT'S UP TO ME TO WELCOME THEM TO THE 'HAVEN.
GUHHK!

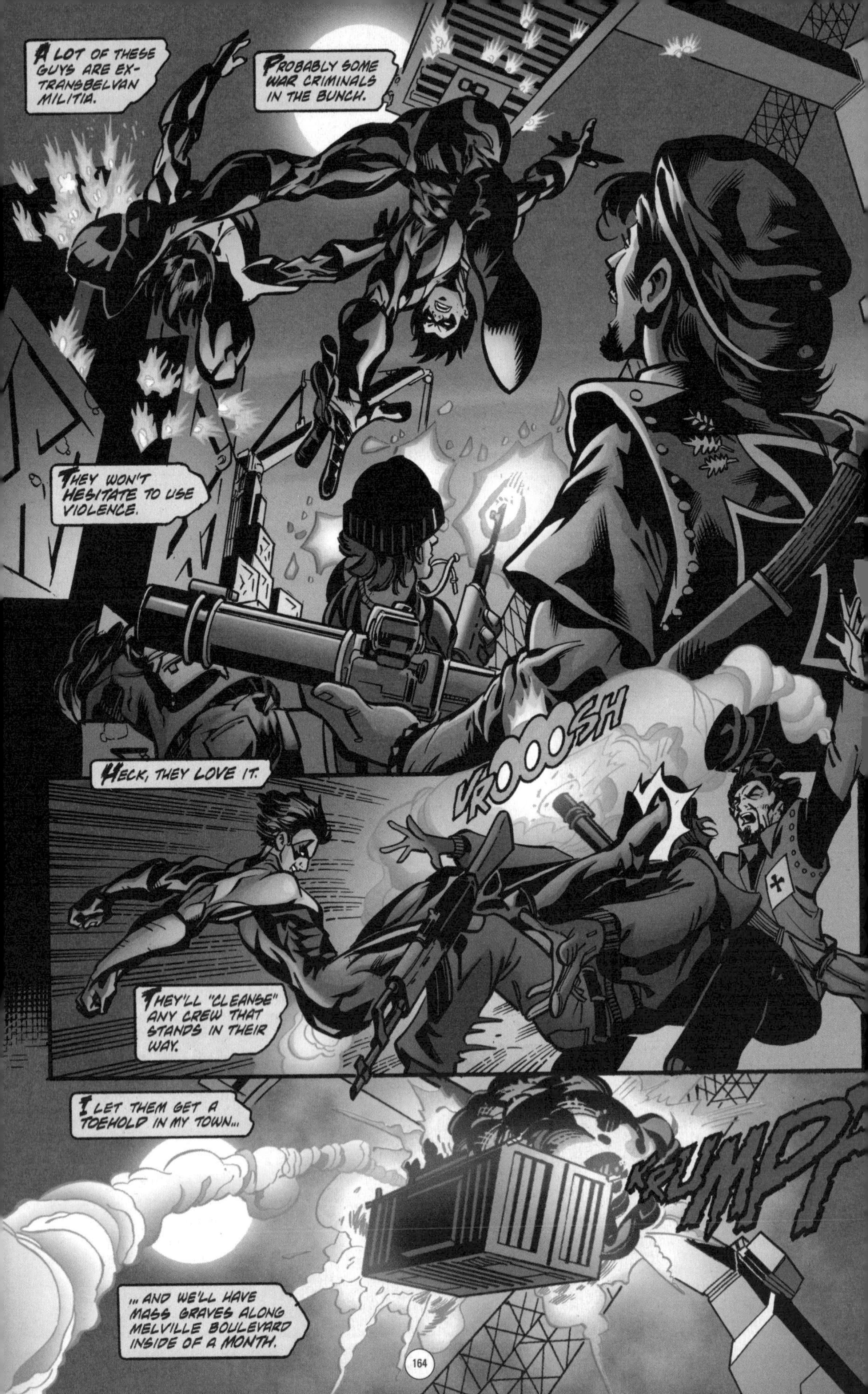
A LOT OF THESE GUYS ARE EX-TRANSBELVAN MILITIA.
PROBABLY SOME WAR CRIMINALS IN THE BUNCH.
THEY WON'T HESITATE TO USE VIOLENCE.
VROOOOSH
HECK, THEY LOVE IT.
THEY'LL "CLEANSE" ANY CREW THAT STANDS IN THEIR WAY.
I LET THEM GET A TOEHOLD IN MY TOWN...
KRUMP!
...AND WE'LL HAVE MASS GRAVES ALONG MELVILLE BOULEVARD INSIDE OF A MONTH.

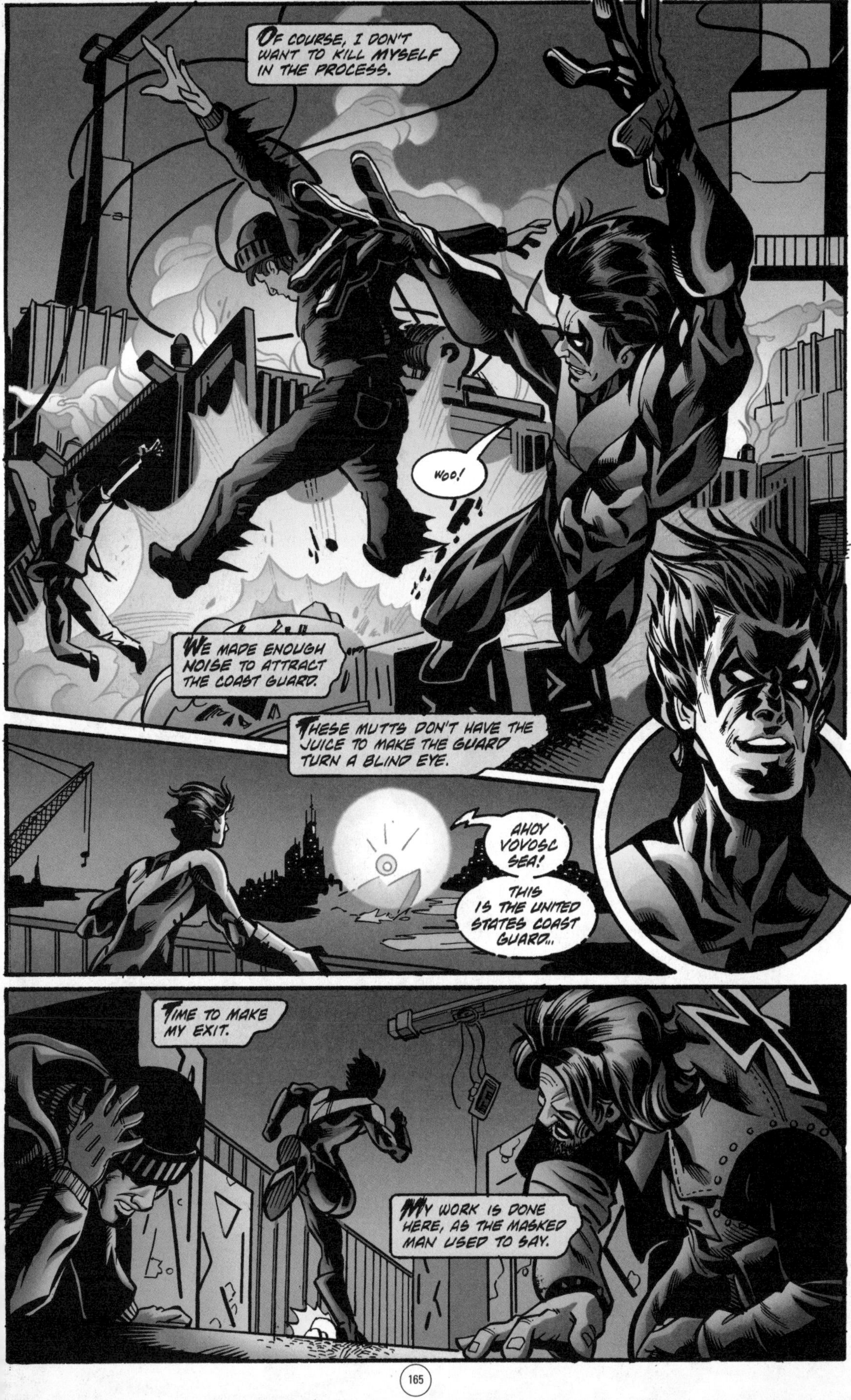

OF COURSE, I DON'T WANT TO KILL MYSELF IN THE PROCESS.
WOO!
WE MADE ENOUGH NOISE TO ATTRACT THE COAST GUARD.
THESE MUTTS DON'T HAVE THE JUICE TO MAKE THE GUARD TURN A BLIND EYE.
AHOY VOVOSC SEA!
THIS IS THE UNITED STATES COAST GUARD...
TIME TO MAKE MY EXIT.
MY WORK IS DONE HERE, AS THE MASKED MAN USED TO SAY.

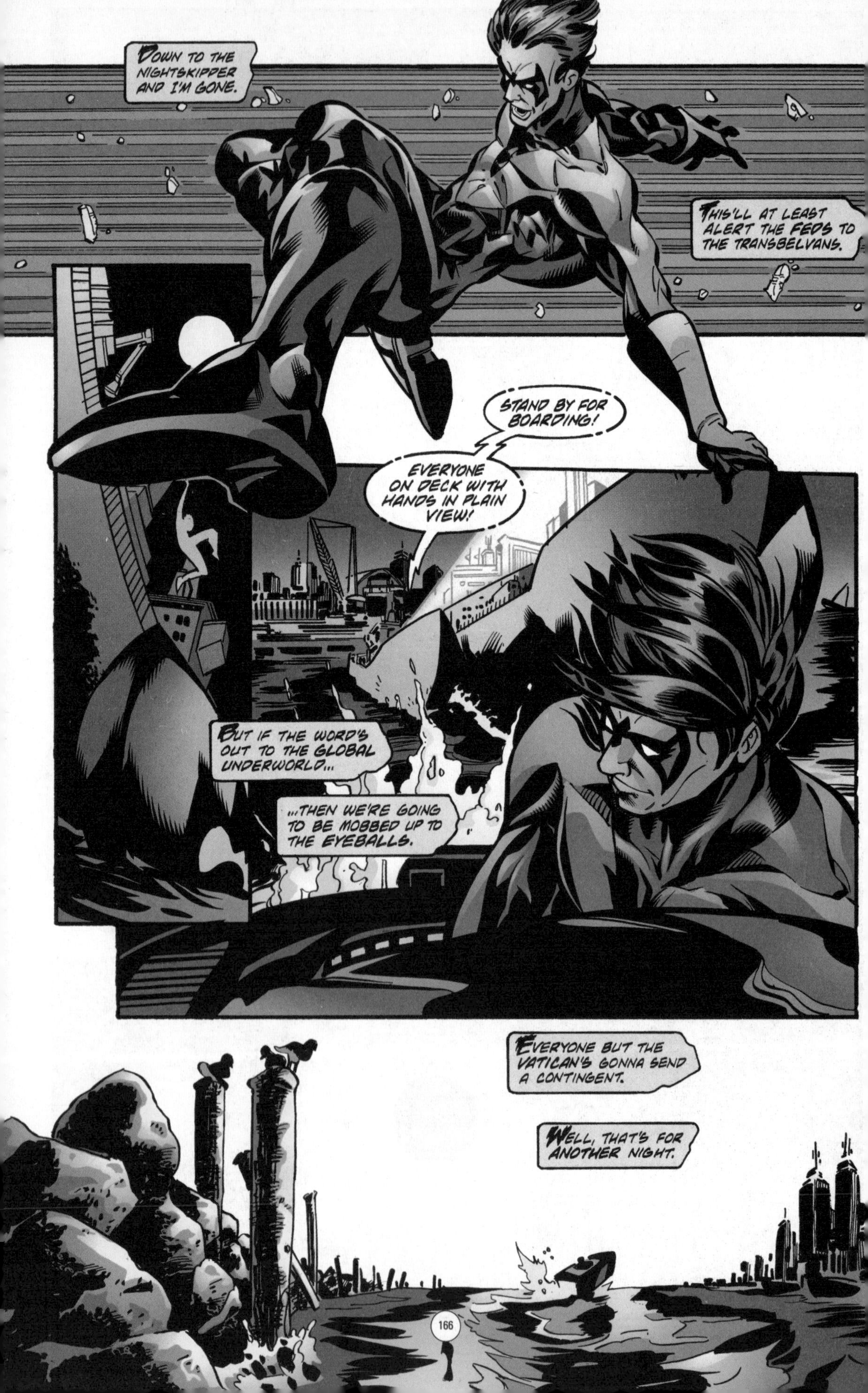

DOWN TO THE NIGHTSKIPPER AND I'M GONE.
THIS'LL AT LEAST ALERT THE FEDS TO THE TRANSBELVANS.
STAND BY FOR BOARDING!
EVERYONE ON DECK WITH HANDS IN PLAIN VIEW!
BUT IF THE WORD'S OUT TO THE GLOBAL UNDERWORLD...
...THEN WE'RE GOING TO BE MOBBED UP TO THE EYEBALLS.
EVERYONE BUT THE VATICAN'S GONNA SEND A CONTINGENT.
WELL, THAT'S FOR ANOTHER NIGHT.

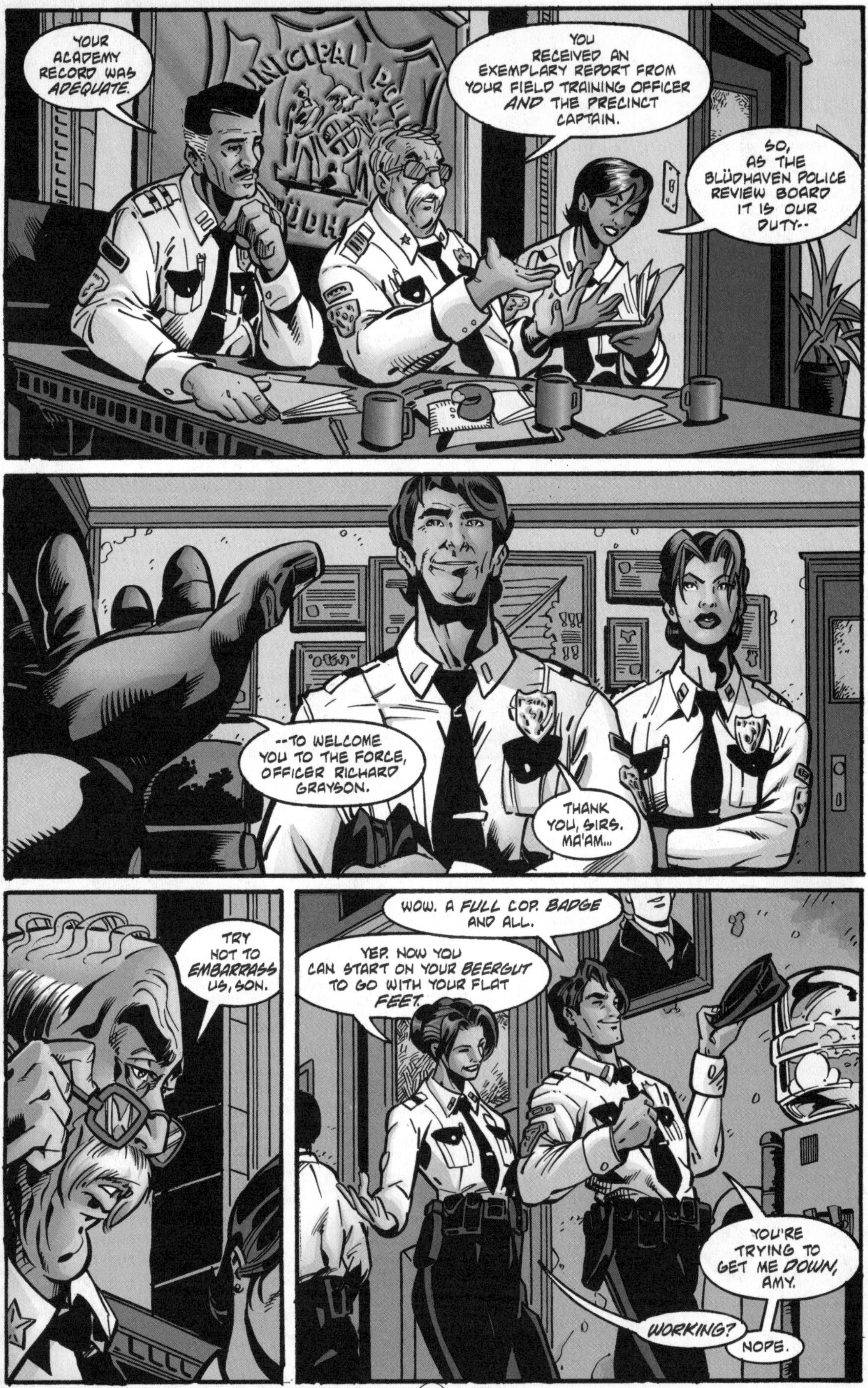
YOUR ACADEMY RECORD WAS *ADEQUATE.*
YOU RECEIVED AN EXEMPLARY REPORT FROM YOUR FIELD TRAINING OFFICER *AND* THE PRECINCT CAPTAIN.
SO, AS THE BLÜDHAVEN POLICE REVIEW BOARD IT IS OUR DUTY--
--TO WELCOME YOU TO THE FORCE, OFFICER RICHARD GRAYSON.
THANK YOU, SIRS. MA'AM...
TRY NOT TO *EMBARRASS* US, SON.
WOW. A *FULL COP. BADGE* AND ALL.
YEP. NOW YOU CAN START ON YOUR *BEERGUT* TO GO WITH YOUR FLAT *FEET.*
YOU'RE TRYING TO GET ME *DOWN,* AMY.
WORKING?
NOPE.

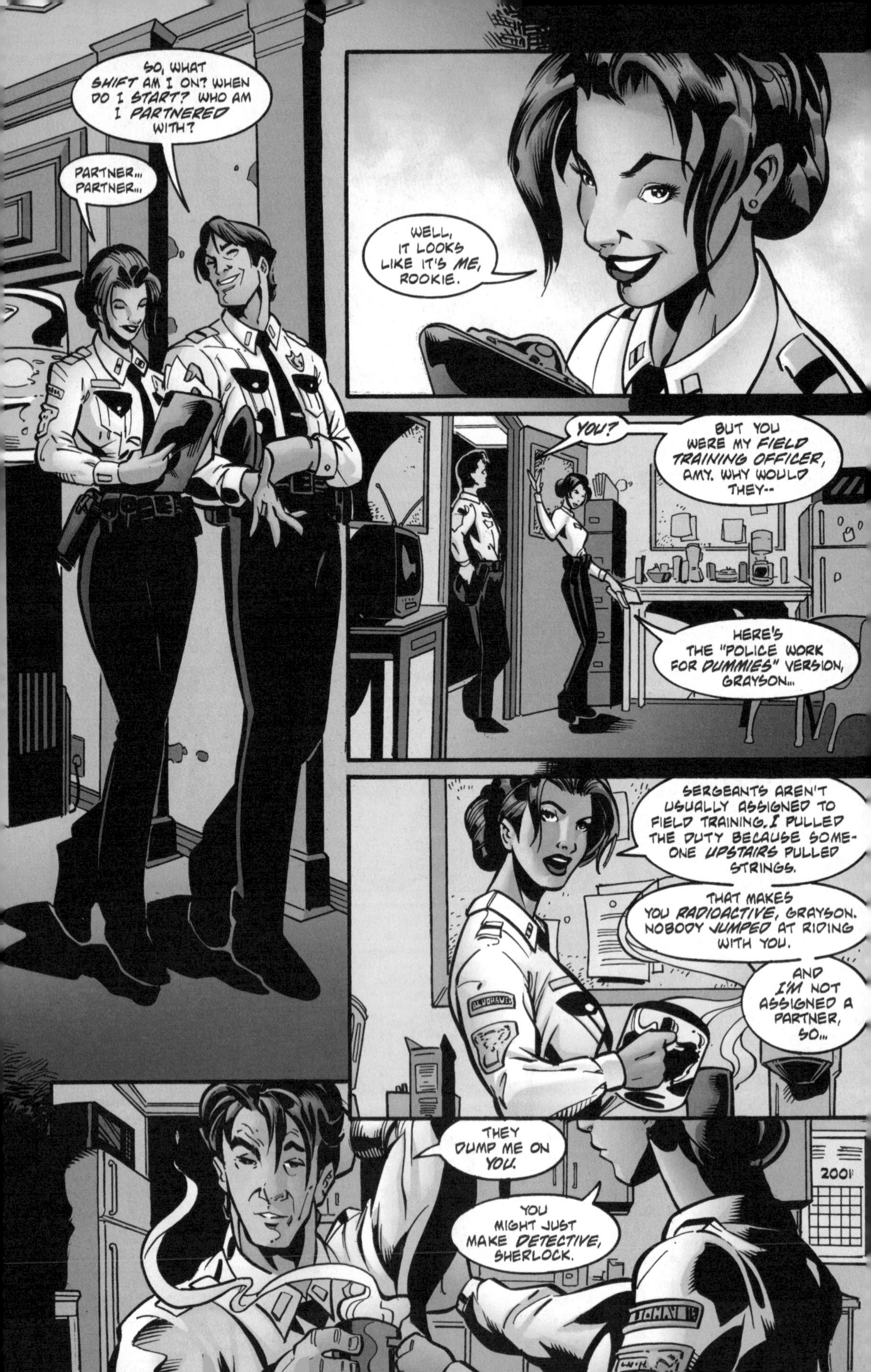
SO, WHAT SHIFT AM I ON? WHEN DO I START? WHO AM I PARTNERED WITH?
PARTNER... PARTNER...
WELL, IT LOOKS LIKE IT'S ME, ROOKIE.
YOU?
BUT YOU WERE MY FIELD TRAINING OFFICER, AMY. WHY WOULD THEY--
HERE'S THE "POLICE WORK FOR DUMMIES" VERSION, GRAYSON...
SERGEANTS AREN'T USUALLY ASSIGNED TO FIELD TRAINING. I PULLED THE DUTY BECAUSE SOME-ONE UPSTAIRS PULLED STRINGS.
THAT MAKES YOU RADIOACTIVE, GRAYSON. NOBODY JUMPED AT RIDING WITH YOU.
AND I'M NOT ASSIGNED A PARTNER, SO...
THEY DUMP ME ON YOU.
YOU MIGHT JUST MAKE DETECTIVE, SHERLOCK.
2001

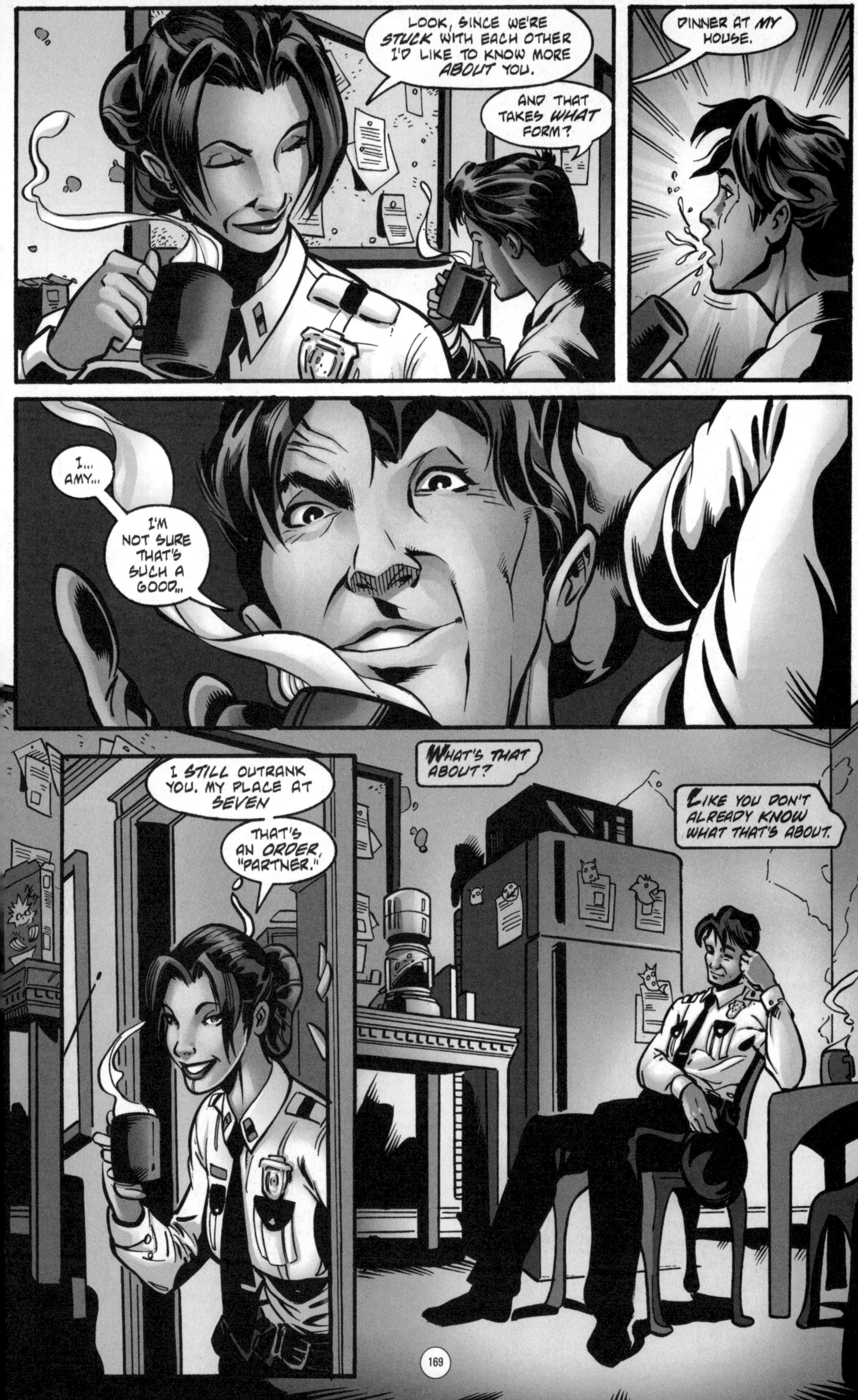
LOOK, SINCE WE'RE STUCK WITH EACH OTHER I'D LIKE TO KNOW MORE ABOUT YOU.
AND THAT TAKES WHAT FORM?
DINNER AT MY HOUSE.
I... AMY...
I'M NOT SURE THAT'S SUCH A GOOD...
I STILL OUTRANK YOU. MY PLACE AT SEVEN
THAT'S AN ORDER, "PARTNER."
WHAT'S THAT ABOUT?
LIKE YOU DON'T ALREADY KNOW WHAT THAT'S ABOUT.

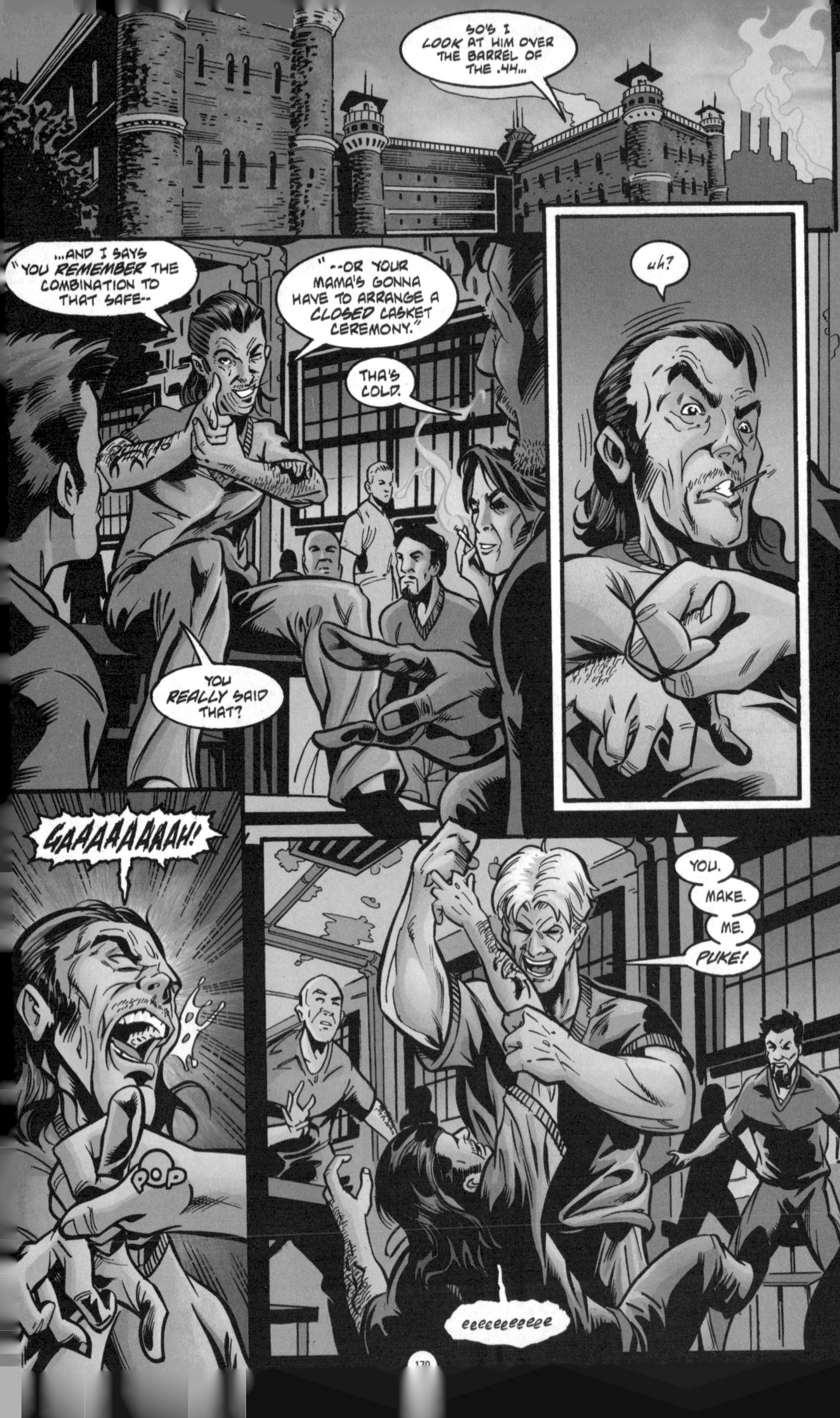

SO'S I LOOK AT HIM OVER THE BARREL OF THE .44...
...AND I SAYS "YOU REMEMBER THE COMBINATION TO THAT SAFE--
"--OR YOUR MAMA'S GONNA HAVE TO ARRANGE A CLOSED CASKET CEREMONY."
THA'S COLD.
YOU REALLY SAID THAT?
uh?
GAAAAAAAAH!
POP
YOU.
MAKE.
ME.
PUKE!
eeeeeeeeeee

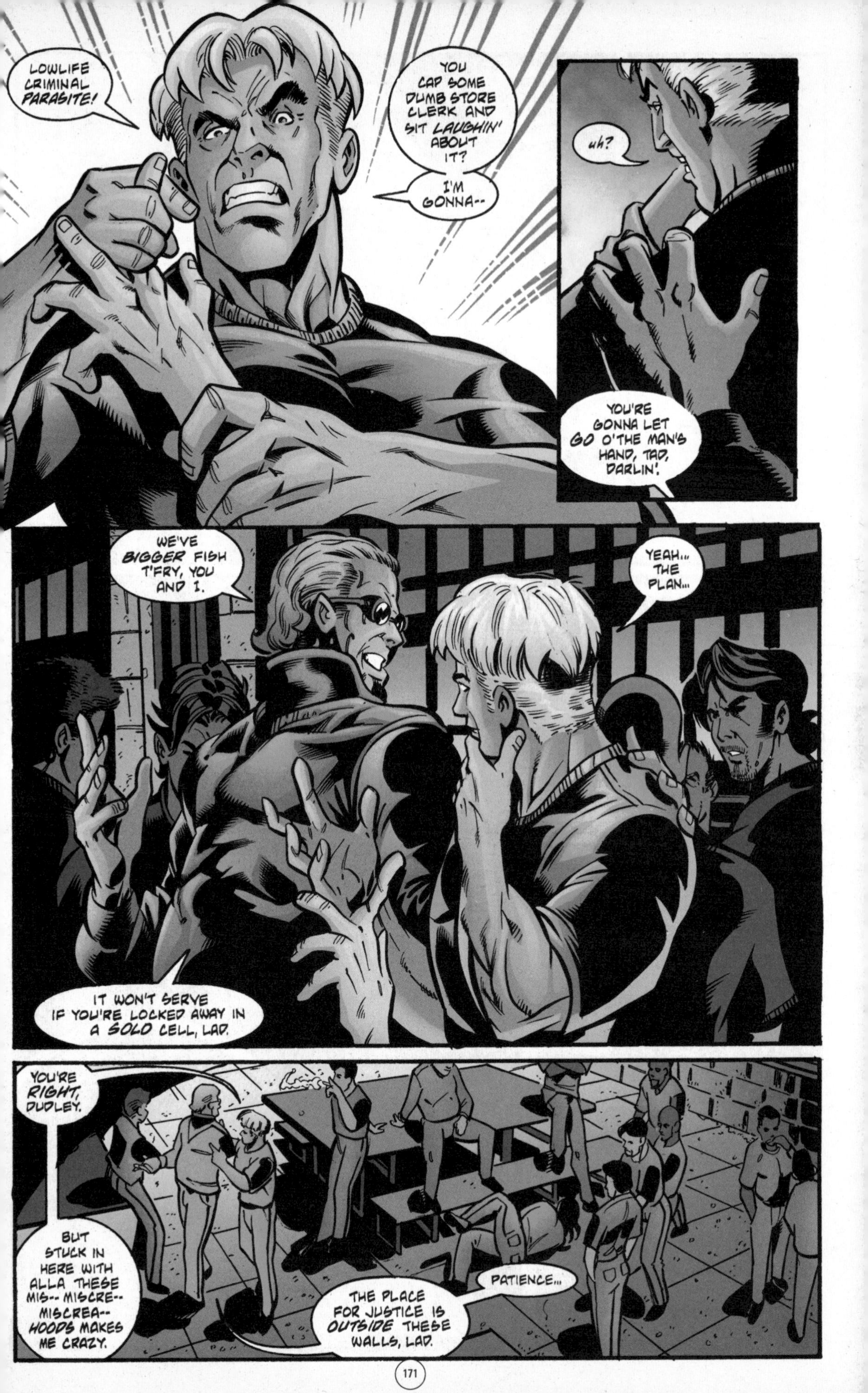
LOWLIFE CRIMINAL PARASITE!
YOU CAP SOME DUMB STORE CLERK AND SIT LAUGHIN' ABOUT IT?
I'M GONNA--
uh?
YOU'RE GONNA LET GO O'THE MAN'S HAND, TAD, DARLIN'.
WE'VE BIGGER FISH T'FRY, YOU AND I.
YEAH... THE PLAN...
IT WON'T SERVE IF YOU'RE LOCKED AWAY IN A SOLO CELL, LAD.
YOU'RE RIGHT, DUDLEY.
BUT STUCK IN HERE WITH ALLA THESE MIS-- MISCRE-- MISCREA-- HOODS MAKES ME CRAZY.
PATIENCE...
THE PLACE FOR JUSTICE IS OUTSIDE THESE WALLS, LAD.

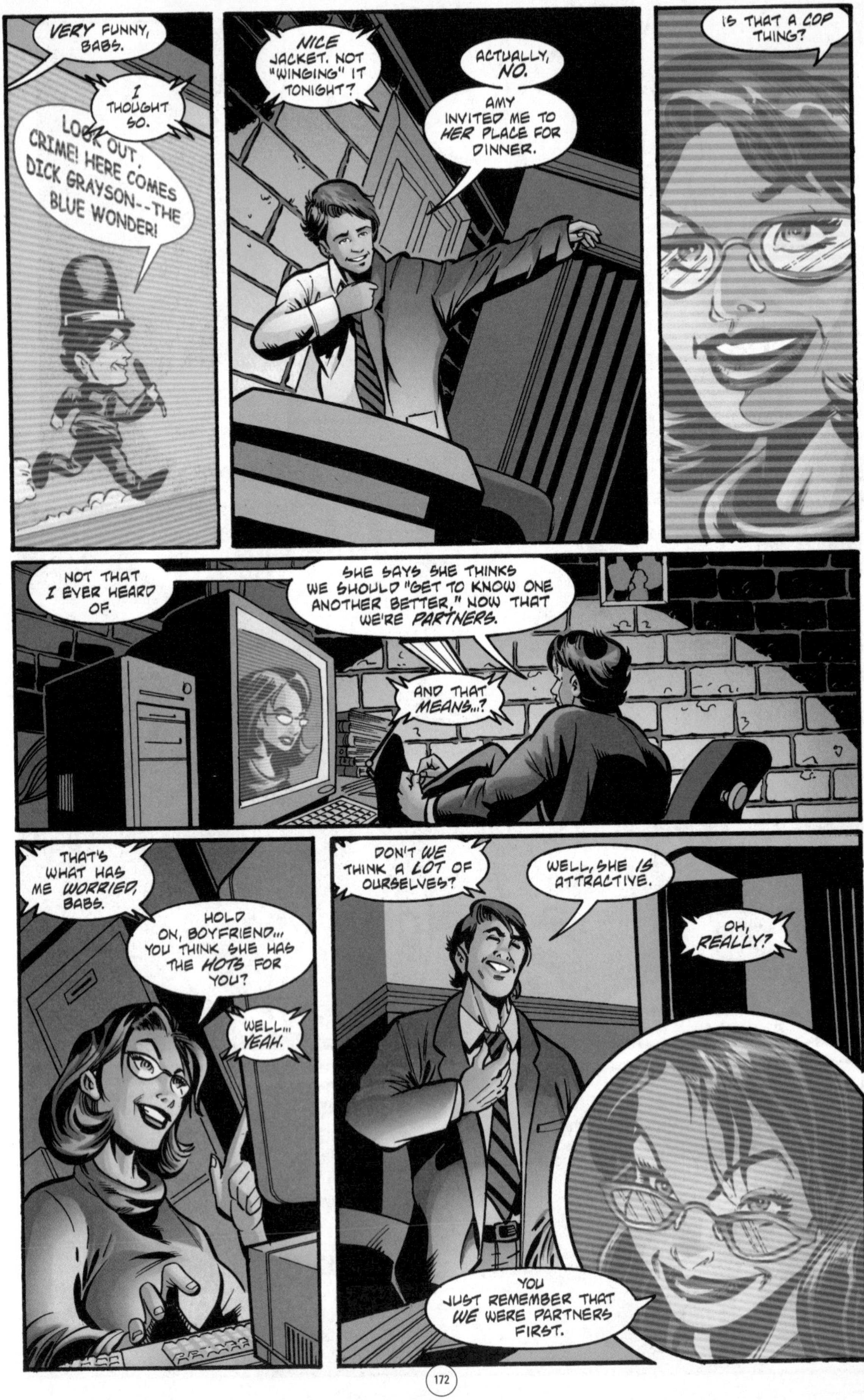
VERY FUNNY, BABS.
LOOK OUT, CRIME! HERE COMES DICK GRAYSON--THE BLUE WONDER!
I THOUGHT SO.
NICE JACKET. NOT "WINGING" IT TONIGHT?
ACTUALLY, NO.
AMY INVITED ME TO HER PLACE FOR DINNER.
IS THAT A COP THING?
NOT THAT I EVER HEARD OF.
SHE SAYS SHE THINKS WE SHOULD "GET TO KNOW ONE ANOTHER BETTER," NOW THAT WE'RE PARTNERS.
AND THAT MEANS...?
THAT'S WHAT HAS ME WORRIED, BABS.
HOLD ON, BOYFRIEND... YOU THINK SHE HAS THE HOTS FOR YOU?
WELL... YEAH.
DON'T WE THINK A LOT OF OURSELVES?
WELL, SHE IS ATTRACTIVE.
OH, REALLY?
YOU JUST REMEMBER THAT WE WERE PARTNERS FIRST.

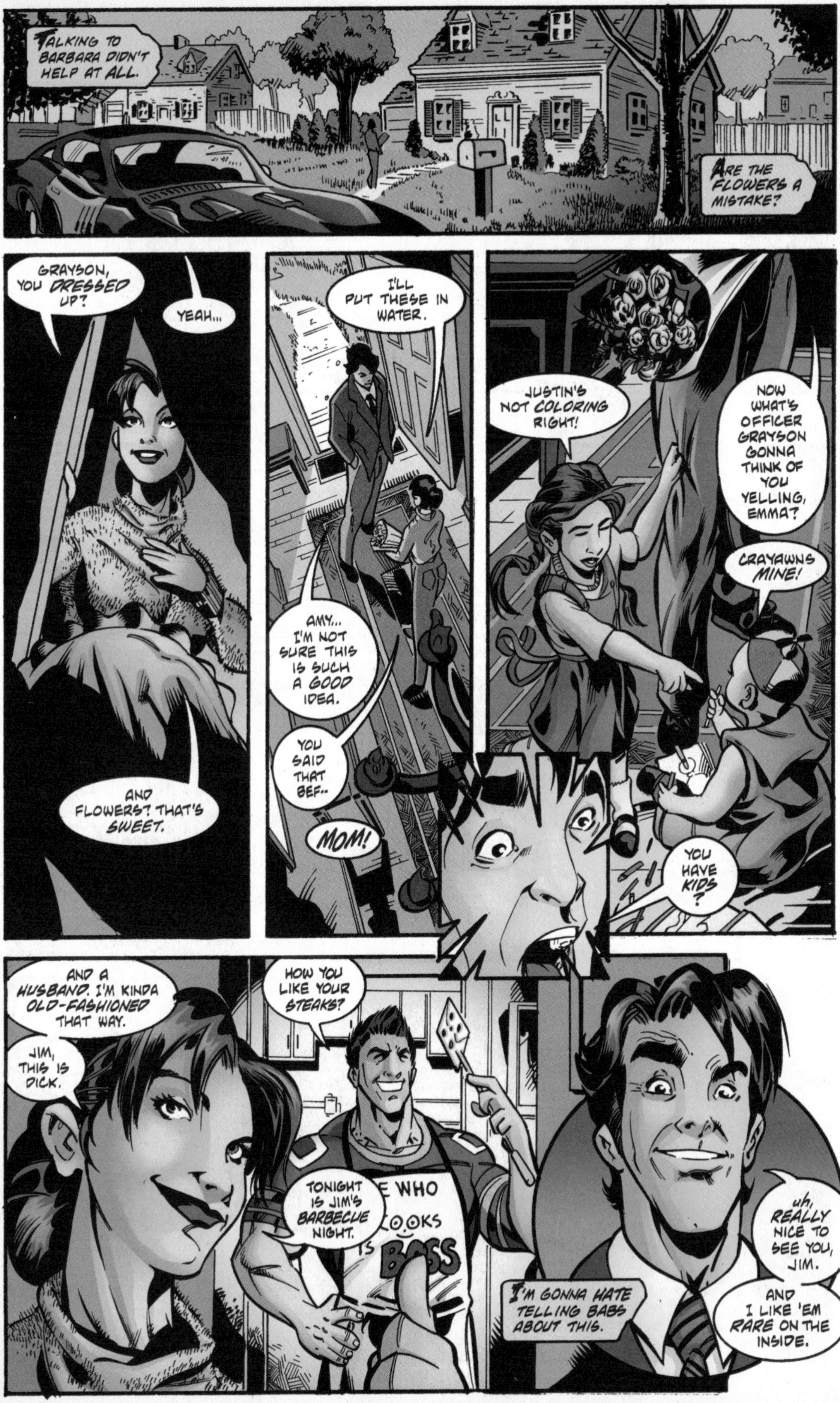

TALKING TO BARBARA DIDN'T HELP AT ALL.
ARE THE FLOWERS A MISTAKE?
GRAYSON, YOU DRESSED UP?
YEAH...
AND FLOWERS? THAT'S SWEET.
I'LL PUT THESE IN WATER.
AMY... I'M NOT SURE THIS IS SUCH A GOOD IDEA.
YOU SAID THAT BEF..
MOM!
JUSTIN'S NOT COLORING RIGHT!
NOW WHAT'S OFFICER GRAYSON GONNA THINK OF YOU YELLING, EMMA?
CRAYAWNS MINE!
YOU HAVE KIDS?
AND A HUSBAND. I'M KINDA OLD-FASHIONED THAT WAY.
JIM, THIS IS DICK.
HOW YOU LIKE YOUR STEAKS?
TONIGHT IS JIM'S BARBECUE NIGHT.
E WHO
C OOKS
IS BOSS
uh, REALLY NICE TO SEE YOU, JIM.
AND I LIKE 'EM RARE ON THE INSIDE.
I'M GONNA HATE TELLING BABS ABOUT THIS.

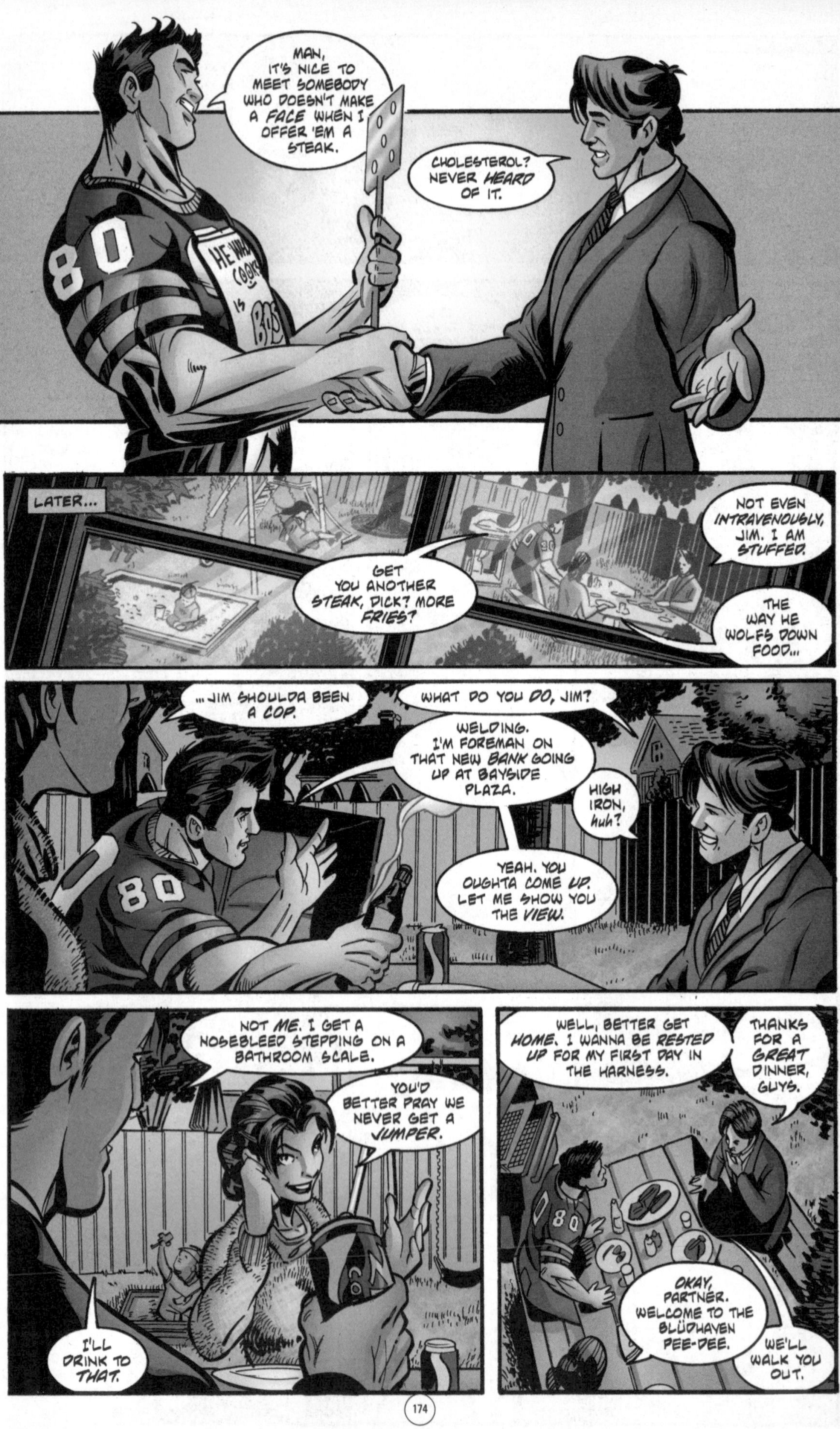
MAN, IT'S NICE TO MEET SOMEBODY WHO DOESN'T MAKE A FACE WHEN I OFFER 'EM A STEAK.
HE WHO COOKS IS BOSS
CHOLESTEROL? NEVER HEARD OF IT.
LATER...
GET YOU ANOTHER STEAK, DICK? MORE FRIES?
NOT EVEN INTRAVENOUSLY, JIM. I AM STUFFED.
THE WAY HE WOLFS DOWN FOOD...
...JIM SHOULDA BEEN A COP.
WHAT DO YOU DO, JIM?
WELDING. I'M FOREMAN ON THAT NEW BANK GOING UP AT BAYSIDE PLAZA.
HIGH IRON, huh?
YEAH. YOU OUGHTA COME UP. LET ME SHOW YOU THE VIEW.
NOT ME. I GET A NOSEBLEED STEPPING ON A BATHROOM SCALE.
YOU'D BETTER PRAY WE NEVER GET A JUMPER.
I'LL DRINK TO THAT.
WELL, BETTER GET HOME. I WANNA BE RESTED UP FOR MY FIRST DAY IN THE HARNESS.
THANKS FOR A GREAT DINNER, GUYS.
OKAY, PARTNER. WELCOME TO THE BLÜDHAVEN PEE-DEE.
WE'LL WALK YOU OUT.

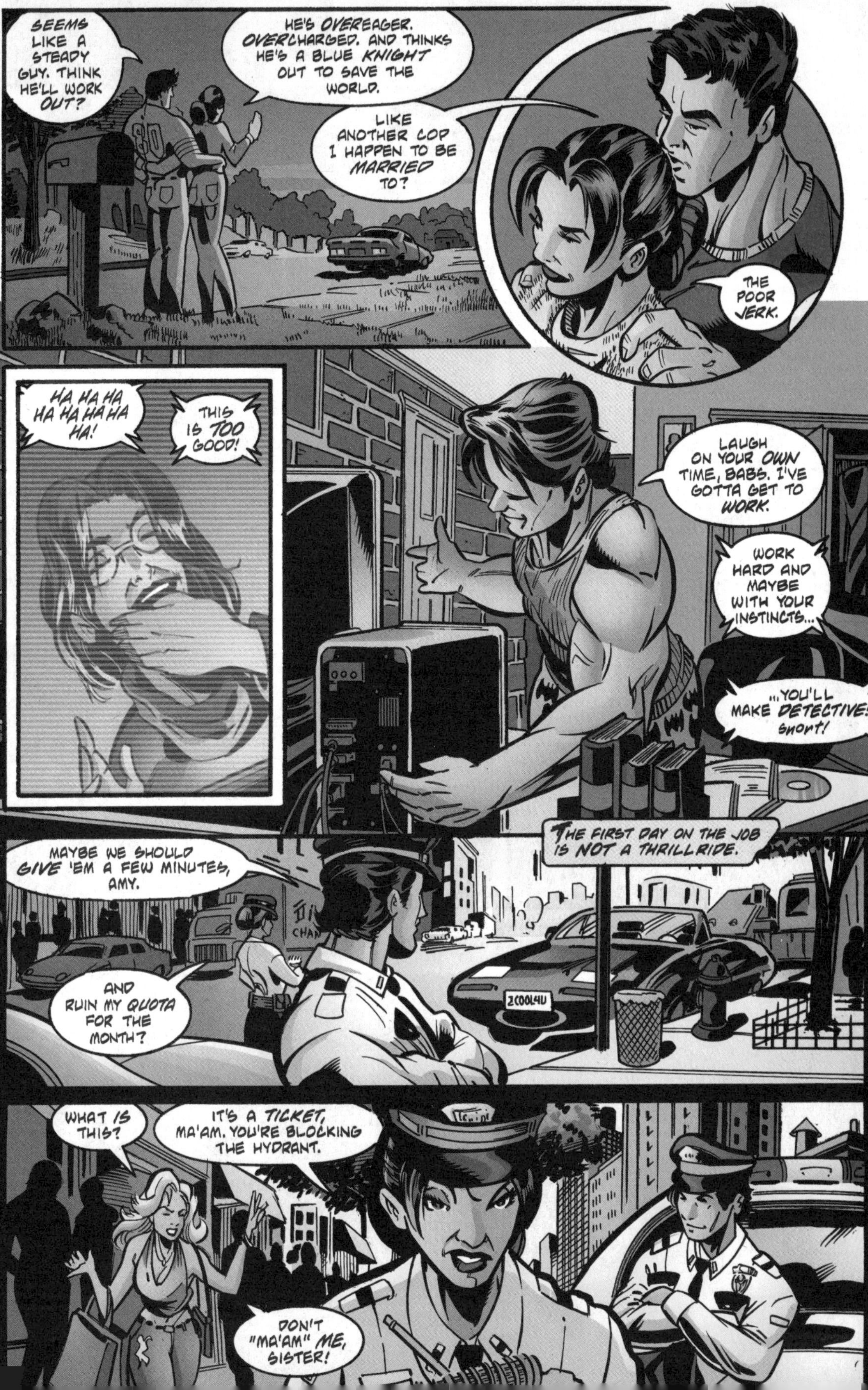
SEEMS LIKE A STEADY GUY. THINK HE'LL WORK OUT?
HE'S OVEREAGER. OVERCHARGED. AND THINKS HE'S A BLUE KNIGHT OUT TO SAVE THE WORLD.
LIKE ANOTHER COP I HAPPEN TO BE MARRIED TO?
THE POOR JERK.
HA HA HA HA HA HA HA HA!
THIS IS TOO GOOD!
LAUGH ON YOUR OWN TIME, BABS. I'VE GOTTA GET TO WORK.
WORK HARD AND MAYBE WITH YOUR INSTINCTS...
...YOU'LL MAKE DETECTIVE! snort!
THE FIRST DAY ON THE JOB IS NOT A THRILLRIDE.
MAYBE WE SHOULD GIVE 'EM A FEW MINUTES, AMY.
AND RUIN MY QUOTA FOR THE MONTH?
2COOL4U
WHAT IS THIS?
IT'S A TICKET, MA'AM. YOU'RE BLOCKING THE HYDRANT.
DON'T "MA'AM" ME, SISTER!

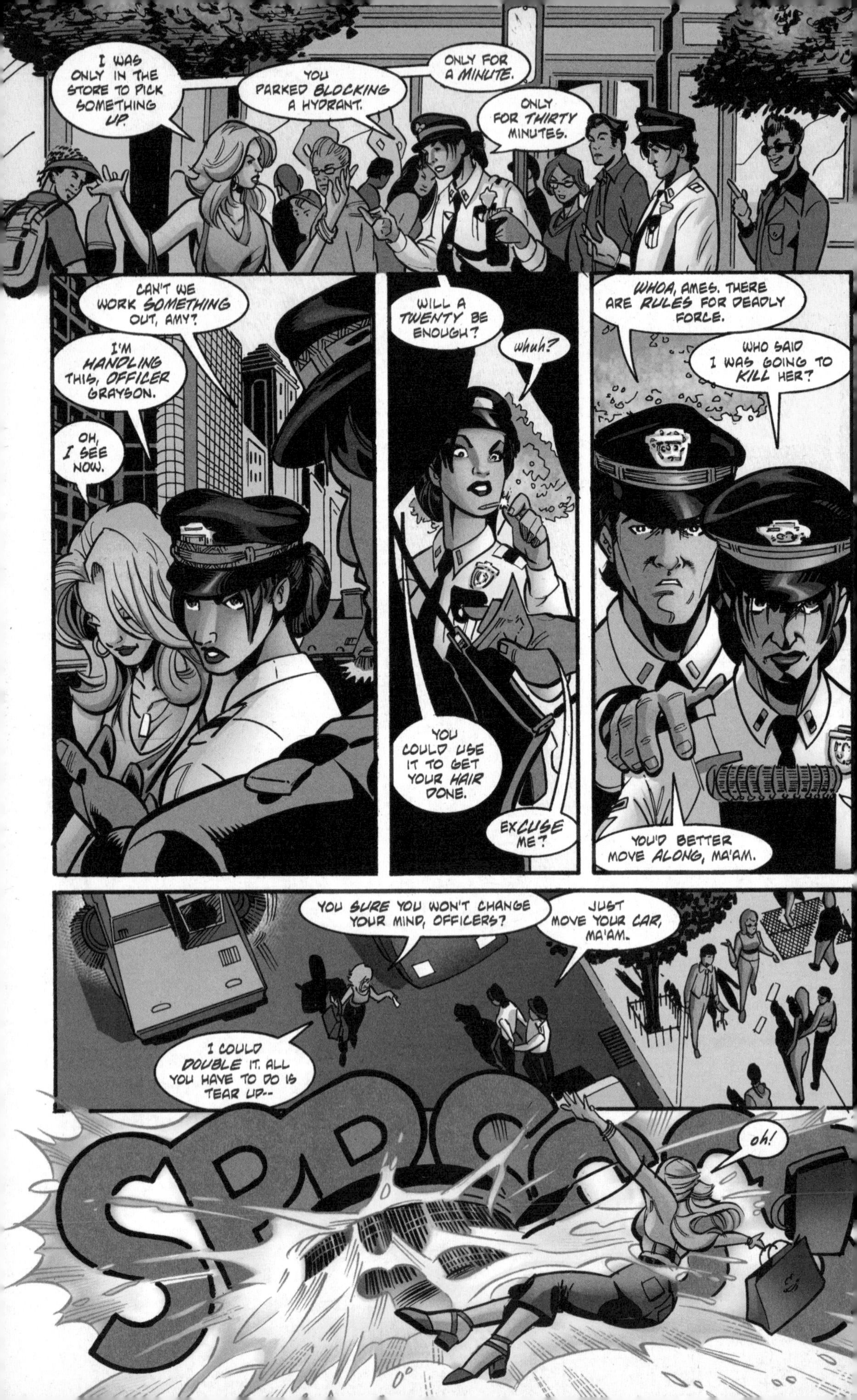
I WAS ONLY IN THE STORE TO PICK SOMETHING UP.
YOU PARKED BLOCKING A HYDRANT.
ONLY FOR A MINUTE.
ONLY FOR THIRTY MINUTES.
CAN'T WE WORK SOMETHING OUT, AMY?
I'M HANDLING THIS, OFFICER GRAYSON.
OH, I SEE NOW.
WILL A TWENTY BE ENOUGH?
whuh?
YOU COULD USE IT TO GET YOUR HAIR DONE.
EXCUSE ME?
WHOA, AMES. THERE ARE RULES FOR DEADLY FORCE.
WHO SAID I WAS GOING TO KILL HER?
YOU'D BETTER MOVE ALONG, MA'AM.
YOU SURE YOU WON'T CHANGE YOUR MIND, OFFICERS?
JUST MOVE YOUR CAR, MA'AM.
I COULD DOUBLE IT. ALL YOU HAVE TO DO IS TEAR UP--
SPROOOO
oh!

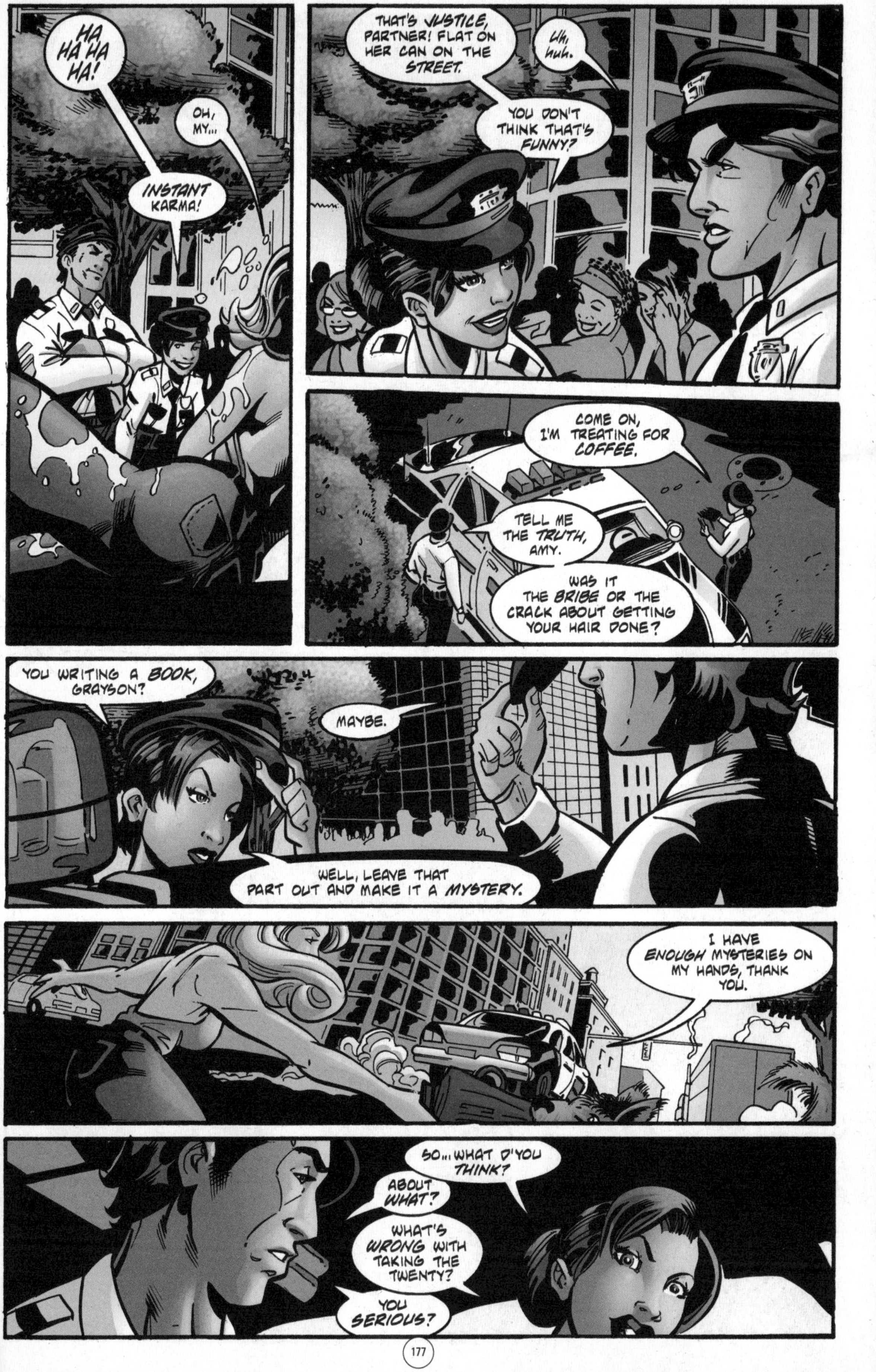

HA HA HA HA!
OH, MY...
INSTANT KARMA!
THAT'S JUSTICE, PARTNER! FLAT ON HER CAN ON THE STREET.
Uh, huh.
YOU DON'T THINK THAT'S FUNNY?
COME ON, I'M TREATING FOR COFFEE.
TELL ME THE TRUTH, AMY.
WAS IT THE BRIBE OR THE CRACK ABOUT GETTING YOUR HAIR DONE?
YOU WRITING A BOOK, GRAYSON?
MAYBE.
WELL, LEAVE THAT PART OUT AND MAKE IT A MYSTERY.
I HAVE ENOUGH MYSTERIES ON MY HANDS, THANK YOU.
SO... WHAT D'YOU THINK?
ABOUT WHAT?
WHAT'S WRONG WITH TAKING THE TWENTY?
YOU SERIOUS?

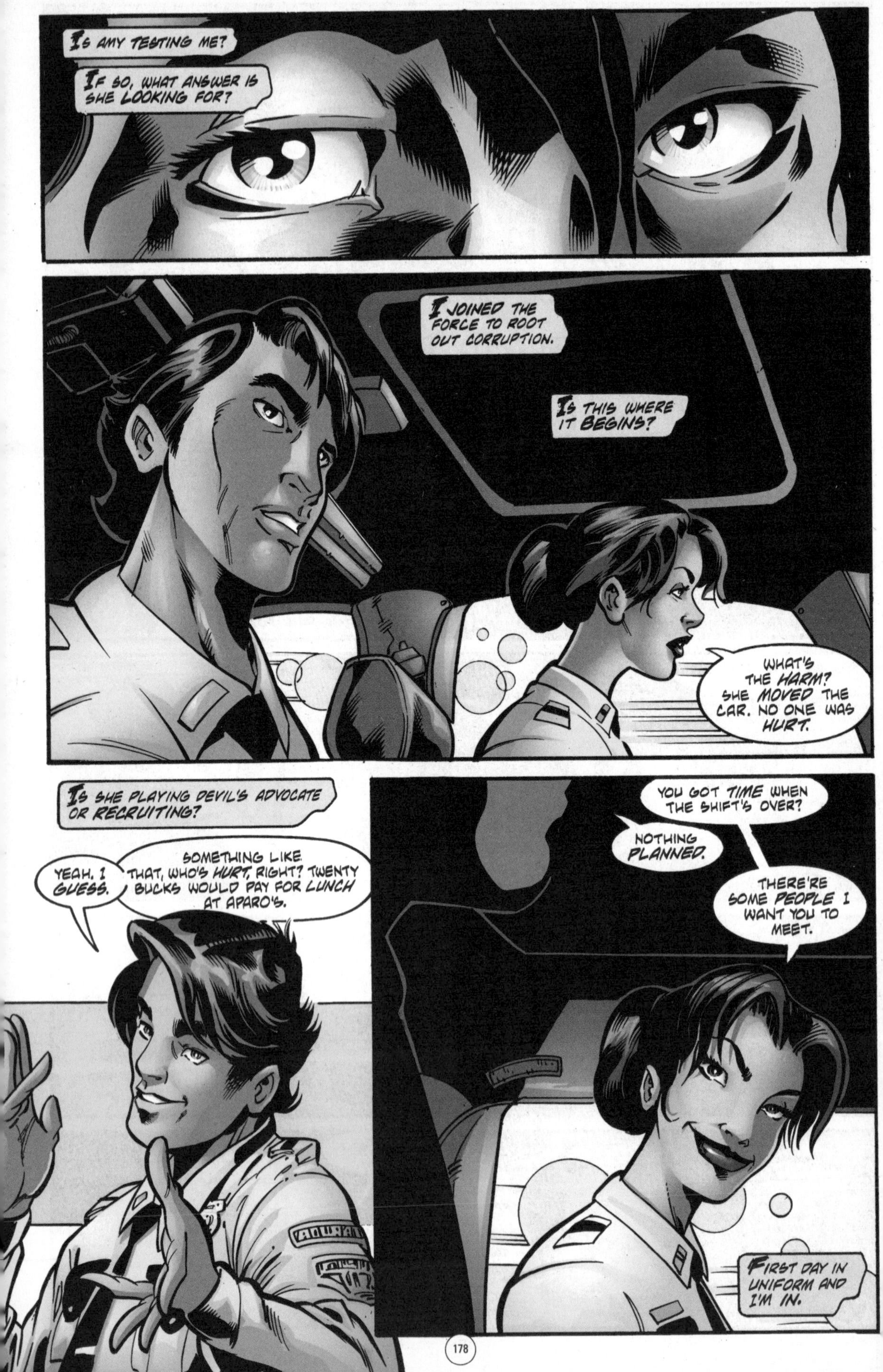

Is Amy testing me?
If so, what answer is she looking for?
I joined the force to root out corruption.
Is this where it begins?
What's the harm? She moved the car. No one was hurt.
Is she playing devil's advocate or recruiting?
Something like that, who's hurt, right? Twenty bucks would pay for lunch at Aparo's.
Yeah. I guess.
You got time when the shift's over?
Nothing planned.
There're some people I want you to meet.
First day in uniform and I'm in.

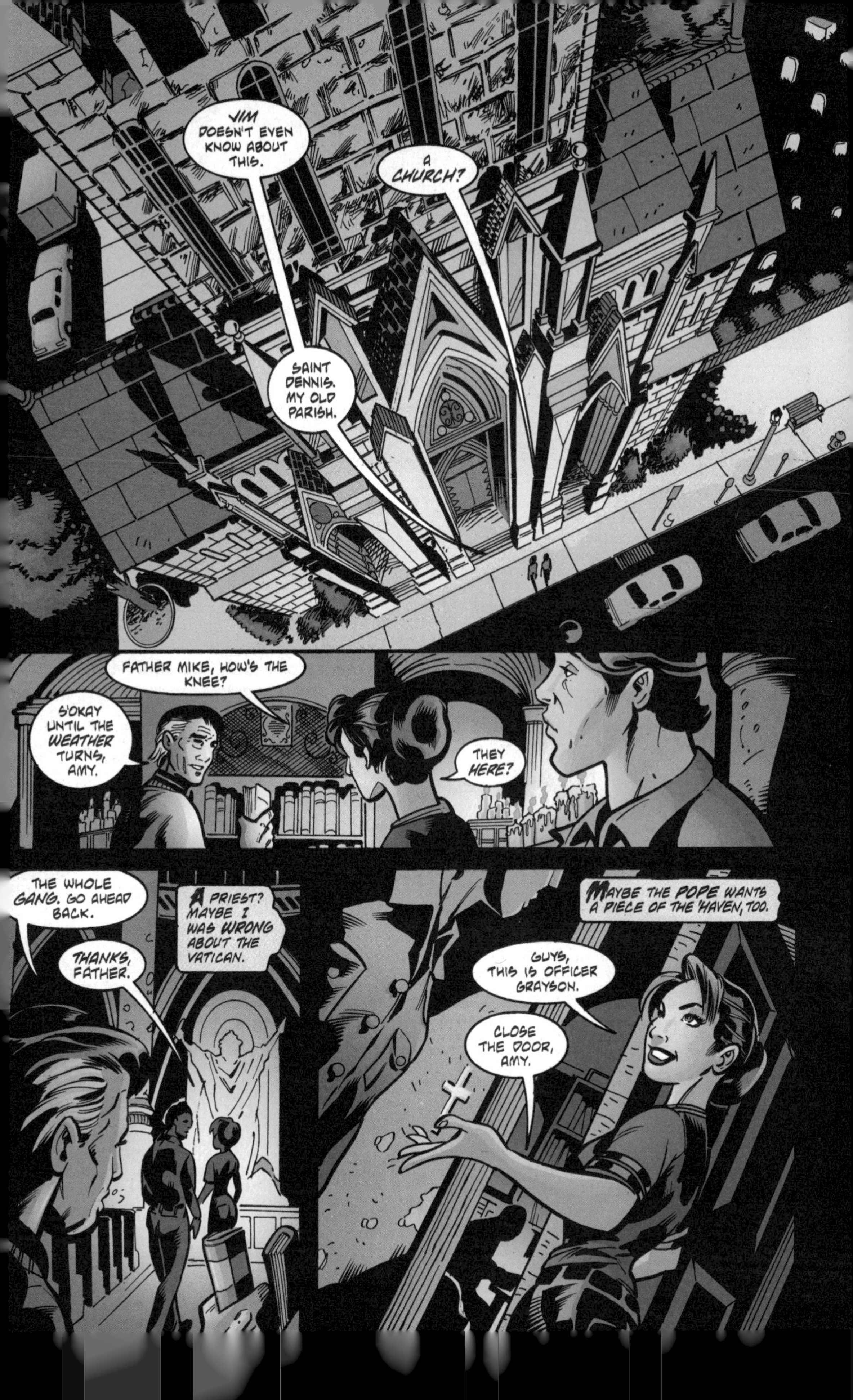

JIM DOESN'T EVEN KNOW ABOUT THIS.
A CHURCH?
SAINT DENNIS. MY OLD PARISH.
FATHER MIKE, HOW'S THE KNEE?
S'OKAY UNTIL THE WEATHER TURNS, AMY.
THEY HERE?
THE WHOLE GANG. GO AHEAD BACK.
THANKS, FATHER.
A PRIEST? MAYBE I WAS WRONG ABOUT THE VATICAN.
MAYBE THE POPE WANTS A PIECE OF THE 'HAVEN, TOO.
GUYS, THIS IS OFFICER GRAYSON.
CLOSE THE DOOR, AMY.

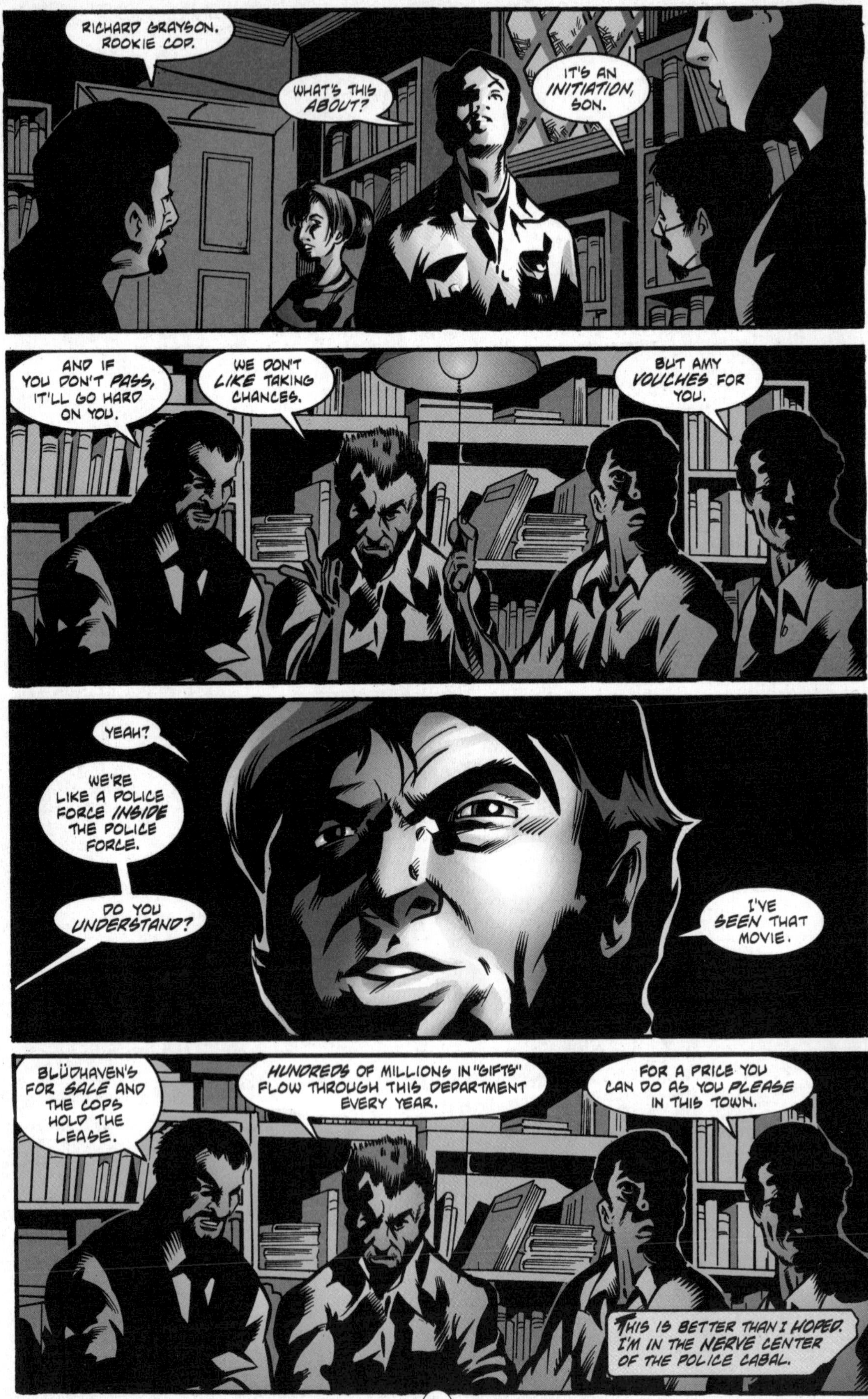
RICHARD GRAYSON. ROOKIE COP.
WHAT'S THIS ABOUT?
IT'S AN INITIATION, SON.
AND IF YOU DON'T PASS, IT'LL GO HARD ON YOU.
WE DON'T LIKE TAKING CHANCES.
BUT AMY VOUCHES FOR YOU.
YEAH?
WE'RE LIKE A POLICE FORCE INSIDE THE POLICE FORCE.
DO YOU UNDERSTAND?
I'VE SEEN THAT MOVIE.
BLÜDHAVEN'S FOR SALE AND THE COPS HOLD THE LEASE.
HUNDREDS OF MILLIONS IN "GIFTS" FLOW THROUGH THIS DEPARTMENT EVERY YEAR.
FOR A PRICE YOU CAN DO AS YOU PLEASE IN THIS TOWN.
THIS IS BETTER THAN I HOPED. I'M IN THE NERVE CENTER OF THE POLICE CABAL.

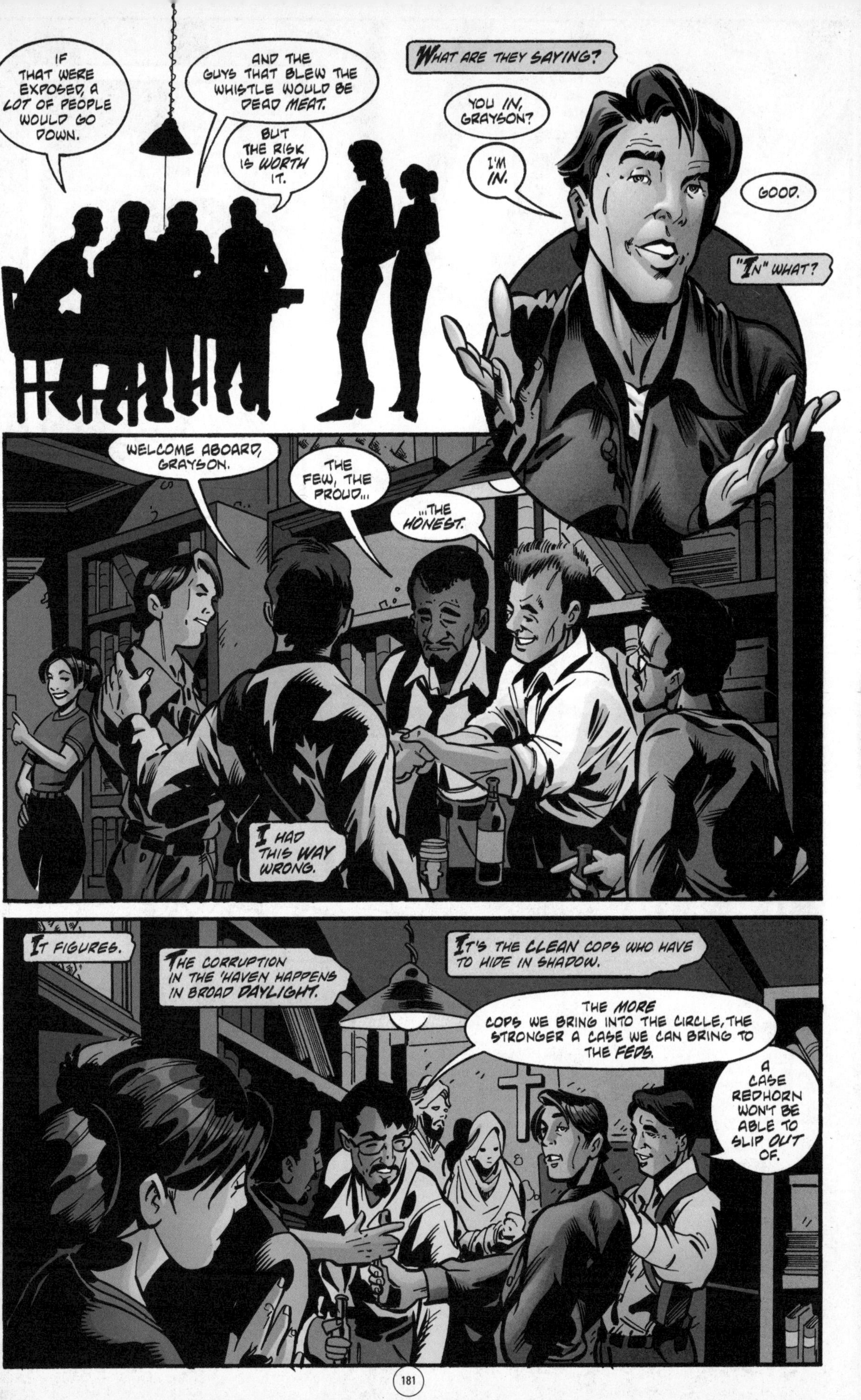

IF THAT WERE EXPOSED, A LOT OF PEOPLE WOULD GO DOWN.
AND THE GUYS THAT BLEW THE WHISTLE WOULD BE DEAD MEAT.
BUT THE RISK IS WORTH IT.
WHAT ARE THEY SAYING?
YOU IN, GRAYSON?
I'M IN.
GOOD.
"IN" WHAT?
WELCOME ABOARD, GRAYSON.
THE FEW, THE PROUD...
...THE HONEST.
I HAD THIS WAY WRONG.
IT FIGURES.
THE CORRUPTION IN THE 'HAVEN HAPPENS IN BROAD DAYLIGHT.
IT'S THE CLEAN COPS WHO HAVE TO HIDE IN SHADOW.
THE MORE COPS WE BRING INTO THE CIRCLE, THE STRONGER A CASE WE CAN BRING TO THE FEDS.
A CASE REDHORN WON'T BE ABLE TO SLIP OUT OF.

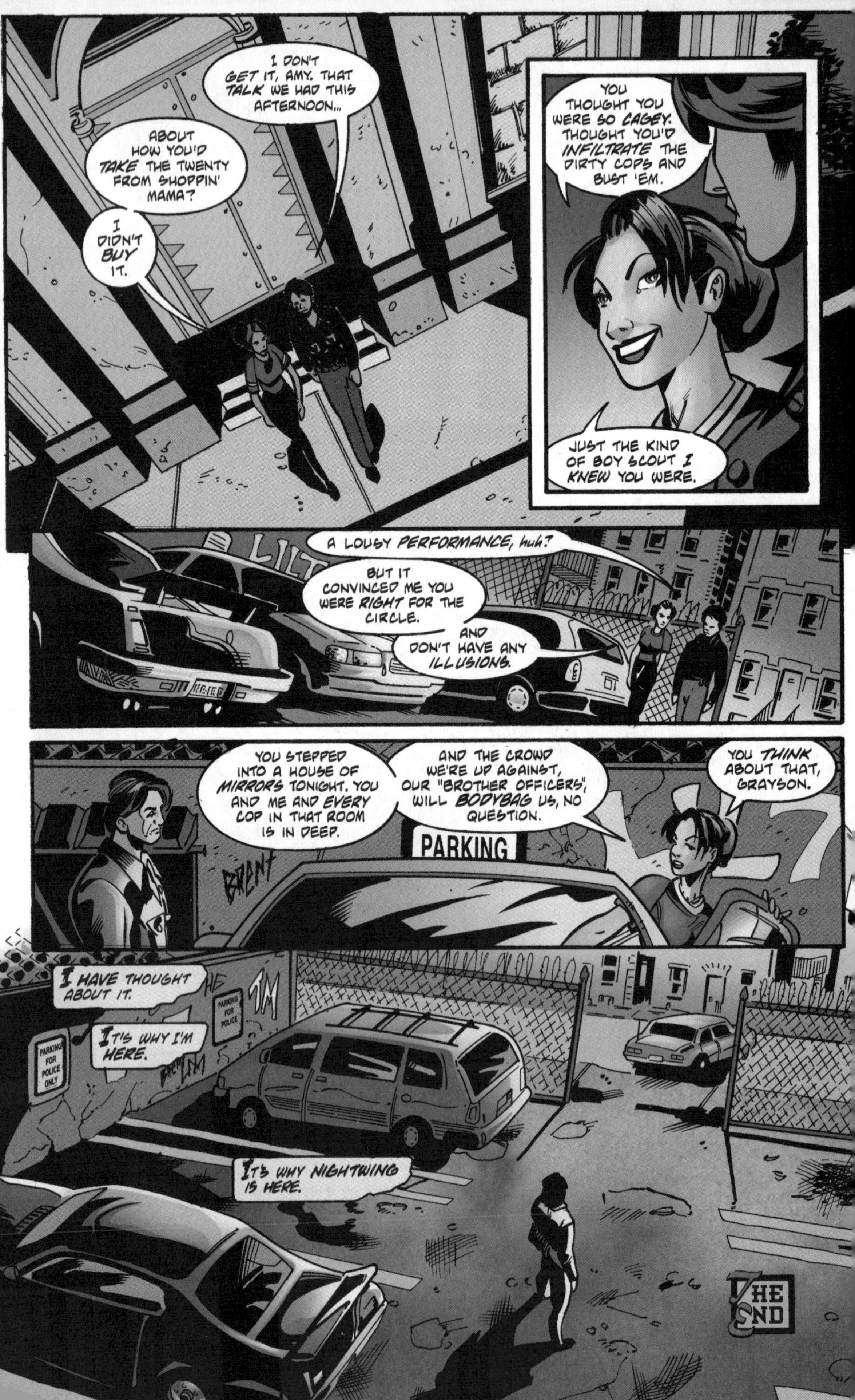
I DON'T GET IT, AMY. THAT TALK WE HAD THIS AFTERNOON...
ABOUT HOW YOU'D TAKE THE TWENTY FROM SHOPPIN' MAMA?
I DIDN'T BUY IT.
YOU THOUGHT YOU WERE SO CAGEY. THOUGHT YOU'D INFILTRATE THE DIRTY COPS AND BUST 'EM.
JUST THE KIND OF BOY SCOUT I KNEW YOU WERE.
A LOUSY PERFORMANCE, huh?
BUT IT CONVINCED ME YOU WERE RIGHT FOR THE CIRCLE.
AND DON'T HAVE ANY ILLUSIONS.
YOU STEPPED INTO A HOUSE OF MIRRORS TONIGHT. YOU AND ME AND EVERY COP IN THAT ROOM IS IN DEEP.
AND THE CROWD WE'RE UP AGAINST, OUR "BROTHER OFFICERS", WILL BODYBAG US, NO QUESTION.
PARKING
YOU THINK ABOUT THAT, GRAYSON.
I HAVE THOUGHT ABOUT IT.
PARKING FOR POLICE
PARKING FOR POLICE ONLY
IT'S WHY I'M HERE.
IT'S WHY NIGHTWING IS HERE.
THE END

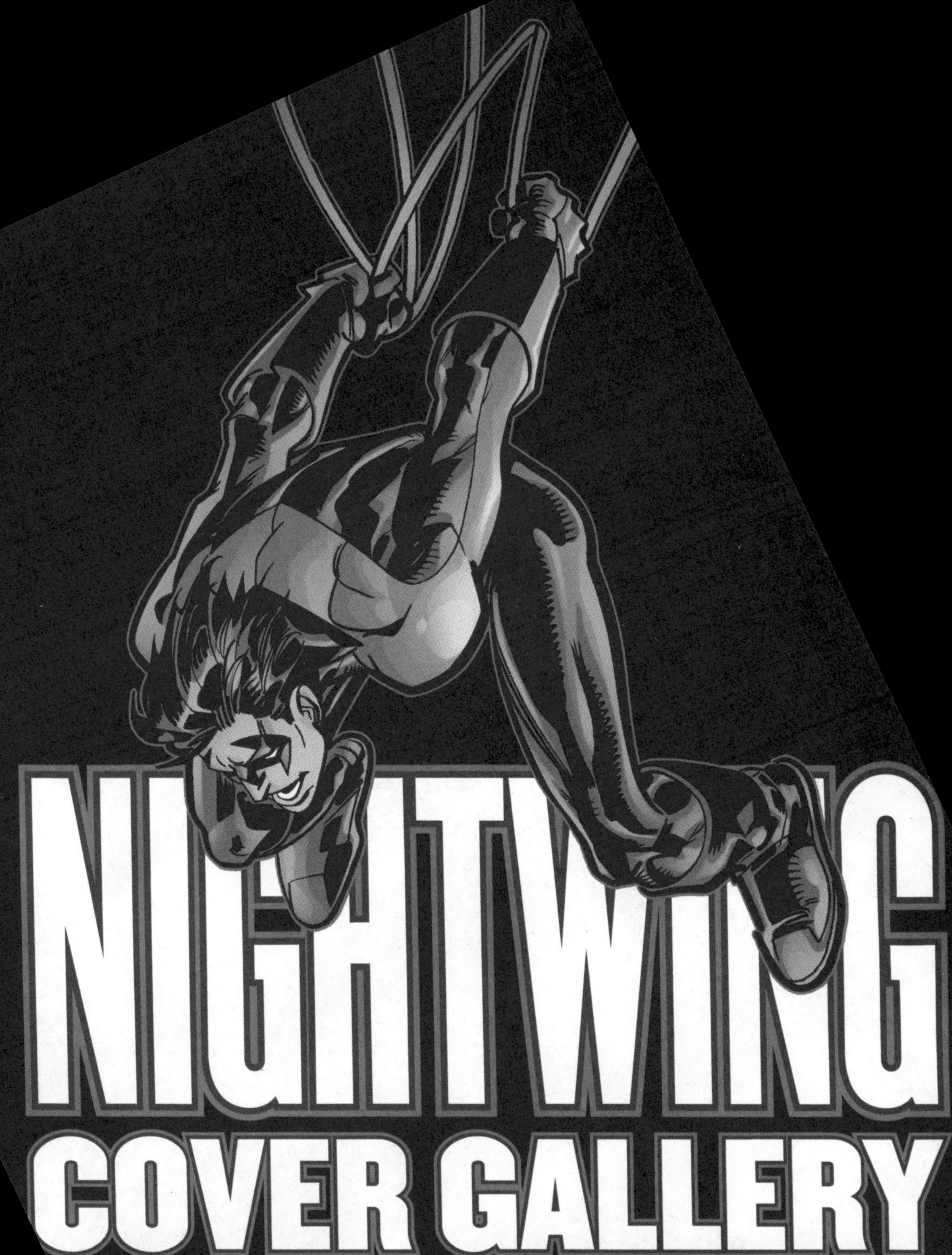

NIGHTWING COVER GALLERY

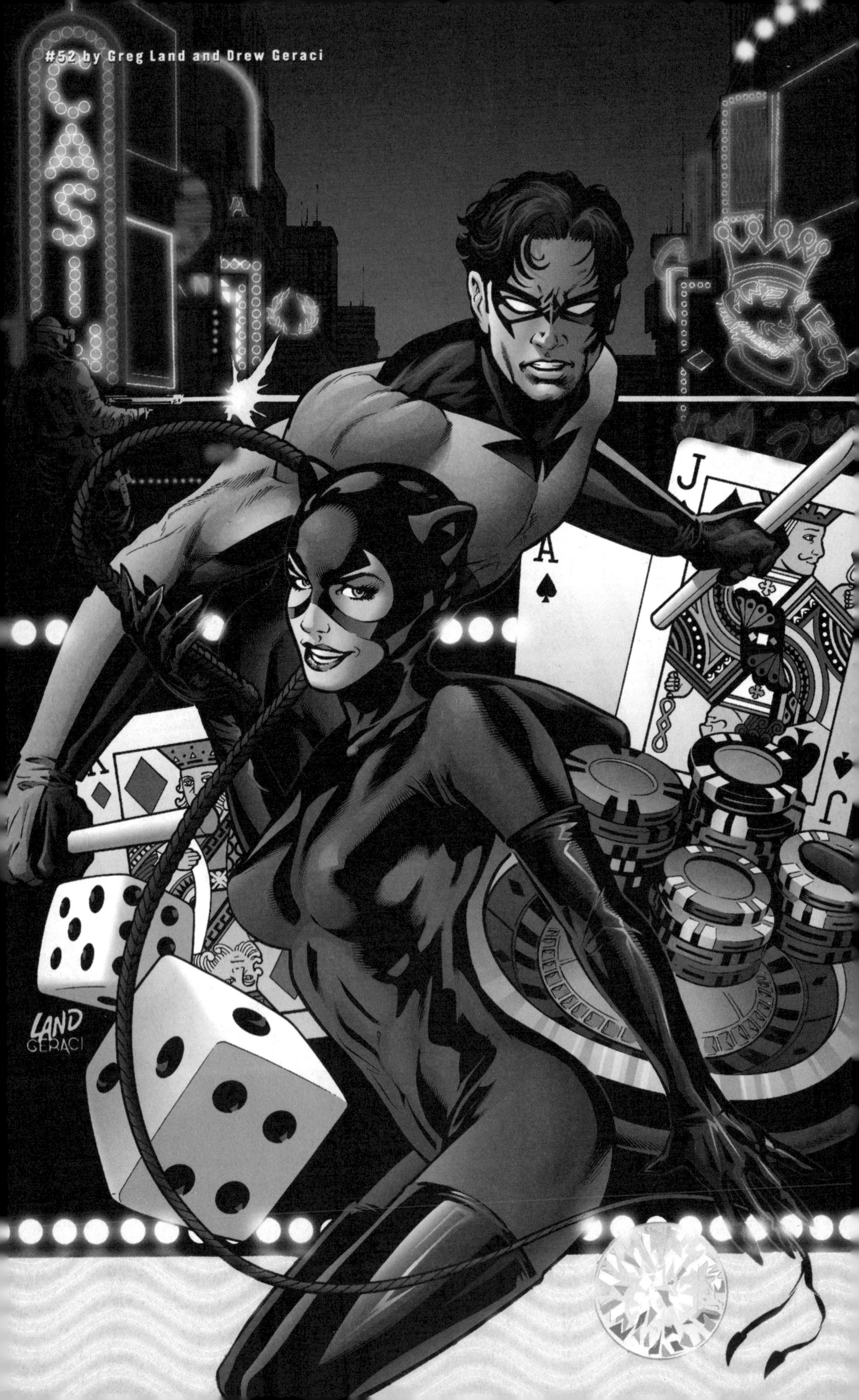
CASI
LAND
GERACI

#52 by Greg Land and Drew Geraci

#54 by Greg Land and Drew Geraci

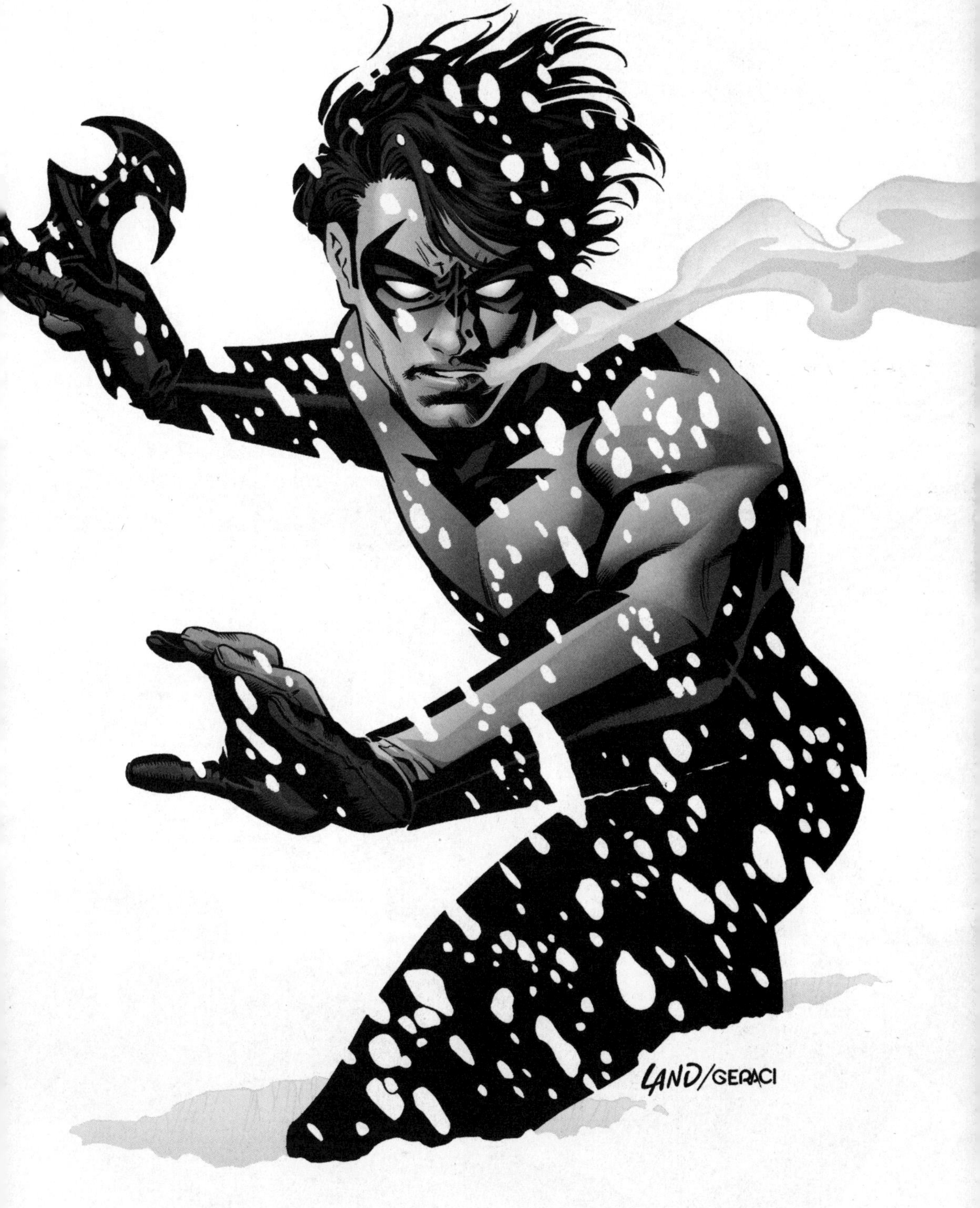
LAND/GERACI

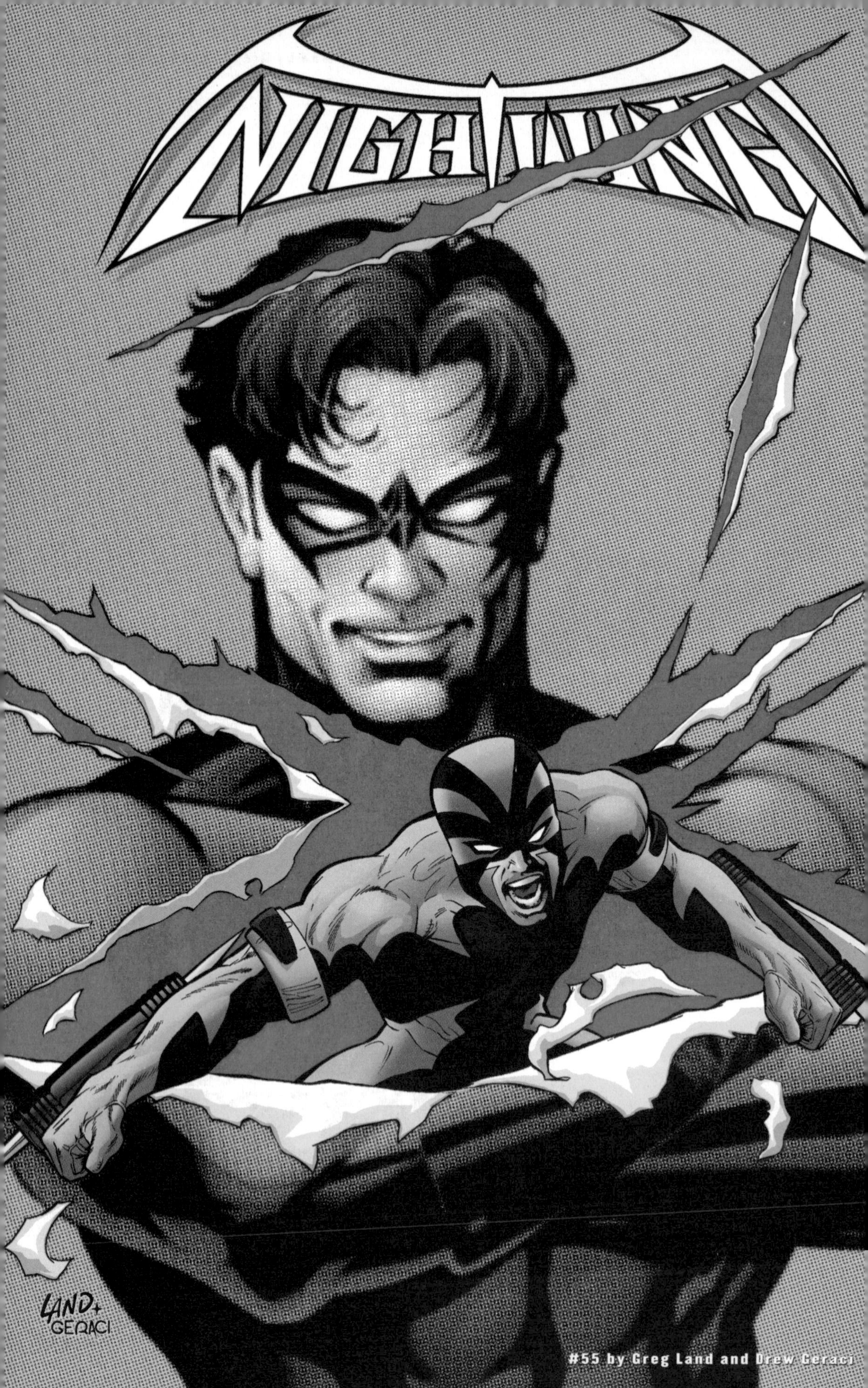
NIGHTWING
LAND+
GERACI

#55 by Greg Land and Drew Geraci

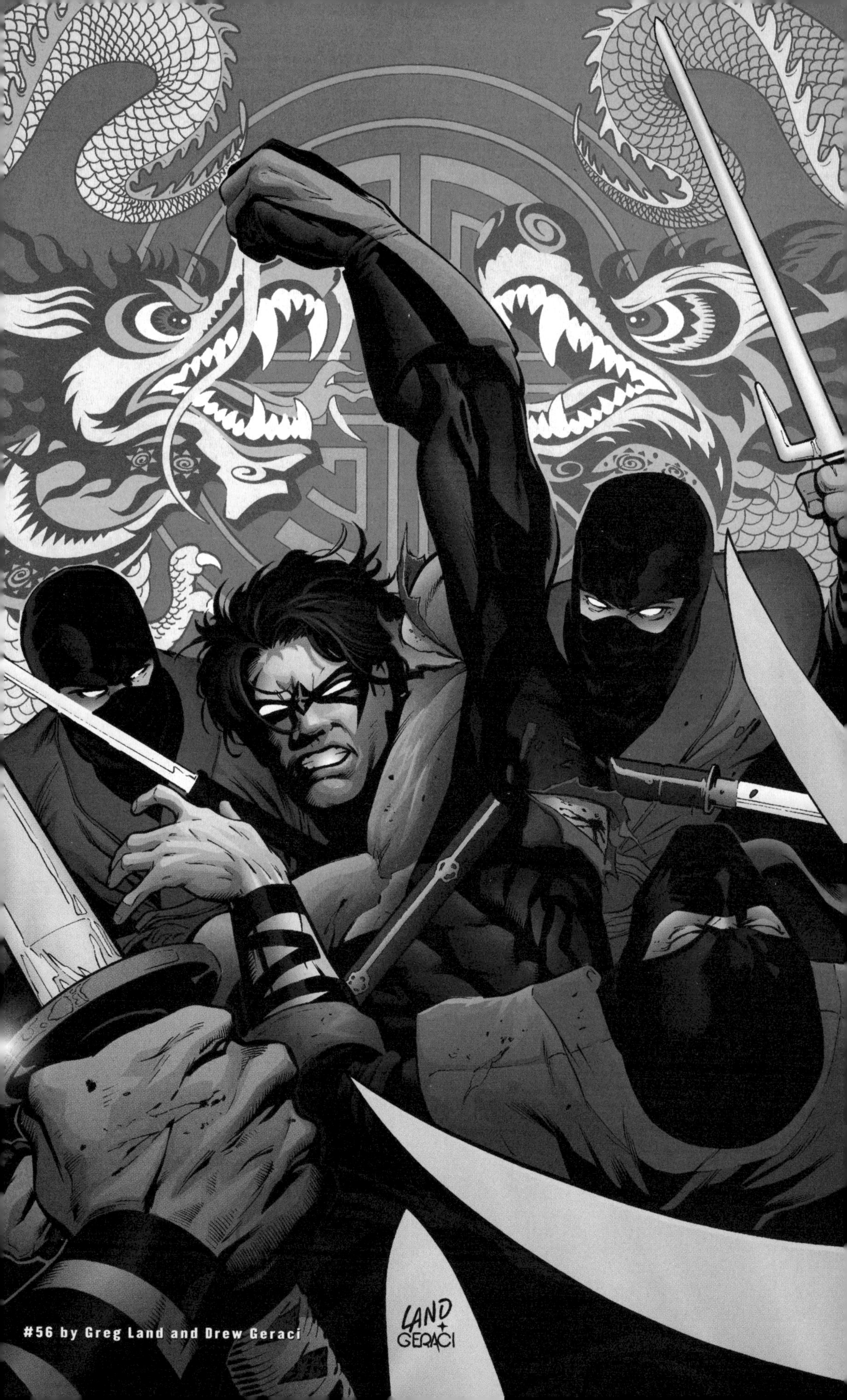
LAND
GERACI

#56 by Greg Land and Drew Geraci

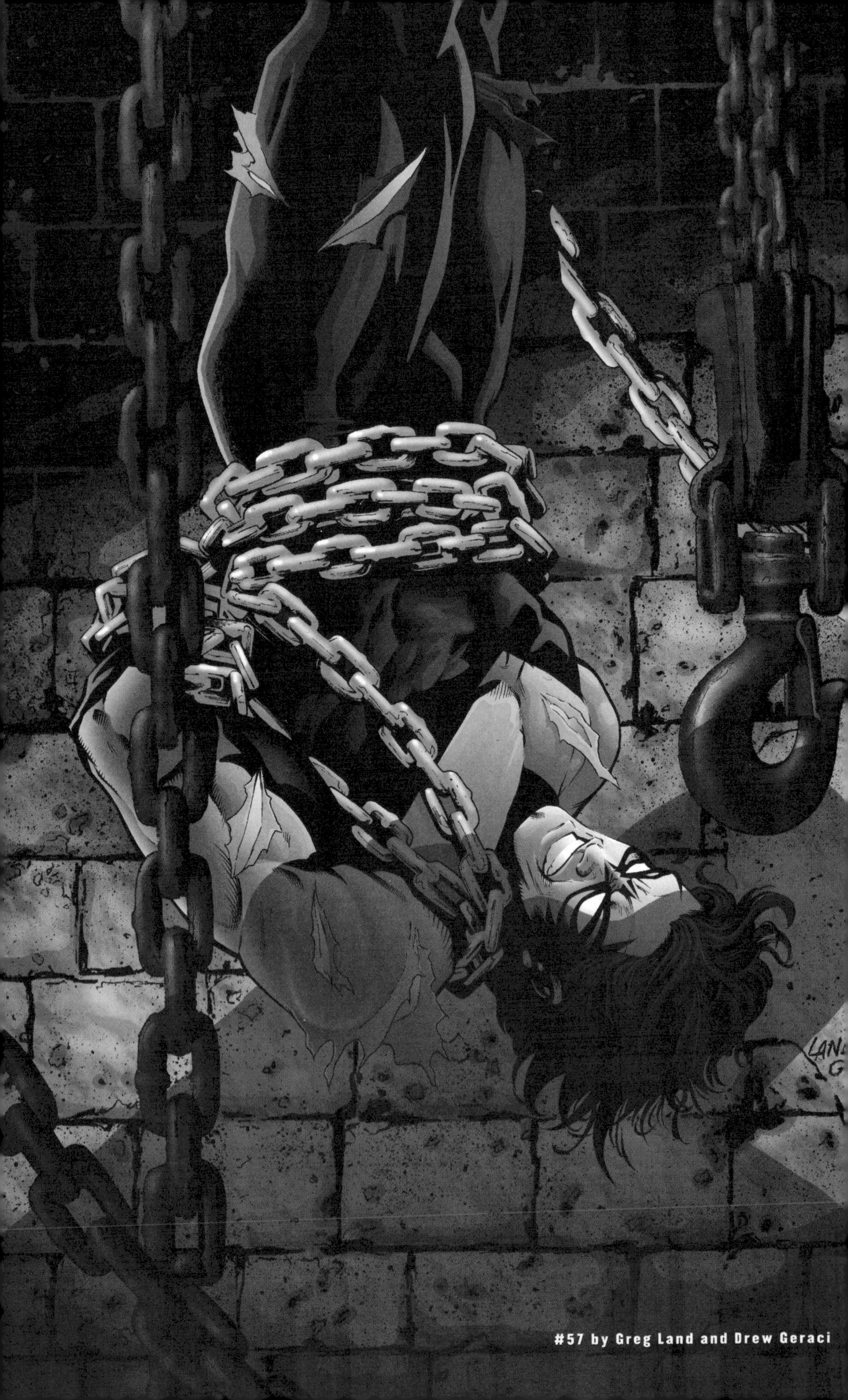

#57 by Greg Land and Drew Geraci

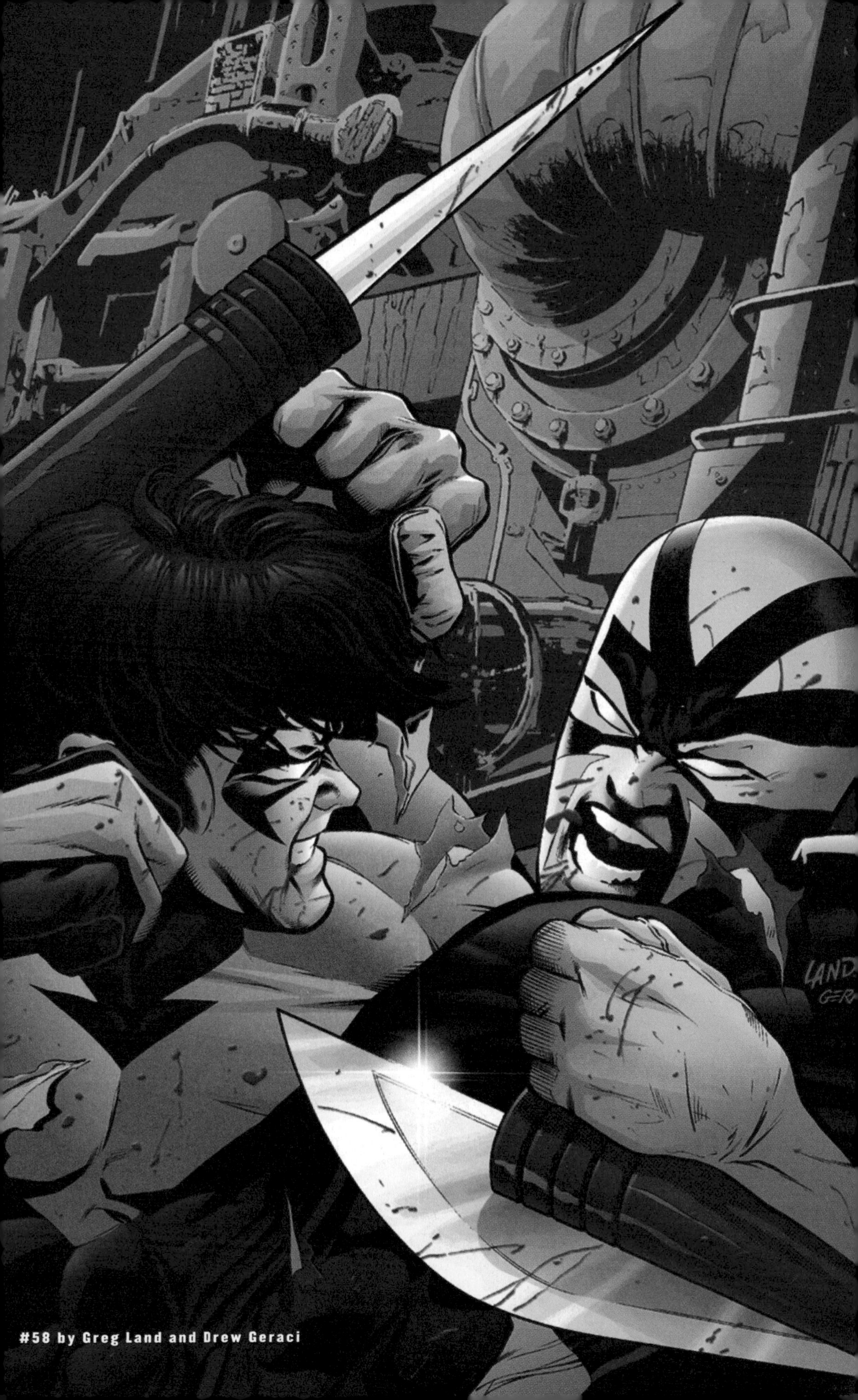

#58 by Greg Land and Drew Geraci

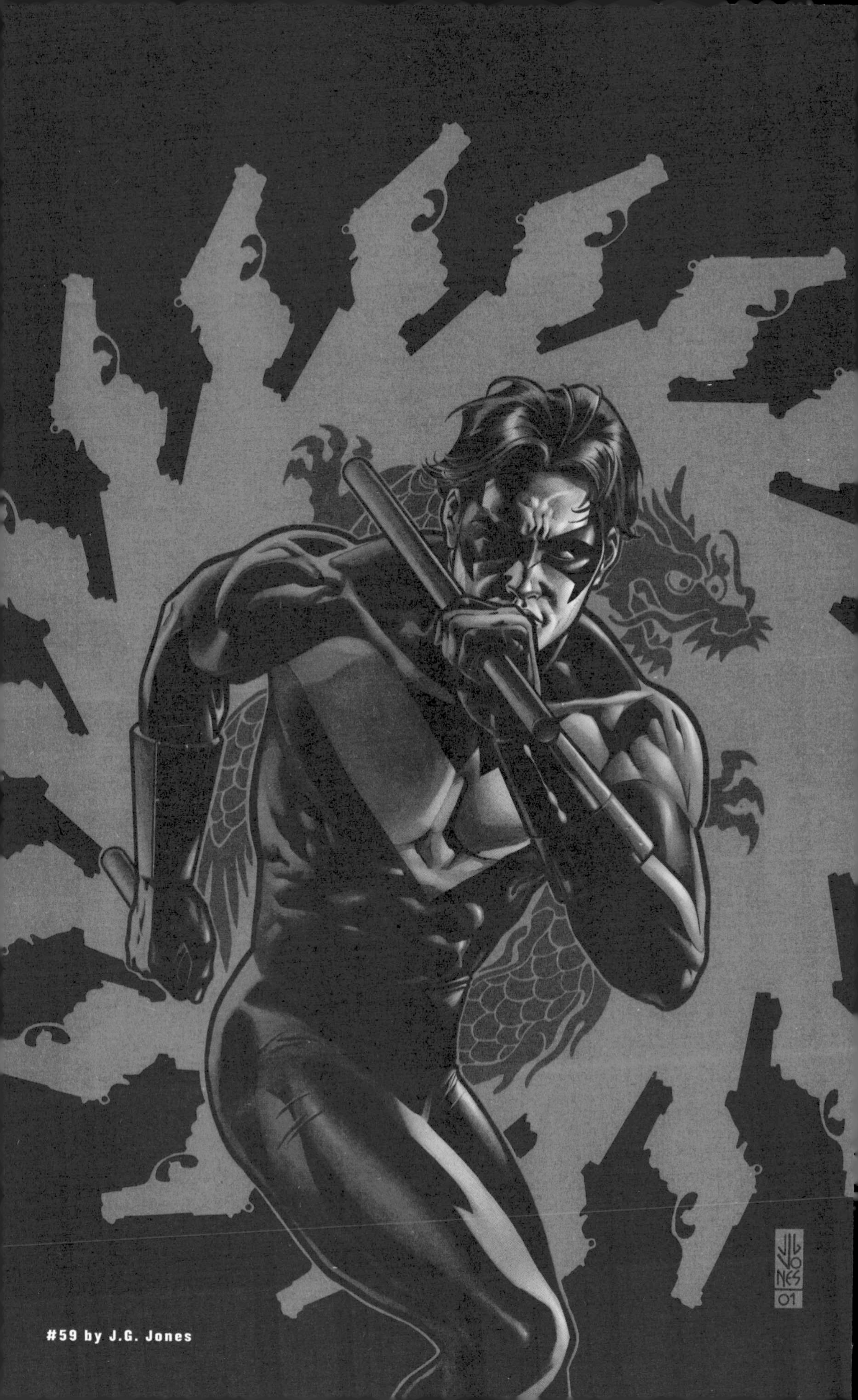

#59 by J.G. Jones

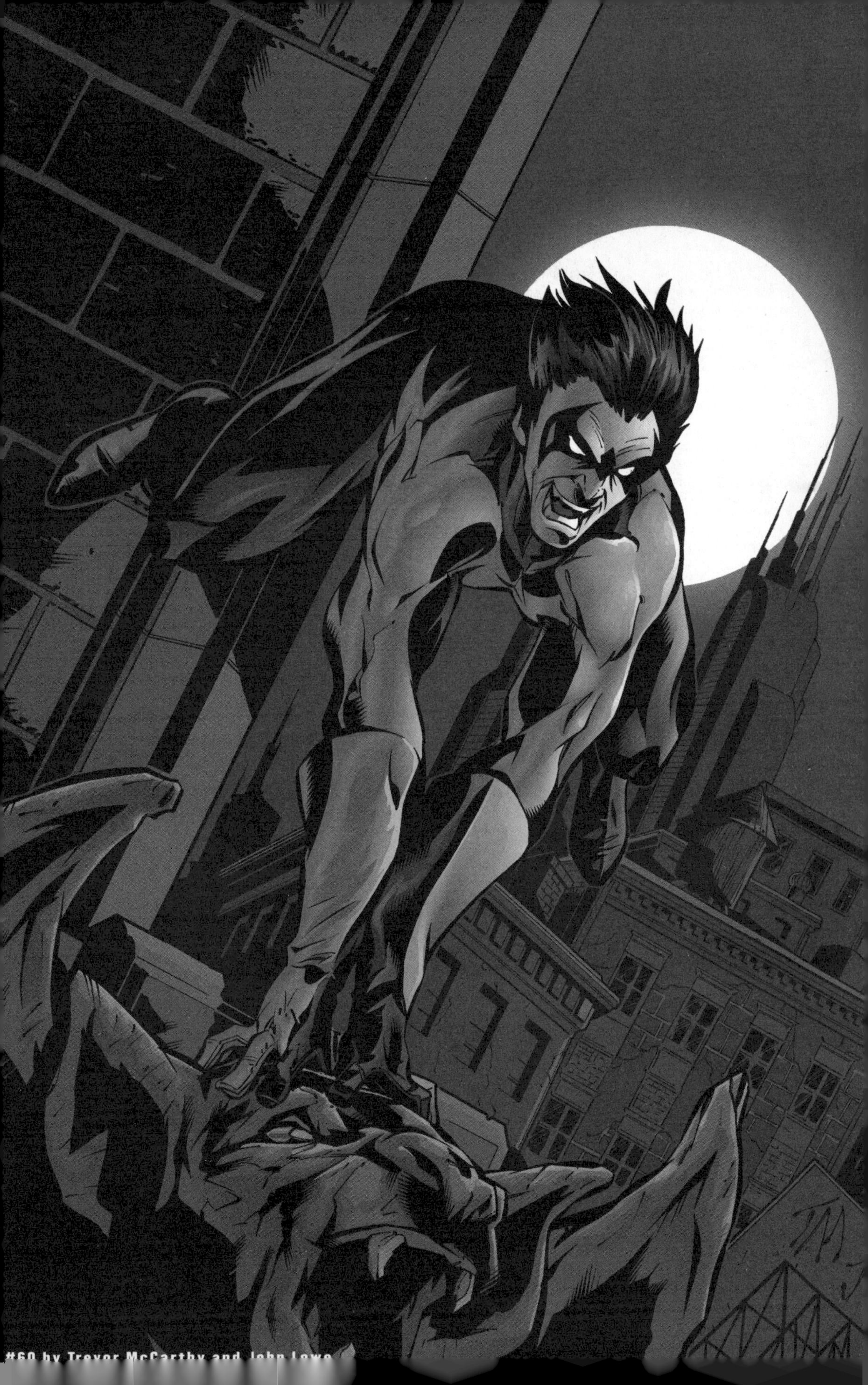

#60 by Trevor McCarthy and John Lowe

BATMAN
THE QUEST FOR JUSTICE CONTINUES IN THESE BOOKS FROM DC: